The Ruse of Techne

Series Board

James Bernauer

Drucilla Cornell

Thomas R. Flynn

Kevin Hart

Richard Kearney

Jean-Luc Marion

Adriaan Peperzak

Thomas Sheehan

Hent de Vries

Merold Westphal

Michael Zimmerman

John D. Caputo, *series editor*

PERSPECTIVES IN
CONTINENTAL
PHILOSOPHY

DIMITRIS VARDOULAKIS

The Ruse of Techne
Heidegger's Magical Materialism

FORDHAM UNIVERSITY PRESS
New York ■ 2024

Copyright © 2024 Fordham University Press

All rights reserved. No part of this publication may be reproduced, stored in a retrieval system, or transmitted in any form or by any means—electronic, mechanical, photocopy, recording, or any other—except for brief quotations in printed reviews, without the prior permission of the publisher.

Fordham University Press has no responsibility for the persistence or accuracy of URLs for external or third-party Internet websites referred to in this publication and does not guarantee that any content on such websites is, or will remain, accurate or appropriate.

Fordham University Press also publishes its books in a variety of electronic formats. Some content that appears in print may not be available in electronic books.

Visit us online at www.fordhampress.com.

Library of Congress Cataloging-in-Publication Data available online at https://catalog.loc.gov.

Printed in the United States of America

26 25 24   5 4 3 2 1

First edition

for Andrew, again

Contents

	Exordium	*xiii*
	Preamble: The Ineffectual and the Instrumental	*1*
	1. The ineffectual, 1 ▪ 2. The instrumental, 4	
1	**Introduction: What is the Ruse of Techne?**	*10*
	3. The ruse of techne, 10 ▪ 4. Metaphysical materialism (the metaphysics of morals), 14 ▪ 5. The reception of Heidegger and the ruse of techne, 16 ▪ 6. The repression of instrumentality, 31 ▪ 7. The underground current of a materialism of instrumentality, 35 ▪ 8. Effects of the ruse of techne (or, why the repression of instrumentality still matters today), 39 ▪ 9. On method, 42	
2	**The Problematic of Action Within a Single, Unified Being: Monism in Heidegger's Thought**	*44*
	10. Heidegger's other path, 44 ▪ 11. The first problem: How to be a different materialist?, 47 ▪ 12. The second problem: How is action possible within a monist ontology?, 52 ▪ 13. The third problem: Can monism provide qualitative distinctions between actions?, 55 ▪ 14. Two kinds of monist materialism, 57 ▪ 15. Two historical difficulties arising from Heidegger's solution to the problematic of action in monism, 61 ▪ 16. The double bind of the repression of instrumentality: Between the vacuous and the self-contradictory, 66 ▪ 17. Why Heidegger's solution to the problematic of action in monism matters, 72	

**3   The Conflation of Causality and Instrumentality:
      Phronesis and the Genesis of the Ruse of Techne   76**
18. Heidegger's bildungsroman, 76 ▪ 19. The truth of phronesis as the combination of calculation, emotion, and situatedness, 79 ▪ 20. The two ends of action in Aristotle (*Nicomachean Ethics* 1139a32), 82 ▪ 21. Techne and phronesis distinguished through their ends, 86 ▪ 22. The distinction between final and instrumental ends and the problematic of action in monism, 90 ▪ 23. A Greek-hating philhellene, 91 ▪ 24. The context of Heidegger's interpretation of phronesis, 94 ▪ 25. Heidegger's mistranslations of the *hou heneka*, 98 ▪ 26. Heidegger's discussion of *hou heneka* and *heneka tinos*: The repression of instrumentality, 101 ▪ 27. The genesis of the ruse of techne: sophia as the virtue of techne, 105 ▪ 28. Teleocracy, 112 ▪ 29. Phronesis, resoluteness, and temporality: The "either/or", 115

**Excursus: Through the Looking Glass of the Distinction
Between Causality and Instrumentality   119**
30. Acting and the other: The politics of instrumentality, 119 ▪ 31. The repression of instrumentality in metaphysics, 126 ▪ 32. Causal and instrumental ends in monist materialism, 133

**4   The Concealment of Instrumentality: The Conception of
      Action in *Being and Time*   144**
33. The reason for focusing on the examples of action in *Being and Time*, 144 ▪ 34. The epigraph and the problem of action in the *Sophist*, 146 ▪ 35. Destruction and monism, 149 ▪ 36. Inauthentic, indifferent, and authentic action, 151 ▪ 37. Hammering and the concealing of instrumentality (*Being and Time* §15), 155 ▪ 38. The breakdown of ends (*Being and Time* §16), 160 ▪ 39. Sign and reference, understanding and interpretation (*Being and Time* §17), 164 ▪ 40. Dictatorship, 169 ▪ 41. The temporality of death and the myth of Care, 172 ▪ 42. Techne as the virtue of theory, 176 ▪ 43. Subjectum absconditum, 184

5   The Ontology of Conflict: Conjuring Authority   186
44. The "turn" and action, 186 ▪ 45. Authority as the means to repress instrumentality, 189 ▪ 46. Conflict and the three senses of techne, 193 ▪ 47. The subjectivism of authority (*Prometheus*), 196 ▪ 48. The problem of the metaphysico-political conflict, 202 ▪ 49. The historical decision and phusis (*Oedipus Rex*), 204 ▪ 50. Apolis and the spontaneous creation of authority (*Antigone* 1), 208 ▪

51. The human as *deinon* and the repression of instrumentality (*Antigone* 2), 213 ■ 52. A politics without reaction or an agonistic politics, 219 ■ 53. The preservers and the magical founding of the city, 222

6 The Ontology of the Ineffectual: The Purloined Letter of Instrumentality   *229*

54. The reversal of the critique of monism, 229 ■ 55. The turn, the return, and the other turn (the critique of Sartre as self-critique), 234 ■ 56. Transformations of the ruse of techne, 238 ■ 57. Instrumentality incorporated into causality (the first sense of techne), 239 ■ 58. The ambivalence of the calculable and enframing (the second sense of techne), 244 ■ 59. The killing power of the saving power (the third sense of techne), 248 ■ 60. Metaphysical or materialist monism?, 252 ■ 61. The French appropriation of the repression of instrumentality, 256 ■ 62. The new Kantianism, 260 ■ 63. Technophobia and the repression of instrumentality, 263 ■ 64. The paradox of the final end, 266

Peroratio   *272*

Acknowledgments   *279*

Works by Martin Heidegger   *283*

Bibliography   *287*

Index   *301*

Exordium

ξυνόν ἐστι πᾶσι τὸ φρονέειν
Heraclitus, D113

Heraclitus's fragment 113 does not mean merely that phronesis is common to all; it also, and primarily, indicates that commonality is constituted by the capacity to make the instrumental judgments that the Greeks called phronesis.

Heidegger started *Being and Time* by suggesting that philosophy had forgotten the question of being. He failed to add that the notion of the single, unified being that he discovered in Greek thought faced a problem recognized since antiquity, namely, the problem of how to account for action: Can actions be different if they are part of the all-encompassing and hence unchanging being? Can anything be other than a mere modification of being if it constitutes a totality outside of which nothing exists? By repressing this problem, Heidegger instituted a forgetting of the answer that the ancients provided, which emphasized the ethical and political import of instrumental judgment, or phronesis. The Greeks thought that we can account for action only by understanding being through its effects. Heraclitus's fragment points out, in this context, that the effects of being register in thinking that the ends of action are always situated in a material context of relations that includes others. Phronesis is an ethical and a political virtue, grounded in a materialist ontology.

Instrumentality has, for too long, been condemned as complicit in the production and perpetuation of power. It is rarely noted that, if existence consists in the unfolding of power relations, then instrumentality ought to be a—nay, *the*—key term of ontology, ethics, and politics. For this to be possible, we need to understand how Heidegger—who sets the matrix of the presentation of ethics and politics in continental philosophy—precipitated the forgetting of instrumentality.

The Ruse of Techne

Preamble
The Ineffectual and the Instrumental

1. The ineffectual

The Ruse of Techne is concerned with a single idea in Heidegger—an idea, however, with far-reaching implications. This is the idea that there is a kind of action without ends or effects, or what I call *the ineffectual*. The positive articulation of his philosophy is inextricable from the ineffectual that denotes a series of terms that Heidegger uses over the years to refer to an action without effects and ends. For example, authenticity in *Being and Time* encapsulates the reference to the ineffectual; art or poetry are the most common articulations of the ineffectual in the years from around the mid-1930s; and his late work typically refers to the ineffectual as simply thinking or the thinking of being.

Heidegger frames his project by staging a series of oppositions. In the opening chapters of *Being and Time*, he talks about the "destruction of metaphysics"; elsewhere he describes his conception of ontology as resisting the reduction of being to mere presence. So, to evaluate the idea of the ineffectual, we need to understand what Heidegger is arguing against. The real target of Heidegger's rejection of metaphysics is not religion as such, given that the notion of an action without effects, or the ineffectual, plays a significant function in mysticism, which explains his fascination with Meister Eckhart.

The real target is technoscience as the key to modernity. Heidegger holds that the end-oriented actions, characteristic of modern science and technology, may be necessary for providing us with the notion of the world within which we live, such as the world of tools in *Being and Time* or the world of the housing crisis in "Building, Dwelling, Thinking." But this experience can go two ways: either we are lost in the world of instrumental calculation, or we take the step beyond instrumental calculation to join the path of the ineffectual that leads to being. Thus, the real target of Heidegger's thought is the end-oriented kind of action and thinking, or what I call *the instrumental*, because he holds that it leads us astray from uncovering being.

Against Heidegger, I hold that it is reductive and distorting to confine the prevalence of the instrumental in modern technoscience. Crucially, the instrumental plays a critical role in ancient Greek thought. At this point, we can observe a curiosity: the instrumental is indispensable for phronesis as presented in book 6 of Aristotle's *Nicomachean Ethics*, and yet it is precisely in his reading of Aristotle's phronesis that Heidegger adumbrates the ineffectual. I will demonstrate that the historical basis of the discovery of the ineffectual in ancient Greek thought is mistaken, and that in fact the ineffectual *does not exist* in the Aristotelian texts where Heidegger claims to discover it.

This has major repercussions for his ontology since Heidegger's conception of being requires the ineffectual to account for action. If the ineffectual does not exist, then Heidegger's ontology faces the prospect of being pure theory without a practical philosophy. To put this in terms of his own diagnosis of metaphysics as the forced separation of theory and praxis, if the ineffectual does not exist, then Heidegger's ontology loses its practical side and thus lapses back into metaphysics.

The Ruse of Techne examines Heidegger's technique to identify the ineffectual, starting with his interpretation of phronesis. In chapter 3, I offer a close analysis that shows the "blind spot" in Heidegger's reading of book 6 of *Nicomachean Ethics*, which enables him to identify phronesis with the ineffectual. I will explain how Aristotle distinguishes between two actions according to their different kinds of ends. The action that Aristotle calls techne is governed by the final ends of causality, whereas phronesis is determined by the calculation of instrumental ends. By contrast, Heidegger argues that all ends—both causal and instrumental—belong to techne. This allows Heidegger to argue that phronesis is purified of all ends of action. In this interpretation of phronesis, Heidegger constructs the ineffectual.

I argue in *The Ruse of Techne* that the conflation of causality and instrumentality in techne is a move that persists throughout Heidegger's work as we see, for example, in "The Question Concerning Technology," and that it is fundamental in the construction of the ineffectual. I call Heidegger's blindness to the function of the instrumental in this history *the forgetting of instrumentality*, and I call the way in which this obscuring of the instrumental leads to a conception of the ineffectual that traverses the entirety of Heidegger's thought *the repression of instrumentality*. In chapters 1 to 3, I show how Heidegger constructs the ineffectual through the forgetting and repression of instrumentality.

Techne is pivotal in Heidegger's technique to construct the ineffectual. Through his conception of techne, he performs the kind of "trick" that I call *the ruse of techne*. Specifically, the ruse of techne employs three meanings of techne from ancient Greek to make instrumentality disappear. First, techne as implicated in the singularity of being in Greek ontology. Heidegger holds that Greek thought does not know of metaphysical transcendence, which also means that it posits a single, unified being. For short, I refer to this conception of the single, unified being without transcendence as monism. Second, techne as technology. This includes all activities that are oriented toward ends, according to Heidegger, that is, it includes the instrumental. Third, techne as artistic practice exemplifies an activity unconcerned with any ends and effects. This is the ineffectual that leads, according to Heidegger, to the truth of being. Thus techne, a single term, can denote three distinct positions that are critical for Heidegger's philosophical position: monism, the instrumental, and the ineffectual.

The three senses of techne furnish Heidegger with his typical argumentative strategy. This consists in saying that if one is to accept the first sense—monism—then the second sense denotes, at best, a preliminary step toward the truth of being, as described for instance in Division 1 of *Being and Time*; or, at worse, a decisive deviation from being, which is responsible for the "nihilism of modernity." In either case, the only way to the truth of being is through the ineffectual or the kind of action free of all ends that characterizes the third sense of techne. This argumentative strategy is endlessly repeated in Heidegger's works, as we will see. The strategy, however, is a trick or ruse involving the second and the third meanings of techne—the instrumental and the ineffectual. A conjurer's trick makes something disappear and something else appear in its place. Heidegger's ruse of techne makes instrumentality disappear with the ineffectual taking its place.

Karl Löwith records how students at Marburg University saw "Heidegger's personality," the young teacher who sought to change philosophy. According to Löwith, the students used to call him "the magician" due to his lecturing *technique*: "He knew how to perform magic by making what he had just demonstrated disappear before the eyes of his audience. The technique of his lecturing consisted in building thought constructs that he then drew away so as to leave the enchanted listener suspended in a vacuum before a riddle."[1] Löwith's description of Heidegger's magic fits the technique of the ruse of techne to present before us a thought construct of action that is promptly withdrawn, leaving his readers suspended in a vacuum, that is, in a place devoid of action—the ineffectual.

Heidegger was never entirely satisfied with his determination of the ineffectual. As I will show, this leads Heidegger to develop three distinct versions of the ruse of techne. I will present each separately in chapters 4 to 6, and I will further argue that they all remain unconvincing, resulting in a conception of action that is either trivial or self-contradictory.

2. The instrumental

The ineffectual is of paramount importance for Heidegger's influence in subsequent philosophy. If there is one feature that unites the diverse array of positions and approaches of the whole tradition of thought that received the name "continental philosophy" in the aftermath of World War II, it is the assumption that an action without ends is indispensable for a conception of the ethical and the political. In other words, Heidegger's ineffectual has been widely accepted in an array of variations that organize the conception of praxis in continental philosophy. For example, Levinas determines the Other as transcendent whereby it is separate from the application of specific rules; Blanchot conceives of an outside that establishes a community distinct from everyday action; Derrida compulsively returns to an unconditioned beyond calculation; Deleuze adumbrates a pure immanence that is sheer potentiality; and Badiou imagines an event that ruptures the instrumental field of politics. These pivotal thinkers—and many others—in continental philosophy may disagree, by and large, but all concur on the centrality of an action without ends, or the ineffectual, to counter modernity's technoscientific threats.

This unquestioned acceptance of the ineffectual is inseparable from Heidegger's forgetting and repression of instrumentality. More precisely, Heidegger's ineffectual is part of the broader "critique of instrumentality," which has been one of the, if not *the*, main avenues of approaching the ethics and politics of modernity. We can summarize this critique as follows: The successes of science and technology in modernity established a naturalism according to which we can determine what to do by neutrally examin-

---

1. Karl Löwith, *Mein Leben in Deutschland vor und nach 1933: Ein Bericht* (Stuttgart: J. B. Metzlersehe, 1986), 42, 43.

ing causes and effects. But actually, causality is anything but neutral as it is always implicated with the instrumental calculations of means and ends that are responsible for the consolidation of structures of power and oppression. Causality and instrumentality intermesh to produce a "dialectic of Enlightenment" that is nothing but a project of domination.

Heidegger's major contribution to the critique of instrumental reason consists in its radical historicization. In most cases, the critique of instrumental reason is narrowly circumscribed within the Enlightenment project that culminates with Hegel, and the kind of historical materialism reliant on teleology that arises through a particular interpretation of Marx. For example, Weber and Adorno take the Reformation as the starting point of their castigation of instrumental reason. In the wake of Heidegger's historicization of ontology, the critique of instrumental reason can extend all the way back to ancient Greek thought. As we discussed earlier, Heidegger discovers the conflation of causality and instrumentality already in Aristotle's conception of techne (§1). Heidegger's discovery of the ineffectual in Greek thought extends the philosophical critique of modernity back to antiquity. This opens up exciting possibilities for the philosophical diagnoses of contemporary issues to resonate with problems and questions that have exercised thought for centuries, such as the question of the one, unified being.

It is significant that we can locate, with some precision, the sites of Heidegger's critique of instrumentality as intertwined with the discovery of the ineffectual in antiquity. It then becomes possible to analyze these sources, such as his pivotal reading of Aristotle's phronesis, to show that the ineffectual can only be discovered by forgetting and repressing instrumentality. This enables us to question the function of the ineffectual in Heidegger's thought as a whole, as well as its unquestioned acceptance by continental philosophy. From this perspective, *The Ruse of Techne* is *both* a close exegesis of how Heideggerian texts determine the ineffectual, *and* a recognition that the critique of Heidegger is also applicable to the repression of instrumentality in continental philosophy. Thus, *The Ruse of Techne* suggests that the question "what would it be like to challenge the ineffectual and to unravel the forgetting of instrumentality today?" signifies a fundamental question for philosophy. It is the task that Heidegger's astonishingly successful conception of the ineffectual bequeaths us today.

Differently put, *The Ruse of Techne* suggests that the most significant effect of Heidegger's thought in subsequent philosophy, and the reason for his pivotal position in twentieth-century philosophy, is the prevalence of the ineffectual. Such an *effects of the ineffectual* suggests that the ineffectual, as such, never existed and it cannot exist. This is consistent with my position that an action without ends, or the ineffectual as conceived by Heidegger, ends up being *either* a trivial, vacuous conception of action which amounts to a disavowal of the possibility of thinking ethically and politically, *or* it presupposes instrumentality, which makes the ineffectual at best self-contradictory and at worse complicit in perpetuating existing power structures. I will demonstrate that this oscillation between triviality and complicity plays an analytic function to distinguish the three different versions of the ruse of techne (§1).

It would be impossible to undo the forgetting and repression of instrumentality without an understanding of how instrumentality functions in the philosophical discourse. *The Ruse of Techne* is part of a long project that seeks to unearth the philosophical potency of instrumentality, or to redeem the value of instrumental or calculative thinking.

Two insights structure such a project. The first insight is a historical one. The notion of the instrumental today is circumscribed by the conception of consequentialism in nineteenth-century utilitarianism, according to which calculative or instrumental judgments aspire to certainty. Thus, Bentham strives to develop a calculus to validate the consequences of calculation. It is customary to take this utilitarian conception of instrumentality as the only possible one. For example, Hannah Arendt does not see any need to refer to anything other than utilitarianism for her critique of instrumentality in *The Human Condition*.[2] However, the instrumentality of the kind of knowledge and virtue that the Greeks called phronesis is decidedly opposed to the possibility that instrumental calculation can lead to certainty. Instead, phronesis in Greek thought is inherently fallible.

A significant part of the project to undo the forgetting of instrumentality is to reexamine its function in the history of thought. For example, it is critical to discover the role it plays in the conception of praxis in antiquity, especially in the notion of phronesis.[3] This allows us also to reconsider the function of instrumentality in modernity. A key feature of the radical politics of Spinoza is to translate the discourse of phronesis into his conception of the good, or virtue, in terms of the calculation of utility.[4]

The second insight concerns the importance of instrumentality. It is *because* of all the perils of instrumentality, well-documented in the numerous

---

2. See in particular §43 of Hannah Arendt's *The Human Condition* (Chicago: University of Chicago Press, 1998).
3. See Dimitris Vardoulakis, *The Logic of Living: The Materialism of Greek Thought* (forthcoming).
4. See Dimitris Vardoulakis, *Spinoza, the Epicurean: Authority and Utility in Materialism* (Edinburgh: Edinburgh University Press, 2020).

discourses against "calculative or instrumental reason," that instrumentality is a pivotal concept in ethical and political discourse. Instrumentality becomes even more central following the historical argument that the ineffectual cannot be found in the ancient conception of praxis. From this perspective it is necessary to work through the repression of instrumentality by discovering how instrumentality is critical for fundamental ethical and political concepts, such as sovereignty and democracy.[5]

Such a new perspective on instrumentality requires that we overcome the utilitarian prejudice that calculation presupposes certainty, or to put it positively, it requires that we embrace the fallibility of phronesis. What Foucault says about power—that it is neither good nor bad, but rather should be measured by its effects—also applies to the fallibility of phronesis. One of the essential effects of phronesis, which is constitutive of its democratic potential, is that its lack of certainty entails that practical judgments are subject to dispute. Thus, the democratic politics of phronesis are built on a ground that accepts the inevitability of conflict. The instrumental leads to an agonistic conception of human interaction.[6]

The historical and ethico-political insights about instrumentality are intertwined in a materialist ontology. This becomes visible as soon as we discern what I call *the problematic of action*. If we accept the "secular" hypothesis that there is no transcendence, or that existence has one quality—if being is one and unified, as Heidegger put it—then, regardless of whether this one existence is referred to as substance or being, as god or the plane of immanence, the difficulty is always the same, namely, that all actions within the one appear as simple variations of that one. Difference becomes an epiphenomenon rather than real. The "existential vacuum" experienced in the "materialist culture" of high capitalism can be traced back to this problematic.

In ancient Greece, there was a specific response to this problematic. Difference is not located in existence but rather in the effects of existence. The ontological question that allows for the link between theory and praxis is not the "what is?" question, but rather the "what are the effects of what is?" question.[7] There are numerous versions of this argument. For example, the epicurean tradition formulates this idea through the distinction between

---

5. See Dimitris Vardoulakis, *Sovereignty and Its Other: Toward the Dejustification of Violence* (New York: Fordham University Press, 2013), and *Stasis Before the State: Nine Theses of Agonistic Democracy* (New York: Fordham University Press, 2018).
6. See Dimitris Vardoulakis, *The Agonistic Condition* (Edinburgh: Edinburgh University Press, 2025).
7. See Vardoulakis, *The Logic of Living*.

causality and instrumentality: the one—substance, god, or nature—can be conceived in terms of causality, whereas action is accounted for through instrumentality.[8] Without a conception of the instrumental, it is impossible to forge a link between theory and praxis within a materialist ontology that posits a single and unified existence.

I refer to the tradition of thought that resonates with the problematic of action as *monist materialism*. It is monist in the sense that it denotes existence without transcendence. It is materialist in the sense that praxis is discernible in its effects. The resonances with Heidegger are obvious. He posits a single, unified being that is determined through the ontological difference between being and beings. In this sense, Heidegger is a monist materialist. But, unlike earlier monist materialists, his conception of the ineffectual precludes the standard response to the problematic of action with recourse to instrumentality. I find Heidegger's approach unsatisfactory for two reasons that I have already mentioned: first, ontologically, the ineffectual does not exist; and second, in terms ethics and politics, the ineffectual leads to either a trivial or a self-contradictory conception of action. The huge influence of Heidegger's ineffectual blocks contemporary philosophy's ability to see the solution to the problematic of action offered by earlier forms of monist materialism.

To call Heidegger a monist can be construed as both self-evident and preposterous. It is self-evident in the sense that monism can designate his notion of the unity of being that lacks transcendence in any metaphysical sense. It is preposterous in the sense that Heidegger views his ontology as doing away with all preestablished metaphysical assumptions about being, which includes rejecting all "labels" and nomenclature in favor of developing a new way to speak about being. Developing such a new vocabulary for philosophy was particularly relevant in the early twentieth century, when philosophy was undergoing a radical transformation that demanded a rupture with the past. It also characterized various modernisms that boldly advocated for actions such as doing away with museums as a means to create an entirely new artistic vocabulary. Unfortunately, this modernist attitude has led to a constraining imperative in Heidegger studies today, which we can express as: "When one speaks not in Heidegger's terms, one better remain silent about Heidegger."

I resolutely disagree with such an approach. Even though I am committed to immanent critique—the critique of another's position in the context of their own terms—as indispensable to a rigorous critical attitude, a

---

8. See Vardoulakis, *Spinoza, the Epicurean*.

vigorous critique cannot set it as a rule that no terms from lateral discourses can possibly be introduced and incorporated. Besides the dreaded "performative contradiction" if this imperative implies a radical nominalism and hence a return to metaphysics, it alienates "nonexpert" scholars and diminishes the influence of Heidegger's thought. Contrary to this approach, then, I hold that there is no greater service to Heidegger's thought than placing it in seemingly lateral registers, such as monist materialism. This keeps his thinking alive and relevant in new and unexpected places while probing its limits.

The Ruse of Techne is a contribution to such a task. It shows how the ineffectual is constructed through the ruse of techne in such a way that both affirms Heidegger as a monist materialist and demonstrates the deficiency of his approach to respond to the problematic of action in materialism. His notion of the ineffectual is not merely an action conceived as separated from the effects of calculative thinking; it is also, unfortunately, a conception of action that is, plain and simple, ineffectual.

1

Introduction
What is the Ruse of Techne?

3. The ruse of techne

By the term "the ruse of techne" I denote a technique that Heidegger uses to argue that instrumentality reduces being to mere presence, which according to Heidegger prevents action from attaining to the truth of being. This is not, I hold, one among many other techniques, but rather *the* critical technique for Heidegger to account for praxis in the matrix of the unified being that he discovers in Greek thought. The ruse of techne is the technique of Heidegger's ontology of praxis, and as such it is distinct from the ontology of being while being inseparable from it since it organizes the nodal points of Heidegger's discourse as well as their relations. The technique of the ruse of techne and the ontology of being mutually determine each other, such as that a conception of praxis in Heidegger cannot be complete without examining the ruse of techne.

The distinctive move of the ruse consists in removing instrumentality from all ethical and political action proper, which simultaneously constructs the kind of action free of ends, that I refer to as *the ineffectual*. The ruse can be understood as *the*—as opposed to *a*—technique employed by Heidegger for collapsing praxis into ontology, whereby action proper is presented as essentially the thinking of being.

The ruse relies on the fact that techne can denote three different senses in ancient Greek. Its trick starts with conflating the causes and effects of causality with the means and ends of instrumentality so as to confine both within one sense of techne; opposed to that, a separate sense of techne denotes an action that is free of all ends. The truth of being is then supposed to be attained only through the action without ends, or the ineffectual. This is like a conjurer's trick because something before our eyes is made to disappear through a technical maneuver. Specifically, what disappears is the function of instrumentality in the account of action in connection to the thinking of being. To see this trick, we need to grasp the three senses of techne that Heidegger employs.

The first sense of techne denotes the monism of Greek thought. The great achievement of the ancient Greeks, according to Heidegger, is that they thought that being in its oneness and unity could be expressed in a multiplicity of particular beings. This leads to the critical Heideggerian distinction between the one being and the many particular beings. The claim is that this enabled the Greeks to think of truth in a different way—other than the realist insistence on truth as the correspondence between subject and object, and other than the idealist way as the coherence of the external world with the categories of human understanding. Instead, the Greeks thought of truth as the *aletheia* of being, which Heidegger translates literally as the *unforgetting, unconcealment,* or *disclosure* of the single, unified being. The discovery of this alternative notion of truth in Greek thought is hugely significant for Heidegger's overall philosophical project, as it allows him to understand the history of thought as the trajectory of the progressive forgetting of being characteristic of what Heidegger calls metaphysics or onto-theo-logy. This forgetting starts with the distortion of the thinking of the one, unified being through the translation of Greek terms into Latin. The first sense of techne, then, taps into a historical root that carries the promise of a retrieval of the single, unified being and an undoing of its forgetting.

The second sense of techne denotes a distortion of being. This distortion is accentuated in modernity with the rise of modern technology and its delusion, as Heidegger holds, that its calculations can represent the world. Heidegger's second sense, then, is techne as technology. As technology, techne includes not only causality, but also the instrumentality characteristic of calculation. In fact, instrumentality assumes two distinct forms in this second sense of techne (§13). *Either* instrumentality is presented as a preliminary to the activity that discloses being, as in Division 1 of *Being and Time*, where there is an essential connection between tools or equipment and the way in which we are in the world. Instrumentality points to the everyday activities of the subject, or what Heidegger calls the *ontic*. The move to the *ontological* leaves instrumentality behind. This technical realm where Heidegger confines instrumentality is merely a first step that never leads to authenticity. *Or* instrumentality is presented as the major hindrance toward the unconcealment of being. There are many forms of concealment, that is, activities that cover over the truth of being. Some forms of concealment block any potential access to being. None more so than modern technology, or what Heidegger calls "machination." The second form of the sense of techne as technology has the most pernicious ethical and political consequences that Heidegger denotes under the name "nihilism of modernity."[1]

There is a third sense of techne that points in the opposite direction from the instrumentality characteristic of technology. Its main feature is that it is free of means and ends calculations, whereby it is purified of instrumentality. This makes it the antithesis of the second sense of techne as technology. The action without ends is constitutive of the path that leads to the truth of being, according to Heidegger, whereby the truth of being is premised on a *forgetting of instrumentality* in authentic action. Increasingly since the 1930s, Heidegger associates the third sense of techne with the kind of artistic activity that indicates a privileged access to being. There is an established Heideggerian pantheon of artists that are said to facilitate such an unbridled drive to disclosure. First among them is perhaps Hölderlin, but not far behind come Sophocles as well as the pre-Socratics, thinkers such as Parmenides whose philosophy has been preserved in poetic form. Art broadly conceived—or rather, the specific artists that populate Heidegger's work—are said to oppose the authority of reason to fit being into preestablished formulas of means and ends, thereby preserving the essential mystery of being. Since the ineffectual arises within the third sense of techne, this sense plays a decisive role in Heidegger's philosophy and from thereon into continental philosophy, as it is critical for their conception of praxis.

We can understand the trick of the ruse of techne as presenting an either/or. Either the technical conjunction of causality and instrumentality represented by the second sense of techne, or a conception of the single, unified being of the first sense of techne. The trick in this either/or consists in that it is not obvious at all why Heidegger thinks that we should conflate causality and instrumentality, which is a constitutive characteristic of the second sense of techne. In fact, as I will show (§§24–25), Heidegger initially derives this conflation through a mistranslation of Aristotle; and

---

1. Heidegger's invective against modern technology resonates with the so-called "radical conservatism" prevalent in Germany from the beginning of the twentieth century, which explains his comments on Spengler or his admiration for Jünger. This cultural and intellectual milieu has been well documented, so I leave it aside here.

when he returns to it later on several occasions—perhaps most notably in "The Question Concerning Technology"—he never provides a comprehensive argument for this conflation (§57). The problem with the absence of a comprehensive argument to demonstrate why causality and instrumentality are conflated is that without this conflation it is impossible to demarcate an area of action that is free of all ends—it is impossible to determine the third sense of techne and the ineffectual. Or, more forcefully, without a clear determination of the conflation of causality and instrumentality, the notion of technology in Heidegger becomes opaque, as a result of which the notion of the ineffectual also collapses as it is defined in opposition to the second sense of techne—as that which is free of the ends of causality and instrumentality.

The ruse relies on the mutual determination of the three senses of techne. As I will explain in more detail later (see chapter 2), the three senses of techne are interdependent: one sense does not stand on its own but in relation to the other two (§13). This also means that there is no sequential order between the three senses of techne, none of them comes strictly speaking "first" or "second" or "third." What matters is the effects produced by their relations, and the most important effect is the forgetting of instrumentality in an account of action in a monist ontology. This forgetting, as I show, functions like a repressed content that structures Heidegger's thought by remaining invisible (§6).

Why does Heidegger need the ruse of techne? I will answer this question in detail in chapter 2. In short, the answer becomes clear as soon as we realize that Heidegger faces a testing problem as a result of his monism: If being is one and unified, then how can one account for action that effects change? Clearly, for being to be one and unified, it cannot be subject to change itself nor can it allow for difference within itself. The danger is that any action of particular beings may appear as a mere variation of the single, unified being without real difference, whereby action is of no consequence and the human is deprived of freedom. This is not merely a paradox of quantity like those we find in Zeno and Eleatic monism. This is major threat to the distinction between a single, unified being and multiple particular beings, for if beings are mere variations of being, then difference disappears, and we end in Hegel's "night where all the cows are black." Unless a satisfactory answer to this question is found, the relation between being and beings collapses, and with it Heidegger's entire philosophical enterprise. I refer to this problem as "the problematic of action" (see chapter 2).

Heidegger never discovered a satisfactory answer to this problematic (§§15–16, §43, §47, §53, §60). He developed instead a technique, the ruse of techne, to cover it up and consign it to obscurity and oblivion. We will see that the Greeks, and a series of materialists in modernity, had in fact developed an answer about how action allows for change and difference within a single, unified being (§7, §§12–13, §§19–23, §§30–32, §42, §§51–52). Their conception relies on sustaining the distinction between causality and instrumentality, whereby they could not have accepted the conflation of causality and instrumentality according to Heidegger's second sense of techne, nor the possibility of an action without ends as postulated in the third sense. Thus, their conception foregrounds the ethical and political import of instrumentality. The ruse of techne consists in all the maneuvering in Heidegger's philosophy to equate the thinking of being with action so as to obscure the materialist answer to the problem of action within a monist ontology. *The Ruse of Techne* will have succeeded if it forces the reader to recognize the need to choose between two incompatible accounts of action within a monist ontology: one that foregrounds and the Heideggerian one that forgets instrumentality (§7, §14, §29, §52, §60).

4. Metaphysical materialism (the metaphysics of morals)

Heidegger's ruse of techne reverts to a metaphysical conception of action. The so-called "destruction" of metaphysics, announced in the opening pages of *Being and Time*, structures Heidegger's project. But this destruction facilitates the overcoming only of the *epistemology* of traditional onto-theo-logy by rejecting transcendence and the reduction of being to mere presence, by bridging the gap between subject and object, and by overcoming the separation of form and content. However, the castigation of instrumentality on the grounds that it prevents the disclosure of being, remains mired in a metaphysics of *morals*—that is, of action—because it follows the typical, anti-materialist rejection of instrumentality in Judeo-Christian metaphysics (see the Excursus). Differently put, whereas the first sense of techne (being as one and unified) makes possible an epistemological break with metaphysics, the second and third senses of techne (techne as technology and techne as the ineffectual) evince the continuity with the ethics and politics of onto-theo-logy that is stringently anti-instrumental.

This Janus-faced relation to metaphysics arises in Heidegger's early lectures on Aristotle. The key idea enabling the *epistemological* break is that techne is a modality of theoretical knowledge. One of the hallmarks of metaphysics, as Heidegger presents it, is the separation of theory and praxis. By inscribing techne to knowledge, Heidegger forcefully imbues theory with praxis. This move is consummated in the powerful description of the "world" in *Being and Time*. The human does not find itself in the "world" as a detached observer, but rather through its use of the tools that the world offers it in any specific circumstance. The key idea that aligns Heidegger's existentialism with the *morals* of metaphysics is the association of techne exclusively with instrumentality, which amounts to the determination of the ineffectual, the action without ends. To put it pithily, both metaphysics and Heidegger concur that no action characterized by the calculation of means and ends, or the calculation of one's utility, can ever aspire to moral rectitude or to authenticity. They also concur that moral rectitude or authenticity require a renunciation of the means and ends action.

There is a whole discourse about the key metaphysical conception of action and morality as based on adherence to certain transcendent principles or rules. From this perspective, a Heideggerian would object to any similarity of the metaphysics of morals with authenticity that is radically incompatible with any rules or principles. Such a response misses what is most important in the metaphysics of morals. As Nietzsche describes it, the adherence to rules or principles, characteristic of Judeo-Christian metaphysics, is only an effect of something deeper that he denotes as "asceticism." Even though Nietzsche rejects the scientism that celebrates the supposed certainty of calculation, he still insists that the basis of morals or action is debt (*Schuld*) as a calculation that is never complete or certain. The Judeo-Christian metaphysics of morals turns debt inward to transform it into guilt (signified by the same word *Schuld* in German). This inward movement consists in saying "no" to life as an attitude that celebrates the refusal to participate in worldly activities. The asceticism of the morals of metaphysics renounces the instrumentality that is constitutive of action. Without Heidegger admitting it, the ineffectual is a central Christian concept for a metaphysical conception of morals.[2] From such a perspective, Heidegger's repression of instrumentality appears imbued in metaphysics.[3]

The ruse of techne, as Heidegger's technique to provide an account of action, equivocates about metaphysics. Through the first sense of techne, Heidegger can reject an epistemology that relies on transcendence, which places Heidegger within the materialist tradition. With the contrast between the second and the third senses of techne, Heidegger follows the

---

2. See Ian A. Moore, "The End of Instrumentality? Heidegger on *Phronēsis* and Calculative Thinking," *Australian Philosophical Review* 6, no. 3 (2022): 255–61.

3. The prompt to think of Heidegger's conception of being in terms of the ascetic ideal was Charles E. Scott's, *The Question of Ethics: Nietzsche, Foucault, Heidegger* (Bloomington: Indiana University Press, 1990). Even though Scott does not see clearly the connection between the ascetic ideal and anti-instrumentalism, his analysis of the ascetic ideal in Heidegger remains valuable and insightful.

metaphysical conception of action according to which morality must be separated from instrumentality. With the first move, Heidegger sidesteps a series of keystones of the epistemology of metaphysics—such as the separation of subject and object, or of form and content. With the second, he follows metaphysics in castigating instrumentality. From this perspective, Heidegger develops a position rife with tensions, an ontology that is both opposed to metaphysics while also adopting the anti-instrumentalism of its morals. I use the term *metaphysical materialism* to denote this ambivalent attitude to metaphysics and the tensions that it generates.

Heidegger's metaphysical materialism fails to provide a satisfactory account of action. Understanding action as the thinking of being is supposed to be liberating. And yet, as we will see, such an account wavers between either being so thin as to be trivial, or in fact, surreptitiously retains the effects of action as integral to the thinking of being, thereby contaminating the ineffectual with instrumentality. If the former is a vacuous conception of action, the latter easily becomes complicit in the reproduction of the prevalent power. This metaphysical materialism is intertwined with Heidegger's magical materialism in the sense that the ruse functions like a conjurer's trick that hides instrumentality within the sense of techne as technology (the second sense), resulting in the vacuous or complicit sense of action mired in the metaphysics of morals. Thus, the ruse also hides the metaphysics of morals entailed by Heidegger's construal of the third sense of techne and leads to a contradictory and unsatisfactory conception of action.

The forgetting or repression of instrumentality, and the obscuring of the metaphysics of morals, are two sides of the same coin—the ruse of techne. From this perspective, the ruse appears critical in Heidegger's overall project.

5. The reception of Heidegger and the ruse of techne

If we peruse the reception of Heidegger's work, it quickly becomes clear that there is a uniform lack of attention to the ruse of techne. The result is that his metaphysical materialism has also remained unexamined. Thus, despite an enormous secondary literature, the technique organizing Heidegger's ontology, that is, the ruse of techne, has never been presented with any clarity and as a consequence it has never informed the exegesis of his work.

We can broadly identify three distinct categories of reception, all of which fail to recognize the ruse of techne: Readings that a) pay no attention to Heidegger's practical philosophy, focusing instead on the epistemological break with metaphysics; b) approach his practical philosophy by presupposing the ineffectual; and c) engage with his conception of technology (or the second sense of techne) without a clear conception of its relation to metaphysical materialism. I will provide a typology of the variants of each of these three categories of reception in relation to the ruse of techne. The typology cannot possibly be exhaustive. Instead, the aim is to signpost the vast scholarship on Heidegger in relation to the ruse of techne.

a) Approaches that do not pay particular attention to Heidegger's conception of action. I identify four relevant variations of this category:

1. An emphasis on *intentionality* that is often informed by a renewed interest in phenomenology. The tendency here is to downplay the way in which praxis is crucial in Heidegger's thought. The impetus is often to construct a materialist epistemology, often referred to as naturalism, following the highly influential work of Dan Zahavi. Within this context, the notion of intentionality seems to take over any concern for instrumentality's role in a conception of action.[4]

2. There are other approaches to Heidegger's *theoretical philosophy and epistemology without extensive attention being paid to ethics and politics*. Some of the most interesting work on this has been the argument about the "transcendental Heidegger" that we find in Steven Crowell.[5] Here belongs, also, the topological approach to Heidegger. Spearheaded by Jeff Malpas, it shifts the emphasis from time to place, and from the early to the later Heidegger. It contains an implicit acknowledgment of calculative reason in the distinction between space (which is calculable) and place (which is not), but this distinc-

---

4. See, indicatively, Sascha Golob, *Heidegger on Concepts, Freedom, and Normativity* (Cambridge: Cambridge University Press, 2014); and for a response, Aaron James Wendland, "Rethinking Intentionality in *Being and Time*," *International Journal of Philosophical Studies* 29, no. 1 (2021): 44–76. An earlier example of this general approach is Burt Hopkins, *Intentionality in Husserl and Heidegger: The Problem of the Original Method and Phenomenon of Phenomenology* (Dordrecht: Kluwer, 1993). A collected volume indicative of this approach is Julian Kiverstein and Michael Wheeler, eds., *Heidegger and Cognitive Science* (New York: Palgrave Macmillan, 2012).

5. Steven Galt Crowell, *Husserl, Heidegger, and the Space of Meaning: Paths Toward Transcendental Phenomenology* (Evanston, IL: Northwestern University Press, 2001). For an appraisal of this approach from the perspective of its connection to a theory of praxis, see William Blattner, "Ontology, the A Priori, and the Primacy of Practice: An Aporia in Heidegger's Early Philosophy," in *Transcendental Heidegger*, ed. Steven Crowell and Jeff Malpas (Stanford, CA: Stanford University Press, 2007), 10–27.

tion is employed to address primarily epistemological and ontological concerns, not concerns about Heidegger's account of action.[6]

3. In the examination of Heidegger's engagement with *Greek philosophy*, particularly with the pre-Socratics, Plato, and Aristotle, the emphasis tends to be on the ways in which Heidegger's work revolutionized the way that Greek thought offered a premetaphysical conception of existence. There is some truly erudite work here by scholars such as Walter Brogan and William MacNeil.[7] John Sallis deserves special mention as conducting his own readings of ancient philosophy based on a Heideggerian approach.[8] However, these readings fail to note the problem of how to connect being and action in a monist ontology, and consequently fail to recognize the ruse of techne.

4. Finally, there are approaches to the *history of philosophy* that rely on Heidegger's methodologies and presuppose the ineffectual, which traps them in the ruse of techne. Some of them amplify and explain Heidegger's own account of past thinkers on this basis.[9] Others revise his reading of the canon, suggesting amendments by discovering the equation of thinking and action in areas that Heidegger castigated as onto-theo-logical, such as the theological tradition.[10] An alternative questioning of Heidegger's reading of the history of thought, while remaining within the purview of Heideggerian philosophy, is Ernesto Grassi's work that presents the Italian humanists as anti-metaphysical

---

6. Jeff Malpas, *Heidegger's Topology: Being, Place, World* (Cambridge, MA: MIT Press, 2006), and *Heidegger and the Thinking of Place: Explorations in the Topology of Being World* (Cambridge, MA: MIT Press, 2012).

7. Walter Brogan, *Heidegger and Aristotle: The Twofoldness of Being* (Albany: SUNY Press, 2005); William McNeill, *The Glance of the Eye: Heidegger, Aristotle, and the Ends of Theory* (Albany: SUNY Press, 1999), and *The Time of Life: Heidegger and Ethos* (Albany: SUNY Press, 2006).

8. John Sallis, *Being and Logos: Reading the Platonic Dialogues* (Bloomington: Indiana University Press, 1996), and *Echoes: After Heidegger* (Bloomington: Indiana University Press, 1990).

9. See, for example, Ian Alexander Moore, *Eckhart, Heidegger, and the Imperative of Releasement* (Albany: SUNY Press, 2019).

10. Some of the most influential works here are Hans Jonas, "Heidegger and Theology," *Review of Metaphysics* 18, no. 2 (1964): 207–33; Jean-Luc Marion, "Saint Thomas Aquinas and Onto-theo-logy," in *Mystics: Presence and Aporia*, trans. Christian Sheppard and Michael Kessler (Chicago: University of Chicago Press, 2003); John Caputo, *Heidegger and Aquinas: An Essay on Overcoming Metaphysics* (New York: Fordham University Press, 1982).

thinkers.[11] Implicitly, a lot of the work in this variant offers historical support to my argument about Heidegger's lapse into a metaphysics of morals.

In this first category of reception of Heidegger, I have found no evidence of any consideration of his technique that I call the ruse of techne. For the most part, the approaches in this category of reception are positioned in such a way as to ignore the repression of instrumentality.

b) There is a rich tradition that seeks to expand on Heideggerian practical philosophy. I noted above that Heidegger is reluctant to talk about an ethics or a politics. A sizeable part of the secondary literature seeks to provide such an ethics or politics based on Heideggerian philosophy. And yet, the ineffectual is accepted without much ado, so as to form the basis of a Heideggerian ethics or politics. As a result, there is a unanimous castigation of instrumentality and the nine variants that I identify remain unaware of Heidegger's metaphysical materialism produced by the ruse of techne.

5. We can understand the entire *hermeneutical tradition* that starts with Gadamer as developing the practical implications of Heidegger's philosophy. The importance of phronesis here is indisputable—a point that will have added significance in light of the argument that Heidegger develops his ruse of techne through his interpretation of phronesis (see chapter 3). In fact, during the time that Gadamer was his student, Gadamer admits the profound influence of Heidegger's interpretation of phronesis.[12] This influence is apparent in *Truth and Method*, where the analysis of phronesis plays a central role.[13] Despite the positive move to attend to the practical implications of Heidegger's philosophy, Gadamer is following his teacher in emptying all instrumentality from the Aristotelian conception of phronesis and depositing it instead into techne.[14] This reading relies on a mistranslation of Aristotle's own determination of the truth of phronesis—as I will explain in chapter 3.

---

11. Ernesto Grassi, *Heidegger and the Question of Renaissance Humanism* (Binghamton, NY: Center for Medieval and Early Renaissance Studies, 1983).
12. Hans-Georg Gadamer, *Philosophical Hermeneutics*, ed. and trans. David E. Linge (Berkeley: University of California Press, 1976), 201–202.
13. Hans-Georg Gadamer, *Truth and Method*, rev. trans. Joel Weinsheimer and Donald G. Marshall (New York: Continuum, 1989), 312.
14. Gadamer, *Truth and Method*, 318–19.

6. Adorno's *The Jargon of Authenticity* argues that Heidegger's "philosophical banality" is disguised by a jargon that appears sublime but is, in fact, vulgar, leading to a profound disconnection from historical reality.[15] The argument grew out of the critique of idealism in *Negative Dialectics*. Adorno accuses Heidegger of a radical inwardness, akin to idealism, which deprives his subjects of any possible political engagement. Despite the perceptive analysis, Adorno grounds his accusations against Heidegger in the implicit—and thus all the more unquestioned—embrace of the ineffectual. As a result, Adorno cannot acknowledge the significant overlap of their respective anti-instrumentalism and, as such, falls short of recognizing the ruse techne.

7. A similar reluctance to question the ineffectual, and consequently an inability to see the ruse of techne, characterizes the extensive literature on Heidegger's *involvement with National Socialism*. There are roughly four main trends here: First, the "Heidegger affair" or "Heidegger controversy" is carried out through studies that compile the documentary evidence of Heidegger's involvement leading to the condemnation of his involvement.[16] These are useful studies, but they tend to have a limited engagement with Heidegger's philosophy. Second, there is a long line of responses to Heidegger's involvement with National Socialism that seek to find an essential connection between his ontology and Nazi ideology.[17] Heidegger's forgetting of

---

15. Theodor W. Adorno, *The Jargon of Authenticity*, trans. Knut Tarnowski and Frederic Will (Evanston, IL: Northwestern University Press, 1973), 51.

16. The two most prominent exponents of this approach are Victor Farias, *Heidegger and Nazism*, trans. Paul Burrell and Gabriel R. Ricci (Philadelphia: Temple University Press, 1989); and Emmanuel Faye, *Heidegger: The Introduction of Nazism into Philosophy in Light of the Unpublished Seminars of 1933–1935*, trans. Michael B. Smith (New Haven, CT: Yale University Press, 2009). Among the many significant responses to the new documentary evidence, Richard Wolin's *The Heidegger Controversy: A Critical Reader* (Cambridge, MA: MIT Press, 1991) was particularly significant in the English-speaking context.

17. In this kind of approach, we can find important readers of Heidegger who are major philosophers in their own right. See, for instance, Jacques Derrida, Hans-Georg Gadamer, and Philippe Lacoue-Labarthe, *Heidegger, Philosophy, and Politics: The Heidelberg Conference*, trans. Jeff Fort (New York: Fordham University Press, 2016); Philippe Lacoue-Labarthe, *Heidegger, Art and Politics: The Fiction of the Political*, trans. Chris Turner (Oxford: Blackwell, 1990); Jacques Derrida, *Of Spirit: Heidegger and the Question*, trans. Geoffrey Bennington and Rachel Bowlby (Chicago: University of Chicago Press, 1989); Jean-François Lyotard, *Heidegger and "The Jews,"* trans. Andreas Michel and Mark S. Roberts (Minneapolis: University of Minnesota Press, 1990); Alain

instrumentality tends to be sheltered from any substantial critique, as the commentators in this approach tend to espouse some version of the ineffectual, largely under the influence of Heidegger's thought. Third, there are readings that offer a more contextual approach to Heidegger's thought and politics.[18] They provide useful social and historical grounding, but again, we will look in vain for a description of the technique of the ruse of techne. Finally, there is a burgeoning literature, following the publication of the *Black Notebooks*, that combines the previous three approaches using the new material made available.[19] Here, either the engagement with National Socialism is assumed as a critique of Heidegger's philosophy, or his ontology is questioned in light of his politics as if there is a seamless connection between the two. It is important to shed light on Heidegger's involvement with National Socialism, but it is a petitio principii to collapse his political actions into his ontological commitments. Philosophically, it is more pertinent to note that, as we learn for instance in *Introduction to Metaphysics*, the Nazi party represented for him an alternative to the technologization of experience in modernity. The ruse of techne, then, becomes critical to think through the connection between Heidegger's anti-instrumentalism and his engagement with National Socialism (see chapter 5).

8. The *left* Heidegger is understandable in the context of the materialist basis of his ontology. The emphasis on finitude and the rejection of transcendence already place Heidegger on a path that shares a similar orientation to Marx's, as Axelos and Marcuse observe.[20] Žižek has

---

Badiou and Barbara Cassin, *Heidegger: His Life and His Philosophy*, trans. Susan Spitzer (New York: Columbia University Press, 2016); Richard Wolin, *The Politics of Being: The Political Thought of Martin Heidegger* (New York: Columbia University Press, 1990).

18. See, in particular, Pierre Bourdieu, *The Political Ontology of Martin Heidegger*, trans. Peter Collier (Cambridge: Polity Press, 1991); Hans Sluga, *Heidegger's Crisis: Philosophy and Politics in Nazi Germany* (Cambridge, MA: Harvard University Press, 1993); James Phillips, *Heidegger's Volk: Between National Socialism and Poetry* (Stanford, CA: Stanford University Press, 2005).

19. Peter Trawny, *Freedom to Fail: Heidegger's Anarchy*, trans. Ian Alexander Moore and Christopher Turner (Cambridge: Polity Press, 2015), and *Heidegger and the Myth of a Jewish World Conspiracy*, trans. Andrew J. Mitchel (Chicago: University of Chicago Press, 2015); David Ferrell Krell, *Ecstasy, Catastrophe: Heidegger from Being and Time to the Black Notebooks* (Albany: SUNY Press, 2015); Donatella Di Cesare, *Heidegger and the Jews: The Black Notebooks*, trans. Murtha Baca (Cambridge: Polity Press, 2018).

20. Kostas Axelos, *Introduction to a Future Way of Thought: On Marx and Heidegger*, trans. Kenneth Mills (Lüneburg: Meson Press, 2015); Herbert Marcuse, *Heideggerian*

also often been seen as advancing a "left Heideggerianism," not only because of his explicit and implicit references to Heidegger but also because of his early association with the Yugoslav Heideggerian school.[21] This left Heideggerianism is characterized by a profound mistrust of technology. Thus, for instance, Axelos's book on Marx examines the early notion of alienation where technology is a causal factor, which is why the editor in the introduction notes the influence of Heidegger, despite scant references in the text itself.[22] As such, the left Heideggerians embrace the anti-instrumentalism that presupposes Heidegger's metaphysical materialism.[23]

9. A different approach to a potential theory of action in Heideggerian is to argue that his *ontology is primarily a theory of praxis*. Perhaps the most influential exponent of this approach is Reiner Schürmann. His *Heidegger on Being and Acting* starts by emphasizing how the historical import of Heidegger's overcoming of metaphysics consists in the dismantling of the distinction between theory and praxis, which entails the primacy of praxis in his ontology.[24] This is in accord with the epistemological materialism in Heidegger, while Schürmann is also fully committed to anti-instrumentalism: "What is the given that radical phenomenology deconstructs? The arrangements among phenomena as they have had currency in the West—the economies of presence." Among these economies there is one that guides the entire enterprise of Schürmann's deconstruction, namely, "contemporary technology."[25] The reason Schürmann offers is political: "Technology attests that in its beginning and its essence

---

Marxism, ed. Richard Wolin and John Abromeit (Lincoln: University of Nebraska Press, 2005).

21. See, for example, Slavoj Žižek, *In Defense of Lost Causes* (London: Verso, 2008).

22. Kostas Axelos, *Alienation, Praxis and Techne in the Thought of Karl Marx*, trans. Ronald Bruzina (Austin: University of Texas Press, 1976). For an important work that brings Heidegger and Marx into conversation and is indebted to Axelos, see Laurence Paul Menning, *Heidegger and Marx: A Productive Dialogue Over the Language of Humanism* (Evanston, IL: Northwestern University Press, 2013).

23. Thomas Brockelman notes how Žižek's engagement with Heidegger revolves around technology in *Žižek and Heidegger: The Question Concerning Techno-Capitalism* (London: Bloomsbury, 2008).

24. Or, as Hans-Georg Gadamer puts the same point in a review of *Heidegger on Being and Acting*, Schürmann manages "to find true acting in thinking itself—in a non-prescriptive thinking." *Graduate Faculty Philosophy Journal* 13, no. 1 (1988): 156.

25. Reiner Schürmann, *Heidegger on Being and Acting: From Principles to Anarchy*, trans. Christine-Marie Gros (Bloomington: Indiana University Press, 1987), 284.

violence is actually more than a matter of concept of theory."²⁶ The condemnation of instrumentality on the grounds that it is inextricable from violence arises from Heidegger's critique of the nihilism of modernity, which in turn relies on his ruse of techne that remains unnoticed in Schürmann's discourse (§28).

10. I treat the *ethical* and the *political* Heidegger as a single variant not to diminish or downgrade the significant work that has been done on this topic, but rather because these discourses are premised on a shared series of well-established moves, despite widely divergent results (§§61–64). For expediency, I refer to Jean-Luc Nancy's article "Heidegger's 'Originary Ethics'" since it rehearses these moves with exemplary clarity. First move: the acknowledgment that Heidegger himself questions the possibility of an ethics, as well as a political philosophy. Second, the acknowledgment that Heidegger erred, both ethically and politically, in his involvement with National Socialism. The first two moves are discursive and historical contextualizations that lead to the next two moves that form the basis of a Heideggerian ethics. Third move, the ontologization of action characteristic of the ineffectual. Nancy states this as self-evident at the very beginning of his article: "what is at issue is the logic by which a thinking sought to analyze what constitutes man as the one through whom 'Being' has as its original 'sense' (or ethos) the choice and conduct of existence."²⁷ Ontology *is* an ethos, according to this move. Being and action become indistinguishable. This is celebrated as Heidegger's major achievement: "With Heidegger . . . philosophy understood itself (once again) as 'ethics.' . . . The 'thinking of Being' . . . is nothing other than a thinking of what Heidegger called 'original ethics.'"²⁸ The fourth move consists in a—or, in *the*—anti-instrumentalism: "the thinking of 'technics' [is] a retreat from moral foundation and the delivery of a different ethical demand."²⁹ This "originary" ethical demand is an ethics beyond technology and calculation, in short, an ethics that forgets instrumentality. No recognition here that the metaphysical of morals also presupposes an anti-instrumentalism. The third and fourth moves, then, are entirely in the thrall of the ruse of techne, seduced or enchanted by it, unable

---

26. Schürmann, *Heidegger on Being and Acting*, 276.
27. Jean-Luc Nancy, "Heidegger's 'Originary Ethics,'" in *Heidegger and Practical Philosophy*, ed. François Raffoul and David Pettigrew (Albany: SUNY Press, 2002), 65.
28. Nancy, "Heidegger's 'Originary Ethics,'" 66.
29. Nancy, "Heidegger's 'Originary Ethics,'" 66.

to break its spell.³⁰ Originary ethics presupposes Heidegger's metaphysical materialism—which is to say that it is in the thralls of magical materialism.

11. I indicate a distinct category for largely *poststructuralist* attempts to think about social and political phenomena within a Heideggerian framework. These attempts are based on readings of Heidegger without attempting to be faithful to his word. We can mention here Jean-Luc Nancy again, in particular his work on thinking community and the social from an ontology that emphasizes singularity.³¹ But perhaps the most significant contribution in this variant is the notion of the event. The event, as François Raffoul shows, is intertwined with Heidegger's philosophy but it also branches out to include all sorts of different thinkers and concerns that Heidegger himself did not tackle directly.³² The reach of this concept can be seen in the well-known interview that Derrida gave about 9/11. The analysis of the terrorist attacks is framed in terms of the event: from a geopolitical perspective—which Derrida describes perspicaciously in detail—the terrorist attack was predictable; and yet, he also insists, as an event, it was simultaneously entirely unpredictable and unexpected, which is to say, it cannot fit into instrumental thinking. Derrida reformulates this double aspect of the event—its predictability and anti-instrumentalism—into the concept of "autoimmunity."³³ But the anti-instrumentalism of autoimmunity finds it hard to avoid self-contradiction, due to the suspicion that, in fact, it presupposes and requires instrumentality.³⁴

---

30. From this vast literature, I single out the following works: Joanna Hodge, *Heidegger and Ethics* (London: Routledge, 1995); Frederick Olafson, *Heidegger and the Ground of Ethics: A Study of Mitdasein* (Cambridge: Cambridge University Press, 1998); and the edited collection by François Raffoul and David Pettigrew, *Heidegger and Practical Philosophy* (Albany: SUNY Press, 2002).

31. Jean-Luc Nancy, *Being Singular Plural*, trans. Robert D. Richardson and Anne E. O'Byrne (Stanford, CA: Stanford University Press, 2000).

32. François Raffoul, *Thinking the Event* (Bloomington: Indiana University Press, 2020).

33. Jacques Derrida, "Autoimmunity: Real and Symbolic Suicides," in *Philosophy in a Time of Terror: Dialogues with Jürgen Habermas and Jacques Derrida*, ed. Giovanna Borradori (Chicago: University of Chicago Press, 2003), 85–136. See especially Derrida's further development of these ideas in *Rogues: Two Essays on Reason*, trans. Pascale-Anne Brault and Michael Nass (Stanford, CA: Stanford University Press, 2005).

34. Dimitris Vardoulakis, "Autoimmunities: Derrida, Democracy and Political Theology," *Research in Phenomenology* 48 (2018): 29–56.

12. *Levinas's reading of Heidegger* has been deeply influential, so I designate it as a category on its own.[35] After studying with Heidegger in the late-1920s, Levinas gradually weaned off the influence of his teacher, ultimately arriving at a critique that can be summarized as follows: Heidegger was wrong that the fundamental question of philosophy is the question of being; rather, the fundamental question is the relation to the Other. Differently put, ethics precedes ontology. This argument takes many different forms and it is refracted and reworked in various writings by Levinas that exercised a significant impact on the "French" reception of Heidegger.[36] Another way in which the Levinasian argument has been expressed is by saying that, due to his insistence on the question of being, Heidegger fails to escape the metaphysics of presence, and hence his philosophy lapses into "sameness."[37] Levinas's critique became a major source of the reading of Heidegger for at least two generations of scholars.[38] The importance of this approach, in relation to the ruse of techne, consists in that Levinas casts doubt on the equation of the thinking of being with action. Its drawback is the unawareness of

---

35. There is a sizeable literature on the relation of Heidegger and Levinas. I cannot deal with this in detail here, mentioning only the recent collection edited by John E. Drabinski and Eric S. Nelson, *Between Levinas and Heidegger* (Albany: SUNY Press, 2014); and the excellent article by Michael Fagenblat, "Levinas and Heidegger: The Elemental Confrontation," in *The Oxford Handbook of Levinas*, ed. Michael L. Morgan (Oxford: Oxford University Press, 2019), 103–33.

36. The influence of Levinas is felt, not so much in the way in which his critique of Heidegger is explicitly referred to, but even more so when it is taken for granted. Here is an example from Blanchot where, without referring explicitly to Heidegger, the possibility of philosophy is identified with the question of the other as opposed to the question of being: "But we must not despair of philosophy. In Emmanuel Levinas's book [*Totality and Infinity*]—where, it seems to me, philosophy in our time has never spoken in a more sober manner, putting back into question, as we must, our ways of thinking and even our facile reverence for ontology—we are called upon to become responsible for what philosophy essentially is, by entertaining precisely the idea of the Other in all its radiance and in the infinite exigency that are proper to it, that is to say, the relation with *autrui*. It is as though there were here a new departure in philosophy and a leap that it, and we ourselves, were urged to accomplish." Maurice Blanchot, *The Infinite Conversation*, trans. Susan Hanson (Minneapolis: University of Minnesota Press, 1997), 51–52.

37. See Emmanuel Levinas, *Totality and Infinity: An Essay on Exteriority*, trans. Alphonso Lingis (Pittsburgh, PA: Duquesne University Press, 1969).

38. The influence of this argument is visible in Jacques Derrida's famous paper on *Being and Time*, "*Ousia* and *Gramme*: A Note on a Note from *Being and Time*," in *Margins of Philosophy*, trans. Alan Bass (Chicago: University of Chicago Press, 1984), 29–67. Or see Andrew Benjamin's reading of Heidegger in *The Plural Event: Descartes, Hegel, Heidegger* (London: Routledge, 1993).

the historical background of monism and the unquestioned embrace of anti-instrumentalism, which leaves the ruse of techne to operate unseen in the background.[39]

13. I have discovered only one book that attempts to question Heidegger's anti-instrumentalism, Stuart Elden's *Speaking Against Number*. It has taken someone who does not work in a philosophy department, and hence is not beholden to the "Heidegger industry," to even attempt to break the hold of the idea that instrumentality blocks the path to the truth of being and to undo the forgetting of instrumentality. Elden's approach is clearly stated at the beginning: "grasping this determination of the world—that *to be, is to be calculable*—is useful in understanding the modern notion of the 'political' as a whole, not sociologically, empirically, or ontically, but ontologically."[40] In other words, calculation or instrumentality is not merely ontic but also ontological. Even though the suggestion of the ontological import of calculation is an iconoclastic position within the reception history of Heidegger, Elden still fails to discern the ruse of techne involved in obscuring this ontological import of instrumentality for a conception of action.

I have distinguished here nine variants to the attempt to find a theory of praxis or a systematic account of action in Heidegger. They all start by noticing how Heidegger did not sufficiently develop the ethical and political implications of his thought, but they also operate within a Heideggerian framework that repress, with Heidegger, the function of instrumentality in an account of action. This means that ultimately these approaches are unable to see the ruse of techne. Beholden to Heidegger's magical ma-

---

39. Symptomatic of this lack of awareness about the connection between anti-instrumentalism and the ruse of techne is Catherine Malabou's *The Heidegger Change: On the Fantastic in Philosophy*, trans. Peter Skafish (Albany: SUNY Press, 2011). Malabou argues that the discourse of change in Heidegger is more primary than the discourse of difference, suggesting to the reader that "Henceforth, you will no longer be able to keep in focus the difference between being and beings but only the difference between *differing* and *changing*. The center of gravity of your reading has already been displaced. You have, without realizing it, *exchanged difference for change*" (16). Even if this argument succeeds in demonstrating that Heidegger tackles the difficulties of instrumentality through this conception of change, still Malabou is thoroughly unaware of a—or *the*—profound refusal of change in Heidegger's metaphysical materialism, namely, his persistence with the typical metaphysical argument about action, according to which instrumental action is always lacking, or ethically dubious.

40. Stuart Elden, *Speaking Against Number: Heidegger, Language and the Politics of Calculation* (Edinburgh: Edinburgh University Press, 2006), 2.

terialism, their key common characteristic emerges as the repression of instrumentality.

c) A third category of reception of Heidegger are the readings that engage with his account of the second sense of techne as technology. In some of these readings, techne is related to epistemological questions and thus is largely unconcerned with practical questions; and in others, the engagement with techne has a decidedly practical intention. In none of these approaches is there a conception of the repression of instrumentality in action, leaving the ruse of techne unrecognized.

14. The *epistemological significance of techne* was forcefully asserted by Hubert Dreyfus in *Being-in-the-World*. This influential book makes the bold assertion that the best worked-out part of Heidegger's philosophy is Division 1 of *Being and Time*. It is there that we find the description of the subject's "world" in terms of the way that one uses tools or equipment.[41] In other works, Dreyfus develops the implications of this reading of Division 1. For instance, he attempts a reading of the differences between techne, technology, equipment, and other cognate terms.[42] Or he applies the reading of equipment to the notion of authenticity from Division 2 of *Being and Time*.[43] In all this influential work, Dreyfus never seriously considers the ethical and political implications of Heidegger's anti-instrumentalism, and he never explores the sources of Heidegger's notion of tools and equipment in Greek thought about action. As a result of not paying attention to this background, the ruse of techne is not even an issue that arises within Dreyfus's framework.

15. Don Ihde has opened up a new, postphenomenological approach to Heidegger's conception philosophy of technology that broadens Dreyfus's insights. Ihde's approach is characterized by two related moves. The first combines an empirical interest in the historical development of technologies with a phenomenological analysis of technology. In this, Idhe's work is pioneering and hugely influential. The second consists in what Idhe refers to as the "inversion" in the

---

41. Hubert L. Dreyfus, *Being-in-the-World: A Commentary on Heidegger's Being and Time, Division 1* (Cambridge, MA: MIT Press, 1991).

42. Hubert L. Dreyfus, "Between Techne and Technology: The Ambiguous Place of Equipment in *Being and Time*," *Tulane Studies in Philosophy* 32 (1984): 23–35, and "Heidegger's History of the Being of Equipment," in *Heidegger: A Critical Reader*, ed. Hubert Dreyfus and Harrison Hall (Oxford: Blackwell, 1992), 173–85.

43. Hubert L Dreyfus, "Interpreting Heidegger on Das Man," *Inquiry* 38, no. 4 (1995): 423–30.

relation between technology and science. Whereas a usual account emphasizes the priority of science, inspired by Heidegger's *Being and Time* and "The Question Concerning Technology," Ihde reverses the relation to demonstrate the priority of technology over science.[44] This argument is clearly aligned with the trajectory of Heidegger's conception of techne as I will describe it, both challenging the repression of instrumentality generally and, more specifically, supporting my argument that, whereas in *Plato's Sophist* from 1924 episteme is presented as the virtue of techne (§27), in *Being and Time* techne is transformed into the virtue of episteme (§42). Ihde could not know the important connection between Heidegger's earlier lectures on techne in Greek philosophy, and Aristotle in particular, as these works were published after his major book on the philosophy of technology.[45] As a result, Ihde does not describe with sufficient clarity the connection between the three senses of techne and he does not recognize the ruse of techne.

16. Another approach that briefly attracted attention was the so-called *Object-Oriented Ontology*—or OOO, as it came to be known—that Graham Harman developed through his own reading of Division 1 of *Being and Time*. The idea has a catchy battle-cry: "Back to the Objects themselves!" Harman suggests that Heidegger's real message was the attempt to construct an ontology devoid of the human, an ontology of the object as such. The overcoming of metaphysics is not, according to Harman's reading, the dismantling of the separation of theory and praxis. Rather, it consists in the expulsion of praxis from ontology altogether. Methodologically this means that we have "to abandon the view that human praxis was ever the theme of the tool-analysis" in Division 1 of *Being and Time*.[46] The fact that Harman's reading of tools—or what I call the second sense of techne—in *Being and Time* is so stretched as to not accord with Heidegger's position can be forgiven, since Harman admits that he wants to go beyond Heidegger. The problem is that the exclusion of praxis makes the tool analysis unstainable and self-contradictory. If OOO has nothing to say about action,

---

44. Don Ihde, *Heidegger's Technologies: Postphenomenological Perspectives* (New York: Fordham University Press, 2010).

45. Don Ihde, *Technics and Praxis: A Philosophy of Technology* (Dordrecht: Reidel, 1979). Heidegger's early lecture on Aristotle and techne did not become available until the 1990s.

46. Graham Harman, *Tool-Being: Heidegger and the Metaphysics of Objects* (Chicago: Open Court, 2002), 7

then what is the point of such an ontology other than as an excuse for a litany of self-aggrandizing claims about its novelty and radicality.[47] Such claims seem blissfully—or conveniently—unaware that they are most concerned with certain kinds of practice, thereby undermining the "revolutionary" ontology of objects devoid of the human that they proclaim for themselves. Finally, reading Heidegger as if techne has nothing to do with praxis, moves OOO to a sphere in which the ruse of techne is in complete command because it can never be questioned without examining the ineffectual in Heidegger's conception of action.

17. A completely different approach consists in *elevating techne to the cypher of being and action*. This is consistent with Heidegger's own account of poetry like Hölderlin's as the supposedly hidden meaning of technology, such as in "The Question Concerning Technology." Here, the mystery of being is transformed into the mystery of great poetry. Alain Badiou discerns the repercussions of making art the cipher of action: "What culminated with Heidegger is the antipositivist and anti-Marxist effort to put philosophy in the hands of the poem."[48] The elevation of art to the mystery of being is a political act that is decidedly polemical against specific, identifiable positions (§55, §61). The context here is important. It is first in France that this argument takes a significant hold through the contribution of thinkers such as Georges Bataille, whose *Accursed Share* develops a fiercely anti-instrumentalist account of social being, while elevating the artist to the new kind of sovereign since artistic production is meant to disclose more about being than any instrumental discourse.[49] This argument has played a significant role in interpretations of Heidegger in English. I am thinking here of works such as Krzysztof Ziarek's *The*

---

47. For example, Harman proclaims that his analysis of "tool-being" contains "enough puzzles to fuel a revolution." Harman, *Tool-Being*, 7. Or another statement whose meaning is its own hyperbole: "I invite the reader to participate in the liberation of objects from the philosophical ghetto where they have been confined for far too long" (11). And another, from the many to choose from: "The meaning of being is tool-being, and the near future of philosophy may hinge in large part on the further exploration of this Heideggerian insight" (16).

48. Alain Badiou, *Manifesto for Philosophy*, trans. Norman Madarasz (Albany: SUNY Press, 1992), 66.

49. Georges Bataille, *The Accursed Share: An Essay on General Economy*, volumes 2 and 3, *The History of Eroticism* and *Sovereignty*, trans. Robert Hurley (New York: Zone Books, 1993), see especially the end to volume 3.

Force of Art and Andrew Mitchell's *Heidegger Among the Sculptors*.⁵⁰ They both advocate the ontological priority of art because it is ineffectual, which helps it escape the instrumentalism of tools and the pernicious effects of machination. The stringent anti-instrumentalism of this approach celebrates the third sense of techne, whereby it is under the spell of the ruse of techne (§53).

18. The most consequential approach insofar as thinking of techne's three senses where Heidegger is concerned, comes from the work of Bernard Stiegler, whose important, three-volume *Technics and Time* has been critical for a renewed attempt to think about technology within continental philosophy using a Heideggerian framework.⁵¹ Admittedly, Stiegler's work is not immune to a certain technophobia and a noticeable anti-instrumentalist bias, but his work opened the way for subsequent scholars to further develop a philosophy of technology. Foremost among them is Yuk Hui, whose work has a certain basis in Heidegger—and Stiegler's interpretation of Heidegger—but is a distinct philosophy in its own right.⁵² I will return to this literature in due course (§§63–64). I merely note here, that despite all the significant advances of this approach, the ruse of techne still lurks in the shadows, without being illuminated in any significant way.

I have outlined here eighteen distinct approaches to Heidegger, organized under three general categories. In this typology of the reception of Heidegger, one thing is clear: *the all too quick unquestioned acceptance of the ruse of techne leads to the forgetting of instrumentality*. The ruse has been so successful that it has remained unnoticed and unseen by generations of scholars reading the same texts that I will be reading to demonstrate its operative presence. In that sense, I am making a claim about the ruse that is not dissimilar to the claim that Heidegger makes about being: namely, the ruse of techne organizes Heidegger's discourse, no less than the entire philosophical discourse about techne and instrumentality in the wake of

---

50. Krzysztof Ziarek, *The Force of Art* (Stanford, CA: Stanford University Press, 2004); Andrew Mitchell, *Heidegger Among the Sculptors: Body, Space, and the Art of Dwelling* (Stanford, CA: Stanford University Press, 2010).

51. Bernard Stiegler, *Technics and Time, 1: The Fault of Epimetheus* (Stanford, CA: Stanford University Press, 1998), *Technics and Time, 2: Disorientation* (Stanford, CA: Stanford University Press, 2009), and *Technics and Time, 3: Cinematic Time and the Question of Malaise* (Stanford, CA: Stanford University Press, 2010).

52. See Yuk Hui, *The Question Concerning Technology in China: An Essay in Cosmotechnics* (Falmouth: Urbanomic, 2017).

Heidegger, even if the ruse is forgotten. Or, perhaps, it is more accurate to say that the ruse of techne has been operative by effecting the forgetting of instrumentality.

6. The repression of instrumentality

We can also employ a psychoanalytic vocabulary to speak of the repression of instrumentality so as to highlight the effects of the ruse of techne.[53] As we know from psychoanalysis, the repressed content determines one's actions and, so long as it remains repressed, it will always return to haunt one's decisions. The repressed is most present and impactful where it is less visible. This seems to be the case with the way that instrumentality is construed in Heidegger's thought and its reception. Let me offer one example.

In "The Political Myths of Martin Heidegger," Jeff Love and Michael Meng argue that there is an important, radical, political potential in Heidegger's rectoral address that is still relevant today. This purported radicalism consists in his anti-instrumentalism. The rectoral address contains a "more radical imagining of the state, as a sustained enactment of philosophical pedagogy . . . [that] seeks nothing less than to eradicate the fraught relation between philosophy . . . and politics."[54] Politics here stands for any action that exhibits instrumental thinking. On this basis, Love and Meng proclaim: "Heidegger is a revolutionary. His philosophy is revolutionary. This revolutionary philosophy requires a revolutionary politics. . . . *Surely*, the rectoral address is sufficient evidence of this."[55] Surely? *Surely* such a "revolutionary" collapse of politics—a politics supposedly without ends—into philosophy—understood as the thinking of being—will have something important to teach us. But Love and Meng merely indulge in a banal technophobia: "Heidegger feared that metaphysics in its modernist, technological iteration as *Machenschaft* (machination) might be successful in declaring itself as the end of history and thus perpetually foreclosing the

---

53. I use the vocabulary of the "repression of instrumentality" referring to the discourse of agonistic democracy in political theory in *The Agonistic Condition* (Edinburgh: Edinburgh University Press, 2025). This vocabulary is indebted to Nicole Loraux, *The Divided City: On Memory and Forgetting in Ancient Athens*, trans. Corinne Pache and Jeff Fort (New York: Zone, 2006).
54. Jeff Love and Michael Meng, "The Political Myths of Martin Heidegger," *New German Critique* 42, no. 1 (2015): 57.
55. Love and Meng, "The Political Myths," 58, emphasis added.

possibility of any new way of thinking from ever emerging."[56] In fact, there is nothing new in the magical materialism of anti-instrumentalism: The robots will take over, as Karel Čapek feared in the 1920s; the algorithms will control our lives, as a more recent version of such fearmongering proclaims.[57] *Surely*, there is nothing more hackneyed and cliched than such anti-instrumentalism.[58] *Surely*, a radical revolutionary who manages to merge ontology and action, as Love and Meng claim about Heidegger, would offer something perhaps a bit less stale and trite.

I am not disparaging Love and Meng. I am pointing out that their article is a perfect symptom—in a *surely* immanently predicable fashion—of the repression of instrumentality. They are staring directly at the ruse of techne without recognizing it and thus unquestioningly appropriating it—a process that Freud and Lacan would have called denegation. For instance, Love and Meng are acutely aware that Heidegger's anti-Semitism of the *Black Notebooks* is intermeshed with his anti-instrumentalism. As they paraphrase Heidegger's point, "Judaism threatens the world as a manifestation of instrumental rationality."[59] Nonetheless, this is still not sufficient grounds for them to question why Heidegger purifies all ethical and—supposedly revolutionary—political action from instrumentality in the name of a philosophical renewal that is also supposedly radical. Such blindness is precipitated by a ruse that represses the function of instrumentality in Heidegger's thought. We encounter here a curious phenomenon: whereas in Heidegger the ruse is the technique producing the repression of instrumentality, in his epigones the obverse appears to be the case, namely, their repression of instrumentality invites the technique of the ruse of techne, with all its familiar moves, to return and dominate their thought, even without their awareness. This continuing effectivity of the ruse of techne through its repression of instrumentality ineluctably returns in a thought that mixes causes and means with effects and ends to solidify a phantasmagoric view of reality.

The obvious objection one could raise against the repression of instrumentality is that the opposition to instrumentality is not confined to Heidegger

---

56. Love and Meng, "The Political Myths," 66.

57. See Jeff Orlowski, dir., *The Social Dilemma*, Netflix, 2020.

58. For instance, Bourdieu traces the sources of this technophobia to the "reactionary revolutionaries" who were equally opposed to liberal democracy and Marxism in Germany from the beginning of the twentieth century to World War II. See Bourdieu, *The Political Ontology of Martin Heidegger*, chapter 1.

59. Love and Meng, "The Political Myths," 64.

but rather characterizes a broad spectrum of thought in the twentieth century. It is surely understandable that the horrors of the first half of the twentieth century facilitated by increasing technological efficiency—from the battlefield to the gas chambers—made thinkers suspicious of instrumentality. As the Frankfurt School eloquently expressed it in a series of influential texts, the technological use of means and ends is the main feature of the "dialectic of Enlightenment" that can lead to devastating destruction.

There is a double response to this objection. First, following a materialist politics, the Frankfurt School is concerned with the *effects* of the use of the technology (§57). The dialectic of Enlightenment presents the way in which the supposedly neutral reason and science are, in fact, imbued with structures of power and domination through the way in which they use the instrumental calculation of means and ends. Theodor Adorno, who is just as a vociferous critic of instrumentality as Heidegger, approaches instrumentality through its effects, such as, for instance, the effect of the dialectic of Enlightenment in the history that leads to the Holocaust. What is absent in Adorno is the glorification of an unhistorical action "without effect," as Heidegger puts it.[60] This makes for a critique of instrumentality in Adorno that is notably different from what I call the repression of instrumentality in Heidegger.[61] Adorno points to the uses of instrumentality in the particular context of the history of modernity. Heidegger positions instrumentality within the constitution of being as such. The Adornian emphasis on use and effects foregrounds the many failures of instrumentality within a technoscientific context. The repression of instrumentality in Heidegger seeks, instead, to overcome the effects of instrumentality. The former addresses the effect in history, the latter wants to cure some purported cause understood as the ground of history (§49).[62]

Second, a materialist ontology and politics that pays attention to the effects of action surely needs to point out that instrumentality has precipitated

---

60. Martin Heidegger, "The End of Philosophy and the Task of Thinking," in *Basic Writings*, trans. David Farrell Krell (London: Routledge, 2000) = *GA* 14, 449/89.

61. For a perspicacious comparison of Heidegger and Adorno, see Alexander García Düttmann, *The Memory of a Thought: An Essay on Heidegger and Adorno*, trans. Nicholas Walker (London: Continuum, 2002).

62. Adhering to the principle that a critique of instrumental practices need not be a critique of instrumentality, I have explored the effects of the instrumental reasoning characteristic of sovereignty, but without this being an argument against instrumentality. See Dimitris Vardoulakis, *Sovereignty and Its Other: Toward the Dejustification of Violence* (New York: Fordham University Press, 2013).

great disasters in modernity. But this is not an argument against instrumentality as such. In fact, an argument against instrumentality—as opposed to specific uses of instrumental reason—is vulnerable to the response that it merely proves the opposite of what it claims, namely, any consideration of the practical expression of power is only possible on the condition that we include instrumentality. If the argument against instrumentality is that it is imbued in the construction of power structures, then any political discourse that does not believe that there is an outside to power and that, instead, is concerned with engaging with forms of power is *ipso facto* obliged to get its hands dirty with instrumentality. If power operates through instrumentality, then one engages with the political by engaging also with instrumentality, and the repression of instrumentality is another way of saying that one wants nothing to do with the political.

A useful illustration of the importance of engaging with instrumentality so as to develop a politics, while remaining attuned to the critique of instrumentality in modernity, is the work of the technology theorist Andrew Feenberg. Initially, he pursued a critique of instrumentality without distinguishing between Heidegger and the Frankfurt School.[63] But he later developed his "instrumentalization theory" acknowledging the importance of instrumentality in the unfolding of power. His theory relies on the distinction between "primary" and "secondary" instrumentalization. Primary instrumentalization refers to technological advances that are causal but always embedded within a social context; whereas secondary instrumentalization consists in the specific application of the technological.[64] Feenberg describes how this distinction was central to the use of technology in his political activism.[65] Ultimately, Feenberg's primary instrumentalization refers to the causes and effects of technology, and secondary instrumentalization to the instrumental ends of action as they adapt technology to given circumstances through specific uses. Such a distinction between causality and instrumentality is unavailable to Heidegger because of the repression of instrumentality. Such a distinction highlights the positive, phronetic use of instrumentality in the tradition that goes back to Greek thought.

---

63. Andrew Feenberg, *Alternative Modernity: The Technical Turn in Philosophy and Social Theory* (Berkeley: University of California Press, 1995).

64. Andrew Feenberg, *Between Reason and Experience: Essays in Technology and Modernity* (Cambridge, MA: MIT Press, 2010).

65. Andrew Feenberg, *Technology, Modernity, and Democracy* (London: Rowman & Littlefield, 2018).

7. The underground current of a materialism of instrumentality

The distinction between causality and instrumentality plays a significant role in a thought in history that focuses on the function of instrumentality in action and which, to paraphrase Althusser, forms the underground current of a materialism of instrumentality. The ruse of techne that represses instrumentality makes this tradition invisible—one could wonder whether it is this tradition that Heidegger feels compelled to repress. Let me sketch some key features of this tradition as a counterpoint to the repression of instrumentality.

Monist materialism provides an account of action that allows for change and difference within the one being by distinguishing between instrumentality and causality. Whereas means and ends calculations are provisional, reliant on an assessment of the circumstances within which they are made, causes and effects lay claim to universality and are independent from specific circumstances. Attuned to the distinction between causality and instrumentality, the Greeks recognized the necessity of means and ends calculations for any account of action, and they never countenanced the possibility that either instrumentality is an inherent obstacle to the truth of being, nor that it is possible to carve out a realm of human action that is immune from calculation.[66] We will see how this distinction is fundamental to Aristotle's account of phronesis (§§19–22) and that Heidegger systematically mistranslates all references to this distinction in his reading of book 6 of *Nicomachean Ethics*, which thus marks the genesis of the ruse of techne (§§24–27).

The distinction between causality and instrumentality is a commonsense distinction that is, in fact, assumed in our thinking, even if we tend to ignore its significance. Let me provide a couple of examples to illustrate this. Consider the relation between design and construction. A specialist can design a machine, a building, or a chemical process in the laboratory. Such a design relies on the operation of causes and effects. The actual construction and implementation of the design requires the operation of instrumentality. For instance, the logistics of obtaining suitable material for the implementation of the design refers to the calculations one makes about how to obtain the means to construct the design. This shows that causality and instrumentality are distinct, even though they are not separate. There is no way to reconcile, let alone conflate, causality and instrumentality, as the repression of instrumentality does through the ruse of techne.

---

66. See Vardoulakis, *The Logic of Living: The Materialism of Greek Thought* (forthcoming).

Or another example: As astronomers know, the laws that govern the movement of celestial bodies are regular, making it possible to observe a phenomenon and reconstruct its causes. That is why telescopes that look into the past are useful for reconstructing the creation of the universe. No such accuracy can ever be hoped for when we attempt to reenact the instrumental calculations of human beings. This is not only because the variables in the calculation of utility are too numerous and dependent on contingent circumstances; in addition, instrumental calculations are fallible, which means that the actors may miscalculate the desired end or the means toward its achievement. Unlike the critique of scientism in modernity, and contrary to utilitarianism, the instrumental here is understood as unstable and impossible to calculate with certainty. This entails that "the starry sky above us" and the patterns of thought that govern our actions can never be completely separated—no one is outside causality—but they can never be reconciled either.

The distinction between causality and instrumentality plays a particularly important role in Epicurus because he privileges phronesis, as the instrumental kind of practical thinking, above all other kinds of knowledge.[67] This requires the distinction of phronesis from theoretical knowledge. For example, Epicurus illustrates this distinction by pointing to phenomena such as thunder and lightning. If we do not have a causal explanation of such phenomena, he argues, we must still provide likely explanations, no matter how many, so as to prevent superstitious belief in vengeful gods who send thunder and lightning to punish us (§32). Thus, the causality that describes material reality, and the instrumentality that describes how we act in response to this reality, are intertwined and yet distinct. The epicureans offer the most significant articulation of the monist materialist distinction between causality and instrumentality because of Epicurus's insistence on the primacy of phronesis.[68]

The distinction between causality and instrumentality is crucial in the account of action that we find in the monist materialist tradition. Perhaps the most famous illustration in the history of political thought is Machiavelli's distinction between fate and virtue.[69] Fate refers to causality, such as the meteorological phenomena that produce rain, causing the river to

---

67. Diogenes Laertius, *Lives of Eminent Philosophers*, trans. R.D. Hicks (Cambridge, MA: Harvard University Press, 1931), X, 132–33.
68. See Vardoulakis, *The Logic of Living*, chapter 4.
69. Niccolò Machiavelli, *The Prince*, ed. Quentin Skinner and Russell Price (Cambridge: Cambridge University Press, 1988), chapter 25.

swell. Virtue consists in preempting a flood by calculating what kind of dams or canals need to be built to irrigate the excess water. The interaction of fate and reason provides Machiavelli with an account of political action, typical of the materialist tradition. Virtue consists in practical judgments as they relate to the natural causes that determine fate.

A notion of practical judgment that relies on instrumental calculation, and is derived from the epicurean phronesis reemerges with modern philosophers such as Spinoza, who describes it by using the word "utilitas" and its cognates.[70] When Spinoza defines the good as what is useful in Definition 1 of Part IV of the *Ethics* and then goes on to aver that "the human is like god to other humans" because of the mutual utility that we afford each other, Spinoza grounds his ethical and political thought on instrumental reasoning and the reciprocal calculation of utility. This is not to suggest that instrumentality is *ipso facto* good. In fact, a critical point in Spinoza's philosophy is that the calculation of utility is fallible, and we regularly "see the better but do the worse." His *Theological Political Treatise* is largely devoted to tracing patterns of the miscalculations of instrumentality, especially in how people become enchanted by figures of authority, thereby lapsing into superstition so as to become "voluntary slaves." Despite these difficulties, it is crucial to recognize the function of the calculation of utility for a materialism that starts with the ontological principle that being is one. Monism requires the distinction between causality and instrumentality because causality can provide a definition of the one substance, as we see in Part I of Spinoza's *Ethics*, while instrumental judgment can account for difference in human action, as Spinoza demonstrates in Part IV of the *Ethics* and in the *Theological Political Treatise*.

From the vantage point of monist materialism, it is not surprising to see that Marx and Engels define the class struggle in the "Communist Manifesto" as the conflict between two different constructions of social, political, and economic interest, represented by two different classes—the bourgeoisie and the proletariat.[71] The discourse of interest in the nineteenth century is the translation of the idea of the calculation of utility, or phronesis, that Marx would have been exposed to with his doctoral dissertation on Epicurus and ancient materialism.

---

70. See Vardoulakis, *Spinoza, the Epicurean: Authority and Utility in Materialism* (Edinburgh: Edinburgh University Press, 2020).

71. Karl Marx and Friedrich Engels, "Manifesto of the Communist Party," in *Collected Works of Karl Marx and Friedrich Engels, 1845–48*, vol. 6 (New York: International Publishers, 1976), 474–519.

The conflation of causality and instrumentality in Heidegger's second sense of techne as technology that precipitates the forgetting of instrumentality means, in historical terms, the forgetting of this entire materialist monist tradition. The repression of instrumentality is the repression of the epicurean legacy in monism, which foregrounds the importance of instrumentality in an account of action. It is this tradition that shows how instrumentality need not be reduced to a metaphysics of presence. Heidegger is silent about this tradition. Despite thousands of pages on ancient Greek thought in his *Gesamtausgabe*, there is nothing on epicureanism. And despite persistently lecturing on early modern thought, the only discussion that we find of Spinoza is roughly twenty pages characterized by a lack of originality and perceptiveness, merely repeating accepted opinions.[72] We see a similar treatment of Marx in the "Letter on Humanism," where he is "celebrated" as a peak of metaphysical thinking and therefore must be rejected in order to achieve an action without ends and effects (§60).

And yet, precisely because of its repression, this tradition and in particular its central distinction between causality and instrumentality—the distinction that the ruse of techne conceals—play a determinative role in Heidegger's thought and produce significant effects in the thought that comes in the wake of the ruse of techne. The present study works through this repression.

---

72. Martin Heidegger, *Geschichte der Philosophie von Thomas von Aquin bis Kant = GA* 23, part 3. This course was delivered at Marburg in 1926. The effective ignoring of this tradition by Heidegger is rarely noticed. There is an intriguing reflection by Derrida on this. During an interview, he points out how important to Heidegger's critique of reason the principle of sufficient reason is, as articulated by Leibniz. But Derrida notes Spinoza "is someone who ferociously critiques all finalism, someone who determines the idea as non-representative—this is his critique of Descartes, that the idea is not a copy; Spinoza's idea is affirmative, precisely, it is an affirmation that is not reproduction or representative copy. It's not a philosophy of certainty, not a philosophy of the subject, not a philosophy of representation, not a finalistic philosophy. And yet, it is a rationalism. It's a great rationalism. Which Heidegger almost never cites. And when he does cite it, to my knowledge, once or twice, it is in the tradition of Schelling, or, at least, he reproduces—very briefly—assessments of early 19th-century German philosophy. So, here once again, what do Heidegger's silences mean?" My contention is that these silences mean that Heidegger is attempting to repress a certain monist materialist tradition in philosophy because it does not fit within his reading of the history of philosophy and because it challenges his repression of instrumentality. See Jacques Derrida, "A Conversation with Jacques Derrida about Heidegger," trans. Katie Chenoweth and Rodrigo Therezo, *Oxford Literary Review* 43, no. 1 (2021): 25.

8. Effects of the ruse of techne (or, why the repression of instrumentality still matters today)

Timothy Campbell raises the stakes about the effects of Heidegger's repression of instrumentality when he notes that "to the degree we speak about biopolitics today, lurking beneath is a conception of technology deeply indebted to Heidegger's ontological elaboration of it."[73] Campbell suggests that Heidegger has marked twentieth-century philosophy and political thought because of his anti-instrumentalist conception of technology, which Campbell associates with thanatopolitics, that is, the kind of thought that privileges death just as "questions of technology grow in importance."[74]

I noted earlier (§2) that the effect of the ruse of techne consists in an almost uniform aversion to instrumentality in continental philosophy. Thus, for Levinas, the Other is absolute by virtue of the fact that it is separated from instrumentality. A not dissimilar suspicion of instrumentality animates the thought of "poststructuralists" such as Blanchot, who is consistently opposed to the cold rationality of what he calls "the day." Agamben joins in by envisaging a politics of means without ends.

Following Campbell, it is too narrow to confine the effects of the ruse of techne and the repression of instrumentality to philosophers working in the phenomenological tradition broadly conceived. Through the influence of his students who moved to the United States, the repression of instrumentality has exercised an enormous influence in political theory as well. Of particular significance in this context are Herbert Marcuse and Hannah Arendt, who spent their careers on the West Coast and in the Northeast, respectively. Marcuse warns about the perils of modern technology in the guise of the "one dimensional man" who is governed by instrumentality. The notion of action in Arendt's *The Human Condition* is free of ends, while instrumental thinking does not belong to the political proper because it is mired in violence, according to *On Violence*.

Anti-instrumentalism—symptomatic of the repression of instrumentality—has marked one of the most influential responses to neoliberalism. The argument is that neoliberalism reduces everything to calculation and subordinates all human activity to instrumentality. As a consequence, it contradicts the very foundation of the political. This argument is most forcefully put forward by Wendy Brown. In *Undoing the Demos*, she argues

---

73. Timothy Campbell, *Improper Life: Technology and Biopolitics from Heidegger to Agamben* (Minneapolis: University of Minnesota Press, 2011), 1.

74. Campbell, *Improper Life*, viii.

that the instrumental thinking characteristic of neoliberalism and exemplified by the figure of the "homo economicus" eliminates the possibility of collectivity and the "demos," thus preventing the flourishing of democracy.[75] In the homo economicus, the neoliberal subject and instrumentality merge as if there is a necessary, causal connection between them.[76] The predominance of the homo economicus results in a profound melancholia on the left, since this line of thought lacks a route to a redemptive politics: economic instrumentalism has become both pervasive and without any outlet to a democratic politics. This is a bleak picture, as it suggests we are deprived of our democratic freedoms, we are imprisoned through our own self-generated, instrumental calculations.

Effectively, the repression of instrumentality that lies at the root of such an approach has allowed for neoliberalism to appropriate for itself the notion of instrumentality. This was an unexpected gift to neoliberal thought. The reason is clear. If, as I argued in the previous section, the only possibility of political change and difference hinges on an account of instrumentality that is not reducible to mere presence, then abandoning instrumentality to neoliberalism is tantamount to abandoning all possibility of political change to it. There is nothing more empowering than controlling instrumentality. Albert Hirschman was pivotal in creating the impression that neoliberalism was the proprietor of instrumental thinking. In *The Passions and the Interests*, he provides a historical underpinning of calculation in terms of the supposed pacifying influence of capitalism, which becomes the philosophico-historical account of neoliberalism's appropriation of instrumentality.[77]

Such an apologetic historicization finds an indispensable prop in the repression of instrumentality: the neoliberal can grant the philosopher all the desired latitude to talk about the ontological mystery of being, so long as the philosopher grants the neoliberal the latitude to permeate human action with a notion of calculation, exempt from ethics and politics. The ruse of techne ineluctably leads to such an alliance where the opposing forces—ontology and neoliberal economics—support each other just as

---

75. Wendy Brown, *Undoing the Demos: Neoliberalism's Stealth Revolution* (New York: Zone Books, 2015).

76. In fact, the term "homo economicus" was invented by neoliberalism as a term of abuse. See Quinn Slobodian, *Globalists: The End of Empire and the Birth of Neoliberalism* (Cambridge, MA: Harvard University Press, 2018), 82.

77. Albert O. Hirschman, *The Passions and the Interests: Political Arguments for Capitalism Before Its Triumph* (Princeton, NJ: Princeton University Press, 1977).

Church and State do in "secularism." The existence and preservation of each of the opposing terms requires that the other thrives too.

The conflation of instrumentality and causality that Heidegger never addresses explicitly (§57) betrays the repression of instrumentality as an instrument of neoliberal ideology.[78] We find the articulation of such an ideology in two expressions that are widely used and unquestionably accepted in biopolitical societies. The first is from the perspective of power and it says that "there is no other way," especially when it comes to harsh social measures that express neoliberal economics. The austerity politics of the European Union in the aftermath of the 2008 financial crisis is just one example of this ideological articulation. The second registers the resignation of the people because "all parties are the same, there is no difference between politicians." This leads to an effective disenfranchisement of voters that only props up neoliberalism. Its end point is inevitably an anti-political battle cry, such as "empty the swamp!"

The common effect of both of these ideological articulations of the repression of instrumentality is the belief that political action is either impossible or futile. Significantly, this mirrors Heidegger's metaphysical materialism. We saw (§4) that this consists in a conception of action that is either trivial and vacuous, whereby it is of no consequence, or it is in fact complicit in the operation and perpetuation of existing forms of power (see also §16, §53). We discover, here, the family resemblance between neoliberal ontology and Heidegger's "being" that is precipitated by the repression of instrumentality through the ruse of techne.

The recognition of this family resemblance may suggest that we retreat from the Heideggerian magical materialism and advance instead toward an epicurean materialism as a way of undoing the ideological effects of the ruse of techne. This is not a normative claim. Rather, it presents the choice between two monist ontologies. The Heideggerian ontology relying on the repression of instrumentality abandons action to those political forces that make normative, moralizing claims to shore up their economic interests.[79] A monism that refuses the reduction of instrumentality to mere presence may offer instead a vocabulary to imagine a political future that is not, of necessity, entangled with neoliberal practice.

---

78. See Roland Végső, "Ends without a Cause: A Response to Dimitris Vardoulakis," *Australian Philosophical Review* 6, no. 3 (2022): 288–94.

79. Jessica Whyte, *The Morals of the Market: Human Rights and the Rise of Neoliberalism* (London: Verso, 2019).

9. On method

A magician tricks our senses to have us believe that a coin has vanished from his hand or that he has pulled a rabbit out of a hat. The ruse is to hide something that is there, or to make something appear out of thin air. Similarly, repression makes us blind to symptoms and effects that are staring us in the face (such as phronetic instrumentality), and makes us see things that do not exist (such as the ineffectual). The most expedient way to counter the ruse is the same method that psychoanalysis suggests in countering the symptoms of repression—we have to work through it.

In terms of the exegesis of Heidegger's ruse of techne, this means that we need to work through his texts to locate the traces of the movements of his thought that effect our repression of instrumentality. This can only be accomplished through close readings of key texts where we can discern the traces of the technique of the ruse of techne.

A consequence of this approach is that the technique of the ruse of techne emerges as the principle that structures of Heidegger's entire philosophical project. Specifically, I will identify three phases in the deployment of the ruse of techne according to the conception of action that they generate or its metaphysical materialism, as I call it. Initially, up to around the early 1930s, the concealment of instrumentality presents action as trivial or vacuous (see chapter 4). Then, from the mid-1930s, Heidegger's ontology assumes a more polemical guise leading to a conception of action that cannot help but become complicit with the political actors representing the "historical destiny" of a people (see chapter 5). Finally, the later Heidegger, especially after World War II, reverts to a description of action as vacuous, devoid of ethics and politics, and without effects (see chapter 6). As I argue, this progression and retrogression depends on how Heidegger deploys the ruse of techne in his thought, and his putative "turn" in the 1930s is merely a way to perpetuate the repression of instrumentality, a product of the ruse of techne.

For this close reading of the ruse of techne in Heidegger's works to be effective, it is necessary to start with an analysis of the creation of its symptoms. There are two important aspects to this. First, I show how Heidegger's conception of the single, unified being faces a significant series of problems to account for action (chapter 2). Then, I demonstrate that Heidegger finds a solution to the problematic of action in monism in his reading of Aristotle's conception of phronesis in book 6 of *Nicomachean Ethics*, which signifies the genesis of the ruse of techne (see chapter 3).

In between the analysis of the causes and the symptoms of the ruse of techne, I will offer a panoramic view of the issues that Heidegger's repression of instrumentality raises. Perhaps Heidegger's greatest achievement is to have shown us a path down a monist ontology that is a blind alley, but which is nonetheless highly enticing because it reproduces familiar themes from the conception of action in onto-theo-logy (see the Excursus). In this sense, Heidegger's importance emerges as the attempt to marry a monist materialism with metaphysics, making him the last great metaphysical thinker.

2

The Problematic of Action Within a Single, Unified Being
Monism in Heidegger's Thought

10. Heidegger's other path

Heidegger's trajectory is customarily presented as a renewal of phenomenology. As the name suggests, phenomenology is the analysis of phenomena or what exists in its appearance to us. Its founding father, Edmund Husserl, captured its impetus in the shibboleth "back to the things themselves." This suggests that phenomenology is an attempt to rethink the foundations of theoretical knowledge without any recourse to transcendent entities or to any kind of knowledge unconnected to experience. Husserl's influence is clear on Heidegger. Indeed, *Being and Time* describes itself as a work of phenomenology and it is dedicated to Husserl "in friendship and admiration." There is no doubt that, while he worked as Husserl's assistant at Freiburg University, Heidegger followed along the path of a renewal of epistemology, characteristic of phenomenology.

And yet, understanding Heidegger merely as radicalizing Husserl's project leaves at least one issue unexamined. For already in *Being and Time*, Heidegger is not content to frame his project solely as a renewal of theoretical knowledge. In addition, it is a renewal of praxis. The focus on the practical suggests that phenomenology was perhaps not the only path followed by Heidegger. If there is another path, then discovering such a parallel path becomes more pressing as soon as we examine Heidegger's later philosophy, where genuine action is customarily described as the thinking of being. A well-known articulation of this idea is the opening of the

"Letter on Humanism," where Heidegger also argues that both ethics and politics are impossible and that they need to be incorporated within ontology.[1] There is, however, something fundamentally strange, even oxymoronic, in a practical philosophy without an ethics or a politics, and this strangeness necessitates an exploration of the other path that led to Heidegger's coarticulation of being and action.

I will argue here that it makes sense to think of Heidegger's other path as "monism." This is not to suggest a history of influence: I am not suggesting that specific monist thinkers inclined him toward specific positions in his philosophy. Rather, I take a basic observation as my starting point, that the central idea that organizes Heidegger's entire thought is that there is a single, unified being distinguished from particular beings. This is also the central idea of monism as it can be found in Greek thought. Even though he does not use the term monism, David Furley agrees, expressing the idea by saying that "no one in the early history of Greek philosophy ever asserted that an existing thing, such as the world, came into being out of 'the non-existent' in the sense of nothing at all."[2] In other words, ancient Greek thought eschews a creationist metaphysics. Or in positive terms, monism implies that existence is a totality outside of which nothing exists, or that existence is of one quality.[3] This insight is crucial for Heidegger's understanding of the Greek thought as premetaphysical, such as when he argues in *Introduction to Metaphysics* that Greek philosophy refuses to separate being and seeming or being and becoming.

Taking monism as the other path of Heidegger's thought provides a significant context, not only for the provenance of his conception of a single, unified being, but for his conception of praxis, as well. We will see that the problematic of action is pivotal for monism, especially in early modernity. The starting question of this problematic is: if there is a single, unified being, then how can we account for difference in action? Or why are actions not simply variations or modifications of the one being? Without a satisfactory answer to these questions, a monist will have to renounce the possibility of an ethics and a politics—which is precisely where Heidegger ended up after the so-called "turn." My suggestion will be that Heidegger's rejection of the traditional monist answer to the problematic of action is responsible

---

1. Martin Heidegger, "Letter on Humanism," in *Basic Writings*, trans. David Farrell Krell (London: Routledge, 2000) = *GA* 9.
2. David Furley, *The Greek Cosmologists: The Formation of Atomic Theory and Its Earliest Critics* (Cambridge: Cambridge University Press, 1987), 45.
3. Cf. Furley's discussion of the whole (*to pan*) in *The Greek Cosmologists*, 136–40.

for his need to repress instrumentality. This explains the impetus to manufacture the ruse of techne.

Thus far, I have described *what* the ruse of techne is and its most important effects. The ruse is a technique that relies on three distinct areas of signification of techne. Techne denotes: 1) the single, unified being; 2) the conflation of causality and instrumentality characteristic of the critique of modern technology; and 3) the activity that is free of ends or the ineffectual that Heidegger associates with art, broadly conceived. The trick of the ruse consists in repressing instrumentality by confining it to techne as technology, whereby instrumentality is reduced to mere presence and hence to onto-theo-logy.

Following Heidegger's footsteps on the path of monism will show us *why* he needed to employ the ruse of techne so as to repress instrumentality. As I will show, Heidegger's solution to the problematic of action in monism is fraught with two major difficulties. Specifically, he describes an action free of ends that is too close for comfort to metaphysics; and, as soon as his conception of action is placed within the purview of the problematic of action in monism a glaring weakness becomes visible, namely, that the Heideggerian conception results in a double bind between the trivial and the self-contradictory.

My aim is not to argue that Heidegger's conception of action was simply "wrong." Instead, by contextualizing Heidegger's thought within the path of monism, I want to shed a different light on Heidegger's philosophy of action. This is particularly significant, given that the monism of Heidegger's thought remains unacknowledged, despite a burgeoning literature on his ethics and politics (§5).

The path of monism is significant because it challenges the commonly held view that continental philosophy can be understood to have only two sources, one in rationalism and the other in phenomenology.[4] Even though such an account may well be possible in terms of epistemology, it is inadequate with respect to continental philosophy's approach to practical knowledge. My suggestion will be that Heidegger's response to the problematic of action in monism has dominated subsequent continental philosophy and it has thereby obscured another possibility contained in epicurean monism. Heidegger's solution repressed the function of instrumentality, whereas the epicurean solution, adopted by Spinoza in modernity, relies on instrumentality.

---

4. See Know Peden, *Spinoza Contra Phenomenology: French Rationalism from Cavaillès to Deleuze* (Stanford, CA: Stanford University Press, 2014).

I will present the problematic of action within being, conceived as single and unified, as a series of three interlocking problems that Heidegger is facing in developing his thought. Understanding these problems sheds new light on elements of Heidegger's philosophy as solutions to them, highlighting both the originality and the weaknesses.

11. The first problem: How to be a different materialist?

The first problem is related to what *Being and Time* calls the "destruction of metaphysics."[5] One vital aspect of what Heidegger means by "metaphysics" is that it involves the separation of theory and praxis. It involves the separation of a kind of knowledge that claims universality for itself and that assumes a knowing subject, conceived as an independent observer from the material world, and from the body's actions within that world. Heidegger's fundamental ontology claims to bridge the gap between theory and praxis, between subject and object, between mind and body.

A key implication of the overcoming of the separation of theory and praxis is the rejection of the idea that there is anything transcendent, such as a god, who can create something out of nothing. The dialectical opposite of positing the possibility of transcendence is insisting on mere presence, the simple presence and availability of beings, which Heidegger singles out as yet another sure marker of metaphysics or what he also calls onto-theo-logy.[6] The overcoming of the metaphysical opposition of theory and praxis requires also the overcoming of the binary opposition between transcendence and mere presence. The rejection of that binary accords with the definition of materialism in the neo-Kantian Friedrich Lange's *Geschichte des Materialismus*, published in 1866, which presents the most detailed history of materialism to date and with which Heidegger certainly would have been familiar, given its widespread influence on nineteenth-century thinkers, including Nietzsche.[7]

---

5. By the word "destruction" Heidegger is not suggesting a "complete separation" from metaphysics since "any attempt at demolition that would always deal with the same materials would be pointless." Dominique Janicaud and Jean-François Mattei, *Heidegger: From Metaphysics to Thought* (Albany: SUNY Press, 1995), 2. See also Sean Kirkland, *The Destruction of Aristotle: Reading the Tradition with the Early Heidegger* (Evanston, IL: Northwestern University Press, 2022).

6. Martin Heidegger, *Identity and Difference*, trans. Joan Stambach (New York: Harper & Row, 1969) = *GA* 11.

7. Friedrich Albert Lange, *Geschichte des Materialismus und Kritik seiner Bedeutung in der Gegenwart* (Iserlohn: Baedeker, [1866], 2nd rev. ed. 1887).

It would be misleading, however, to identify Heidegger's destruction of metaphysics simply or immediately with materialism as it was determined in the first quarter of the twentieth century, in Germany. The reason is that the notion of materialism branched in three directions in Germany at that time: first, it signified a kind of naturalism, or the positivist attitude according to which scientific explanation becomes the final court of arbitration in epistemological matters; second, it denoted neo-Kantianism, favorable to scientific knowledge too, with the difference that it also posited a moral and cultural realm separate from nature; and, third, there was Marxism, whose materialism turns into social critique based on dialectics. Safranksi insists that a main impetus of the early Heidegger is "to avoid . . . the crash into materialism" understood according to these three specific directions that it had taken in Germany at that time.[8] That is Heidegger's first problem: how to "destruct" metaphysics without lapsing into these prevalent materialisms. Heidegger needs a different kind of materialism to ground his conception of the history of philosophy.

It is at this point that monism is important. Heidegger's materialism differs from the materialisms prevalent in Germany at the time in that it is monist. By monism, I mean, here, the usual materialist rejection of transcendence and mere presence *plus* the position that there is one (*monos*) kind of existence outside of which nothing exists. Heidegger names "being" this one existence.

Some may find it objectionable to describe Heidegger's destruction of metaphysics using terms such as monism and substance that are usually reserved for metaphysics. Heidegger himself avoids the term monism, even when he discusses texts such as Parmenides's Fragment 8, often taken to be the first articulation of monism, suggesting that he regards monism as trapped within onto-theo-logy and, hence, as inappropriate to apply to his destruction of metaphysics. In response to such an objection, the first thing to note is that I regard it as a sign of the strength and importance of Heidegger's thought that it can survive, and even thrive, in discourses that are not organized by his chosen vocabulary. This does not mean that any arbitrary vocabulary can be applied to Heidegger's thought, but merely that, *in principle*, a thinker of real philosophical depth and richness like Heidegger can be discussed in alternative vocabularies. Indeed, I would even suggest that, *in practice*, it is impossible for exegesis to avoid doing so.

---

8. Rüdiger Safranksi, *Martin Heidegger: Between Good and Evil*, trans. Ewald Osers (Cambridge, MA: Harvard University Press, 1999), 39 and 26–37.

Those who object to using different terminology to interpret Heidegger and presuppose that only his own terminology can be used effectively create a silo of "Heideggerese" that acts against the promulgation of his philosophy. To this attitude, supposedly adhering to Heidegger's self-assessment that he has moved beyond philosophy whereby traditional concepts are supposedly inadequate to describe his thinking, I use Heidegger's own words as a response: "I have learned to see that these very terms were bound to lead immediately and inevitably into error. For the terms and the conceptual language corresponding to them were not rethought by readers from the matter particularly to be thought; rather, the matter was conceived according to the established terminology in its customary meaning."[9]

Heidegger himself makes one interesting use of the term monism in his habilitation on Duns Scotus. It occurs in the context of discussing the importance of the categories of "unum et diversum" (the one and the many, or unity and multiplicity). Heidegger observes that it is this distinction that prevents the overcoming of dualism because it "lapses that back into an impossible monism [*in einen unmöglichen Monismus zurückzusinken*]."[10] The impossible monism that Heidegger rejects is ignorant of the distinction that a few years later he will formulate as the ontological difference between being and beings. Thus, Heidegger reserves the term monism to denote the medieval philosophical position where the one (*unum*) fails to be distinguished from the many particular beings. We will soon see that Heidegger, in fact, finds it hard to dismiss such an "impossible monism" (§11), despite the offhanded dismissal of it in his dissertation.

When Heidegger turns to pre-Socratic thought, he discovers the ontological difference in Parmenides's Fragment 8—often the text designated as the first articulation of monism. Thus, even though he does not describe Parmenides as monist, we can readily glimpse an important affinity between Heidegger's notion of the unified being that he derives from his early readings of Greek thought.[11] For example, in the important course *The Beginning of Western Philosophy* from 1932, Heidegger reiterates the monist position that being cannot be negated: "Being is utterly [*schlechthin*] without

---

9. Heidegger, "Letter on Humanism," 259.
10. Martin Heidegger, *Die Kategorien- und Bedeutungslehre des Duns Scotus*, in *GA* 1, 263.
11. Following Heidegger's own practice, scholars who examine the source of Heidegger's idea of the single, unified being in the monism of Greek thought, such as in Parmenides, and trace this idea in the entirety of his work, avoid the term monism to refer to Heidegger. See Jussi Backman, *Complicated Presence: Heidegger and the Postmetaphysical Unity of Being* (Albany: SUNY Press, 2015).

a 'not,'" or "Being is utterly [*schlechthin*] un-negative."¹² There is nothing outside being. Simultaneously, this single being can be expressed in many different ways: "The manifold accruing to the ἕν [one] is merely a manifold of unities that precisely unfold out of the 'one' as unity [*eine Vielfalt von Einheiten, die eben aus dem Einen als Einheit sich entfalten*].... This multiplicity does not destroy the unities but, instead, forms them in their full essence."¹³ Heidegger discovers in Eleatic monism the ontological difference, according to which the one, that is, being, can be expressed in many different ways (*pollachos legomenon*), thereby resolving the problem of the impossible monism that he had identified in medieval thought. Parmenides is one of the key references for Heidegger to argue that Greek thought presents the unity of a single being, which entails that there is no separation between subject and object, nor between theory and praxis—there is, to put it in Heidegger's terms when referring to Parmenides, no separation of thinking and acting.¹⁴ The origin of the position about the convergence of thinking and action in the opening of the "Letter on Humanism" is thus, in fact, Eleatic monism (§50).

This is unsurprising if we recall that the idea that existence, as a totality outside of which nothing exists, is a staple of Greek thought. This idea seems so uncontestable that Aristotle passes it over without much ado in *Metaphysics*.¹⁵ This monism is clearly articulated, not only in Parmenides. We can find the precise formulation that there is a unified totality outside of which nothing exists in Democritus.¹⁶ It is also the starting point of Epicurus's epistemology outlined in the letter to Herodotus.¹⁷ Furley, in his magisterial *The Greek Cosmologists*, traces the various articulations of

---

12. Martin Heidegger, *The Beginning of Western Philosophy: Interpretation of Anaximander and Parmenides,* trans. Richard Rojcewicz (Bloomington: Indiana University Press, 2012) = *GA* 35, 125–26/162.

13. Heidegger, *The Beginning of Western Philosophy*, 114/147–48.

14. See for instance, the discussion of Parmenides in "Moira (Parmenides VIII, 34–41)," in *Early Greek Thinking*, trans. David Farrell Krell and Frank A. Capuzzi (New York: Harper Collins, 1984) = *GA* 7. Anaximander is another important reference here. See Richard Colledge, "Heidegger on (In)finitude and the Greco-Latin Grammar of Being," *Review of Metaphysics* 74, no. 2 (2020): 289–319.

15. Aristotle, *Metaphysics*, trans. Hugh Tredennick (Cambridge, MA: Harvard University Press, 1933), 986b.

16. Diogenes Laertius, "Democritus," in *Lives of Eminent Philosophers*, trans. R.D. Hicks (Cambridge, MA: Harvard University Press, 1931), IX, 44.

17. Diogenes Laertius, "Epicurus," in *Lives of Eminent Philosophers*, X, 39.

this idea in Greek thought from the Ionians to Aristotle.[18] For the development of Heidegger's own monist position the key figure is Aristotle because that is where he discovers the "twofoldness of being," as Walter Brogan calls is—the idea that being is both single and manifold.[19]

If we reject the impossible monism of medieval thought, which has no conception of the ontological difference in the relation between "the one and the many," and if we understand by monism the philosophical position that posits one being in its relation to the multiplicity of beings, then the term monism comes to designate a key feature of Heidegger's overcoming of metaphysics. This is perhaps best discerned in his criticism of Nietzsche as still trapped within metaphysics. As Heidegger understands it, Nietzsche's rejection of metaphysical transcendence in favor of immanence is still trapped in metaphysics because a simple negation presupposes the term negated.[20] Besides the rejection of transcendence, it is also necessary to have a conception of being as one and unified—a being that, as Heidegger discovered in Parmenides, is impervious to a "not." Heidegger claims that Nietzsche conducts a critique of metaphysics within metaphysics because Nietzsche fails to adumbrate a monist ontology that rejects the possibility that there is negation within being.[21] For Heidegger, a monism that is aware of the ontological difference is the only way to work around metaphysics.

Heidegger "destructs" metaphysics, I suggest, by adhering to a monist materialism. This is a materialism (overcoming the divide between theory and praxis while also rejecting transcendence and mere presence) that is also monist since it insists on the unity of one being that is distinct from

---

18. Furley, *The Greek Cosmologists*. Sadly, the second volume, which would have dealt with philosophy after Aristotle, remained incomplete at Furley's death.

19. Walter Brogan, *Heidegger and Aristotle: The Twofoldness of Being* (Albany: SUNY Press, 2005). Note the metaphor of the fold, a favorite of Deleuze's, another philosopher with the monist conception of a plane of immanence.

20. We find this argument in his lectures and essays on Nietzsche, collected in *Nietzsche I: The Will to Power as Art*, trans. David F. Krell (New York: Harper & Row, 1979) = GA 43; *Nietzsche II: The Eternal Recurrence of the Same*, trans. David F. Krell (New York: Harper & Row, 1984) = GA 44; *Nietzsche III: The Will to Power as Knowledge and Metaphysics*, trans. Joan Stambaugh, Frank A. Capuzzi, and David F. Krell (New York: Harper & Row, 1987) = GA 47; *Nietzsche IV: Nihilism*, trans. Frank A. Capuzzi (New York: Harper & Row, 1982) = GA 6.

21. I disagree with such an assessment of Nietzsche as I hold that, at least, this theory of action is based on a monist ontology. I touch on this point in §6, §16, §26, and §36 of *The Agonistic Condition* (Edinburgh: Edinburgh University Press, 2025).

its articulations in a multiplicity of beings. But the solution to the first problem leads to the further problem of how to account for action within a monist ontology.

12. The second problem: How is action possible within a monist ontology?

The suspicion concerning its ability to provide an account to action has haunted monism since antiquity.[22] The problem is clear to see: If all that there is exists within a one that has no negation, then any action that we undertake ultimately would make no difference to existence. Sometimes I use a riddle to explain this point to my students: I ask them to imagine that there is a planet whose mass is one trillion tons. A city is built on it that weighs 100,000 tons. What is the mass weight of the planet now? The answer is, the same as before, as all the activity to build the new city has not altered the mass of the planet, it has merely redistributed it. There is no negation, there is merely variation. The logic of this joke illustrates the problem of action in monism. No matter what actions one undertakes, one is left with the same unified existence lacking difference. No change is possible, rendering action meaningless and futile.

Before I proceed, let me note that recent discussions of monism tend to be framed through the distinction between substance monism, existence monism, and priority monism. I want to make three observations regarding these distinctions. First, since these distinctions that have proliferated in analytic philosophy postdate Heidegger's contribution, it is to be expected that this is never the way in which he frames the question of the single and unified being. Second, there has recently been a significant challenge to all these versions of monism through the work of Michael Della Rocca, putting into question whether the distinctions between the different kinds of monism can be sustained.[23] Third, and most importantly, in all these different monisms, one thing is conspicuously absent: an account of action. Usually, monism is treated as an epistemological issue, avoiding entirely any discussion of praxis. Or monist accounts of action within this analytic tradition, such as "value monism," are simplistic and lacking in resources to

---

22. See Vardoulakis, *The Logic of Living: The Materialism of Greek Thought* (forthcoming).

23. Michael Della Rocca, *The Parmenidean Ascent* (Oxford: Oxford University Press, 2020).

provide a credible way of thinking about the world.[24] By contrast, historically and conceptually, the question of monism is never a purely epistemological issue, but also a practical one.[25] The problem of action is not an incidental addendum to monism; without an adequate response to the problematic of action, monism is merely a theoretical mind game. The problematic of action is constitutive of monism.[26]

Heidegger's ontological difference is far from an adequate solution to the problem of action in monism: the unity of being persists at the ontological level, whereas multiplicity can be discovered at the ontic level where there is a plurality of beings. But the ontological difference merely evades the real problem. Difference is still inscribed only on the side of beings, very much like what Heidegger called in his dissertation (§10) the impossible monism of medieval metaphysics. Taking the one seriously, it actually becomes tricky to arrive at any conception of difference in the many, or multiplicity other than as a mere variation of the one.

This is a major problem for two reasons. The first has to do with Heidegger's destruction of metaphysics. If the destruction relies on the overcoming of the distinction between theory and praxis, then a postmetaphysical ontology requires a postmetaphysical determination of praxis. If the ontology is monist, then Heidegger has to respond to the problem of how to conceive action such that it allows for change and difference within a unified being. Symptomatic of the enormity of this problem is Heidegger's reticence, not only to refuse to develop an ethical and political theory. It is noteworthy—even astonishing—that in the huge mass of secondary literature on the ethical and political implications of Heidegger's conception of being (§5), there is total silence about the enormous internal pressure that this problem poses within Heidegger's own system.

The second reason is a historical one. The reception of Spinoza, *the* major monist in modernity, is marked by the problem of difference in action within a single totality. The pivotal figure here is Pierre Bayle. The opposition to Spinoza after the posthumous publication of his work was ferocious. Two decades later, Bayle summarized the reaction in his *Dictionary*. The

---

24. See my comments on Della Rocca's *The Parmenidean Ascent* at the Critical Antiquities Workshop, University of Sydney, November 13, 2020, https://www.youtube.com/watch?v=ZJnQRQBWzm4.

25. See for instance, Socrates's response to the Eleatic monist that I discuss in §34.

26. For an account of the theological context in the constitutive relation of monism and action, see Mary-Jane Rubenstein, *Pantheologies: Gods, Worlds, Monsters* (New York: Columbia University Press, 2018).

crux of the refutation of "Spinozism" consists in the argument that it is impossible to provide an account of difference in action from within a monist ontology. Bayle tirelessly returns to this point, which he formulates in different ways. Here is one: given their monism that insists on one unified and immutable substance, Spinozists "would have to claim that there has not been, and there never will be, any change in the universe, and that all change, the very greatest or the very smallest, is impossible."[27] And here is an extravagant second articulation as an *ad absurdum* argument: "in Spinoza's system all those who say, 'The Germans have killed ten thousand Turks,' speak incorrectly and falsely unless they mean, 'God modified into Germans has killed God modified into ten thousand Turks,' and the same with all the phrases by which what men do to one another are expressed."[28] The inference is unequivocal: monism is unable to provide a theory of action that accounts for difference.

Given the ban on Spinoza's works, Bayle's entry on Spinozism became the main source of knowledge about Spinoza until the publication of the Paulus edition at the beginning of the nineteenth century. As a result, Bayle's argument about the impossibility of action within monism was firmly established as philosophical dogma.[29] I have not been able to discover any serious challenge since the seventeenth century to the dogma that monism cannot account for difference in action.

Friedrich Jacobi revitalized the argument that monism lacks a conception of action in two major controversies about Spinozism that he initiated at the end of the eighteenth century. In the course of these controversies, Jacobi invented the term "nihilism" to designate the problem of meaningless action within a monist ontological framework.[30] These controversies had a major impact on idealism. Jacobi's conception of nihilism—namely, that monism is unable to account for action and hence lacks an ethics and a politics—reinforced Bayle's rejection of monism on the grounds that it finds it impossible to account for difference and change. Thus, Hegel's entire reading of Spinoza as lacking a "determinate negation" and as being

---

27. Pierre Bayle, *Historical and Critical Dictionary: Selections*, trans. Richard H. Popkin (Indianapolis, IN: Bobbs-Merrill, 1965), 327.

28. Bayle, *Historical and Critical Dictionary*, 312.

29. See Dimitris Vardoulakis, "The Invention of Nihilism: Political Monism, Epicureanism, and Spinoza," *Crisis and Critique* 8, no. 2 (2021): 510–35.

30. I discuss all the relevant literature in the creation of the term nihilism in Vardoulakis, "The Invention of Nihilism." For a fascinating historical account of nihilism from antiquity to modernity, see Gideon Baker, *Nihilism and Philosophy: Nothingness, Truth and World* (London: Bloomsbury, 2018).

"acosmist," is nothing but a reformulation of Jacobi's nihilism.[31] This issue was still alive in Germany in the first third of the twentieth century, as demonstrated, for instance, by one of Heidegger's students, Leo Strauss, whose doctoral dissertation was on Jacobi's epistemology and whose first book proposed a refutation of Spinoza that relies on the discourse about the impossibility of differentiating action in monism.[32]

The problem about how to account for difference in action in monism is not only a pressing concern from within Heidegger's own system, it is also a concern that had a significant role in the development of idealism, led to the invention of the term nihilism, and continued to reverberate in Germany at the time that Heidegger started lecturing in Freiburg while he was aligning himself with Husserl and phenomenology in an attempt to develop his own materialism. Within this context, one would expect Heidegger to tackle the problem of action within monism head on. But both in the published writings and in the lecture courses of the early Heidegger, the problem is never even formulated. I have not found anywhere a discussion that explains what is at stake in the problematic of action in a monist ontology.[33] On the rare occasion that Heidegger lectures on monist thinkers from modernity, his presentations are formulaic and unadventurous, following established exegetical patterns without ever stating the problem of differentiating action within a single, unified being.[34]

13. The third problem: Can monism provide qualitative distinctions between actions?

Even though Heidegger does not address the problem of how to account for different actions within a single, unified being, still he repeatedly and compulsively returns to a third problem intertwined with the second one,

---

31. For one example of this argument, see G.W.F. Hegel, *Lectures on Logic: Berlin, 1831*, trans. Clark Butler (Bloomington: Indiana University Press, 2008), 49.

32. Leo Strauss, *Das Erkenntnisproblem in der philosophischen Lehre Fr. H. Jacobis*, in *Gesammelte Schriften*, Band 2: Philosophie und Gesetz, Frühe Schriften, ed. Heinrich Meier (Stuttgart: J.B. Metzler, 2013 [1921]), 237–92, and *Die Religionskritik Spinozas als Grundlage seiner Bibelwissenschaft: Untersuchungen zu Spinozas Theologisch-politischem Traktat* (Berlin: Akademie Verlag, 1930). For discussion, see again Vardoulakis, "The Invention of Nihilism." After World War II, Emmanuel Levinas mounts his attack on Spinoza based on the same accusation of acosmism. See *Alterity and Transcendence*, trans. Michael B. Smith (London: Athlone, 1999), 69–70.

33. I take up this topic in *The Logic of Living*, §15.

34. See for example, the discussion of Spinoza in part 3 of Martin Heidegger, *Geschichte der Philosophie von Thomas von Aquin bis Kant* = GA 23.

namely, how to ascribe quality to actions within a monist ontology. How can we distinguish the quality of actions if they are all part of the single unified totality? It is not simply that the problem of the qualities of action is intertwined with the problem of the possibility of different actions within monism. More forcefully, we can say that Heidegger displaces the second problem into the third one.

We can understand this as the problem of "beyond good and evil in monism." I do not take this name from Nietzsche but rather from the Preface to Spinoza's Part IV of the *Ethics*. How is action to be qualified within a monist metaphysics where there is only one totality, "God, or Nature"? From such a position, says Spinoza, action can be, strictly speaking, neither good nor evil, because these are nothing but "modes of thinking, or notions we form because we compare things to one another."[35] A monist ontology cannot ascribe qualities to action without simultaneously introducing different qualities within the one and thereby introducing negation within the one and refuting monism. Being as such has no qualities.[36]

Heidegger is acutely aware of the problem of the untenability of qualitative distinctions within a conception of the one, unitary being. Monism makes it impossible to think of any kind of value or quality within being. Moreover, the general direction of Heidegger's response to this problem is similar to Spinoza's solution—and it is, in fact, the only tenable solution to the problem of how to evaluate action within a monist ontology that I am aware of within the history of thought. Specifically, the starting point of the solution consists in identifying as "good" those actions that are attuned to monism. Spinoza proposes to continue using the term good to denote that by which "we may approach nearer and nearer to the model of human nature we set before ourselves," that is, the model of nature that accords with monism.[37] Similarly, Heidegger designates as "inauthentic" the kind of activity that stops short of the "truth of being," which is only a short step from holding that thinking and acting are the same.[38]

Beyond this starting point, Spinoza and Heidegger take two fundamentally divergent routes that lead to different—one is tempted to say diametrically opposed—conceptions of action. The difference has to do with instru-

---

35. Spinoza, *Ethics*, trans. Edwin Curley (London: Penguin, 1996), Preface to Part IV, 115.
36. Cf. Della Rocca, *The Parmenidean Ascent*.
37. Spinoza, *Ethics*, 115.
38. Jean-Marie Vaysse explores these similarities in *Totalité et Finitude: Spinoza et Heidegger* (Paris: Vrin, 2004), but he fails to discern the fundamental divergence of their thought that I will describe.

mentality, or the calculation of means and ends. Instrumentality becomes the mechanism that Spinoza uses to identify which actions adhere to a monist conception of being. His answer, schematically, is the following: if there is nothing inherently "good or evil" in any action, then we need to examine the effects of actions. That is why at the beginning of Part IV of the *Ethics*, Spinoza defines the good as that which is "utilius."

Conversely, Heidegger vehemently rejects any means and ends calculation as having any chance to attain the truth of being. Rather, calculation marks for Heidegger an instrumental action that conceals being and which results in the malaise of modernity consisting in the domination of technology that Heidegger calls "machination" (*Machenschaft*). Heidegger argues for a different kind of action, free of ends and purified of instrumentality, the kind of praxis that *Being and Time* calls authenticity, and which is subsequently associated with poetry and the event. This is the kind of action that the late works described as without effects—or the ineffectual.

14. Two kinds of monist materialism

Through the divergent answers to the third problem about the qualities of action, we arrive at two fundamentally different, and ultimately incompatible, versions of monism. Either a monism where action is determined through its *differential effects*, or a monism where action is determined through the *qualitative differentiation* between actions that determine being as mere presence and ineffectual actions that lead to unconcealment.

More specifically, the epicurean monism that Spinoza espouses provides an account of action with recourse to instrumentality. The task of such an epicurean monism is to examine the effects of action. Actions are different because they produce different effects. Heidegger's version, by contrast, seeks to determine action through the supposition that instrumental praxis blocks access to the truth of being—or to monism. The Heideggerian task then becomes determining the conditions for the disclosure of the truth of being, which requires that we can qualitatively distinguish between actions in a way that explicitly precludes instrumentality. Importantly, Heidegger cannot locate difference in being itself, since he regards this as Nietzsche's error: Nietzsche attempts a transvaluation of values by inscribing value in being, whereas Heidegger holds that being knows of no negation and hence has no different qualities (§11).

The epicurean solution followed by Spinoza requires the distinction between causality and instrumentality (§7) so as to avoid recourse to any qualitative distinction between actions. From within a strictly monist ontology, it is absurd to impute any ends to a single substance. God exists, says Spinoza in the Preface to Part IV of the *Ethics*, "for the sake of no end."[39] Within a monist epistemology, the one has no intentions or ends. The one simply is. The one simply is, in the sense that it encompasses the entirety of causes and effects, which is why in Part I of the *Ethics* Spinoza calls it the "immanent cause" of existence. However, staying at the level of causality makes it impossible to account for difference in action. That is where the distinction between causality and instrumentality becomes critical. Definition 1 of Part IV of the *Ethics* defines the good as the useful, or utilius. Actions are not good or bad due to an inherent quality in them, since the qualities of action are all part of the same immanent causality—which is why nothing is good or evil absolutely. Rather, actions are good or bad depending on their utility, that is, depending on the effects they produce.

Spinoza's entire ethics and politics revolve around the calculation of utility as the kind of instrumentality that allows him to differentiate actions. He insists that human action requires that we calculate which actions are good or which ones are least evil (*Ethics* IV, P54). But Spinoza is also, and always, fully aware that the instrumental thinking that starts with the supposition that the good is that which is utilius is liable to miscalculation.[40] Thus, a sizeable portion of the *Theological Political Treatise* is devoted to examining those miscalculations that lead to what he calls "superstition" and whose effect is voluntary servitude or the phenomenon that "people act for their servitude as if they act for the salvation," as the Preface of the *Treatise* memorably puts it. Despite the fallibility of instrumental calculation, I hold that Spinoza regards democracy as possible, so long as democracy is not understood as merely a constitutionally defined regime, but rather as the conflicts that arise in the process of determining the utility of the community and the polity. We find then in Spinoza, an ethical and political monism that provides an account of different actions depending on their effects while rejecting the possibility that difference can be attained through qualitative distinctions.

Spinoza is actually following the ancient tradition of how to account for difference within a monist ontology. Cicero's book 5 of *On Ends* presents a synoptic view of this approach. He explores the most significant question of philosophy, or more accurately, the question that, when it is properly settled or rightly constituted, will also settle all other philosophical questions. This is the question of the good, understood in terms of the ends (*de fini-*

---

39. Spinoza, *Ethics*, 114.

40. As I explain in *Spinoza, the Epicurean*, Spinoza's position is not reducible to utilitarianism if by that term we understand a school of thought that develops in nineteenth-century England, precisely because utilitarianism remained wedded to the ideal of a correct calculation.

bus) of action. The participants in the dialogue agree on the philosophical question that resolves all philosophical questions, namely, the question about the good that conjoins thought and praxis. They agree, as Cicero puts it, that the good is the question about the "logic of living" (*ratio vivendi*) that governs how action leads either to good or evil effects. Finally, it seems entirely uncontentious that the issue of the good is, in fact, the question about ends (*rerum finibus*) because it is the ends of our actions that determine the logic of living—notes Cicero, repeating this curious phrase. Philosophical disagreement arises only about what these ends are, so as to reach good and bad effects—but they all agree on the pivotal position of the ends in solving the ethical and political dilemma of the good.[41]

We can summarize this approach by saying that the response to the problematic of action shows that the question "what is?" is not the proper ontological question. If ontology is not to be separated from praxis, then the proper ontological question is "what are the effects of what is?" Given that existence, as such, admits of no different qualities, the question of being is intertwined with the question of the effects of being. Difference is a property of the effects of being, not of being itself.[42]

Like Spinoza and the monist tradition, Heidegger holds that there are no inherently "evil" actions as such so as not to have to inscribe any qualitative distinctions within being. Unlike Spinoza, the "mystery of being" is paramount for Heidegger and this means that any calculation is doomed. As a result, Heidegger has to hold that the examination of the effects of action is futile in the pursuit of the truth of being, irrespective of whether the effects are causal or instrumental. By conflating causality and instrumentality, Heidegger holds that any calculation of the effects has no chance to lead to a democratic politics but only ever entrenches the concealment of being and the domination of technoscience.

The contrast between the two approaches to action within a monist ontology can be presented in terms of the different conceptions of calculation. Spinoza, adhering to the distinction between causality and instrumentality, can present the effects of action in terms of the fallibility of instrumentality. Heidegger, by conflating causality and instrumentality through the ruse of techne, argues that calculation is always concerned with certainty so as to align it with the theoretical knowledge of science. This opens the way for Heidegger to posit an action unconcerned with certainty because it is free

---

41. Cicero, *De Finibus Bonorum et Malorum*, trans. H. Rackham (Cambridge, MA: Harvard University Press, 1931), 5,15–16.

42. For further discussion, see Vardoulakis, *The Logic of Living*.

of all calculation. Through the distinction between causality and instrumentality, Spinoza can designate a calculation that is fallible, not because of some kind of existential mystery, but rather because of the prosaic fact that humans lack the natural power to calculate correctly the effects of their actions. By contrast, Heidegger shields the mystery of being from all calculation, which leaves no room for the effects of action. Instead, all calculation is confined to the technoscientific pursuit of precise measurement (§42). This difference in the conception of calculation manifests in Heidegger's divergent conception of action in monism. His insistence on the mystery of being is the obverse side of the repression of instrumentality.

Departing from this fundamental difference, Heidegger arrives at a powerful and influential solution to the problem of action in monism, which at first glance may appear highly original but, as I will argue, has a significant structural affinity with the metaphysics of morals (§15). It consists in displacing the qualitative distinction from being to different forms of concealment. While being remains mysterious, some forms of concealment are conducive to leading toward the truth of being, whereas others are hopelessly deviating away from being. We find this idea in many different texts, including *Being and Time*, where the instrumental realm, described through the analysis of tools in Division 1, can lead either to authenticity or to being lost in an amorphous multitude (§36). The qualitative distinction is not drawn according to two qualitatively distinct states—an authentic and inauthentic one—as this would blatantly contradict the impossibility of making qualitative distinctions within being. Rather, the qualitative distinction is drawn according to the kind of praxis undertaken within the instrumental realm. Either one loses oneself within this realm, or one transcends the instrumental—or rather represses it, as I would say—to arrive at authenticity (see chapter 4). Differently put, the qualitative distinction is about orientation: either one is disoriented and trapped within the instrumental that is supposed to presuppose precise measurement and calculation, or one is oriented toward disclosing the truth of being because one has abandoned the pursuit of calculation altogether.

I will turn to Heidegger's 1942–43 seminar on Parmenides to provide an illustration of this solution. Parmenides's monism places Heidegger's solution in the context of the problematic of action. The seminar starts with the categorical statement that "for a long time now the world has been out of joint and man is on the path of error."[43] This is due to modernity's

---

43. Martin Heidegger, *Parmenides*, trans. Andre Schuwer and Richard Rojcewicz (Bloomington: Indiana University Press, 1992) = *GA* 54, 8/11.

instrumental thinking that is "a technical attack [*ein technischer Angriff*] on a being and an intervention for purposes of an 'orientation' toward acting, 'producing,' wheeling and dealing."[44] This error signifies a technical obsession with the correct calculation indicative of an orientation away from the mystery of being. But there is another form of concealment that "preserves" the mystery of being: "The concealment holding sway here is close to the concealment characteristic of the secret, which may have, though not by necessity, the basic character of mystery." The distinctive feature of this concealment is that it preserves "the openness of the open mystery" or the truth of the one, unified being. By contrast, the technological concealment becomes "the horizon of scientific and technical discoveries" that prevent "access to the truth of being."[45] Both kinds of concealment, then, are within being. Their qualitative difference does not indicate different qualities of being. Rather, it indicates two qualitatively different responses to the mystery of being. Or, differently put, quality is not a property of being but a property of praxis. With this, Heidegger has arrived at an account of difference within action through a qualitative distinction between different actions.

We encounter here, then, two different responses to the problematic of action within monism, depending on how they deal with instrumentality. One determines different actions by focusing on the effects of instrumental calculation. The other draws a qualitative distinction between actions according to whether they are calculative or not, which produces the conception of an action without ends, or the repression of instrumentality. Maybe the greatest achievement of the ruse of techne has been to obscure the philosophical importance of the distinction between these two different approaches to the problematic of action in monism.

15. Two historical difficulties arising from Heidegger's solution to the problematic of action in monism

To start evaluating Heidegger's solution, I need to make two observations about his qualitative distinction between two acts, depending on how they approach being.[46] First, the qualitative distinction between the two kinds of praxis in response to concealment hinges on the relations established between the three senses of techne operating in Heidegger's discourse. We

---

44. Heidegger, *Parmenides*, 4/5.
45. Heidegger, *Parmenides*, 63–64/93–94.
46. I evaluate the epicurean and Spinozian approach in *Spinoza, the Epicurean*.

can see the immediate connection between these three senses of techne by examining one sentence from "The Age of the World Picture."

Heidegger writes that "in the age of the Greeks, the world can never become picture [*im Griechentum die Welt nicht zum Bild werden kann*]."[47] Three interrelated claims can be extracted from this statement, corresponding to the three meanings of techne. In this programmatic essay, world as a picture indicates the conception of existence as measurable and quantifiable. This is the key characteristic of the meaning of techne as technology. The fact that the Greeks lack this conception of world as picture indicates the other two meanings. Techne signifies the singularity and unity of being, or what I refer to as Heidegger's monism. Further, the Greeks have a conception of praxis that, as understood by Heidegger, is free of all ends and hence free of all the measurement and calculation characteristic of modern technoscience. This meaning aligns with the sense of techne as art. We see here, then, how in one sentence all three meanings of techne coalesce. Such a tight interrelation is critical for the ruse of techne.

Let me provide one example of this, again from the *Parmenides* lectures of 1942–43 that I noted earlier. Heidegger distinguishes Parmenides from modern philosophers on the grounds that he does not need "400 or more pages" to arrive at the "essential."[48] In this remark, the same three meanings of techne are again operative. Parmenides is the great monist for whom being is one and unified. He is contrasted to the modern philosopher seduced by technoscience to offer theories of truth and verification that are disoriented in mere presence leading to the forgetting of being. And Parmenides's philosophy was written in the form of a poem, like a work of art, that can more succinctly and directly express the truth of being. The ruse of techne larks behind every sentence that Heidegger writes. In some more explicitly than in others, but always there as the technique that regulates the logic of Heidegger's thought.

In the second observation, Heidegger never uses the vocabulary of quality. Rather, Heidegger uses the term "essence" to denote the qualitative distinction within praxis as pertaining to the relations between the three meanings of techne. For instance, he famously argues in "The Question Concerning Technology" that the essence of technology is nothing technological (§57). The reason is that the essence of technology has nothing to do with the meaning of techne as technology, but rather with the meaning

---

47. Martin Heidegger, "The Age of the World Picture," in *Off the Beaten Track*, trans. Julian Young and Kenneth Haynes (Cambridge: Cambridge University Press, 2002) = *GA* 5, 69/91.

48. Heidegger, *Parmenides*, 8/11.

of techne as art, insofar as it relates to the single, unified being or the meaning of techne indicating monism. With this move, Heidegger excludes all calculation and instrumentality from techne as art through the translation of the qualitative distinction into the discourse of essence. From this perspective, the Heideggerian notion of essence is yet another instrument effecting the repression of instrumentality.

At this point, it is hard to say whether the ruse of techne produces the qualitative distinction between actions or whether it is the other way around. As we will see in Heidegger's interpretation of phronesis in book 6 of the *Nicomachean Ethics* (see chapter 3), the two come together at the same time. What concerns me here, instead, are the difficulties Heidegger encounters as a result of his solution to the problematic of action in monism by drawing a qualitative distinction between two actions according to how they are oriented toward being. Specifically, he faces two difficulties when placed within a historical context: 1) Greek thought insists on the instrumentality of action; and 2) Heidegger's solution has a structural affinity with the metaphysical rejection of instrumentality.

First difficulty: Let me frame it with a personal anecdote. As a student in the "classical stream" of high school in Greece, my teachers explained (in the course reading many Greek texts from Homer to Aristotle) the importance of instrumental calculation for the ancient Greeks. The figure of Ulysses comes straight to mind, as well as Prometheus and Antigone. These are figures who are constantly calculating. The notion of phronesis itself, as it is presented in book 6 of Aristotle's *Nicomachean Ethics*, is also defined in terms of instrumentality. I was deeply shaken in my first year as graduate student when I encountered Heidegger's interpretation of the Greeks as being inimical to calculation. For a long while, I believed that my teachers at school had deceived me, or at least presented a distorted picture.

But then I started comparing Heidegger's interpretations of the Greeks with the texts themselves, and I started noticing some strange translation or paraphrase choices that systematically obscured, or distorted, the importance of means and ends calculations conveyed in the texts. Let me take phronesis as an example, as it is of acute importance here, because Heidegger's conception of the three meanings of techne emerges for the first time in his analysis of phronesis in Aristotle. In this context, Heidegger makes techne a modality of theoretical knowledge, thereby bridging the gap between theory and praxis via techne (§27); empties phronesis from instrumentality to define an action without ends (§29); and suggests, for the first time, the solution to the problem of action in monism by drawing a distinction within praxis (§24). But Heidegger relies on a mistranslation of a key passage about the truth of phronesis. Where Aristotle quite plainly insists on the instrumentality of phronesis, Heidegger translates the position as its opposite, that is, as the anti-instrumentalism of phronesis (§§25–26). Heidegger constructs the ruse of techne for the first time through this mistranslation.

The mistranslation about the instrumentality of phronesis cannot be corrected with an *erratum*, as it reflects Heidegger's solution to the problem of action in monism and hence challenges Heidegger's entire conception of the history of thought. As he summarizes his understanding of the history of philosophy in "The Age of the World Picture," for instance, the connection of thought and action with calculation is a characteristic of modernity, or what he calls nihilism in his lectures on Nietzsche. Heidegger insists that Greek thought has contrastingly a pure access to the single, unified being. The whole discourse of the destruction of metaphysics and the unforgetting of being is premised on this conception of the history of philosophy as first having access to being, and then losing it via the Latin translations of Greek thought. However, this conception, intermeshed with mistranslations, facilitates the genesis of the ruse of techne.

If being, in its singularity and unity, is thought in terms of instrumentality in Greek thought, then at least three important considerations follow: First, it requires an examination of the technique that Heidegger uses to propagate his account of the history of thought that represses instrumentality. My argument here is that the ruse of techne is precisely this technique. Second, this shakes the foundations of Heidegger's ontology, as the historical conception of philosophy is integral to his philosophical project. It would require nothing less than a revision of the entire conception of being and its unconcealment. Third, we need to reconsider the alternative historical account of monism (§7 and §14) that rectifies the distorted picture precipitated by Heidegger's resolution to the problematic of action.[49]

Second difficulty: Heidegger's solution to the problem of "beyond good and evil"—the third problem I noted above—consists in confining all end-oriented action to the technoscientific insistence on measuring, thereby separating a qualitatively distinct action that is purified of instrumentality, and inferring that the criterion for "good and bad" is the way in which it preserves this qualitative distinction. Clearly, there is a circularity in this argument, but I leave this consideration for later (§16). The remarkable

---

49. The third consideration essentially requires the history of monist conceptions of action from antiquity onward. The present book is a contribution to such a huge task, as is also *Spinoza, the Epicurean*, *The Logic of Living*, and *The Agonistic Condition*.

feature of the structure of Heidegger's argument that I want to note here is that it mirrors the answer to the problem of the existence of evil in Christian metaphysics.

In the fourth century, when dogma was consolidated, Christianity faced a major conceptual difficulty that threatened its metaphysical foundations. The problem is nothing but a reformulation of the third problem of action within monism: If there is one god who is all-encompassing of existence, then how can we account for the existence of evil? The Pelagians might argue that sin is something given to humans by god—thereby being in danger of making evil a property of god. Or the Manichaeans might suppose that there is a second, evil deity—whereby the god is no longer one. Ultimately, all these ideas were castigated as heresies and the orthodox answer was provided by Augustine, who argued that sin is a property of human action (§31). Using the story of the Fall as his primary example, Augustine described sin as the choice that arises from the free will, such as the calculation of Adam and Eve that they can eat the forbidden fruit without god's knowledge. Such instrumentalism is always bound to fail because the divine is purified from calculation—which is why no knowledge was needed in the Garden of Eden.

Following the Fall, no one is free of sin, but there are two kinds of humans: those who are on the path to the city of god—Augustine calls them pilgrims—whose sins ultimately do not eliminate their path; and pagans who are not on the right path and act in way that threatens the pilgrims' progress.[50] Sin, as the negative of the one—omniscient, omnipotent and omnipresent—god is ineliminable from the mortal world, but there are two qualitatively different attitudes to sin, depending on whether one's actions are oriented toward the city of god or not.

The parallel expositions about action in Heidegger and Augustine are conspicuous. There is the one (being or god). The one is not amenable to valuation or is not liable to negation (being is "beyond good and evil" and evil is not a property of god). "Evil" is action characterized by instrumentality and calculation (modern technology or the prompting of the "serpent"). There are distinct qualitative actions in the realm of calculation (in concealment or the Fallen world). Some of these actions are on the right path (Heidegger's path to being or the pilgrimage of Augustine), while others block the way (technology as the "bad" concealment and the

---

50. Augustine, *The City of God Against the Pagans*, ed. and trans. R.W. Dyson (New York: Cambridge University Press, 1998).

"pagans").[51] The strategy in both cases is the same: to give an account of action by avoiding a qualitative distinction within the one and displacing it instead into praxis according to the criterion of whether acting is oriented toward the one or not. And the criterion to recognize the different orientation is also the same: if an action is calculative or instrumental, it is on the wrong path. This thought culminates in Christian mysticism, such as in Meister Eckhart, where the action to approximate god is entirely without effects—not unlike Heidegger's notion of the ineffectual.[52]

It is certainly the case that Heidegger's epistemology has no room for a transcendent god, and his conception of time cannot tolerate eschatology. I would readily agree that his ontology successfully overcomes an onto-theo-logical conception of knowledge (§4). Heidegger destructs the epistemology of metaphysics. But that is not the case with the onto-theo-logical theory of action or the morals of metaphysics. Here, the Christian influence is palpable, and it is located precisely in the castigation of instrumentality. His metaphysical materialism captures this ambivalence: *overcoming of the epistemology of metaphysics through materialism while remaining trapped in metaphysics because instrumentality deviates from the path toward unconcealment.* From the perspective of his conception of action, Heidegger is neck deep into onto-theo-logy.

16. The double bind of the repression of instrumentality: Between the vacuous and the self-contradictory

Heidegger's association of instrumentality with the deviation from the path toward being, as a result of the qualitative distinction between actions, results in the impossible choice between, on the one hand, a trivial conception of action and on the other, one that actually relies on effects whereby it is self-contradictory and thus appears to support established forms of power. I will illustrate this unpalatable dilemma with recourse to the 1942–43 lecture course on Parmenides.

---

51. Is it a coincidence that the best philosophical descriptions of Augustine's position are still to be found in the work of Hannah Arendt, who studied with Heidegger and who had a fraught relationship with his thought? See Hannah Arendt, "What is Freedom?" in *Between Past and Future: Six Exercises in Political Thought* (New York: Viking, 1961), 143–71, and *The Life of the Mind* (New York: Harcourt, 1978). For an account of the relation between Arendt and Heidegger see Dana R. Villa, *Arendt and Heidegger: The Fate of the Political* (Princeton, NJ: Princeton University Press, 1996).

52. See Ian Alexander Moore, "The End of Instrumentality? Heidegger on *Phronēsis* and Calculative Thinking," *Australian Philosophical Review* 6, no. 3 (2022): 255–61.

I already mentioned *Parmenides* in presenting Heidegger's solution to the third problem about the quality of actions. In the same lecture course, Heidegger illustrates the qualitative distinction between one kind of action that blocks access to the truth of being, and another that facilitates the openness of the mystery of being through the contrast between handwriting and the typewriter: "The typewriter veils the essence of writing and of the script." The reason is that "the typewriter is . . . a withdrawing concealment [*eine . . . sich entziehende Verbergung*] . . . and through it the relation of Being to the human is transformed."[53] In other words, the typewriter, unlike the writing hand, is an instrument, a form of technology, and as such traps the human in concealment. Writing by hand puts the human in a position to potentially experience the disclosure of being. Using a typewriter dooms the human to a concealment that withdraws from being.

This is a much-discussed example. For instance, Don Ihde notes the irony that Heidegger sold the manuscript of *Being and Time*, thereby instrumentalizing his handwriting in the pursuit of profit.[54] In a less personal approach, Friedrich Kittler questions the distinction between handwriting and the typewriter by noting how Nietzsche's writing was both rescued and transformed by the typewriter. It was rescued because his deteriorating eyesight meant that handwriting was difficult for him, so acquiring a typewriter enabled him to continue working. It transformed his writing because it was the use of the typewriter that led to the aphoristic style that Nietzsche pioneered and is famous for.[55] Kittler's point amounts to saying that technology—and by extension instrumentality—cannot be good or bad as such. We can only judge its effects—which is as we saw the point about action in epicurean monism.

The critical issue is where to draw the line between what is technological and what is not. One could ask, is handwriting not a form of technology too? The instruments of handwriting, for instance, radically change over the centuries. Writing on clay is different from writing with a stylus, and that is again different from a fountain pen, and then different from a plastic pen such as the Pilot G–2 that I prefer. The distinction between handwriting and the typewriter cannot be a distinction between a practice that is bereft of technology and one that is dominated by it. It is impossible to draw this distinction by referring to the quantity of domination that a specific technology

---

53. Heidegger, *Parmenides*, 85/126.
54. Don Ihde, *Heidegger's Technologies: Postphenomenological Perspectives* (New York: Fordham University Press, 2010), 125–26.
55. Friedrich Kittler, *Gramophone, Film, Typewriter*, trans. Geoffrey Winthrop-Young and Michael Wurz (Stanford, CA: Stanford University Press, 1999).

has over the writer, since the connection between writer and the technologies of writing is contextual and fluid. For instance, does the typewriter "dominate" the writer "less" than a laptop? This raises the question: If technology is a necessary and ineliminable prosthesis to our actions, then how can one draw the line between one technology—such as handwriting—that is supposedly more suited *qualitatively* to the disclosure of being, and another—such as the typewriter—that is meant to make being withdraw? One senses that this is an intractable sorites that can only be solved by the arbitrary decision of the one who, by virtue of drawing that line, wants to establish their own personal authority. Perhaps, then, the contrast between handwriting and the typewriter is not primarily about writing instruments, but rather about power relations. I will return to this shortly.

The difficulty of quantifying the domination by technology and instruments of writing so as to produce a qualitative distinction between actions can be seen by a counterexample that reverses Heidegger's: the fetishization of handwriting can be more dominating than any gadget used as a writing device. At the 2019 Sydney Writers' Festival, Behrouz Boochani explained how he wrote *No Friend but the Mountains* using WhatsApp on his mobile phone, since writing was prohibited in the Manus Island Regional Processing Centre, where he was detained.[56] Writing on a smuggled mobile phone that could easily be hidden, and texting immediately to collaborators, was the most expedient way to write his book. During the question and answer period, an old, silver-haired gentleman asked Boochani—who was still detained then and participated via video link—whether he would start writing by hand when he was released from the detention center (I feared that he was about to offer to donate a $5,000 fountain pen and acid free paper to him). Thankfully, Boochani laughed him off by explaining that he was just describing the writing process, that he in fact liked writing on his mobile phone, and that he intended to continue writing on his mobile even after being released from detention. The instrument of writing—manual, mechanical, or electronic—can offer no quantitative distinctions between levels of technological domination and hence no qualitative distinctions between different actions. Other than in a purely *trivial* way, no essential distinction can be drawn from within the practice of employing different technologies of writing.

56. On Boochani's *No Friend by the Mountains*, see J. M. Coetzee, "Australia's Shame," *New York Review of Books*, September 26, 2019, www.nybooks.com/articles/2019/09/26/australias-shame/; and Dimitris Vardoulakis, "Behrouz Boochani and the Biopolitics of the Camp: The New Primo Levi?" *Public Seminar*, February 16, 2019, https://philarchive.org/archive/VARBBA.

The students present at the seminar on Parmenides must have showed signs of incredulity at the distinction between handwriting and the typewriter, because Heidegger breaks the flow of his lecture to note that "you, as is proven to me by your reaction, though well-intended, have not grasped what I have been trying to say."[57] Were they thinking that the distinction was trivial for a conception of action? Alternatively, perhaps, they were aghast at the other possibility, namely, that even though Heidegger was suggesting a qualitative distinction between the different forms of concealment in action, *in fact the distinction was mired in effects, presupposing the instrumentality from which the action oriented toward being was meant to be purified.* Remember the date: winter semester of 1942–43. The young men were at the battlefront, the classroom was full of young women, who were aware that they were unlikely to ever become philosophy professors like Heidegger, who writes with his fountain pen, but one of them might become his secretary, taking notes and then typing his lectures or his essays on a typewriter in preparation for publication.[58] Maybe this class, full of female students, could grasp (too well) the gender politics of the distinction between the fountain pen—did I hear a Lacanian whisper, "the phallus"?—and the typewriter, even while the professor remained blissfully oblivious.

Hidden behind the possible triviality of this example lies the potential that instrumentality, which is supposed to provide the measure for the evaluation of the different kinds of concealment, is actually inscribed in being, and that if we are to discern the truth of being, we need to examine the effects of instrumentality. It is this instrumentality that, despite itself,

---

57. Heidegger, *Parmenides*, 85/125. I note the uniqueness of this apostrophe to the students. I do not recall a similar apostrophe that records the students' incredulity in any other lecture course notes published in *GA*.

58. Heidegger justifies his rejection of the job offer from Berlin on the grounds that his philosophy was close to the solitude of the peasant life, away from the busy city that distracts from what is "essential." Martin Heidegger, "Why Do I Stay in the Provinces?" in *Philosophical and Political Writings*, ed. Manfred Stassen and trans. Thomas Sheehan (New York: Continuum, 2003), 16–18. At the same time, correspondence between Heidegger and the dean of philosophy, preserved in the Freiburg University archives, shows that Heidegger negotiated certain benefits to stay at Freiburg University, one of which was the use of a typist. See Antonia Grunenberg, *Hannah Arendt and Martin Heidegger: History of Love*, trans. Peg Birmingham et al. (Bloomington: Indiana University Press, 2017), 92. For the role of women as typists in the Weimar Republic, see Angelika Führich, "Woman and Typewriter: Gender, Technology, and Work in Late Weimar Film," *Women in German Yearbook* 16 (2000): 151–66. There is extensive literature on the gender politics of the typewriter. For example, see Margery Davies, *Woman's Place is at the Typewriter: Office Work and Office Workers, 1870–1930* (Philadelphia: Temple University Press, 1982).

Heidegger's fountain pen denotes. Thus, Heidegger's words—written, typed, and printed—may, in fact, entail the opposite of what they explicitly want to say, namely, the ontological import of instrumentality. Moreover, the concealment of instrumentality, its repression in the contrast between handwriting and the typewriter, emerges as complicit in perpetuating the prevailing power structures that the very constitution of the classroom manifested. In both cases, the contrast between handwriting and typewriter evidences a disregard of the ethical and political import of action.

Undaunted by the potential reversal of his monism to the epicurean position, and by the puzzled looks of his students, Heidegger presses on: "I have not been presenting a disquisition on the typewriter itself, regarding which it could justifiably be asked what in the world that has to do with Parmenides. My theme was the modern relation (transformed by the typewriter) of the hand to writing, i.e., to the word, i.e., to the unconcealedness of being. A meditation on unconcealedness and on being does not merely have something to do with the didactic poem of Parmenides, it has everything to do with it [*hat freilich alles, nicht nur einiges, mit dem Lehrgedicht des Parmenides zu tun*]. . . . This situation is constantly repeated everywhere, in all relations of modern man to technology [*in allen Bezügen des neuzeitlichen Menschen zur Technik*]."[59] The typewriter, insists Heidegger, has everything to do with Parmenides's monism, with his assertion of the one, because of its relation to the unconcealment of being. The way in which the typewriter prevents such unconcealment is not a point about typewriters as such but rather about the relation of technology, "constantly repeated everywhere," to the truth of being. We can evaluate an action—explains the professor—only in relation to how a technical action leads or blocks the way to the disclosure of being.

Maybe sensing that he is repeating himself—which he was, and repetition is an important element of the qualitative distinction between actions in monism that I will return to shortly—or maybe that his students are still incredulous, Heidegger feels that he needs another example: "He who has ears to hear. i.e., to grasp the metaphysical foundations and abysses of history and to take them seriously *as* metaphysical, could already hear two decades ago the word of Lenin: Bolshevism is Soviet power + electrification. That means: Bolshevism is the 'organic,' i.e., organized, calculating (and as +) conclusion of the unconditional power of the party along with complete technization [*Technisierung*]."[60] The passage from the apostrophe

---

59. Heidegger, *Parmenides*, 85–86/126–27.
60. Heidegger, *Parmenides*, 86/127.

to his students to the determination of "Bolshevism" had to be cited extensively, as it is not simply about what it says, but also about how it is said. By the time we have reached the description of Bolshevism as presumably the political counterpart of the typewriter as the kind of technology, or "technization," that deviates from the path toward being, the professor's grammar barely holds together, the sentences become almost spasmodic. One senses that, unlike the typewriter example, the reference to Bolshevism was *ex tempore*, in a moment of near exasperation toward the unreceptive students without ears attuned to the call of being—are ears technical instruments too, perhaps?[61] One senses, further, that the incredulous, calculating looks of the female students undermined the professor's authority, which had to be imminently restored with reference to a presumed shared nationalist sentiment against Bolshevism as the enemy.

The students could not have failed to hear the professor's words *in tempore*, uttered in early 1943 after the Bolsheviks had recently encircled the German army outside Stalingrad, only days away from delivering the Third Reich its first major defeat in WWII (a defeat that was a catastrophe not only because of the immense loss of life, but also for its military implications). The path to the unconcealment of being does pass, after all, via the *effects* of action. It is such effects that determine the choice of example and tone in which it is delivered. One is tempted to ask: Is it maybe such effects that also determine the qualitative distinction between actions within the one being? Is it, moreover, such effects that determine how the typewriter and Bolshevism are examples of the forms of concealment that prevent access to the truth of being? Even if one hesitates to answer "yes" to the above question, one still could not deny the *instrumental* and *effective* way in which the supposedly noninstrumental and noneffective path to the truth of being is presented. And this is assuredly self-contradictory in an immanently political way that supports persisting social inequalities and the sovereign determination of Bolshevism as the enemy.

So here is, in a sentence, the ethical and political effect of the qualitative distinction between actions within the monism of the ruse of techne: it yields an account of action that is either trivial and hence *vacuous* or instrumental and hence *self-refuting*, while enforcing an ideological reproduction of the prevailing power structures.

---

61. See Peter Szendy, *Listen: A History of Our Ears*, trans. Charlotte Mandell (New York: Fordham University Press, 2008).

17. Why Heidegger's solution to the problematic of action in monism matters

The difficulties that I outline above are not meant to diminish Heidegger's achievement. After all, no philosopher succeeds in presenting a coherent enough position, free of "mistakes." In fact, it seems to me that what I regard as the difficulty in his position about action in monism, is also his greatest achievement. Heidegger's monist ontology reversed the traditional way in which monist ontologies account for action, which had consisted in emphasizing the effects of action, proposing in its stead, a conception of action that is free of effects.

This position has had a huge impact in continental philosophy, sidelining instrumentality and calculation from ethical and political discourse. But as soon as we locate the provenance of this conception of action in monism, we may arrive at a surprising conclusion. Maybe the most significant effect of Heidegger's work has been to promulgate an answer to the solution of action in monism that obscures the traditional answer that relied on instrumentality. It is as if, after Heidegger, instrumentality became the taboo word for ethics and politics, leading to a uniform castigation of instrumentality in continental philosophy. The reception of Spinoza and the epicurean monist tradition is symptomatic of this taboo: commentators have silenced the importance of utility in his ethics.

It appears, then, that Heidegger's solution to the problematic of action in monism through the repression of instrumentality and the forgetting of the epicurean monist tradition, are mutually supportive. We can see this in Gilles Deleuze. Not only does his influential interpretation of Spinoza thoroughly silence the discourse of utility in Spinoza, to the extent that *Expressionism in Philosophy* has nothing to say about instrumentality, displacing the issue of action in monism to a polemic against Platonism. Moreover, when he develops his own theory of action, Deleuze resolutely insists on the ethical import of an action without ends, which is indebted to Heidegger's qualitative distinction to repress instrumentality. The clearest illustration of this is, perhaps, his celebration of Bartelby. In a late essay that summarizes all the key themes of his practical philosophy, Deleuze presents Bartelby's "I prefer not to" as the paragon of ethical action that is supposed to offer a blueprint for the dismantling of structures of domination.[62] In celebrating Bartleby's action without effects, Deleuze works in

---

62. Gilles Deleuze, "Bartleby; or The Formula" in *Essays; Critical and Clinical*, trans. D. Smith and M. Greco (Minneapolis: University of Minnesota Press, 1997), 68–90.

the shadow of Heidegger's solution to the problem of action in monism: the qualitative distinction between instrumental actions and actions supposedly purified from instrumentality.

The repetition of the ruse of techne is *the* means that Heidegger scholars use to perpetuate his conception of action that affirms, simultaneously, the repression of instrumentality and an action free of ends. Its three nodal points should be familiar by now, and they can easily be discovered in scholarship on Heidegger.

The ruse of techne usually starts with the critique of instrumentality, technology, and calculation as leading to concepts that are closed off or occluded. Any means and ends process is supposed to be a "picture," to use the term from "The Age of the World Picture." For instance, any philosophy that has recourse to instrumentality for an account of action is immediately castigated as leading to conceptual closure. Calculation is supposed to strive to establish the crippling domination of technology and science.

Art is celebrated as the antithesis of techne as technoscience. Poetry, painting, drama, any chosen work of art, can be singled out as providing an open reflection on being that preserves its "mystery." As such, art is presented as providing privileged access to the truth of being. And this means that works of art are celebrated as giving us a more profound access to the realm of action—both politics and the ethical nature of our actions. We can only free ourselves through actions on the path to the truth of being, of which art is exemplary. Real liberation needs great poets.

This is supported by the side of techne that gives a historical thickness to the other two sides by showing how techne is intertwined in the Greeks with the singularity and unity of being. Most often, this meaning of techne is constructed by repeating Heidegger's readings of the ancient Greeks without even checking the Greek texts, but simply repeating Heidegger's readings.

The repetition of the ruse of techne, by now, has become a kind of *incantation* that pays scant—nay, *no*—attention to a monist account of action that relies on a qualitative distinction between actions that are instrumental and actions that are without effect. This is particularly problematic when art is celebrated as the privileged path to being. In these cases, what is called art becomes an alibi for a lack of political positions—which can easily be co-opted to become a political apologetic that castigates any political opponent for "technologization." As opposed to reducing politics to a mystical veneration of poets, maybe we need to question the assertion that calculation necessarily establishes the closure of thinking and hence political domination. In fact, the very opposite seems to be the case—what authority cannot tolerate is calculation,[63] such as the calculation registered in the looks of the female students in reaction to the distinction between handwriting and the typewriter—looks that were more powerful than Heidegger's appeal to a shared nationalist opposition to Bolshevism.

When we hear the incantations repeating the ruse of techne we need to remember three things. First, the monist tradition that has recourse to instrumentality to construct a theory of action does *not* presuppose that calculations require clear and secure ends. In fact, as I argue in *Spinoza, the Epicurean*, the opposite is the case. What is attractive about instrumentality is its fallibility, which reflects our mistakes and missteps whenever we act and fail, not only to reach our goal, but more often to even be able to articulate a coherent goal. From within the history of monism, the repeated assertion that instrumentality offers a closed system is merely a red herring. By contrast, instrumentality is used to provide an account of action as a means to liberation because it is the only way to undercut what La Boétie calls "voluntary servitude," and to undermine authority. As Spinoza shows, the possibility of democracy stands or falls alongside the possibility of instrumentality.

Second, denying that art has no privilege in ethics and politics is not meant to diminish art, but rather to wrench it away from its exile in the mystery of being and bring it back to solid ground. Art is part of the way in which we assess the world around us. It offers us ways to conceive why "we see the better and do the worse," as Ovid puts it, and it is useful, as Bernard Williams notes, because real life examples about action, when inserted within an ethical or political narrative, resemble less real life and more "bad literature."[64] Differently put, the value of art may not be in its imperviousness to effects but, to the contrary, in the uncanny ways it has to register the effects of the instrumental.

Third, from the perspective of the ruse of techne, Heidegger's path of monism emerges as more significant than the path of phenomenology today. The phenomenological roots of Heidegger's thought, and his mark on the development of phenomenology and postphenomenology are well noted and much discussed. But the monist path has remained obscure, hidden from scrutiny. It has remained repressed, and we know that the

---

63. Dimitris Vardoulakis, "The Antinomy of Frictionless Sovereignty: Inverse Relations of Authority and Authoritarianism," *boundary 2 online*, August 20, 2020, www.boundary2.org/2020/08/dimitris-vardoulakis-the-antinomy-of-frictionless-sovereignty-inverse-relations-of-authority-and-authoritarianism/.

64. Bernard Williams, *Shame and Necessity* (Berkeley: University of California Press, 1993), 13.

repressed has a habit of returning to haunt our decisions and actions. Heidegger's solution to the problematic of action in monism matters, especially, for continental philosophy because it has regulated discourse by virtue of being repressed and hence unnoticed. It has become an incantation.

Philosophy will not free itself from such repeated return of an action without effects until it contends with Heidegger's ruse of techne. We can break the enchantment of the Heideggerian incantation as soon as we understand the trick of the ruse of techne. *The Ruse of Techne* is devoted to this task: to describe this technique and bring it to light so as to loosen its grip on our thought and imagination. It is only then that we will be in a position to see the real power of Heidegger's magical materialism, which consists inter alia in obscuring the other account of action in monism that relies on the effects of acting. But dispelling the enchantment of the ruse of techne forces philosophy to seriously consider the choice presented by the path of monism: *either* Heidegger's repression of instrumentality *or* the ethical and political central to the instrumental, according to epicurean monism.

3

The Conflation of Causality and Instrumentality
Phronesis and the Genesis of the Ruse of Techne

18. Heidegger's bildungsroman

Let me start with a familiar story about Heidegger so as to indicate how it relates to the problematic of action in monism that I explained in chapter 2. This is the story of how a young, promising scholar in Germany came to prominence as one of the preeminent philosophers of the twentieth century. After finishing his habilitation on Duns Scotus, the young Martin Heidegger decided to move to Freiburg to align himself with Edmund Husserl, the founder of the new, exciting, philosophical school in Germany called phenomenology. Working as Husserl's assistant was never going to be enough to satisfy Heidegger's ambition. He soon turned to Greek philosophy to find ways to extend the main insight of phenomenology—namely, that truth resides in phenomena.

Aristotle held a special significance during Heidegger's tenure as Privatdozent in Freiburg. His lectures on Aristotle lead to the notion of truth as *aletheia* or the unconcealment of being (an idea with implications for the history of philosophy), while also forging a philosophical program distinct from Husserl's. Moreover, his seminars on a variety of texts such as *Physics* and *Metaphysics*, established his reputation as a magnificent teacher.[1] His

---

1. See Hannah Arendt, "Martin Heidegger at Eighty," in *Heidegger and Modern Philosophy*, ed. Michael Murray and trans. Albert Hofstadter (New Haven, CT: Yale University Press, 1978), 293–303. The English translation first appeared in *New York*

reputation reached Paul Natorp in Marburg, who in 1922 was looking to fill a position in ancient philosophy. The revered scholar of ancient Greek philosophy wrote to Husserl to inquire about his young protégé. Husserl responded with his strongest possible endorsement, meaning that Heidegger was in contention for the position which would set him up for the academic career that he so fervently craved.

The appointment was anything but straightforward. The problem was not only that Heidegger had published nothing since his habilitation but, as Husserl informed Natorp, Heidegger was still searching for his own position and his own voice, not feeling confident yet to commit it to paper. There was Heidegger's plan for a book on Aristotle, based on his lecture courses, however the book would never be ready in time for the appointment at Marburg. To resolve this complication, the two professors devised a creative solution: they asked Heidegger to write a summary of his projected book that would present his original interpretation and be submitted in lieu of the forthcoming publication.

Under immense pressure, Heidegger wrote the text titled "Phenomenological Interpretations with Respect to Aristotle" within three weeks, in October 1922.[2] This text, often referred to as the "Natorp report," can be regarded as the first, preliminary draft of *Being and Time* in the sense that we find here, for the first time as Theodore Kisiel notes, "the double-pronged program familiar to us in *Being and Time* of 1) a fundamental ontology and 2) a destruction of the history of ontology."[3] This intellectual breakthrough, coupled with the professional success of being awarded the position at Marburg University, paved the way for Heidegger's magnum opus that would solidify his position as a key philosopher of the twentieth century.

Review of Books, October 21, 1971, 50–54, available at www.nybooks.com/articles/1971/10/21/martin-heidegger-at-eighty/. See also Leo Strauss, "An Introduction to Heideggerian Existentialism," in *The Rebirth of Classical Political Rationalism: An Introduction to the Thought of Leo Strauss,* ed. Thomas L. Pangle (Chicago: University of Chicago Press, 1989).

2. Martin Heidegger, "Phenomenological Interpretations with Respect to Aristotle: Indication of the Hermeneutical Situation," trans. Michael Baur, *Man and World*, 25 (1992), 355–93 93 = "Phänomenologische Interpretationen zu Aristoteles (Anzeige der hermeneutischen Situation)," *Dilthey-Jahrbuch*, 6 (1989), 235–74.

3. Theodore Kisiel, *The Genesis of Heidegger's Being and Time* (Berkeley: University of California Press, 1995), 249. The importance of Aristotle for the early Heidegger is well documented in excellent works such as: Walter Brogan, *Heidegger and Aristotle The Twofoldness of Being* (Albany: SUNY Press, 2005); and William McNeill *The Glance of the Eye: Heidegger, Aristotle, and the Ends of Theory* (Albany: SUNY Press, 1999).

We can add a layer of complexity to this well-known story which will put it in the orbit of Heidegger's monism: The importance of Aristotle consisted in showing Heidegger the possibility of understanding being as one and unified.[4] Without such a notion of being, the conception of aletheia, or truth as unconcealment, is impossible. We can see this idea progressively becoming clearer and its importance being recognized in the lectures from the first period that Heidegger spent at Freiburg working with Husserl. What is missing from all these texts is an answer to the question of how to link the conception of the single being that can be expressed by particular beings in many different ways, with the possibility of action. In other words, during his early lectures on Aristotle at Freiburg, Heidegger solves the first problem that I identified in chapter 2—moving past metaphysics through a monist materialism that is irreducible to the prevalent materialisms of his day—but he is paralyzed by the second problem—how to account for action in monism—and unable to find a solution to it.

The Natorp report is the circuit breaker that foregrounds the notion of phronesis from book 6 of the *Nicomachean Ethics*.[5] Aristotle argues there that aletheia (truth) does not apply only to the various forms of knowledge such as episteme and sophia. He also talks about the aletheia of two forms of activity that he calls techne and phronesis. This helps Heidegger realize that the problem of how to account for action in monism is not intractable, it does not even need to be answered directly. Rather, it can be displaced to the third problem of monism, namely, the distinction between two qualitatively different actions (§§13–14). Thus, techne emerges in Heidegger's interpretation of Aristotle as a modality of theoretical knowledge that can never attain to the truth of being, an idea that will be fully developed in Division 1 of *Being and Time*; while phronesis as the kind of action free of ends provides the conception of an existential analytic of praxis that will become Division 2, as it is the action that can lead to authenticity and the truth of being. Techne is a first step toward aletheia that can only be realized in a qualitatively different kind of action exemplified by phronesis. The qualitative difference in Heidegger's interpretation is that techne is an end-oriented action, whereas phronesis is free of ends.

After years of painstakingly slow toil, the three weeks in late 1922 in which he developed his interpretation of phronesis provided Heidegger with his conception of action within a single, unified being upon which the

---

4. See Martin Heidegger, *Being and Time*, trans. Joan Stambaugh (Albany: SUNY Press, 2010) = *GA* 2, 2/3.

5. See Heidegger, "Phenomenological Interpretations with Respect to Aristotle," 377–84.

philosophical project of the rest of his life would be built. Crucially, the distinction between techne and phronesis also led to the first adumbration of the triangle of techne: techne as pointing to a Greek monism that is ante-metaphysical; techne as an end-oriented action does not attain to the truth of being; and phronesis as the alternative action to techne that is free of all ends to action whereby it is oriented toward unconcealment, which Heidegger would later align with art.

To qualitatively distinguish between actions with ends and actions without ends that thereby lack effects, Heidegger associates all ends to action solely with techne, which conflates causality and instrumentality. Incorporating both in techne purifies phronesis of any vestige of instrumentality. This is consistent with Heidegger's solution of the problematic of action (§§13–14). The problem is that such a solution sits uncomfortably next to Heidegger's position of a single, unified being. A qualitative separation suggests that difference is inscribed in being itself, which contradicts its singularity (§15). We will see that Heidegger makes several attempts to resolve this difficulty. In particular, I will sketch three distinct strategies that he pursues, all ultimately unsuccessful (§9). I hold that Heidegger's strategy can provide no solution to the problematic of action, which is why I describe this strategy that conflates techne and phronesis as "Heidegger's mistake" (§2).

By contrast, Aristotle draws a distinction between the ends of techne and phronesis. The ends of techne are the final ends characteristic of causality, whereas the ends of phronesis operate at the level of means and ends characteristic of instrumentality (cf. §14). I will demonstrate in this chapter that Heidegger consistently mistranslates the passages in Aristotle in which this distinction between ends occurs. *These mistranslations are symptomatic of Heidegger's mistake*: the mistranslations cause the mistake, not vice versa—the two mutually support each other and give rise to each other.

In the present chapter, I will show how the symptomatic relation between the mistranslations about the ends of techne and phronesis and the mistake about praxis functions as the condition of the possibility of the repression of instrumentality, and hence gives birth to the ruse of techne. This will lead in chapter 4 to the description of the first systematic presentation of the mistake in *Being and Time*, before turning to the second attempt in chapter 5, and the third in chapter 6.

19. The truth of phronesis as the combination of calculation, emotion, and situatedness

To grasp Heidegger's mistranslation, we have to first examine Aristotle's conception of the truth of phronesis as it is presented in book 6 of the

Nicomachean Ethics. The first two chapters of book 6 delineate a series of distinctions that provide the matrix for the examination of the truth of action that he calls phronesis. It is important to pay attention to these opening distinctions, not only because it is here that Aristotle determines the notion of the truth of phronesis, but also because, as we will see, Heidegger skims over the first two chapters of book 6, starting his reading with chapter 3, even though the pivot of his reading is the truth of phronesis that Aristotle outlines in chapter 2.

The distinction between techne and phronesis organizes the opening of book 6. These are the two intellectual virtues, that is, virtues that involve a certain ratiocination about how an action is to be successfully enacted; or they are intellectual in the sense that they do not happen merely by disposition (1138b–1139a).[6] Intellectual virtues are different from "natural" virtues like justice or temperance that can be acquired by habit.[7] Notably, the terms techne and phronesis themselves are not introduced until chapter 3, with their distinction drawn explicitly in chapters 4 and 5. Nonetheless, the opening two chapters of book 6 distinguish between action (*praxis*) and production (*poiesis*), which are the activities characteristic of phronesis and techne respectively.

The distinctions between action and production, and between phronesis and techne refer to another distinction between *ergon* and *energeia* introduced in the first few sentences of *Nicomachean Ethics* (1094α). Aristotle notes that every techne and every examination, every praxis and every judgment, aims at the good. In other words, rational activity is not pure theoretical knowledge, but always directed at something practical that can take many forms. The pursuit of the good, or virtue, with rational activity, however, indicates that actions can have two distinct kinds of ends. This is not *the* end as metaphysical entelechy (cf. §28). Instead, Aristotle draws a distinction between the ends of *erga* that are the products of activity—or independent of the activity—and the ends of *energeiai* that are commensurate with its enactment (1094a).[8] This initial distinction is carried over in book 6, where techne is the intellectual virtue that corresponds to *ergon*,

---

6. Aristotle, *Nicomachean Ethics*, trans. H. Rackham (Cambridge, MA: Harvard University Press, 2003).

7. We will see the importance of this distinction between natural and rational virtue in §51, where I discuss *to deinon* in *Nicomachean Ethics*.

8. The description of energeia as commensurate with its enactment can also be found in *Metaphysics* Theta. Thus, this distinction between ergon and energeia is constitutive of Aristotle's ontology. I take up this issue in Vardoulakis, *The Logic of Living: The Materialism of Greek Thought* (forthcoming), chapter 3.

while the ends of phronesis are provisional as they arise in the process of their enactment, thereby corresponding to *energeia*.

This is a pivotal distinction for Aristotle to avoid an unpalatable separation between theory and praxis. If the good is not to be purely intellection, then it has to be connected to activity. This in turn encounters the problematic of action in monism. In the absence of transcendence in Aristotle's philosophy, or if being is one and unified, then how is it possible to account for difference in action? As we saw earlier, the ancient response was to account for difference through the distinction between ends (§7, §14). Aristotle establishes this distinction in terms of *ergon* and *energeia* at the beginning of *Nicomachean Ethics*, and then explains the distinction within the matrix of the intellectual virtues in book 6. So, even though the distinction between techne and phronesis is only explicitly addressed in chapters 4 and 5 of book 6, still it is pivotal to Aristotle's conception of the practical. His conception of ethics and politics stands on the grounds established by the distinction between an end that is independent of its enactment (the activity of ergon and the end of techne), and an activity whose ends are commensurate with its enactment (the activity of energeia and the end of phronesis).

Aristotle makes it clear that he regards phronesis as much more significant than techne insofar as the ethical and the political are concerned. The ends of techne are products of skill, artifacts that are separated from their creator and thereby achieve a life of their own. In contrast, by being commensurate with their enactment, the ends of phronesis can never be separated from the person who enacts them nor from the context within which they are enacted. Consequently, phronesis provides a sphere of action as an interaction. The ends of phronesis forge those links that we call "community." Understandably, then, Aristotle's focus in book 6 is on phronesis. And this is also the case in the first two chapters of book 6 where he establishes the truth of praxis as the activity characteristic of phronesis.

Aristotle discusses the truth of praxis in terms of knowledge. It is not the scientific knowledge (τὸ ἐπιστομονικὸν) that examines universals that remain the same, irrespective of the circumstances of their enactment. Rather, it is a calculative knowledge (τὸ λογιστικὸν) that consists in making judgments about changeable things (1139a). A calculative judgment requires three components to determine the truth of praxis: sensation, intellect, and emotional disposition (αἴσθησις, νοῦς, ὄρεξις, 1139a20). These three elements all need to be present; sensation alone cannot be the motivator of action (ἡ αἴσθησις οὐδεμίας ἀρχὴ πράξεως, 1139a20). Sensation provides the setting within which the calculative faculty operates by employing both rationality and emotion. In other words, practical judgments are situated, their calculations arise from within the circumstances that one finds oneself—that is, from within one's field of sensation. But for action to take place, this setting provided by sensation requires both rationality and emotion.

After all these distinctions, it is now possible to determine the truth of phronesis. It is the practical judgment (προαίρεσις) that combines a correct thinking with an appropriate emotional disposition (τὸν τε λόγον ἀληθῆ εἶναι καὶ τὴν ὄρεξιν ὀρθήν, 1139a24). Aristotle repeats this point in various ways. For instance, he notes that practical truth requires a corresponding correct desire (ἡ ἀλήθεια ὁμολόγως ἔχουσα τῇ ὀρέξει τῇ ὀρθῇ, 1139a31). At the conclusion of this discussion, he further observes that as far as instrumental reasoning is concerned, it matters little if the starting point of judgment is thinking or desire (διό ἢ ὀρεκτικὸς νοῦς ἡ προαίρεσις ἢ ὄρεξις διανοητική, καὶ ἡ τοιαύτη ἀρχὴ ἄνθρωπος, 1139b5–6). It can be either thought moving desire or desire moving thought. The key idea is not simply the copresence of thinking and emotion—such a copresence is taken for granted by Aristotle—rather, the key point is that we can talk about the truth of action only so long as both calculation and emotion are the correct responses to the given circumstances, a point in common in Greek thought in general (§23). The truth of the practical judgment that makes action possible is to be discovered in the relation between the mind and the body within a specific setting.

So, the first two chapters of book 6 of *Nicomachean Ethics* argue that all action concerns certain ends, and that the intellectual virtues use the calculative faculty (*to logistikon*) to determine the correct emotion within a specific setting. This combination gives us the truth of praxis.

20. The two ends of action in Aristotle (*Nicomachean Ethics* 1139a32)

Within the context of the explanation of the truth of praxis, Aristotle draws a significant distinction between two kinds of ends of action. This is consistent with the first distinction of *Nicomachean Ethics* between the ends of production (*ergon*) and activity (*energeia*). The Greek text reads:

> πράξεως μὲν οὖν ἀρχὴ προαίρεσις (ὅθεν ἡ κίνησις ἀλλ' οὐχ οὗ ἕνεκα), προαιρέσεως δὲ ὄρεξις καὶ λόγος ὁ ἕνεκά τινος. (1139a32–33)

Let me start by providing a translation that corresponds to the common understanding of this passage, but which falls short of acknowledging the distinction between the two ends of production and activity:

> The origin of action is choice—hence what moves action is the for-the-sake-of-which—while the origin of choice is a desire and a rational understanding that is for the sake of something.

If we turn to the published translations of *Nicomachean Ethics*, we will find variations of this translation. Ian Moore summarizes the interpretation of this passage that justifies a variant translation: "the parenthetical remark is meant to clarify the type of cause that choice is, namely, an efficient cause. Choice moves us into action, but we do not act for the sake of the choice, which would make it a final cause. Rather, we act both for the sake of the proximate ends that reason determines *and* for the ultimate end of living well."[9] Thus, this translation understands the passage as drawing a distinction between the efficient cause of action and final cause of action. Grammatically, this is perfectly correct.

A translation such as Moore's presupposes an interpretation of the passage that ignores how the distinction between ergon and energeia from the opening of *Nicomachean Ethics* corresponds to the distinction between techne and phronesis that Aristotle is about to introduce. By failing to recognize that Aristotle is making here a distinction between the different ends of action, it obviates the crucial role played by the distinction between the ends of techne and phronesis, which is critical to resolve the problematic of action (§14). In other words, such a translation carries an exegetical baggage that ignores the critical distinction between different ends to respond to the problematic of action.

We will soon see that Heidegger's own mistranslation reproduces the exegetical baggage that ignores the importance of the distinction between the different ends of action, which allows him to introduce a different solution to the problematic of action, one that relies on the qualitative distinction between actions (cf. §13). Thus, his mistranslation is intertwined with the mistake of conflating the different ends in his way of accounting for difference in action by repressing instrumentality.

By contrast, I hold that the philosophical background of the problematic of action in monism, as I explained it in chapter 1, entails an alternative translation that is consistent with a different understanding of the grammar and syntax of this passage. Let me start with my proposed translation:

> Judging determines acting (it instigates the movement of action, not its final end), and judging is determined by desire and rationality toward a certain specific or provisional end.

I also provide a paraphrase that links this passage with the discussion of the truth of phronesis in first two chapters of book 6 of *Nicomachean Ethics*:

9. Ian Alexander Moore, "The End of Instrumentality? Heidegger on *Phronēsis* and Calculative Thinking," *Australian Philosophical Review* 6, no. 3 (2022): 256.

Praxis requires a judgment about ends. Such a calculative judgment is necessary so that one is moved to act. But the end of the practical judgment [of phronesis] is not a final end [because such a final end belongs to techne and is independent of the circumstances]. Rather, practical judgment [which is situated in our circumstances given by our sensation and] consists in the combination of an emotional disposition with calculative rationality that articulates itself as a provisional end [that arises from within the action and its context, whereby, unlike the final end, it is not independent of the context in which it is arises].

The key is the distinction between two kinds of ends, rendered through the stark contrast between two uses of ἕνεκα followed by the different pronouns. This is the contrast between οὗ ἕνεκα and ἕνεκά τινος, or in transliteration *hou heneka* and *heneka tinos*, respectively.

Heneka is a common word in Greek, always followed by a genitive, and pronouns are often used next to *heneka* to refer either to an antecedent or to "something," "what," and the like. It indicates that something is done for a certain aim. In other words, *heneka* is a preposition employed to indicate the ends of action. So, both *hou heneka* and *heneka tinos* are common enough expressions in Greek and in everyday language they are not used in a narrowly technical sense.

What is strange and unusual is the use of the preposition with two different pronouns within the same sentence. Aristotle uses the *heneka* in a technical sense within his theory of the four causes: his most common way of referring to the final cause is as *hou heneka*. But it is rare to contrast this established use of the preposition *heneka* with the preposition followed by a different pronoun. It raises the question about the antecedent of each pronoun highlighted by the contrast. My contention is that the striking contrast between *heneka* followed by two different pronouns stages the distinction between causal and instrumental ends that is critical for dealing with the problematic of action.[10] Heidegger consistently mistranslates the distinction between the ends because he responds differently to the problematic action, namely, by conflating the two ends (§§24–29).

Aristotle, then, says that the instrumental judgment of praxis is what moves one to act, but this movement does not pertain to the kind of end he refers to as *hou heneka*. Here, Aristotle uses the relative pronoun *hou* to

---

10. We find a similar use of the rare contrast between *hou heneka* and *heneka tinos* in *Metaphysics*, in the famous passage about philosophy arising from wonder. See Aristotle, *Metaphysics*, trans. Hugh Tredennick (Cambridge, MA: Harvard University Press, 1933), 982b. I discuss this passage in *The Logic of Living*.

indicate that there is a kind of action that is not of the nature of phronesis. We can act for certain ends that are relative to the action but independent of it. Conversely, the practical judgment characteristic of phronesis is a calculation about a contingent end (*heneka tinos*) given within the situation (or the "sensation") in which the action unfolds. Here, the interrogative pronoun *tinos* indicates that the end of acting is not pregiven but arises within the acting. The end of the action is part of the action itself and to be determined in the process of acting.

This interpretation of the grammar as staging a distinction between two ends, one of phronesis and praxis and another of techne and poiesis, accords with what immediately follows the contrast between *hou heneka* and *heneka tinos*. Aristotle makes two qualifications that lead to the first distinction between praxis and poiesis in book 6. The qualifications are, first, that the practical judgment of praxis involves intellection; and second, that because intellection on its own does not lead to action, praxis needs to have certain ends. Aristotle uses again the preposition *heneka* to make this point (διάνοια δ' αὐτὴ οὐθὲν κινεῖ, ἀλλ' ἡ ἕνεκά του καὶ πρακτική, 1139a35–1139b1). This merely repeats the point made both at the beginning of *Nicomachean Ethics* and in the beginning of book 6 that action is to be understood in terms of its ends.

No sooner has Aristotle indicated the necessity of considering the ends to determine the practical—using the preposition *heneka*—than he draws a distinction between poiesis and praxis, based on their different ends. In fact, he makes this point using the distinction between three different ends. Poiesis or productive activity, just like praxis, requires a certain end (ἕνεκα γάρ του, 1139b1). The end of production is not the same as the end in general (οὐ τέλος ἁπλῶς, 1139b2).[11] An end in general would be the entelechy that, according to Aristotle's ontology, belongs to every single thing, irrespective of human action. Instead of such a general end, clarifies Aristotle, the productive activity is always directed toward a specific end (πρός τι καὶ τινός, 1139b3). Further, unlike the production or poiesis, praxis has a different kind of end. The end of praxis is εὐπραξία, that is, a well-accomplished action (1139b4). The end of praxis is commensurate with the action, since the term *eupraxia* indicates that the end itself also contains the notion of praxis. Soon enough, in chapters 4 and 5, he will define techne in terms of the ends of poiesis, and phronesis in terms of the ends of praxis.

---

11. We will see in §28 how the distinction between the metaphysical notion of telos and the end specific to techne has been obviated in the secondary literature readings of Aristotle, under the influence of Heidegger.

Since contrasting *hou heneka* and *heneka tinos* at the conclusion of the examination of the truth of praxis, then, Aristotle consistently distinguishes between actions depending on their ends, which is consistent with the traditional way of accounting for difference within a monist ontology (§14). *We can identify differences in actions through the different ends of action.* Aristotle does not distinguish between actions directly, by ascribing different qualities to them, but rather between the *effects* of actions. The distinction, then, is between an end to action that is pregiven and independent of it (*hou heneka*), which is characteristic of production and techne; and an end to action that is determined by practical judgment as part of the acting (*heneka tinos*), which is characteristic of praxis and phronesis.

As I will show (§21), the end of techne that is independent of action can be analyzed in terms of Aristotle's theory of causality. The final end refers to one of the four causes in Aristotle's schema of causality. This is the kind of end that designates the end product of techne. The final end is pregiven independently of the action and can be achieved with some certainty. By contrast, the instrumental end of phronesis arises within contingency and hence it cannot be achieved with certainty. It is only ever provisional because the means and ends of instrumentality are contingent. To mark this distinction, I refer to *hou heneka* as final end and to *heneka tinos* as instrumental end.

Undoubtedly, the distinction between the two ends of action has been underplayed in the secondary literature on Aristotle. To understand the reasons, we will have to consider the Thomist interpretation of *Nicomachean Ethics* that sets the framework for the interpretation of Aristotle in the West, and which conformed with the metaphysics of morals that is characterized by the repression of instrumentality. I will provide some brief historical background to this in the Excursus.[12]

21. Techne and phronesis distinguished through their ends

The distinction between the two ends of action in book 6 of the *Nicomachean Ethics* entails that techne and phronesis are different because of their ends. *The distinction is drawn on the basis of the ends, not of the actions themselves.* As a result, what matters in the analysis of praxis is not only an understanding of the action but also of its *effects*. I cannot stress enough the

---

12. See also Dimitris Vardoulakis, "Phronesis and Instrumentality: The Import of Aristotle's Book 6 of *Nicomachean Ethics* Today," *Graduate Faculty Philosophy Journal* 44, nos. 1–2 (2023): 99–122.

importance of this point. This is the point where Heidegger departs from the monist materialist tradition. He constructs two qualitatively distinct actions, techne and phronesis. Heidegger is not able to draw the distinction on the basis of ends because he deposits all ends to techne, as we will soon see. The shift of the distinction from the ends of action to actions themselves that Heidegger produces through a series of mistranslations is what I call Heidegger's mistake. Differently put, Heidegger's mistake is his conflation of causal and instrumental ends, or of causality and instrumentality.[13]

The distinction of actions according to their ends leads to a seemingly paradoxical insight. It means that the *same* action or *process* of actions has both causal and instrumental ends.[14] As soon as we realize that the distinction is between the different ends and not between different actions, this point suddenly appears as rather commonsensical. For instance, the final end of manufacturing a teacup is that it can hold tea. This is an end that preexists and is independent of the specific actions that produce the cup. The end itself—the holding of liquid—can be achieved through different actions, different manufacturing processes, by different technicians, in different places and times. We can be pretty certain that the end has been achieved by pouring tea to test whether or not it leaks from the cup. The instrumental end of this manufacturing process is different from the final end, and it can vary depending on the manufacturer. Thus, an independent teacup maker may want to fulfill a production order so as to pay the rent on her small workshop. By contrast, an industrial manufacturer may want to fulfill a specific order so as to invest the profit to purchase new machinery or employ additional workers. From the perspective

---

13. It is indicative of the repression of the instrumentality of phronesis in the tradition that starts with Heidegger's *Plato's Sophist* that Hans-Georg Gadamer, who was present at the 1924 lecture course as a student, translates 1139a32 in such a way that thoroughly collapses instrumentality into causality: "Die Quelle des Verhaltens ist die Vorzugswahl als Anfang der Bewegung, nicht als Zweckursache." Aristotle, *Nikomachische Ethik VI*, ed. and trans. Hans-Georg Gadamer (Frankfurt am Main: Vittorio Klostermann, 1998), 27. It is also clear in the Introduction to that translation that Gadamer has no awareness of the importance of instrumentality for Aristotle's argument.

14. This point about action has been noted by scholars. For instance, Andrew Feenberg draws a similar distinction in his "instrumentalization theory" by distinguishing between "primary" and "secondary" instrumentalization. See Feenberg, *Between Reason and Experience: Essays in Technology and Modernity* (Cambridge, MA: MIT Press, 2010), and *Technology, Modernity, and Democracy*, ed. Eduardo Beira and Andrew Feenberg (London: Rowman & Littlefield, 2018). However, neither Feenberg nor anyone else that I am aware of notes the significance of this distinction in Aristotle, thereby missing its historical dimension.

of production, the final end is consistent: making an object that can hold tea. From the perspective of the calculative judgment characteristic of phronesis, the instrumental end can vary widely every time that the action is undertaken. Heidegger's mistake misses the distinction between causal and instrumental end (§24).

By drawing the distinction on the basis of the ends, Aristotle can determine the truth of techne and phronesis with recourse to their distinct ends. Thus, the truth of techne for someone who produces teacups can be quite certain and it can be verified experimentally. For instance, when we pour tea into our teacup, we can easily determine whether its final end has been achieved. Such certainty is absent from the end of phronesis. The truth of phronesis—as we saw earlier—arises from the conjunction of calculative judgment, emotional disposition, and the material setting within which the action unfolds. Consequently, there are many variables that determine the end of phronesis, thereby making it difficult to determine its truth.

Further, the technical end of the production of a teacup is constant, but the instrumental end can be variable: for one technician it can be to earn a profit, whereas another may be expecting to produce the cups at a loss but hoping for another profitable commission later on. In addition, the variables themselves can change during the course of their enactment, which can potentially completely change the calculation of phronesis. The final end of production remains the same, irrespective of whether the commissioning client goes bankrupt and cannot pay for the product. But the bankruptcy of the client fundamentally changes the calculation of the instrumental ends of the actions of the cup maker. A good cup maker makes good cups; a prudent one makes cups that meet his instrumental end for a profitable production.

As if this was not enough, the instrumental ends of phronesis are subject to changes that are entirely outside the control of the person making the instrumental calculation. This entails that the instrumental ends of action are not, strictly speaking, "owned" by the person who calculates, as they are determined by the material conditions within which the calculation of ends unfolds. Such material conditions include the others, which is why Aristotle insists that phronesis is not only indispensable for ethics but also for politics. For instance, an earthquake may destroy the workshop manufacturing teacups. From the perspective of the truth of techne, the earthquake is irrelevant. The end is judged through the independent criterion of whether the cup can hold tea or not. By contrast, the earthquake matters to the instrumental end because the end of phronesis is constitutive of the actions undertaken in their totality. It pertains, as Aristotle puts it, to good living as a whole (πρὸς τὸ εὖ ζῆν ὅλως, 1140a27).[15] A prudent technician ought to have chosen an earthquake-proof building for the workshop, and it is a political decision to regulate construction so as to prevent buildings from collapsing in earthquakes.[16] The upshot is that the end of causality—what Aristotle calls *hou heneka*—can be certain, whereas the end of instrumentality—the *heneka tinos*—is fallible.

Heidegger's mistake fails to note the distinction between actions on the basis of their ends as a consequence of which he is subsequently unable to distinguish between techne and phronesis in relation to the ends of action. Instead, Heidegger draws the qualitative distinction between the actions of techne and phronesis themselves.[17] To achieve this, Heidegger transfers all the ends to techne, thus any truth related to ends is understood *only* in terms of the end of production. Heidegger *conflates* causality and instrumentality, thereby concealing the instrumental ends of phronesis within the causal ends of techne. This allows him to designate a different kind of action than techne on the basis that the qualitatively different phronesis is purified of ends. What is lost in the gap that opens up between techne and phronesis is any notion of action that has ends that cannot be determined with any certainty as a matter of their essence. Heidegger represses the fallibility of the end of instrumental actions because he has transferred all ends to the final end characteristic of techne—he has concealed instrumentality into causality. Thus, all end-oriented action, according to Heidegger, is characterized by the prospect of being finished or completed

---

15. We will see in in §26 how Heidegger interprets passage 1140a27 to mean that phronesis is separated from all ends. I will explain why Heidegger's paraphrase of this passage is untenable given the grammar of the Greek text.

16. Cf. the discussion of fate and virtue in chapter 25 of Niccolò Machiavelli's *The Prince*.

17. A hugely influential account of this kind of approach is Hannah Arendt's *The Human Condition*. As is well known, she distinguishes between two end-oriented activities, labor and work, whereas the third kind of activity, action, is freed of ends. Commentators on Heidegger have turned to Arendt's account to examine the separation of poiesis or techne (that includes all ends) and praxis or phronesis (that is free of ends). See for example, Jacques Taminiaux, "Phenomenology and the Problem of Action," *Philosophy and Social Research* 11 (1986): 207–19, and *Heidegger and the Project of Fundamental Ontology*, trans. Michael Gendre (Albany: SUNY Press, 1991), chapter 3. Such accounts are often critical of Heidegger's insufficient determination of action. See a relevant discussion in Brogan, *Heidegger and Aristotle*, 149–51. They fail to note, however, that the basis of the distinction between the actions of poiesis and praxis, drawn on the basis of the separation of the actions as opposed to the ends of action, is a characteristically Heideggerian move. From this perspective, other differences notwithstanding, Arendt ultimately relies on the Heideggerian conception of an action that is end-free.

(§25 and §29; see also §14). What thereby disappears is a huge sway of action that is end-oriented but whose ends are provisional and judgments fallible—that is, what disappears is what Aristotle calls phronesis.

22. The distinction between final and instrumental ends and the problematic of action in monism

I noted earlier how the traditional monist response to the problematic of action has involved the consideration of the effects of action (§14). We see here the importance of the distinction between final and instrumental ends for this solution. As we saw in chapter 2, the problematic of action in monism consists in how to distinguish different actions when one posits a totality outside of which nothing exists. As soon as the distinction between the two ends is entertained, the problematic of action has a straightforward answer. Action matters within a single, unified totality because of its ends—because of the effects of action. The ends of action can occur within that totality but do not coincide with it. That is why Aristotle insists that the ends of production and praxis are not the general end of his metaphysics—they are *not* entelechy or the teleology that characterizes being, in general (§20). The framework for this answer is consistent within the materialist tradition—there is always a distinction on the basis of the ends of action—even though there is considerable variation in how these ends of action are understood to be related to the totality.[18] Its conflation of causality and instrumentality results in the failure to note the solution of the monist materialist tradition.

In the monist materialist tradition, the question of difference in action is dealt with recourse to the ends, not with recourse to action directly. For example (as we saw in §21), the certainty of techne and the fallibility of phronesis do not separate two actions, but rather distinguish two ends. The actions are the same, but they produce different effects from the perspective of their causal and instrumental ends. As we saw in chapter 2, Heidegger was faced with the problem of how to account for action within a single, unified being and his solution was to displace this problem to the question of the qualitative distinction between actions (§13). We see, here, the critical point of departure from the monist materialist tradition. Because he conflates causality and instrumentality, Heidegger cannot draw the distinction on the basis of the ends or the effects of actions. Thus, he draws

---

18. In *The Logic of Living*, I examine the divergent responses to the problematic of action of the four major philosophical schools of antiquity.

the distinction between techne and phronesis on the basis of the actions themselves, which gets him into all sorts of trouble, forcing him to use the ruse of techne to obfuscate the difficulties and contradictions (§27).

We also glimpse, here, why Heidegger's seemingly minor mistranslation of the two ends of action is *symptomatic* of his mistake and how he construes difference and praxis. Richard Lee is correct that the important aspect of Heidegger's mistranslation is the production of the conception of an action without effects and from this perspective the mistranslations are symptomatic of Heidegger's mistake. As Lee puts it, "Heidegger's translation goes wrong on the basis of the diagnosis of Heidegger's mistake in thinking the ethical and the political."[19] In other words, the mistranslation concerning the two ends of action is *not* the cause of Heidegger's mistake of conflating techne and phronesis, or causality and instrumentality. The mistranslations and the mistake offer mutual support to each other, which manifests itself in the conception of an action purified of ends.

As soon as Heidegger's mistake is viewed within the context of his attempts to find an answer to how to account for action within a monist framework, the seemingly minor translation error suddenly appears intermeshed with how Heidegger determines praxis, affecting his entire "destruction" of the metaphysical tradition's separation of theory and praxis. The conflation of the two ends of action allows Heidegger to distinguish actions on the basis of whether they are directed toward ends or whether they are free of ends and effects—never with recourse to their distinctive ends. As I will demonstrate in the rest of this book, Heidegger never abandons the possibility of an action without effects, employing three different strategies to try to define the ineffectual (cf. §9)

23. A Greek-hating philhellene

Starting with Aristotle's painstaking distinctions in the first two chapters of book 6 of the *Nicomachean Ethics,* we have arrived at a sort of "plateau" from which we can survey a certain conception of action within materialist monism. This is the plateau of the distinction between causality and instrumentality for an account of action within a monist framework, that is, within a framework that supposes a single, unified being. The notion of the single, unified being was common in Greek thought, even though it was constructed in many different ways (§15).

---

19. Richard Lee, "Willing the Means: On Vardoulakis on Heidegger on Aristotle," *Australian Philosophical Review* 6, no. 3 (2022): 274.

Consequently, the distinction between causal and instrumental ends was pivotal in the conception of praxis in Greek thought.[20] Let me just offer one further example here, from Plato's *Philebus*. Heidegger's plan was to conclude *Plato's Sophist* with an analysis of this Platonic dialogue, assuming that it is directly connected to the issues raised in book 6 of *Nicomachean Ethics* (§24). In addition, Plato employs the linguistic means of a contrast between *hou heneka* and *heneka tinos* to distinguish between two ends of action. Thus, the distinction in Plato mirrors the linguistic expression in 1139a32 of the *Nicomachean Ethics*.

In *Philebus*, the key position that Socrates argues against is that pleasure is the same as the good (ἀγαθὸν εἶναι . . . καὶ τὴν ἡδονὴν, 11b).[21] Instead, the good for Plato requires a combination of thought and emotion—just like the truth of phronesis in Aristotle. The argument relies on the distinction between being and becoming, which Plato draws by employing *heneka* twice:

> Some beings always exist for an end, while other beings always come into existence for the sake of another end [τὸ μὲν ἕνεκά του τῶν ὄντων ἔστ' ἀεί, τὸ δ' οὗ χάριν ἑκάστοτε τὸ τινὸς ἕνεκα γιγνόμενον ἀεὶ γίγνεται] (53e)

There is an end that belongs to being as such and becoming whose ends are for the sake (χάριν) of something else. The two ends, as distinguished by Plato, refer to essence and becoming respectively (οὐσίαν καὶ γένεσιν, 54α). An essence contains the end in itself, whereas becoming does not.

Based on this distinction, Plato argues that pleasure is not the same as the good. Pleasure is only ever a form of becoming, never an essence. Therefore, pleasure, or any emotion, can only ever provide an end related to something external to it. By contrast, the good has its own end, which is why, claims Plato, we can talk about the essence of the good:

> Now the end for which [οὗ ἕνεκα, *hou heneka*] things are always created belongs to the class of the good [τοῦ ἀγαθοῦ], where the end for [τινὸς ἕνεκα, *tinos heneka*] the creation of something else belongs to a different class. (54c)

That which has a certain stability and regularity across time (ἀεί) has an independent end (*hou heneka*) different in kind from the end of the emotions and another that belongs to becoming that is particular (*tinos heneka*).

---

20. This is one of the major points that I demonstrate in *The Logic of Living*.

21. Plato, *Philebus*, in *Statesman, Philebus, and Ion*, trans. W.R.N. Lamb (Cambridge, MA: Harvard University Press, 1925). I have regularly amended the translation.

The end of the good can be found in itself—the good is self-sufficient, as Plato puts it—whereas the end of becoming is external to it.

Just as in *Nicomachean Ethics*, the distinction between the two ends is drawn between an end that is pregiven and independent from the action, and another end that is provisional because it depends upon the given circumstances. Thus, Plato and Aristotle agree on the need for the distinction between the two ends, so as to distinguish between actions. The distinction is drawn across similar conceptual terrain—one end is independent of action, the other arises from within it. Moreover, *Philebus* and the *Nicomachean Ethics* use the same grammatical formulations—*hou heneka* and *tinos heneka*—to express the two ends.

It is tempting to say that is where the similarities end. There is a significant secondary literature that examines the divergent approaches to phronesis and the good in Plato and Aristotle.[22] For instance, according to Plato, the *heneka tinos*, the provisional end, can never be associated with truth. Conversely, book 6 of the *Nicomachean Ethics* suggests, using the same vocabulary as *Philebus*, that the instrumental end of phronesis is amenable to truth. I acknowledge these differences, but for the point I am making here they are less important than the adumbration of the same distinction between the two ends, using the same contrast between *hou heneka* and *heneka tinos*. Their differences notwithstanding, Aristotle and Plato agree on the importance of the distinction between certain ends independent of the actions performed and other ends that are integral to the action and which can only ever arise in relation to the action. Actions can be distinguished because they have different ends.

It is noteworthy that, whereas the distinction between the end of essence and the end of becoming has been clearly noted in the secondary literature on Plato, I have not been able to find any systematic discussion of the same point in relation to the corresponding passage in the *Nicomachean Ethics*. One may retort that the distinction in *Philebus* is much more detailed. I concur, while adding that this only shows that Aristotle mentions it in passing (1139a32) as a distinction that would have been familiar to his students, whereby he does not need to elaborate. But this means that this distinction is an assumption that structures the entire discourse of phronesis in the *Nicomachean Ethics*.[23] On this count, it merits—it demands—our attention (§32).

---

22. See for example, Hans-Georg Gadamer, *The Idea of the Good in Platonic and Aristotelian Philosophy*, trans. Christopher Smith (New Haven, CT: Yale University Press, 1986).

23. For details, see Vardoulakis, "Phronesis and Instrumentality."

Even if one rejects my all-too-quick analysis of Plato, and even if one refuses to accept the even larger point about the function of the two ends for an account of action in Greek thought, still this does not affect my analysis of Aristotle's *Nicomachean Ethics*, nor my presentation of Heidegger's mistake (§§24–27). If, however, one accepts my point about the function of the two ends in Greek thought, we reach the somewhat paradoxical (even confronting) recognition that Heidegger, the thinker who probably did more than anyone else to place Greek thought center stage in contemporary philosophy in the last century, is nonetheless plagued by a fundamental blindness to how action is conceived by the Greeks. Heidegger vehemently rejects, as constitutive to the truth of being, that which is indispensable for the Greeks, namely, instrumentality. In this sense, we can see Heidegger as a Greek-hating philhellene.[24]

24. The context of Heidegger's interpretation of phronesis

As I will discuss shortly (§§25–26), Heidegger systematically mistranslates all references to instrumentality in Aristotle's presentation of phronesis. These mistranslations evidence the forgetting of the distinction between the two ends of action. This allows Heidegger to separate two kinds of action: techne, whose main characteristic is that it is end-oriented which, according to Heidegger, makes it a modality of theoretical knowledge; and phronesis, understood as without ends because it exhibits the concern for the being of the subject itself.

Heidegger's mistranslations lead to the mistake of the conflation of causal and instrumental ends, which provides him with the basis for the destruction of the metaphysical separation of theory and praxis, since it leads to an interpretation of techne as a modality of theoretical knowledge, whereby theoretical knowledge has a practical component (§27). In his interpretation of Aristotle, this takes a specific form: Techne is never able to achieve disclosure because it is end-oriented, whereas phronesis is oriented toward the truth of being because it is purified of ends. More broadly, the mistake consists in the repression of instrumentality, indicated by the mistranslations. Philosophically, this produces the notion of a kind of action that is free of ends—what in his interpretation of the *Nicomachean Ethics* Heidegger identifies as phronesis, later he associates with techne as art, and after WWII he describes as an action without effects, or the ineffectual.

---

24. I examine the influence of another German thinker, Jacob Burckhardt, in Heidegger's repression of instrumentality within Greek thought in §51.

We see that the mistranslations of the references to instrumentality in book 6 of the *Nicomachean Ethics* and the mistake are intertwined. But whereas one could dismiss the mistranslations as something that inevitably occurs in the "battle of interpretations" of ancient texts, the mistake cannot be so easily dismissed because it is ingrained in Heidegger's position. The reason is that the mistake *provides the structure of Heidegger's conception of action for the rest of his philosophical career.* Heidegger will never rectify the mistake. Heidegger will continue in various ways (that I trace in this book) to conflate causality and instrumentality so as to distinguish between two qualitatively different actions—one that is oriented toward being and one that is not—the criterion always being whether the activity is instrumental. And also, from this point on, Heidegger will attempt to hide the mistake using the ruse of techne.

From this perspective, the conjunction of the mistranslations of the instrumentality of phronesis in book 6 of *Nicomachean Ethics* with Heidegger's mistake becomes pivotal for an understanding of the ruse of techne. This conjunction is the seed from which the ruse springs, it is the moment of its conception. To approach the critical moment, then, let me start with some contextualizing that builds upon the narrative from the beginning of this chapter (§18).

Since arriving at Freiburg as Husserl's assistant, and intent on working in phenomenology, Heidegger repeatedly lectured on Aristotle. His courses, published several years later in the *Gesamtausgabe*, show Heidegger reading Aristotle within the purview of phenomenology, thereby offering both highly innovative interpretations of Aristotle's epistemology and extending the historical scope of phenomenological epistemology. While offering these early courses on Aristotle, Heidegger stumbled upon the idea of the single, unified being. This discovery combined with the project to overcome the metaphysical separation between theory and praxis. But the problem was that Heidegger's focus had been on epistemology and theoretical knowledge. He also needed to find a way to bridge the gap between theory and praxis so as to demonstrate the premetaphysical nature of Greek thought. The "Natorp report" from October 1922 was important because Heidegger, for the first time, turned to phronesis, which gave him an avenue to introduce the practical into the theoretical in a way that remained faithful to the monist insight of the single, unified being while also dismantling the metaphysical separation between theory and praxis.

A few months after the "Natorp report," in the summer semester of 1923—his last semester as Husserl's assistant in Freiburg—Heidegger's seminar was on phronesis. Even though the notes from that seminar have been lost, a year later at Marburg he returned to Aristotle.[25] In the summer semester of 1924, he delivered one of his most famous courses on Aristotle, the so-called "rhetoric lectures."[26] There was no reference to phronesis in those lectures.

For the next semester, the winter semester of 1924–25, he announced a course on Plato's *Sophist*. Despite the course's title, all the seminars until Christmas 1924 were on Aristotle's notion of phronesis. In comparing Gadamer's brief account of Heidegger's interpretation of book 6 of *Nicomachean Ethics* from the lost 1923 seminar at Freiburg with the material presented in 1924, it would appear that Heidegger based his Marburg seminars on the earlier one. Before turning to the question of being through a reading of Plato's *Sophist*, which will provide the opening move of *Being and Time* (§34), Heidegger sought to clarify the question of action by returning to Aristotle's treatment of phronesis.[27]

At the beginning of the winter seminar, Heidegger explained to the students that his methodological supposition for the order of texts was that it was preferable to interpret Plato by starting with the later text by Aristotle, due to "the old principle of hermeneutics, namely that interpretation should proceed from the clear into the obscure" (8/11).[28] The pivotal question of the central text, Plato's *Sophist*, is the one about the single, unified being (§34). This was going to lead to the question of action, presented through the theory of phronesis in Plato's *Philebus*, which was the text that Heidegger planned to examine after the *Sophist*, although, in fact, he ran out of time. This approach seems to suggest, then, that the confused presentation of phronesis in *Philebus* can only be clarified by the clearer one in Aristotle's *Nicomachean Ethics*. The plan for the structure and method of the lectures, as explained by Heidegger, appears to suggest that the question of the single, unified being can only be tackled through the Aristotelian conception of phronesis—or, more precisely, through Heidegger's

---

25. We know of the 1923 seminar in Freiburg through Gadamer's account. See Hans-Georg Gadamer, *Gesammelte Werke* (Mohr: Tübingen, 1985–2010), 2: 485 and 3: 199–200.

26. Martin Heidegger, *Basic Concepts of Aristotelian Philosophy*, trans. Robert D. Metcalf and Mark B. Tanzer (Bloomington: Indiana University Press, 2009) = *GA* 18.

27. To concentrate on phronesis, I avoid tackling, here, Heidegger's reading of the *Sophist*, which is the second part of the seminar. I offer a close reading of Heidegger's reading of Plato's *Sophist* in *The Logic of Living*, §15.

28. Martin Heidegger, *Plato's Sophist*, trans. Richard Rojcewicz and Andre Schuwer (Bloomington: Indiana University Press, 1997) = *GA* 19. Hereafter in this chapter, cited parenthetically, English reference followed by reference to the German edition.

reading of the Aristotelian phronesis as an action without effects, first adumbrated in the "Natorp report."

The connection between the Natorp report and *Plato's Sophist* is also external. Natorp's scheming with Husserl resulted in Heidegger's appointment at Marburg University. Within the first year of Heidegger taking up his first tenured post, Natorp, his senior supporter, had died. His death in August 1924 was barely a month before Heidegger started teaching the course titled *Plato's Sophist*. The course began with a long "in memoriam" to Natorp in which Heidegger reviewed the deceased scholar's contribution to the study of ancient Greek philosophy.[29] The Natorp report was written in Freiburg for the old scholar at Marburg; *Plato's Sophist* was delivered in Marburg with the aura of the recently deceased Natorp present in the classroom. In the early text, phronesis arises in the discussion almost unexpectedly—in the lecture course a few years later, it frames the entire discussion.

Plato's Sophist consolidates the conception of a qualitative distinction between an action concerned with ends and another free of ends. From this perspective, the winter semester course of 1924–25 is critical for the conception of action in Heidegger. Even though the distinction between techne or production and phronesis or praxis has often been noted in the secondary literature, its importance for the conception of action in Heidegger philosophy has never—to the best of my knowledge—been noted. For instance, Brogan, who offers one of the most astute analyses of *Plato's Sophist*, correctly notes that the *logoi* of techne and phronesis are different because they aspire to different truths. The truth of techne is the truth of production and theoretical knowledge, whereas the truth of phronesis is concerned with the human itself. Even though Brogan clearly discerns this distinction, he does not explore its implications for Heidegger's theory of action, but rather, turns his attention to *nous* as a common element in techne and phronesis.[30] As a result of the lack of recognition of how determinative for Heidegger's conception of action his interpretation of phronesis is, Heidegger's mistake has remained unnoticed in the secondary literature—both in relation to *Plato's Sophist* and more broadly for Heidegger's theory of action.

Within the context of Heidegger's grappling with the problematic of action in monism, the lecture course *Plato's Sophist* is much more than

---

29. On Natorp's influence on Heidegger, see Michael Bowler, *Heidegger and Aristotle: Philosophy as Praxis* (London: Continuum, 2008), chapter 3.

30. Brogan, *Heidegger and Aristotle*, see esp. 173–74.

merely the prelude to *Being and Time*. It is also the first time that he develops a consistent answer to this problem, which coincides with the first clear and succinct presentation of the ruse of techne. Consequently, the ruse of techne is—nay, *it can only be*—constructed by the mistranslations, symptomatic of the conflation of the two ends of action signified by the two uses of *heneka* that we saw earlier in the analysis of the passage from 1139a32.

25. Heidegger's mistranslations of the *hou heneka*

Heidegger skims over chapters 1 and 2 of book 6 of the *Nicomachean Ethics* whereby he never discusses explicitly the passage from 1139a32. This is strange in itself. The entire import of the discussion of phronesis, the whole point of almost three months of lecturing on it, was to show that the truth of phronesis can be understood as the unconcealment of being, unlike the truth of techne that can only be the truth of particular beings. This is necessary for Heidegger's construction of a qualitative distinction between two forms of action, one that attains to the truth of being and one that does not. If the truth of phronesis is so important, then it is surprising, even astonishing, that Heidegger elides the opening discussion of the *Nicomachean Ethics* where Aristotle defines the truth of phronesis.

But then, Heidegger cannot refer to the two opening chapters of book 6 of *Nicomachean Ethics*, since phronesis is described there as a calculative rationality, whereas Heidegger wants to expunge calculation from phronesis. We see, here, the enormous tension in Heidegger's reading of book 6 of *Nicomachean Ethics*. To make the argument that phronesis is concerned with the truth of being, whereas techne is concerned with the truth of theoretical knowledge, Heidegger has to ignore chapters 1 and 2 of book 6. It is often remarked how Heidegger is fascinated by Aristotle's description in chapter 3 of five distinct ways in which "the truth of the soul" can appear— namely, techne, phronesis, episteme, sophia, and nous (1139b16–17). But the most striking feature, that Heidegger starts his analysis only in chapter 3, merely glancing at chapters 1 and 2, has not been noted, particularly since it is in chapter 2, in 1139a32, that Aristotle draws the distinction between the two kinds of end, the causal and the instrumental, by contrasting *hou heneka* and *heneka tinos*.

The initial surprise of Heidegger's decision to start his analysis in chapter 3 is soon succeeded by an even bigger surprise. Even though Heidegger never examines, directly, the distinction between the two senses of instrumentality in 1139a32, still he regularly refers to the end of phronesis as the *hou heneka*—instead of *heneka tinos*. Heidegger's use of *hou heneka*, however, has nothing to do with any ends—neither final nor instrumental. Rather, the "*telos* [end] of phronesis is the *anthropos* [the human] as such" (35–36/51). This is the reason that Heidegger explicitly associates phronesis with Dasein that "comports itself to itself" or for which its being is a concern (35/51). The end of phronesis, Heidegger argues, is not a particular end in the world as it has no effects, but is rather the single, unified being itself, whereby the end of phronesis is an end separate from any calculation or the concerns of everyday life. To indicate this end of phronesis that is a comportment toward being, Heidegger cannot use the interrogative *tinos* next to *heneka* as this would suggest an ontic end. The problem is that when Aristotle explains the kind of end that pertains to phronesis in 1139a32, he explicitly says that it is "οὐχ [not] hou heneka."

Let me provide an example of this linguistic use in Heidegger's text. It is, in fact, from the Natorp report, and it is the first description of the end of phronesis as *hou heneka* that I have been able to find: "phronesis makes the location of the one who performs the action accessible: in securing the *hou heneka* (the 'Why'), in making available the particular Towards-what-end, in apprehending the 'Now,' and in sketching out the How [*Die φρόνησις macht die Lage des Handelnden zugänglich im Festhalten des οὗ ἕνεκα, Weswegen, im Beistellen des gerade bestimmten Wozu, im Erfassen des 'Jetzt' und in der Vorzeichnung des Wie*]."[31] The only explicit association of *hou heneka* with the judgment of phronesis in book 6 of the *Nicomachean Ethics* occurs in 1139a32. If Heidegger is referring to that passage, then the mistake in his paraphrase is clear. Heidegger misses the negative preceding the *heneka*. The Greek text says "οὐχ hou heneka." Heidegger misses the "οὐχ." By skipping the negative, Heidegger ascribes to phronesis a characteristic that is absent from Aristotle. In Heidegger's interpretation, the "end" of phronesis is now neither a causal nor an instrumental end, but rather provides the effect-free setting within which the being of beings can unfold. Whereas Aristotle uses *heneka* with distinct pronouns to distinguish between different ends so as to emphasize their effects, Heidegger uses *hou heneka* on its own to indicate how phronesis orients itself toward being because it is free of all ends, so as to indicate the human's concern for itself.

One may object here that *heneka* is a common Greek word and that Heidegger may not have the particular passage of 1139a32 in mind. He may simply be using the relative pronoun, as opposed to the interrogative one, without quoting from the text. In other words, Heidegger may be using

---

31. Heidegger, "Phenomenological Interpretations with Respect to Aristotle," 381/259.

heneka in a nontechnical manner. There is textual evidence, however, that Heidegger is referring to 1139a32, as he continues to use the expression *hou heneka* as a characteristic of phronesis in *Plato's Sophist*. The most revealing use occurs in a context that clearly suggests that Heidegger has the passage from 1139a32 in mind. The reason is that, besides *hou heneka*, Heidegger here explicitly uses the vocabulary from 1139a32, such as the *arche* (starting point or principle) of action that is conjoined with *proairesis*, the kind of judgment that Aristotle says is characteristic of phronesis (101/147–48). This is precisely the vocabulary of 1139a32, and the same three terms—*hou heneka*, *arche*, and *proairesis*—do not occur together anywhere else in *Nicomachean Ethics*. And yet, we find here exactly the same mistranslation as the one in the Natorp report. Heidegger does not place the negative next to *hou heneka*—and exactly the same mistake as a result of this omission, namely, phronesis is emptied out of all ends. The end of the action of phronesis is, says Heidegger, the same as its *arche*, whereby phronesis is oriented toward the truth of being because it is emptied out of instrumentality.

Is this rendering a mere *lapsus calami*? Is the neglect of noting the negative next to *hou heneka* a small lapse, first occurring in the Natorp report, then carried over to *Plato's Sophist*? Or is the mistranslation an error symptomatic of something deeper in Heidegger's thought?[32] I cannot, of course, determine these questions with any certainty if they refer to Heidegger's intentions. But my concern is not to explicate Heidegger's psychological state but rather to trace the effects of his error. From such a perspective, it is significant that the mistranslation occurs for the first time at the point in the text in which Heidegger is working out his solution to the problem of action in monism. Moreover, the mistake of conflating the distinct ends of action is part of the solution. Without this mistranslation, Heidegger would have been unable to hold that techne concerns only the truth of beings whereas the truth of phronesis concerns being irrespective of effects.[33] Eliding the negative next to *hou heneka* allows Heidegger to identify techne with all ends

---

32. I am alluding here to the debate about the potential distinction between mistake and error. See Stanley Corngold, "Error in Paul de Man," *Critical Inquiry* 8, no. 3. (1982): 489–507; and Paul de Man, "A Letter from Paul de Man," *Critical Inquiry* 8, no. 3 (1982): 509–13.

33. Importantly, in the early discussion of Heidegger's interpretation of Aristotle, especially before the publication of volume 19 of the *GA* that contains *Plato's Sophist*, the emphasis was on the distinction between poiesis (production) and praxis (action). See, indicatively, Jacques Taminiaux, "Poiesis and Praxis in Fundamental Ontology," *Research in Phenomenology* 17 (1987): 137–69; and Robert Bernasconi, "The Fate of the Distinction Between Praxis and Poiesis," *Heidegger Studies* 2 (1986): 111–39. These early readings set the stage and, it seems to me, have prevented scholars from noticing what

while making it a modality of knowledge, and at the same time to purify phronesis from all instrumentality.

The objection might persist that, in the absence of an explicit reference to 1139a32, we cannot be sure that Heidegger is actually thinking of this passage. The use of the three terms—*hou heneka*, *arche*, and *proairesis*—may be coincidental. And in any case, the important point in 1139a32 is the distinction between the two ends signified with the two uses of *heneka*, which is not obvious in the use of *hou heneka* on its own in the Natorp report or in the example from *Plato's Sophist* above. Even if Heidegger did not have 1139a32 in mind, still my point stands. Heidegger uses the expression *hou heneka* to empty instrumentality out of phronesis, which is the opposite of what Aristotle says using the same vocabulary.

26. Heidegger's discussion of *hou heneka* and *heneka tinos*: The repression of instrumentality

Despite the text of *Plato's Sophist* never referencing 1139a32 directly, the circumstantial evidence is overwhelming that Heidegger does in fact have the specific passage in mind. At the critical point where he first thematizes phronesis in *Plato's Sophist*, he explicitly contrasts *hou heneka* to *heneka tinos*. The text of *Plato's Sophist* was compiled by combining Heidegger's notes with student notes, so some inaccuracies in referencing are understandable. And 1139a32 is the only passage in *Nicomachean Ethics* where we find the striking contrast between the double *heneka* and the two pronouns.

The passage in which Heidegger contrasts *hou heneka* to *heneka tinos* occurs early in *Plato's Sophist*, in a dense couple of pages that introduce the key themes of phronesis. Heidegger argues that phronesis has nothing to do with utility or instrumentality and summarizes this point through the use of the contrast between *hou heneka* and *heneka tinos*. The entire passage is significant, so let us take it from the beginning. The discussion of phronesis starts with an interpretation of 1140a25–27 in which Aristotle describes the *phronimos*, that is, the human whose action is characterized by phronesis. Here is Heidegger's paraphrase:

> "A *phronimos* is evidently one who can deliberate well, i.e., appropriately," who is *vouleutikos* [i.e., someone who makes judgments or deliberates], and specifically who can deliberate appropriately over

---

was really original in *Plato's Sophist*, namely, the separation of the two, qualitatively distinct actions of techne and phronesis.

"that which is good (full and perfect) and which is, in addition, good *hautō*, for him, the deliberator himself . . ." The object of *phronesis* is hence determined as something which can also be otherwise, but from the very outset it has a relation to the deliberator himself. . . . The *aletheuein* [the process of determining the true] of *phronesis* therefore contains a referential direction to the *aletheuon* [the one who pursues the truth] himself. Yet we do not designate as a *phronimos* the one who deliberates in the correct way *kata meros*, i.e., in relation to particular advantages, e.g., health or bodily strength, which promote Dasein in a particular regard [*Als einen φρόνιμος bezeichnen wir aber nicht denjenigen, der κατὰ μέρος in rechter Weise überlegt, d.h. bezüglich bestimmter Beitraglichkeiten, die in bestimmter Hinsicht, z.B. in Hinsicht auf Gesundheit oder Körperkraft, für das Dasein beiträglich sind*]. Instead, we call *phronimos* the one who deliberates in the right way *poia pros to eu zein olos*, regarding "what is conducive to the right mode of Being of Dasein as such and as a whole." The *vouleuesthai* [deliberating] of the *phronimos* concerns the Being of Dasein itself, the *eu zein*, i.e., the right and proper way to be Dasein. (34/48)

The key idea in this passage is that the phronimos exercises phronesis by being concerned with life as a whole, which Heidegger takes to mean that the phronimos is unconcerned with the specific utility or advantages (*sympheronta*) of acting. Heidegger paraphrases the passage in such a way as to purify phronesis from instrumentality.

Here is the passage in Greek:

Δοκεῖ δὴ φρονίμου εἶναι τὸ δύνασθαι καλῶς βουλεύεσθαι περὶ τὰ αὑτῷ ἀγαθὰ καὶ συμφέροντα, οὐ κατὰ μέρος, οἷον ποῖα πρὸς ὑγίειαν ἢ πρὸς ἰσχύν, ἀλλὰ ποῖα πρὸς τὸ εὖ ζῆν ὅλως. (1140a25–27)

Here is a translation based on the Loeb edition that is as faithful as possible:

Now it is held to be the mark of the *phronimos* to be able to judge/deliberate well about what is good and advantageous for himself, not in some particular part, for instance what is good for his health or strength, but what is advantageous as a means to the good life as a whole.

In drawing the distinction between the two ends of action in §20, I discussed the same passage to argue that the concern of phronesis for "good life as a whole" evidences its instrumental end. So, my interpretation does not accord with Heidegger's which reads the same expression as denying the instrumentality of phronesis, or more emphatically, as the emptying out of all ends from within phronesis other than a concern with the singular, unified being. Is this a matter of different interpretations? I think not. The grammar and syntax of the passage show that Heidegger's reading is untenable. His mistranslation, moreover, evidences his mistake, that is, the obviation of the distinction between the two ends of action.

The syntactical error that structures Heidegger's entire reading is easy enough to see. The word *sympheronta* (advantageous) is attributed only to the partial understanding that Heidegger designates as "particular advantages." When it comes to life as a whole, which is the mark of phronesis, the word *sympheronta* is silenced. Aristotle's text could not be more explicit: the conjunction "*kai*" (and) connects the good and utility. The caveat "*ou kata merous*" (not in some particular part) pertains to both the good and to utility. The *ou kata merous* does not refer to "advantageous" but rather is the rhetorical contrast (*alla*) to "good life as a whole." It is only by ignoring both the parataxis "ἀγαθὰ καὶ συμφέροντα," the things that are good and useful, *and* the rhetorical contrast between "in some particular part" and "life as a whole" that the word *sympheronta*, signifying instrumentality, can be excluded from phronesis. In other words, Heidegger twists a straightforward syntactical conjunction, followed by a clear rhetorical contrast, so as to fit his interpretation that instrumentality pertains only to particular beings whereas phronesis, purified from instrumentality, is associated with the single, unified being.

The meaning in Aristotle is the opposite of Heidegger's paraphrase. The good life as a whole that relates to the single, unified being can only be approached through judgments or calculations that are good *and* instrumental in nature. Or, in a different formulation, there is no conception of acting without regard to the instrumental ends of action. Or, in a different lexical register: *instrumentality is constitutive of the ontology of action*. Aristotle is saying exactly what Heidegger is denying.[34] What I call Heidegger's mistake is not simply the grammatical and syntactical errors that allow for an interpretation of phronesis as purified of all ends. Rather, Heidegger's mistake, symptomatic of his mistranslations, consists in the obscuring of the distinction between casual and instrumental ends that is so crucial for

---

34. Heidegger consistently mistranslates passages in which the word *sympheron* (utility or instrumentality) occurs, and always in such a way as to obscure the instrumental character of phronesis. For another example, see Heidegger, *Plato's Sophist*, 105/155–56. I cannot possibly examine all these instances here, other than noting the consistency of Heidegger's mistake.

a monist account of action. *The mistake effects the repression of instrumentality and its obverse side, the conceptualization of the ineffectual.*

Soon after introducing his conception of phronesis in such a way as to dissociate it from *symferon* (utility, advantage), Heidegger summarizes his interpretation of phronesis by using the contrast of the two forms of the *heneka* that we found in 1139a32:

> The *telos* [end] of phronesis is not a *pros ti* [a particular end] and not a *heneka tinos*; it is the *anthropos* [human] itself. . . . The *telos* [end] of phronesis is a *telos halpos* [a universal end] and a *hou heneka*, a "for the sake of which [*ein Warumwillen*]." Now insofar as Dasein is disclosed as the *hou heneka*, the "for the sake of which," there is a predelineation of what is for its sake and what has to be procured at any time for its sake. In this way, with Dasein as the *hou heneka*, there is grasped with one stroke the *arhce* [starting principle] of the deliberation of *phronesis*. . . . These *archai* [principles] are Dasein itself; Dasein finds itself disposed, and comports itself to itself, in this or that way. Dasein is the *arhce* [principle and beginning] of the deliberation of *phronesis*. And what *phronesis* deliberates about is not what brings *praxis* [action] to an end. A result is not constitutive for the Being of an action; only the *eu* [the well-done], the how, is. The *telos* [end] of phronesis is the *anthropos* [human] itself. (35/50)

The first point to note is that, like the previous example of the use of *heneka*, Heidegger does not acknowledge that he is referring specifically to 1139a32. However, unlike the previous instances from *Plato's Sophist* in which Heidegger says that phronesis concerns the *hou heneka*, here he constructs *hou heneka* with *heneka tinos*. Such a contrast using *heneka* is notable, and the only place that it occurs in *Nicomachean Ethics* is the passage from 1139a32. If Heidegger is not reading directly from 1139a32, then he is quoting it from memory: The passage in which Aristotle distinguishes between the two ends had caught his attention.

The way in which Heidegger presents the contrast between *hou heneka* and *heneka tinos* lays bare his mistranslation, symptomatic of the mistaken conflation of the two ends of action, so as to establish an action free of ends. The divergencies between the Greek text and Heidegger's paraphrases are stark. Whereas Aristotle asserts that the possibility of the truth of phronesis hinges on the *heneka tinos* or the instrumental ends of action as distinct from *hou heneka* or the final end of action, Heidegger avers that the end of phronesis is contained within the human's concern for itself that is separated from both the products and the effects of action, that is, both from causal and instrumental ends. Whereas Aristotle distinguishes between actions relying on their ends, Heidegger distinguishes between actions directly, by separating phronesis from any action that is end-oriented—that is, oriented toward any kind of end. Whereas Aristotle recognizes that all actions have effects and that we can differentiate actions according to their effects, Heidegger distinguishes between two qualitatively distinct actions based on whether they are instrumental, which precipitates the repression of instrumentality.

The mistranslations and Heidegger's mistake support each other: the concealment of the distinction between the two ends of action that conflates causality with instrumentality and effects the qualitative distinction between actions and the conception of the ineffectual. As a result, Heidegger arrives at a position that is the reverse, not only of Aristotle's position, but also from the way that monist materialism has solved the problem of action. Heidegger's mistake is hidden through the technique that I refer to as the ruse of techne.

27. The genesis of the ruse of techne: sophia as the virtue of techne

Heidegger's destruction of metaphysics required overcoming the distinction between theory and praxis (§3, §11, and §18). The conflation of causality and instrumentality is indispensable for the argument in *Plato's Sophist* that theoretical knowledge in Aristotle is the virtue of techne, which Heidegger uses to argue that praxis is inscribed in theoretical knowledge. This will be refashioned into the well-known description of instruments in Division 1 of *Being and Time* (§§37–39), and the same argument with reference to Greek thought will be made in later texts (§47). The problem is not only that this argument about sophia as the virtue of techne relies on the mistranslations of book 6 of the *Nicomachean Ethics*, it also surreptitiously repeats the so-called techne analogy, a key position in metaphysics.

Heidegger's interpretation that for Aristotle theoretical knowledge is the virtue of techne can be understood as explaining the relation between the meaning of techne that refers to the single, unified being, or Heidegger's monism, and the notion of techne as technology or craft. The third meaning of techne characteristic of the ruse, namely, as the kind of action free of ends, is present as Heidegger's extrapolation of phronesis (§29).

Heidegger constructs the single, unified being as a mystery that we can never know in any comprehensive way. But, due to its historical grounding, being is not completely obscure. Even though we have forgotten being, Heidegger holds that the Greeks, and Aristotle in particular, were cognizant of the single, unified being. Heidegger draws a stark inference from this: "This past . . . is nothing detached from us, lying far away. On the contrary, we are this past itself . . . insofar as . . . our philosophy and science live on these foundations, i.e., those of Greek philosophy, and do so to such an extent that we are no longer conscious of it" (7/10). Being as one and unified is always there, even though we are unable to see it. This is so, both in our everyday experience and in the philosophy of the past. Thus, Heidegger's philosophical project becomes uncovering what is hidden in experience that is at the same time hidden in our past. He continues, "Precisely in what we no longer see, in what has become an everyday matter, something is at work that was once the object of the greatest spiritual exertions ever undertaken in Western history" (7/10). The destruction of metaphysics is not a complete rejection of past (§35). Rather, it is the project of the discovery of the single, unified being in the past so as to inform our contemporary experience.[35] This simultaneous proximity to, and distance from, being that is both historical and experiential places the monism of Greek thought center stage in Heidegger's own project.

There is an additional element to Greek thought that Heidegger quickly points out to his students. The Greeks, and Aristotle in particular, have a concept of truth as unconcealment that is attuned to the propensity of being to be both proximate and distant, both visible and concealed. This is the concept of truth as *aletheia*.[36] To demonstrate this, Heidegger points to the etymology of aletheia. This word consists of *lethe* (forgetting) with the privative prefix alpha, "a." Thus, the word literally means "unforgetting." As Heidegger puts it, "*aletheia* means: to be hidden no longer, to be uncovered." He clarifies, "This privative expression indicates that the Greeks had some understanding of the fact that the uncoveredness [*Unverdecktsein*] of the world must be *wrested*, that it is initially and for the most part not available" (11/16). From the perspective of the single, unified being, truth as aletheia is the uncovering, unconcealment, or disclosure of being.

Perhaps it is misleading to speak of *aletheia*, the noun. Maybe it is better to refer to *aletheuein*, the infinitive, so as to draw attention to the effort required for the unconcealment of the single, unified being that is simultaneously the most obvious and the most obscure part of our existence. Heidegger underscores this effort because there is no guarantee that being

---

35. See Ian Thomson, *Heidegger on Ontotheology: Technology and the Politics of Education* (Cambridge: Cambridge University Press, 2005).

36. For the influence of Brentano in Heidegger's understanding of *aletheia* in Aristotle, see David F. Krell, "On the Manifold Meaning of Aletheia: Brentano, Aristotle, Heidegger," *Research in Phenomenology* 5 (1975): 77–94. For the most comprehensive presentation of Heidegger's conception of truth, see Daniel O. Dahlstrom, *Heidegger's Concept of Truth* (Cambridge: Cambridge University Press, 2001).

will be disclosed. As he explains, "everyday Dasein [*das alltägliche Dasein*] moves in a double coveredness [*Verdecktheit*]: initially in mere ignorance [*Unkenntnis*], and then in a much more dangerous coveredness, insofar as idle talk [*das Gerede*] turns what has been uncovered into untruth" (11/15). We see here the configuration of the qualitative distinction between two senses of concealment (§§13–14). The distinction between two kinds of action, one that leads to unconcealment and one that exacerbates concealment, is insufficient to bridge the gap between theory and praxis. Heidegger needs to show also how praxis is inscribed in theoretical knowledge.

The determination of techne as a modality of theoretical knowledge or sophia is the move that forges a confluence of theory and praxis, thereby overturning a key *epistemological* position of metaphysics. The secondary literature on *Plato's Sophist* has downplayed this argument, focusing instead on how phronesis undoes the separation of theory and praxis.[37] This is unfortunate. The argument that episteme is the virtue of techne occurs immediately after the determination of phronesis in §8 of *Plato's Sophist*, that is, immediately after the passages in which Heidegger's mistake occurs (§26). The argument is announced in the title of subsection (c), which says that sophia, as the culmination of theoretical knowledge, is the virtue of techne. Thus, the gap between theory and praxis is bridged through techne.

Most of the argumentation in subsection (c) of §8 in *Plato's Sophist* consists in a comparison between phronesis and techne. Heidegger repeats several times that phronesis is impervious to *lethe*, the forgetting that the privative alpha of *a-letheia* undoes.[38] In other words, Heidegger holds that phronesis is oriented toward being. By contrast, techne is not a genuine *aletheuein*, or unconcealment, because of its end-oriented character. Heidegger offers the production of a shoe as an example of techne: The fact that the shoe can be completed entails that the end of techne does not include its own *arche* or principle of action, whereby the complete product is an object to be used. The truth of techne is its use, which means that it is independent of the act of production (29/41). This preempts the description of equipment in *Being and Time* and explains why end-oriented actions do not lead to the truth of being, according to Heidegger. The causes that produce the shoe can only show the truth of techne through its instrumentality.

The causes and effects employed by the cobbler and the means and ends that function after the shoe is delivered over to someone else are, according

---

37. For a review of this literature, see Panagiotis Thanassas, "Phronesis vs. Sophia: On Heidegger Ambivalent Aristotelianism," *The Review of Metaphysics* 66 (2012): 31–59.
38. Heidegger repeats this point three times in 39/56.

to Heidegger, intertwined in Aristotelian techne. *The conflation of causality and instrumentality within techne is coupled with the designation of techne as a modality of theoretical knowledge.* Thus, the determination of sophia as the virtue of techne in §8 relies entirely on the earlier passage that elides the distinction between causal and instrumental ends—or, on the repression of instrumentality. Heidegger's conception of techne in *Plato's Sophist* is premised on his mistake.

The designation of techne as a modality of theoretical knowledge is again premised on a mistranslation. At the conclusion of §8, after the comparison between phronesis and techne, Heidegger explicitly states the position that techne is a modality of sophia: "What is most striking now is that Aristotle designates *sophia* as the virtue of techne (*Nic. Eth.* VI, 7, 1141a12). The highest mode of *aletheuein* [unconcealment], philosophical reflection, which according to Aristotle is the highest mode of human existence, is at the same time the virtue of techne" (39–40/56–57). The whole passage that Heidegger cites as support for this claim that techne is a modality of sophia reads: "ἐνταῦθα μὲν οὖν οὐθὲν ἄλλο σημαίνοντες τὴν σοφίαν ἢ ὅτι ἀρετὴ ἐστίν." Far from saying that sophia *is* the virtue of techne, this passage plainly says that people say (σημαίνοντες) that the great artists have sophia. Aristotle is pointing to a linguistic usage, not to a philosophical distinction.[39] If we turn to *Nicomachean Ethics* 1141a12, the expression that sophia is the virtue of techne is unambiguously about linguistic use. According to Aristotle, "people say" that a competent artist such as Pheidias has sophia. Sophia in this context is something that we "ἀποδίδομεν," that is, something that "we," the people of Athens that Aristotle has in mind, attribute to great artists, customarily in everyday linguistic usage.

Based on the conflation of causality and instrumentality and on yet another mistranslation, Heidegger asserts that "the arete [virtue] of techne is not phronesis but is precisely sophia" (43/61); and that "sophia is simultaneously the virtue of techne and episteme [science]" (47/68). It is a small step from here to say that "sophia has the priority in relation to beings [*das Seiende*] in themselves, insofar as the beings with which it is concerned have for the Greeks ontological priority" (94/137). The peculiar character of Greek

---

39. Robert Bernasconi points out that there is a precedent in Heidegger's fanciful interpretation of this passage from 1141a12. In the 1850s, Carl Prantl had offered a similar interpretation of sophia as the virtue of techne with recourse to the same passage. However, Bernasconi adds that Eduard Zeller had already pointed out the mistake in this reading by noting the point that I also make, namely, that Aristotle is clearly expressing, here, a common linguistic usage. Bernasconi, "Heidegger's Destruction of Phronesis," *The Southern Journal of Philosophy* 28 (1989): 135.

thought according to Heidegger to understand knowledge based on a conception of being as one and unified, is premised on the conception of sophia as virtue of techne. That is why the Greeks resist the separation of theory and praxis that signals the metaphysical conception of knowledge.

This argument provides Heidegger with a significant historical grounding of his assertion of the forgetting of the single, unified being in metaphysics: The corruption of Greek thought through its translation into Latin breaks the conjunction of techne and sophia, thereby obscuring the connection between theory and praxis, holding, instead, that the "genuine ideal of knowledge appears in theoretical knowledge and that all knowledge receives its orientation from the theoretical" (17/24). Differently put, being remains obscure and concealed in the epistemology of metaphysics because metaphysics does not recognize that theoretical knowledge is the virtue of techne. Or being is consigned to oblivion because metaphysics fails to conflate causality and instrumentality so as to distinguish the ineffectual as a qualitatively distinct kind of action.

And yet, *at least since Aquinas, there is a strong metaphysical tradition that relies precisely on the conflation of causality and instrumentality*. Most prominently, this conflation is the prop and stay of the design argument about the existence of god that relies on the so-called techne or craft analogy from Aristotle (§31). This is a well-known story in the history of philosophy, but I have been unable to discover any examination of Heidegger's destruction of metaphysics that links his conflation of causality and instrumentality to the techne analogy and the design argument.

The key points of the story include the much commented upon peculiarity in Aristotle's account of causality. Aristotle distinguishes between four kinds of causes: the material, the formal, the efficient, and the final cause. But he has a habit of illustrating the four causes with reference to techne (§31). For example—to use Heidegger's example of the shoe from *Plato's Sophist*—the material is the leather, the form can be a boot, the efficient is the cobbler, and the final end is walking in the shoe. Aristotle's habit of using examples from techne to explain causality establishes an analogy between craft and natural causality, and thereby also with the theoretical knowledge concerned with universals. The nature of this analogy is far from obvious. For example, it is not clear whether Aristotle means it as a mere example or whether he actually holds an inherent, ontological sameness between natural causality and the practice of craft.[40] Despite this ambiguity,

---

40. See Sarah Broadie, "Nature, Craft and Phronesis in Aristotle," *Philosophical Topics* 15, no. 2 (1987): 35–50.

the techne analogy has played a fundamental role in the history of thought. Heidegger notes this in "The Origin of the Work of Art" (§64), and other philosophers have demonstrated how ingrained the techne analogy has been in the Western understanding of a series of concepts.[41]

The next key turn in our story occurs in the thirteenth century, at the time when Aristotle's works were introduced back into the West, giving rise to Thomism, the most impactful movement of thought of the late medieval period. The turn consists in Aquinas's adapting of the techne analogy to prove the existence of god. This is the "quinta via," the "fifth way" or the fifth argument for the existence of god, from the *Summa* that is regarded as the first design or teleological argument. It is worth quoting the famous passage: "We see that things which lack knowledge, such as natural bodies, act for an end, and this is evident from their acting always, or nearly always, in the same way, so as to obtain the best result. Hence it is plain that they achieve their end not by chance, but by design. Now whatever lacks knowledge cannot move towards an end, unless it be directed by some being endowed with knowledge and intelligence, as the arrow is directed by the archer. Therefore, some intelligent being exists by whom all natural things are ordered to their end; and this being we call God."[42] It is plain to see that the argument rests on the techne analogy. Aquinas presupposes that it is possible, or even inevitable, to conflate natural causes with the instrumental ends of an intelligent being. The conflation of causality and instrumentality arises from the techne analogy and becomes a keystone of the metaphysical proof of god.

That it is neither inevitable nor possible to conflate causality and instrumentality is made plain in David Hume's *Dialogues on Natural Religion*. The core of Hume's critique of the design argument is his attack on the conflation of causality and instrumentality. He demonstrates that there is no philosophical justification to move from causes and effects to means and ends as if the two are interchangeable, since the techne analogy is "a very weak analogy, which is confessedly liable to error and uncertainty." He continues by noting that "the dissimilitude" between causality and instrumentality "is so striking" that their conflation is "a conjecture, a presumption

---

41. For example, there is significant recent work on the techne analogy and the determination of the female. See Emanuela Bianchi, *The Feminine Symptom: Aleatory Matter in the Aristotelian Cosmos* (New York: Fordham University Press, 2014); and Adriel M. Trott, *Aristotle on the Matter of Form: A Feminist Metaphysics of Generation* (Edinburgh: Edinburgh University Press, 2019).

42. Thomas Aquinas, *The Summa Theological*, trans. Daniel J. Sullivan (Chicago: Benton, 1952); vol. 1 of the Encyclopedia Britannica edition, 1.2.3., 13.

concerning a similar cause."[43] Instead of conjecture, he might as well have said that it is conjuring trick that hides in plain sight the lack of any argument for the conflation of causality and instrumentality other than a peculiar use of Aristotle's techne analogy.

Like Aristotle's techne analogy, which is never argued for, and Aquinas's design argument that simply assumes it is possible to move from causes to means, Heidegger's mistake also conflates causality and instrumentality, which is never argued properly, relying instead on a series of tenuous translations of Aristotle's text. Such mistranslations lead to an epistemology faithful to the single, unified being, which relies on techne as a modality of theoretical knowledge. The conjuring trick in Heidegger's description of sophia as the virtue of techne is that it relies on the techne analogy translated into the position that techne is a modality of theoretical knowledge.

This is the moment of the genesis of the ruse of techne: the employment of the conflation of causality and instrumentality to argue for the bridging of the metaphysical gap between theory and praxis, without mentioning that the conflation of causality and instrumentality is in fact a metaphysical position, functioning as the premise for the design argument and which relies on the techne analogy. Heidegger mistranslates Aristotle using the metaphysical conflation of causality and instrumentality so as to claim that Aristotle's conception of praxis is ante-metaphysical and that Heidegger's recuperation of the Aristotelian argument effects an overcoming of metaphysics. At the moment of the genesis of the ruse of techne, its conjuring trick hides the metaphysical provenance of the claim that sophia is the virtue of techne so as to claim it as an advance against metaphysics. The conjuring trick hides Heidegger's mistake.

Let me conclude with a clarification. Hume's critique, which I regard as correct, does not affect the critique of instrumentality in the Frankfurt School tradition. The reason is that thinkers such as Adorno do not conflate causality and instrumentality. The critique of how science is employed for instrumental ends in Adorno is a critique of power as it articulates in a specific historical setting, which means that it is a critique of the effects of instrumentality. Adorno has no need for the conflation of causality and instrumentality, with all the metaphysical baggage that such a conflation entails, since he is concerned with showing how the combined use of causality and instrumentality affects society, culture, and politics. By contrast, Heidegger cannot do without the conflation of causality and instrumentality

---

43. David Hume, *Dialogues Concerning Natural Religion and Other Writings*, ed. Dorothy Coleman (Cambridge: Cambridge University Press, 2007), 20–21.

so as to determine an action that is free of effect and hence occupies a temporality outside the tumult of politics and social and cultural concerns (§29). And given that the conflation lacks support in an argument, Heidegger needs the ruse to hide it.

I will demonstrate in the rest of this book the persistence of this ruse in the conflation of causality and instrumentality, which Heidegger constructs in his interpretation of book 6 of *Nicomachean Ethics*. The conflation between causality and instrumentality is most acutely obvious in the "Question Concerning Technology" (§57) but it takes several forms in Heidegger's thought, none of which acknowledges Hume's objection that the conjunction of causes and effects with means and ends is unargued for and unwarranted.

28. Teleocracy

Max Scheler invited Heidegger to give a lecture at the University of Cologne in December 1924. Heidegger decided to speak on Aristotle's conception of truth, that is, on the material that he had been teaching as part of the course *Plato's Sophist* since the beginning of the winter semester. The preserved text of the talk at Cologne reads like a summary of the interpretation of Aristotle in the lecture course that he was teaching at the same time.[44] All the important points of the interpretation can be found in the talk—with one critical exception: Heidegger does not put forward the position that sophia is the virtue of techne. This is a curious silence since this is an essential part of his argument that Aristotle's aletheia overcomes metaphysics. Without the conception of techne as a modality of theoretical knowledge, the metaphysical separation of theory and praxis remains intact. What held Heidegger back? Was it diffidence? Or did the older, revered scholar function as a kind of superego that censors the young scholar, fearing that Scheler might expose his trick by asking him about the techne analogy assumed in the determination of episteme as the virtue of techne? Maybe. We will never know.

But maybe it is more important that, half a century later, Heidegger himself occupies that position of the superego censor. And what he censors is any attempt to think of ends other than in terms of the conflation of causality and instrumentality, and of the ineffectual as the action without

---

44. Martin Heidegger, "Being-There and Being-True According to Aristotle," in *Becoming Heidegger: On the Trail of His Early Occasional Writings, 1910–1927*, ed. Theodore Kisiel and Thomas Sheehan (Seattle: Noesis Press, 2007), 211–34 = *GA* 80.

ends as the only possibility to resist the metaphysical foreclosure of thought. The qualitative distinction between techne, as the modality of theoretical knowledge, and phronesis, as the praxis without effect, is taken unquestioningly as the consummation of the overcoming of metaphysics—without noting that the provenance of the conflation of causality and instrumentality is in metaphysics itself. Heidegger has now been transposed to the position of the superego who cannot be questioned. Let me offer here one example with reference to an interpretation of techne and phronesis in book 6 of the *Nicomachean Ethics*.

Reiner Schürmann notes that "In the *Nicomachean Ethics* [we find] the distinction between *poiesis* and *praxis*. In *poiesis* (making), setting to work precedes the work as constructing precedes the edifice. But in *praxis* (acting), setting to work is itself the end."[45] That is why, in Heidegger's terms from *Plato's Sophist*, techne can never aspire to aletheia: its completion makes its end an item of use and thereby cancels it out. Schürmann intensifies this critique of activity as production by linking it to the metaphysical doctrine of entelechy in Aristotle—something that Heidegger does not do in *Plato's Sophist*. Thus, Schürmann notes that the distinction between the end-oriented activity of techne and phronesis ameliorates the ambiguities of entelechy, but ultimately "here again the paradigmatic scheme for understanding arche and telos is production."[46] With this move, Schürmann amplifies Heidegger's move of depositing all ends to techne by linking techne to entelechy. The conflation of causality and instrumentality is even more radical.

We readily find also the qualitative distinction between two actions, depending on whether they are end-oriented. Unlike techne, phronesis—insists Schürmann following Heidegger—is free of ends: "The other acting, which has remained unthought, will necessarily differ from action as conceived by the tradition issuing from Aristotle. It cannot be confused with the praxis assigned its goal by reason and sustained by the will." Phronesis—the kind of action that Heidegger will subsequently associate with artistic activity—is emptied out of instrumentality that is transferred entirely to techne: "Theoretical teleocracy seems rather to be born from reflection about *techne* alone, so that we 'aim at' something, strictly speaking, only in the domain of fabrication. From there the rule of end has imposed itself on reflection about 'inquiries,' and finally on each and every form of acting, each and every form of choice. The rule of end has constituted the

---

45. Reiner Schürmann, *Heidegger on Being and Acting: From Principles to Anarchy*, trans. Christine-Marie Gros (Bloomington: Indiana University Press, 1987), 103.

46. Schürmann, *Heidegger on Being and Acting*, 103.

concepts of scientific investigation as well as those with which we account for moral decisions."[47] All discussion of ends in "the tradition issuing from Aristotle" ultimately leads to productive activity (to techne as technology) and the domination of instrumental thinking that determines both epistemological and moral authority.

On what does Schürmann base his argument about the conflation of causality and instrumentality and the subsequent separation of an activity without ends? The move from entelechy to techne as incorporating all ends is made with breathtaking ease. The only support Schürmann provides in both passages cited above is the opening paragraph of *Nicomachean Ethics*. Aristotle notes there that every practical activity requires an end, but he insists that there is a variety of ends and that the different kinds of activities have correspondingly different ends. Aristotle does not mention entelechy in this passage. Instead, as we saw earlier (§19), this is the distinction between *poiesis* and *praxis* that prefigures the distinction between techne and phronesis in book 6. Not only does this passage not collapse the distinction between entelechy and the ends of action; moreover, it can be understood as indicating how Aristotle preempts the distinction between causal and instrumental ends at the beginning of book 6. Conversely, the collapse of the distinction between entelechy and the end of techne appears merely as the employment of the techne analogy to justify the exclusion of instrumentality from the kind of action that Heidegger understands as phronesis, which in turn leads to the castigation of the ends of techne as the justification of a metaphysical teleology that leads all the way to the nihilism of modernity. This is not only a petitio principii; moreover, it assumes, without arguing for, the techne analogy so as to suggest that metaphysics is overcome, all the while forgetting that the techne analogy is derived from a metaphysical interpretation of Aristotle.

I am not singling Schürmann out for misreading Aristotle—not only because I deeply admire Schürmann's work, but also because I am not interested in pointing out mistranslations as such. Rather, mistakes are interesting when they point to something ingrained in one's thinking that remains unexamined—the kind of repressed content that haunts thought. And what remains unexamined in this reading of techne as "teleocracy" is Heidegger's mistake that conceals the distinction between causal and instrumental ends resulting in the repression of instrumentality, which is premised on the conjectured—or conjured—techne analogy. Teleocracy is the magical word that triggers the repressed content of Heidegger's ruse of techne.

---

47. Schürmann, *Heidegger on Being and Acting*, 83.

29. Phronesis, resoluteness, and temporality: The "either/or"

The position that sophia, as the highest possible knowledge, is the virtue of techne, also provides Heidegger's point of critique of Greek thought. This suggests, according to Heidegger, the danger of understanding being in the purview of theoretical knowledge as mere presence. Or, as he puts it in *Plato's Sophist*, "for the Greeks the consideration of human existence was oriented purely toward the meaning of being itself. . . . The Greeks gathered this meaning of being, being as absolute presence [*als absolutes Anwesendsein*]."[48] This shortcoming mirrors the fault that Heidegger finds with Husserl's phenomenology that is also oriented toward being as it is revealed by phenomena.[49] This paves the way for Heidegger's own project that is first comprehensively articulated in *Being and Time*.

And yet, some of the critical insights of *Being and Time* are chiseled out in the interpretation of phronesis in *Plato's Sophist*. Franco Volpi has been instrumental in showing how Heidegger's interpretation of phronesis provided the foundations of *Being and Time*.[50] What Volpi has failed to note, however, is that phronesis operates as the opposite of techne in the sense that it is freed of all ends, whereby it occupies the third meaning of techne, that is, as the ineffectual. From such a perspective, phronesis is a critical component of the genesis of the ruse of techne in *Plato's Sophist*.

Heidegger translates Aristotle's determination of phronesis as an action that is self-interrogative, or an action whose ends are expressed through its enactment, into the determination of Dasein as the kind of being that is concerned with its own being: "Disclosure, however, in relation to which there is *aletheia*, is itself a mode of being [*Sein*], and indeed not of the beings [*des Seienden*] which are first disclosed—those of the world—but, instead, of the beings we call human Dasein" (12/17). This means, according

---

48. Heidegger, *Plato's Sophist*, 122/178.
49. For a detailed analysis about how Heidegger's reading of Aristotle relates to his critique of Husserl, see Pavlos Kontos, "Aristotle in Phenomenology," in *Oxford Handbook of the History of Phenomenology*, ed. Dan Zahavi (Oxford: Oxford University Press, 2018), 5–24.
50. Franco Volpi, "Dasein as *praxis:* The Heideggerian Assimilation and the Radicalization of the Practical Philosophy of Aristotle," in *Martin Heidegger: Critical Assessments, Volume II: History of Philosophy*, ed. Christopher Macann (London: Routledge, 1992), 90–129, "*Being and Time:* A 'Translation' of the *Nicomachean Ethics*?" in *Reading Heidegger from the Start: Essays in his Earliest Thought*, ed. Theodore Kiel and John van Buren, trans. John Protevi (Albany: SUNY Press, 1994), 195–211, and "In Whose Name? Heidegger and 'Practical Philosophy,'" *European Journal of Political Theory* 6, no. 1 (2007): 31–51.

to Heidegger, that the end of Dasein is without effects, or, which is the same thing, that phronesis has no effects because it is purified of ends. That is why, Heidegger avers, the interpretation of the various possibilities of unconcealment "is accomplished in the sixth book of *Nicomachean Ethics*" (13/19). The truth of being understood as aletheia, or unconcealment, requires a kind of action that is without effects.

From this, Heidegger can draw the qualitative distinction between techne, as modality of theoretical knowledge, and phronesis, as oriented toward the truth of being. Theoretical knowledge posits certain ends accomplished by techne; but as soon as they are accomplished, they belong to use, which only ever submerges the subject in everyday activities that detract from the truth of being. Techne as a modality of theoretical knowledge offers "a determination of beings insofar as they are *finished, complete* [*fertig, voll-ständig*] it is always already constantly there [*das immer ist*] as finished" (85/123). By contrast, "in the case of *phronesis*, the *prakton* [the doing or the action] is of the same ontological character as the *aletheuein* [disclosing] itself. And here, presumably, the *telos* [end] is in fact disclosed and preserved; for it is the Being of the deliberator himself [*es ist nämlich das Sein des Überlegenden selbst*]" (34/49). This entails, according to Heidegger, that phronesis is uniquely oriented toward the truth of being: "there is no *lethe* [forgetting] in relation to phronesis. . . . As regards phronesis, there is no possibility of falling into forgetting. . . . Hence because phronesis does not possess the possibility of *lethe* [forgetting], it is not a mode of *aletheuein* [disclosing] which one could call theoretical knowledge [*als theoretisches Wissen*]" (39/56). Heidegger can only draw the qualitative distinction between techne and phronesis because of his mistake, that is, only because of the conflation of causality and instrumentality that enables the construction of an action without ends repressing instrumentality.

Later in the lecture course, Heidegger describes phronesis, the kind of action free of ends, as resoluteness: "in a momentary glance [*im Augenblick*] I survey the concrete situation of the action, out of which and in favor of which I resolve myself [*ich mich entschließe*]" (114/165). The importance of resoluteness will become clear in *Being and Time* that designates it as the authentic disclosure of Dasein, whereby Heidegger explicitly links resoluteness to the temporality of the moment.[51] But, the essential element is present here already as a characteristic of phronesis, namely, an acting for

---

51. Martin Heidegger, *Being and Time*, trans. Joan Stambaugh (Albany: SUNY Press, 2010), 313/434.

the sake of the acting subject, an acting with no external ends and hence effects.[52] Such an acting takes place in the temporality of the *Augenblick*.[53]

Even if we grant that there is such an action that is free of all instrumentality because it is resolute, how do we recognize that such an action is not simply yet another iteration of instrumentality? Heidegger answers this question with recourse to temporality.[54] "This possibility of failure is constitutive for the development of techne," writes Heidegger. The reason is that, as a modality of theoretical knowledge, techne operates on linear time, where causes and effects, as well as means and ends, are sequentially arranged (38/54). This is the linear time of metaphysics and of its theoretical knowledge that culminates in the scientism and technologization that Heidegger disparages as the nihilism of modernity. By contrast, phronesis—purified of causes and effects as well as of means and ends—knows of no such linear temporality:

> But in the case of phronesis, on the contrary, where it is a matter of a deliberation whose theme is the proper being of Dasein, every mistake is a personal shortcoming [*ist jedes Fehlgehen ein Sich-Verfehlen*]. This shortcoming with regard to oneself is not a higher possibility, not the *teleiosis* [end or completion] of phronesis, but precisely its corruption [*Verderb*]. Other than failure, the only possibility open to phronesis is to genuinely hit the mark. Phronesis is not oriented toward trial and error; in moral action I cannot experiment with myself. The deliberation of phronesis is ruled by the either/or [*das Entweder-Oder*]. (38/54)

Phronesis does not occupy the time of sequential moments but the "the blink of an eye" that makes the action either one that is oriented toward the truth of being, or a "corruption," that is, a failure. There is no in-between. This "either/or" is not carried out in a temporal sequence and

---

52. As William McNeill notes, Heidegger had discovered resoluteness in Aristotle before *Plato's Sophist*. For instance, Heidegger makes the connection clear already in *Basic Concepts of Aristotelian Philosophy*. See McNeill, *The Time of Life: Heidegger and Ethos* (Albany: SUNY, 2006), 86–87.

53. On Heidegger's interpretation of Aristotle and the *Augenblick*, see McNeill, *The Glance of the Eye*.

54. Besides *Being and Time*, the subsequent lecture course *The Basic Problems of Phenomenology* is critical because it contains a more explicit analysis of temporality in Aristotle. See Martin Heidegger, *The Basic Problems of Phenomenology*, trans. Albert Hofstadter (Bloomington: Indiana University Press, 1982) = *GA* 24. For a discussion on temporality and Aristotle in *Basic Problems*, see John Protevi, *Time and Exteriority: Aristotle, Heidegger, Derrida* (Lewisburg, PA: Bucknell University Press, 1994).

hence it is not something that we can verify using the experimental procedures of science. Thus, the either/or marks the point beyond effects characteristic of phronesis in *Plato's Sophist* and in the later Heidegger of techne as art.

Contra Heidegger, there is another either/or that offers philosophy its choice (§2 and §14). *Either* a philosophy that is caught up in the ruse of techne so as to repress instrumentality by failing to note the mistaken conflation of causality and instrumentality. *Or* a materialist philosophy that is mindful of the effects of action, and thus retains the distinction between causal and instrumental ends so as to allow for a philosophy of the political and the ethical. In a different formulation, *either* Heidegger's phronesis as ineffectual *or* Aristotle's phronesis as coextensive with its effects.

The significance of Heidegger's mistake is to present philosophy with this choice. I suggest here that philosophy needs to reject Heidegger's option because of its impoverished conception of action, as I will demonstrate in the second part of *The Ruse of Techne*. Prior to that, I will sketch, in the Excursus, what is at stake in this choice between two different conceptions of action in monism.

Excursus
Through the Looking Glass of the Distinction Between Causality and Instrumentality

Why does the distinction between the causal and the instrumental ends of action matter? Or relatedly, why is it crucial today to confront the choice between a philosophy that represses instrumentality by conflating causality and instrumentality and one that recognizes the significance of instrumentality for the ethical and the political? I will pause my interpretation of Heidegger to consider these questions, which arise through his influential conception of action that represses instrumentality. I will sketch the way in which the distinction between causality and instrumentality, as the other of the repression of instrumentality, is critical for grasping, first, alternative conceptions of action in materialism; second, the pivotal function of the concealment of this distinction in the construction of the morals or theory of action in metaphysics; and third, to nod toward how the underground current of a materialism of instrumentality (§7) that employs this distinction can be of significance today.

30. Acting and the other: The politics of instrumentality

In *The Empty Space*, Peter Brook defines theater in a way that offers an insight into how to understand action. Brook says that the "act of theatre" occurs when one person walks into an empty space *and* at least one other person is watching.[1] A materialist could expand this definition to account

---

1. Peter Brook, *The Empty Space* (New York, Atheneum, 1968), 7.

for action in general by saying that to act is to act with. There is no action without the operative presence of an other. We discover equivalent insights in the phenomenological tradition. As Maurice Merleau-Ponty puts it, "insofar as I have sensory functions . . . I already communicate with others."[2] Even the act of sensing something presupposes the presence of the other.

Such an approach would be unacceptable to a conception of action that relies on the free will of the individual. For an individualist conception of action relying on free will, the presence of the other would be deemed an unnecessary addition. No matter how predisposed we might be to rely on the free will for understanding action nowadays, we should remain alert that an individualist conception of action comes with significant baggage. For instance, it presupposes an autonomous individual, separate from the external world. Such an individual can cognize the external world while also being able to separate its rational from its emotional parts. There are various critiques of such a conception of the individual, not least by Heidegger himself. Not wanting to repeat these well-rehearsed critiques, I will bracket out this conception of the individual from the account of action as an acting with, but I will return to the importance of the free will for the metaphysics of morals later (§31).

The next point to consider is what acting *with* means. What is the nature of the one observing the person who is acting? Under what conditions does such an other become part of one's actions? When we start considering these questions, we eventually reach the realization that an other is always present. Even if one is alone, in a faraway place, one's actions are never completely isolated. There is always an other "watching." For instance, imagine a person far away from others, reading a book in the middle of the night. The reader is completely still. There is no noise, either inside or outside the house. There is no movement, nor an immediately present observer. And yet, the book that one is reading is always a conversation (of sorts) with the author and the particular group of readers that the book is appealing to. The reader may also be reading the book with specific people in mind. She may be reading, for instance, a Heidegger text in preparation for a class later in the week. Other students may be present in her mind as she considers how they might respond to particular passages. The approach in class will also color her reading, leading her to notice different aspects of the text, concentrating on either a critique of Heidegger or a defense against his critics.

2. Maurice Merleau-Ponty, *Phenomenology of Perception*, trans. Donald A. Landes (London: Routledge, 2012), 369.

There is no way of being, no existence, which is not simultaneously an action that presupposes an other. That is why activity is, as Hannah Arendt puts it, the "human condition." The human is always involved in a network of relations. And this involvement is a form of action that includes others. It is impossible to extricate oneself from such a network of relations.

One may object at this point that such a conception of action is firmly ensconced in metaphysics. Isn't the conception of action as always taking place within a totality and as always observed the conception of action that we find in Augustine? His *Confessions* designates this totality as god and describes a series of emotions about the fact that god is always observing him, such as frustration because god never responds. There is, nonetheless, a significant difference. In the metaphysical conception of action, the observer is omnipresent because god is transcendent. By contrast, in the materialist approach to action, the presence of the other is not transcendent; rather, the other is—as we will see shortly—involved in the formation of practical judgments. This is not to suggest that the other is purely immanent either, as the distinction between transcendence and immanence falls flat at this point. The other is not an immediate presence, nor is it "objectively present," as *Being and Time* puts it. Consequently, for materialism, such an other is not the same as the *transcendent* totality. The other is part of the network of relations that persist in a *materialist* totality.

This returns us to the problem of action within a *monist* materialist ontology. As soon as we establish the notion of a totality that has regular laws that cannot be broken, or a totality outside of which nothing exists, there follows the problem of whether action can effect any change within this totality. How can we differentiate between actions within such a totality, since they appear as mere modifications of that totality and hence as lacking difference? This is the problem of how to account for action in monism that I have highlighted since the introduction. This is also the problem that Heidegger had to tackle as soon as he posited a single, unified being that he discovered in Greek thought.

I have also noted the point where Heidegger departs from the monist materialist tradition. The materialists draw the distinction at the level of the ends. The same action has different ends—ends that are final and can be understood in terms of causality and production; and instrumental ends that are contingent and ineliminable from the ethical and the political. The former belong to techne, the latter to phronesis. By contrast, Heidegger attempts to distinguish between actions. Some actions are oriented toward being, and some are not. Heidegger calls the former phronesis and the latter techne in *Plato's Sophist*. Even though the terminology changes over time—for example, Heidegger stops using the term phronesis—the idea remains constant: the action that can disclose being is free of ends. To achieve such a difference between actions, Heidegger absorbs all ends into techne, whereby instrumental ends become subsumed within causal ends, effecting the repression of instrumentality. This is Heidegger's mistake in *Plato's Sophist*—the mistake that facilitates the ruse of techne.

The difference of distinguishing at the level of ends or between actions directly may seem like a minor philosophical squabble. After all, is it not more important to oppose the common enemies, such as individualism and the metaphysics of morals? And yet, if we pause to consider this initial, seemingly minor difference, we will soon note a cumulative effect, whereby a series of important diverges emerge between the two conceptions of action within a monist framework. These differences profoundly affect the nature of one's relation to the other—they affect the "with" of acting. Let me provide a couple of examples.

The first example pertains to the importance of the parallel function of both ends of action. This enables the critique of *both* the production, in all its multifaceted complexity that includes epistemological, social, and economic concerns, *and* the representation of this production, regardless of whether this is done in terms of superstructure, hegemony, or ideology, and so on. Conversely, the forgetting of instrumentality entails that the only way in which the effects of action can be assessed is in consequentialist terms. This is not only a rather impoverished way to think of the effects of action; it is also self-contradictory since the separation of actions that are end-oriented from actions that are oriented toward being, aim *inter alia* toward a critique of the epistemology that pursues a technological employment of knowledge, characterized by the attainment of ends. In other words, we discern, here, the source of the dilemma between a vacuous and a self-contradictory account of action that we have already discovered in Heidegger (§4 and §16). Important political implications follow from this.

A key political implication of the theory of praxis that distinguishes between different ends arises from the fact that the ends of techne and the ends of phronesis are carried out in the same action process. The way that things are produced corresponds to the ends of techne. This may be determined by a network of material and technological relations. But the instrumental end is produced by the provisional ends that we set ourselves in the course of acting. The way that we think about what we are producing, and the aims we might have to participate in a production process, are distinct from that process itself. For instance, the way we might justify to ourselves why we participate in reproducing oppressive processes of production is what Althusser calls ideology. The ends of ideology are accomplished through the same actions as the ends of production, but the ends are in each case distinct. Thus, an ideology critique needs to inquire about both ends. The differentiation of action according to its ends, thus, offers the resources to examine and critique the power structures that underlie action or the action with others in a social, economic, and political field. Differently put, the distinction between causality and instrumentality offers the framework for political thought.

Conversely, the Heideggerian move to distinguish between actions finds it harder to interrogate power structures. Thus, it is harder to develop a political thought when we define actions on the basis of how they are oriented toward being. All production, all end-oriented activity, is excluded as a possible avenue of reaching disclosure. As a result, all technology is seen as an impediment and true freedom is freedom from all ends. What is the value of all end-oriented activity? One might respond that the framing of the political in terms of consequences is a marker of political domination, and that Heidegger develops a politics as a critique of such an enlightenment reason. I concur, and I believe that Heidegger's philosophy provides excellent resources for the kind critique of consequentialist and utilitarian theories that arise from enlightenment's positing of the absoluteness of reason. They all make the move that Heidegger describes, whereby all ends are reduced to the ends of techne that are supposed to be calculated with some certainty because they are independent of the action itself. This is indeed a marker of domination in the sense that it curtails conduct within the purview of such predetermined ends. But this is still insufficient for a critique of power. Simply juxtaposing the consequentialist conception of action to another kind of action that is "useless," or free from consequences, is to conceal the area where the political unfolds—the area demarcated by the ends of instrumentality. What consequentialists and Heidegger alike forget is that the ends of techne and the instrumental ends are distinct because the latter are—as I put it in the previous chapter—fallible in the sense that they can never be derived with any certainty. Such a forgetting is detrimental as it fails to account for instrumental ends, and hence for the part of rational activity that understands action in a framework other than production. The problem then with the Heideggerian critique of end-oriented activity is that it is focused on a consequentialist conception of the end while discarding the instrumental end of action, thereby reducing all end-oriented action to production and offering an impoverished view of the political that falls short of a critique of power.

Let us examine a second significant divergence between the two answers. This concerns the kind of politics that the distinction between causal and instrumental ends makes possible. It is critical to recognize that instrumental ends are shared ends. This is already implied in Aristotle, when he describes phronesis as a situated kind of judgment whose end is part of the action. The fact that it is situated entails that its ends can never be completely owned by whoever makes the practical judgment. The effect of this is both a critique of authority as the figure who suspends judgment and an opening of a path toward a communal or democratic politics.[3] By contrast, the kind of action that is separated from ends and is oriented toward being lacks such a sharing capacity. It is not by accident that Heidegger refers to existential solipsism in the context of describing the care of Dasein in *Being and Time* (§40). To facilitate interaction, such a position requires either great works or great figures that have authority. This is not the naïve obedience to a political leader or Führer, as I will explain in chapter 5, but rather the anti-democratic insistence on the authority of those few who can disclose being.

The instrumental ends—that is, the ends of phronesis—cannot be owned. This makes established power precarious—or, at least, open to critique—and also provides a mechanism to account for the sociality of action. Thus, Machiavelli argues in the *The Prince* that the sovereign is not restricted by any moral precepts independent of the situation. There is no moral precept against killing one's opponents and in fact Machiavelli advocates such actions. If a new sovereign needs to eliminate enemies so as to ensure the preservation of his power, this should be done as early as possible, before they have the opportunity to regroup and so that the crime can be forgotten during the course of his rule. But this instrumental end does not entail that the sovereign's power is absolute. Machiavelli insists that the sovereign ought to ensure that his actions avoid inciting the hatred and the indignation of the people, so that they do not rejoice in his downfall and do not resist him. Because it is impossible to own instrumental ends, the multitude retain some power over the decisions of the sovereign. The way in which the sovereign uses his power is intertwined with the reception of that use by the people—which means that his practical judgments that calculate the ends of his action are never completely his own. This is a critical feature of the practical judgments that involve the calculation of instrumental ends. Such shared ownership of practical judgments is responsible for a sense of community. Phronesis establishes the other's presence that makes action possible, because phronesis shows the way in which instrumental ends are dispersed among everyone who is

---

3. I describe such a conception of democracy within a monist materialism in *Spinoza, the Epicurean: Authority and Utility in Materialism* (Edinburgh: Edinburgh University Press, 2020).

affected by them. This promotes a sense of a democratic community, despite the fact that the ends that affect others can also be responsible for conflicts or the agonism of the political.

The contrast with Heidegger's position could not be sharper here. We can see immediately that he recognizes something like the shared space of ends. That is what he calls "world" in *Being and Time*. No end-oriented action is ever individual. It is, rather, imbued in the field of relations of one's world. But as long as the distinction is drawn between different actions according to the criterion of whether the action is oriented toward being, and as long as this orientation toward being is characterized as freed of ends, then the possibility of the shared end is not available to unconcealment. Further, as soon as Heidegger's project is imbued with the historical sense of techne that refers to the Greek discovery of the single, unified being, the political project of pursuing the truth of being implies that the unforgetting of being is a difficult task that only a few can potentially accomplish. The elitist implications of such a position are not free of political consequences.

Such elitism haunts all conceptions of action that rely on a monist ontology and that account for action by distinguishing between end-oriented actions and actions that are free of ends. We can see this, for example, in Hannah Arendt's works. Despite differences from Heidegger, Arendt remained true to her old teacher's fundamental position about a qualitatively distinct action that is free of ends, which she calls simply "action" in the *Human Condition*, as opposed to the end-oriented activities that she calls "work" and "labor." This explains her difficult relation to democracy. Arendt was never comfortable with a shared space of ends. Her conception of the space in-between, characteristic of end-free action, is of a field of relations that can be essentially purged of instrumentality. That is why the notion of authority is so critical for Arendt. The action proper of the political requires the figures of authority who determine what that action free of ends is. A stark example of this need for authority is her analysis of the Hungarian revolution in the second edition of *The Origins of Totalitarianism*. Ultimately, she argues, it is not the people forming political factions who are responsible for the success of a revolution. Rather, the Hungarian revolution is "the only authentic light we have" because of the "trusted and trustworthy men," that is, the men of authority who run its councils.[4] By contrast, the materialists who distinguish causal from instrumental ends

---

4. Hannah Arendt, *The Origins of Totalitarianism* (Cleveland, OH: Meridian, 1962), 500, 502.

tend to see authority as something that needs to be resisted so as to promote the shared ends of actions characteristic of instrumentality.[5]

What are we to make of these divergences that arise from the acceptance or the concealment of the distinction between final and instrumental ends? A complete thematic analysis of this contrast is beyond the scope of the present study, but I will continue highlighting the contrast and exploring some of its repercussions over the course of the second half of *The Ruse of Techne*. But first, it would be useful to follow a red thread of the contrast in the history of philosophy so as to better grasp the import of the repression of instrumentality that structures Heidegger's conception of action. I will sketch, first, the way in which the metaphysics of morals, or a metaphysical conception of action, relies on a forgetting of instrumental ends; and second, the materialist tradition that, from antiquity to modernity, seeks to preserve the distinction between causal and instrumental ends.[6]

31. The repression of instrumentality in metaphysics

In order to discern the connection between metaphysics and the rejection of instrumentality we need to return to the distinction between the ends of causality and instrumentality that we find in *Nicomachean Ethics* 1139a32 and that Heidegger mistakes. The metaphysical conception of action, or what I call the "metaphysics of morals," undoes this distinction by privileging the causal end. There are various reasons for this. They partly have to do with the fact that Judeo-Christian metaphysics places creation at the start of ontology whereby the end of causality plays a critical role; and partly due to the function of the free will so as to repress instrumentality. I will roughly map this terrain, starting with the function of the causal end in metaphysics.

The description of the end of techne in *Nicomachean Ethics* presupposes Aristotle's influential theory of the four causes—a theory that has remained essentially unchallenged for centuries and which has been of fundamental significance in the history of epistemology. This theory is presented both in *Physics* and in *Metaphysics*. In summary, the four causes are the efficient cause (the agent of the action), the material cause (the stuff acted upon),

---

5. The topic of the conflict between authority and instrumental ends is central to the epicurean understanding of instrumental ends, as I explain in §32.

6. I begin by highlighting Althusser's account of the "underground current" of materialism in philosophy (§1). My version of such a materialism places at center stage the distinction between causality and instrumentality (§32).

the formal cause (the form that the material is given by the agent), and the final cause (the purpose or aim of the formed material).

Following Aristotle—for instance, *Physics* 2.3—the traditional example provided for the four causes comes from art or craftsmanship, or what the Greeks call *techne*. For instance, we can think of the four causes in terms of a statue. The efficient cause is the sculptor, the material cause is the marble, the formal cause is the shape of the artifact (for instance, of a god), and the final cause is the purpose of the sculpture (such as to be venerated in a temple). This kind of example is responsible for the techne analogy (§27).

The final end of causality and the instrumental end can be part of the same action, but they are nonetheless distinct (§22). The instrumental end of the sculptor's actions may be the commission with which she plans to buy a house. This end depends on her practical judgments. But the final end of her actions, the purpose of the sculpture, is pregiven—it can be determined even before a specific sculptor is found to fulfill the commission. Obviously, the fulfillment of one end does not entail the fulfillment of the other as well. The delivery of the complete sculpture to the temple does not necessarily entail that the house the sculptor had in mind will be purchased. The final and the specific ends are distinct—as they are conceivable and achievable independently of each other—even if they are not separated in that they form part of one process of action. Consequently, to understand the actions of the sculptor—to find the truth of her actions in the sense presented at the beginning of book 6 of the *Nicomachean Ethics*—we have to take into account the distinction between final and provisional ends, or between causality and instrumentality.

There is one further implication of monumental importance for the metaphysics of morals. The causal schema allows for a double determination of the subject, the efficient cause. This double determination leads straight into the path of the metaphysical conception of the subject. The agent of action is both all-powerful and entirely powerless (§64). The sculptor is powerful in the sense of being the one who gives shape to the material. The end is in her hands. But at the same time, the sculptor is also determined by external circumstances. For instance, the marble delivered to her workshop may be of inferior quality so that the result of the chiseling may be imperfect. Or "fate"—and I am using this word to allude to Machiavelli, to whom I will turn in the following section—may intervene and a natural disaster destroys the workshop so that the work is not completed.

This double determination of the subject as both all-powerful and powerless creates a huge tension within the efficient cause that follows any notion of subjectivity all the way to modernity, when this double determination is thematized in Immanuel Kant's third antinomy. This is the famous antinomy about freedom in the *Critique of Pure Reason*. The antinomy concerns a totality that is conceived as an indefinite chain of causes and effects. The subject is inserted into this chain. The two sides of the antinomy understand the subject's relation to causes and effects in two diametrically opposed ways. Either the subject is completely determined by causes and effects, whereby freedom is absent; or the subject can break the chain of causality and thereby achieve freedom. Either fully determined and hence powerless (or unfree, in the language of modernity), or releasing itself from causal determination and hence powerful (or free). This is a crippling dilemma: either freedom is deprived by the operation of natural causality, or freedom is supposed to miraculously break free from natural causes. Due to this antinomy, Kant holds that freedom cannot be understood in terms of causality inherent in the agent of action or the efficient cause that is split between unlimited power and powerlessness.

Instead, Kant suggests that freedom ought to be understood as moral action. He insists that freedom is the expression of the moral law that is separate from nature and causality, which also means separate from instrumentality, as any calculation of means and ends reverts back to the operation of causes and effects. Instead, freedom aspires to the universal practical law, or what Kant also calls the "categorical imperative." We are free, by obeying this moral law, even though it is never fully accessible to us. Thus, we have to act "as if" we knew what that law was, despite its absence. What is it that provides the end to action as a way of grasping, ever partially, ever provisionally, the moral law? Nothing but a return to the human in its universality, which makes it an end in itself. This is what Kant calls the "kingdom of ends" in the *Groundwork of the Metaphysics of Morals*. This kingdom consists in the internalization of the moral law. It is the recognition of the inherent worth and dignity of humanity. Given that this end does not refer to specific subjects but to subjectivity, it is never determined as a specific end. The moment that there is an instrumental action, natural causes also come into effect, whereby the subject is no longer obeying the moral law but is thrown back to the antinomy of freedom. This does not exclude the possibility of instrumental calculations; rather, it creates a hierarchy, whereby the universality of practical judgment is purged of instrumentality, allowing for action with ends afterward as a way of implementing the genuine moral judgment.

In order to understand Kant's solution to the riddle of freedom—the internalization of the moral law that purges causal and instrumental ends from moral action—we need to consider the conceptual context within which Kant raises the question about the splitting of the efficient cause between powerlessness and powerfulness. The question we need to consider is what happens to this conception of agency in Christian metaphysics.

Christian metaphysics is a metaphysics of creation. The metaphorics of this creationism resonates with the four causes in Aristotle and the conception of production that we found in *Nicomachean Ethics*. The analogy of god as a creator who molds the human from mud, like a potter, arises from the power that the technician enjoys. The entire Judeo-Christian metaphysics, relying on the possibility of a creation *ex nihilo*, is an expression of the all-powerfulness of the efficient cause. Transcendence can also be defined with recourse to this schema in the sense that it is not subject to the four Aristotelian causes. When the creation is from something, that is, when it has a material cause, it is dependent also on the other three causes. In this instance, the creator is determined by the material or the form that may be imposed, for instance, by a patron. The other causes impose themselves on the creator and curtail her power, thoroughly circumscribing the limits of her action. The human is powerless in the sense that one's action is always determined by external powers.

The distinction between the all-powerful god and the powerless human is further used to expand the conception of action to the interpersonal and historical levels. The divine is providential. Such a metaphysics needs to explain how human action is subordinated to the necessity of the divine will that is both all-powerful and all-encompassing—omnipotent, omnipresent, and omniscient. The solution? The conflation of causality and instrumentality. This is a critical point: to sustain the metaphysics of creationism that requires an omnipotent agent who can create something out of nothing, as opposed to a powerless agent who creates through forming preexisting matter, metaphysics needs to incorporate instrumentality into causality.

To understand the subordination of instrumentality to causality, we need to examine the notion of the end in onto-theo-logy. Augustine is a critical figure at this juncture. He defends a creationist metaphysics, so he needs the final end of causality to conceptualize god as creator. God is the all-powerful efficient cause. Such an all-powerful god, or providence, reintroduces the problem of action within monism that I explored in chapter 2. How can we account for action within a framework where we are all part of an inescapable providential order? It is at this point that Augustine introduces a radically different notion of the end—one that is absent from Greek philosophy, and which will be of immense significance for the Middle Ages. This is the notion that human life is a journey toward the city of god that constitutes the telos of all human action (§15). No human ever reaches the city of god in their lifetime, but there are two fundamental attitudes in how humans comport themselves toward that journey. Those that Augustine calls "pilgrims" strive for the city of god, but their powerlessness makes that end inaccessible. Others, whom Augustine calls "pagans," are not oriented toward the end of reaching the city of god, and moreover, they are predisposed to obstruct the progress of the pilgrims.

The city of god in Augustine becomes an end that is radically different from the end of phronesis in *Nicomachean Ethics*. They are both ends that belong to action—they are not external ends like the final end modeled on the actions of a craftsman. But the instrumental end in Aristotle is something immanently achievable in one's lifetime. One has the capacity to make the right judgments, and to achieve good living as a whole (1140a27; cf. §21 and §26). The city of god is, strictly speaking, not accessible in any mortal lifetime. To approximate it becomes an arduous quest that is more successful when it becomes an ordeal, a struggle through adversity or even a martyrdom. Earthly delights—from luxuries or the company of others—is never the end of life for Aristotle, but they are also not to be rejected outright so long as they do not detract from the attainment of the good life. By contrast, the life of the pilgrim is a quest for the salvation of the soul that needs to eschew all earthly delights and sacrifice the personal good to charity (*caritas*), in service to the community of the pilgrims as a whole. Whereas the materialist model can distinguish between the causal and instrumental ends of actions that are both grounded in actuality, the Augustinian model distinguishes between two kinds of action depending on whether they are oriented toward the city of god that is by definition unreachable in actuality.

But the ultimate difference is not simply that the Greek model of the instrumental end is earthly while the Augustinian is otherworldly. Rather, the ultimate difference is that the Greek model of the instrumental end includes a calculation that is conditioned and includes a rational and an emotional element. By contrast, calculation is scorned in the Augustinian model. The end is given, it is the city of god. The quest to approximate the end is a series of stations. And the quest is all the better accomplished if there is as little emotional investment as possible, since passions are the source of sin. Thus, the end offered by the city of god is stripped of its instrumental character. Ends are either part of creation, in which case they ultimately evidence god, or they are the sinful ends of the pagans who are the "children of the flesh." Instrumentality is not a sign of practical wisdom, but of moral sign. The only acceptable end is the end of causality that evidences god—hence the importance of the cosmological argument. The instrumental end is either incorporated within the final end or taken as the symptom—nay, the *cause*—of sin.

An additional move is needed because the problem of the qualitative distinction between actions stubbornly persists. If there is a providential totality within which all humans subsist, then how can we distinguish, in the fallen, mortal world, the actions of the pilgrim from the actions of the pagan? This is the problem of how to account for action within a monist framework, except that now the totality is transcendent, and this has a significant consequence. Whereas the problem for materialist monism is how to distinguish between human actions, the problem now that the totality is transcendent is how to *avoid* making distinctions within that very totality. Thus, now the problem is transformed into the thorny question of how to account for the existence of evil if god is an omnipotent totality that is good by definition. The transcendence of totality shifts the problem of difference from the human to the divine. The problem of evil was at the center of the numerous heresies that haunted the formation of Christian dogma in the fourth century. It was Augustine who provided the answer to the problem of evil by finding a way to shift the problem back to the human, but without recourse to the instrumental end. The answer consists in the construction of the free will, an idea that was absent from Greco-Roman thought.[7] Evil is a quality of the action, but it is not external to the human; rather, an action is good or evil depending on whether the internal choice of the agent is instrumental. The paradigm of this model is the Fall. Adam and Eve exercised their free will to eat the forbidden fruit, but this was an "evil" choice because it evidenced their instrumental end to gain knowledge. The model of the free will becomes the mechanism whereby the metaphysics of morals can make qualitative distinctions between different actions so as to allow for differences within providence.

The differences between the understanding of action according to the free will, and the determination of action according to the distinction between causality and instrumentality, have far reaching implications. For instance, they produce different senses of community thereby suggesting a different politics. The instrumental end of the epicurean materialist tradition cannot be owned by anyone since it is conditioned in such a way that a practical judgment includes others (§30). The notion of the free will no longer needs conditioning as it is internalized. It is the way in which one is in contact with divine law. The sense of community, related to the Augustinian free will, is determined by the end provided by the city of god. Does one belong to the community of the pilgrims or is one a child of the

---

7. The classic study on this is by Albrecht Dihle, *The Theory of Will in Classical Antiquity* (Berkeley: University of California Press, 1982).

flesh? This is a sense of community that relies on an "us versus them" logic—it is a first articulation of identity politics.[8] A justification of violence against the other is constitutive in such notion of identity. The identity produced by the instrumental end is by contrast differential: a nonstable identity that arises through the interactions that unfold in the course of sharing instrumental ends. The conflict between competing ends is also constitutive within such instrumentality—whence its essential agonism, as I have argued elsewhere—but such a conflict can be productive and it is not amenable to the process of the justification of violence.[9]

It is instructive in this regard to jump forward to the twelfth century to consider the reception of Aristotle during the Middle Ages. The recovery of the Aristotelian corpus posed all sorts of challenges to medieval theologians in the thirteenth century. The great synthesis of Christian metaphysics and Aristotelian philosophy is accomplished by Thomas Aquinas in his *Summa Theologica*. What is most revealing, in terms of the repression of the instrumental end, is to compare his commentary of *Nicomachean Ethics* to the reading that I offered earlier, especially the distinction between the two ends. The fact that Aquinas passes over the specific passage in 1139a32, where Aristotle uses the contrast between *hou heneka* and *heneka tinos* to draw the distinction between the two ends, is not especially significant if we keep in mind that Aquinas was working with the Latin translation, not the Greek original. What is more fundamental is that Aquinas acknowledges that the ends of production are distinct from the ends of the phronesis, but he resolves the ends of phronesis with recourse to the doctrine of the free will. The fact that the end of phronesis is internal to the action does not create a space of shared ends, according to Aquinas. Rather, it is an indication of the internalized choice between good and evil, characteristic of the free will that he derives from his reading of Augustine's *City of God*. For this purpose, it is not surprising that Aquinas translates *prohairesis* as "free will."[10] By contrast, I rendered *prohairesis* as practical

---

8. See William Connolly, *The Augustinian Imperative: A Reflection on the Politics of Morality* (Lanham, MD: Rowman & Littlefield, 2002).

9. I regret that I did not see clearly enough this distinction in *Sovereignty and its Other*. I argue there that a justification of violence always presupposes an instrumental logic, but I failed to note the fundamental difference between a violence that can arise as a result of the conflict of ends and a violence that is justified when an end is posited in such a way as to establish a logic of "us versus them." The reason for this deficiency is that I had not yet fully realized the importance of the distinction between causal and instrumental ends, and the role that this distinction plays in an articulation of action within materialist thought.

10. For a discussion of this point, see Matthias Perkams, "Aquinas on Choice, Will, and Voluntary Action," in *Aquinas and the Nicomachean Ethics*, ed. Tobias Hoffmann,

judgment in chapter 3, or more specifically as the practical judgment that calculates the provisional ends of instrumentality.

We see, then, in Aquinas a double move in relation to the end that characterizes phronesis. First, the end is internalized, whereby it is transformed into the free will. Second, the internalization effects an obliteration of the instrumental end of action. Heidegger's mistake also consisted in a double move. First, the internalization of the end of phronesis that now becomes the self-care of Dasein. Second, the concealment of instrumentality. Now, I am not disregarding Heidegger's critique of the free will, and I profoundly admire his dismantling of the epistemology of metaphysics that includes his critique of the free will. But his so-called "destruction of metaphysics" leaves essentially untouched the structure of the repression of instrumentality characteristic of the metaphysics of morals. For instance, the internalization of the end of the kind of action that is oriented toward the truth of being may not have recourse to the kind of free will that we find in Augustine and Aquinas. But it is nonetheless structurally similar to the Kantian position whereby the end of freedom and moral action is internalized by virtue of concerning humanity as a whole. Heidegger substitutes the being of Dasein for Kant's humanity. Thus, Heidegger's account of action mirrors the structure of the repression of instrumentality in the metaphysics of morals (§15 and §27). For this reason, as I have been arguing, Heidegger may overcome the epistemology of metaphysics, but he is still entrenched in the repression of instrumentality, characteristic of the metaphysics of morals (§4).

32. Causal and instrumental ends in monist materialism

Greek thought, according to Hegel, failed to consider the subject as self-reflective, whereby the human could develop no self-consciousness. From the standpoint of idealism this is a fatal flaw of Greek thought since it prevents it from arriving at the absoluteness of reason. But the self-reflective subject of idealism itself reproduces the split between a determined subject, one that is subjected to natural causality, and an all-powerful sense of agency, the transcendental notion of subjectivity that is universal and

---

Jörn Müller, and Matthias Perkams (Cambridge: Cambridge University Press, 2013), 72–90. The most important study of phronesis in Aquinas is Anthony J. Celano, *Aristotle's Ethics and Medieval Philosophy: Moral Goodness and Practical Wisdom* (Cambridge: Cambridge University Press, 2016). See also Dimitris Vardoulakis, "Phronesis and Instrumentality: The Import of Aristotle's Book 6 of *Nicomachean Ethics* Today," *Graduate Faculty Philosophy Journal* 44, nos. 1–2 (2023): 99–122.

partakes of every individual subject. Further, this is only possible because of the autonomy of the self-reflective subject, which thereby constructs its own interiorized freedom. Hegel is working within the matrix of the metaphysics of morals that absorbs instrumental ends within causality and that employs an interior freedom to repress instrumentality. From this perspective, Hegel's condemnation is in fact an invitation to pay closer attention to phronesis as the kind of instrumental judgment that shows how to form a thought that is not amenable to the metaphysics of morals.

Another way of framing this contrast is by saying that the discourse that determines the subject through this split between powerlessness and all-powerfulness is anthropocentric. As Heidegger recognizes from the four causes, the efficient cause becomes the critical one for metaphysics, whereby the human becomes the measure of all things. The underground current of a materialism of instrumentality (§7) by contrast operates on an anti-anthropocentric conception of the human. The provisional nature of the instrumental end avoids the two extremes of power—all-powerfulness and thorough powerlessness. The agent may make practical judgments that aspire to instrumental ends, but those judgments are fallible, as they are dependent on the given circumstances. Phronesis is a kind of knowledge that is responsive—it responds to the material reality that the human finds itself in. This is the kind of judgment that can never "belong" to an individual, as it belongs just as much to the individual's environment and to the others who influence the individual in making the judgment (§30). Thus, the distinction of instrumentality and causality leads to an anti-anthropocentric conception of action.

One may ask at this point: if the distinction between instrumentality and causality is so important for ancient thought, then why is it mentioned so quickly in a text like *Nicomachean Ethics*? Why doesn't Aristotle, ever the good teacher who delights in clear distinctions, dwell on it? This is a significant question that needs to be addressed in more depth than is possible here. I will only explore here three aspects of a possible response.

First, I have suggested already that Greek thought seems to assume the distinction between causality and instrumentality (§23). Every thought, in every era, makes a series of assumptions that remain largely unexamined. They are, as R.G. Collingwood puts it, the absolute presuppositions that structure thought. The distinction between final and provisional end is one of these for Greek thought. This means that the distinction is important and needs to be examined, and that the failure thus far to do so has been a significant lacuna in our understanding of the Greeks.

The fact that it is a significant distinction that is taken for granted is indicated by Cicero's *De finibus bonorum et malorum* that presents a summary of the theory of action of the major philosophical schools in antiquity. This theory of action is structured, as the title suggests, according to the *ends* of action. It is not actions as such that are good or bad—they are distinct due to the ends. The three philosophical positions that Cicero outlines all *require* the conception of the instrumental end. The fact that, like Aristotle, Cicero presupposes the validity of the distinction between causality and instrumentality and does not bother to thematize it, even though it is critical for his presentation of the different philosophical positions, only means that the distinction appears so obvious as to need no justification.

De finibus gives us a further insight into the fate of the distinction between causal and instrumental ends. This is one of the most influential ethical treatises for centuries because it summarizes the fundamental ethical positions about action in the ancient world. During the Middle Ages, it functions as one of the most authoritative summaries of practical philosophy from antiquity. The reason that the readers of Cicero in the Middle Ages did not notice the presupposition of the distinction between causal and instrumental ends is because their own absolute presuppositions obscured it. As I explained in the previous section, the onto-theo-logical presupposition is the repression of instrumentality.

But—and that is the important point—this also suggests a fundamental difference in how we regard instrumentality today as opposed to the Greeks in antiquity. Whereas we are working in the aftermath of the repression of instrumentality, that was not the case for the Greeks. If metaphysics tends to absorb instrumental ends into causality or to castigate them as sin (§31), then a response to the metaphysics of morals requires a clear distinction between causal and instrumental ends. After metaphysics, such a distinction pertains to nothing less than how we can conceptualize action, ethics, and politics. The stakes for delineating the distinction between causal and instrumental ends were different in the ancient world. The ancients did not know the conflation of causality and instrumentality. When I call for a materialist theory of action that relies on instrumentality, I oppose a centuries old assumption that instrumentality is negative—an assumption ingrained in philosophical training. By contrast, when Aristotle draws a distinction between *hou heneka* and *heneka tinos*, he is not writing against the repression of instrumental ends, but rather against different conceptions of instrumental ends, such as the one in *Philebus* that seeks the virtuous ends of action in an essence that is contrasted to contingency. Who one's interlocutor is determines the structure and emphasis of one's discourse. This factor needs to be kept in mind in an investigation of the distinction between causal and instrumental ends in antiquity.

Second, even though there has been no systematic discussion of the distinction of the final and provisional ends of action in ancient thought that I am aware of, there is nonetheless a body of literature on ancient thought that will be significantly supported by assuming such a distinction. These are the readings of ancient thought that emphasize its practical element, or more emphatically, the primacy of praxis in antiquity. For instance, Pierre Hadot in *What is Ancient Philosophy?* (and elsewhere) has shown the practical orientation of the ancient schools of philosophy. Hadot convincingly demonstrates that philosophical education did not concentrate on what we might call "theoretical knowledge." Of course, knowledge that might be universally applicable was part of the instruction, but the schools were primarily concerned with instructing the students in a way of life. This practical instruction was the primary aim. Does this not suggest that the structure of the major schools of philosophy is essentially instrumental? It is unfortunate that Hadot does not consider this question, nor does he consider what kind of conception of instrumentality underlies the instruction in how to act offered by the ancient schools of thought. Exploring these questions, I suspect, will reinforce Hadot's thesis by exploring the ethical and political underpinning of philosophical instruction as a way of life, that is, by showing how the ancient conception of action lent itself to a conception of education as instruction in the "good life."

Another example is the renewed interest in virtue ethics as an alternative to deontological and utilitarian theories that dominated moral philosophy for a couple of centuries. Alasdair MacIntyre's *After Virtue* was pioneering in this regard, followed by a number of significant studies that examined virtue ethics in antiquity with an eye to how their conception of action might be relevant today—books such as Julia Annas's *The Morality of Happiness*. If we read carefully MacIntyre and Annas, we will notice that they always acknowledge that a certain conception of the end needs to accompany the conception of virtue so that a virtue ethics can actually be a theory of action. This is consistent with the structure of the argument in *Nicomachean Ethics*, where the natural virtues that have become the focus of virtue ethics are complemented by the "intellectual virtues" that examine the ends of action. Even though virtue ethicists acknowledge this point, they eschew a sustained analysis of the ends of actions as articulated in ancient virtue ethics.[11] Such an analysis that acknowledges the distinction between causal and instrumental ends will enrich their argument and make them even more relevant today.

---

11. See Vardoulakis, "Phronesis and Instrumentality."

I would like to suggest that an analysis of the distinction between causal and instrumental ends will not merely enrich discourses such as philosophy as a way of life and virtue ethics. These discourses will also presuppose the distinction between causal and instrumental ends, even though this is not foregrounded. In a strange way, the ancient presupposition of the centrality of the distinction between causal and instrumental ends in a conception of action is reinstated in these approaches. Directing the spotlight onto this presupposition by exploring the function of the distinction between the two ends of action will be a critical step toward showing the fundamental incompatibility between ancient theories of action and the conception of action in onto-theo-logy that represses instrumentality. It will also be indispensable in exposing our own absolute presuppositions today.

Third, I hold that the distinction between final and instrumental ends becomes most central, and hence most developed, in epicureanism, and I will provide three examples from antiquity to support this claim. Further, I also hold that the reemergence of epicureanism in modernity is responsible for reintroducing this distinction into modern discourse and I will again provide three examples of this. Finally, I hold that the epicurean influence has been obscured by the rise of political economy, or more accurately by the idea that economic theory is distinct from the political and moreover is the primary way in which politics unfolds. This indicates the urgent relevance of the distinction between causality and instrumentality today.

There is no clearer way in which Epicurus articulates the distinction between causality and instrumentality than in an argument that he repeats twice, and which will appear utterly nonsensical without this distinction. The argument occurs at the end of his letter to Herodotus, and then again at the beginning of his letter to Pythocles. Epicurus considers the ethical and political effects of "meteorological" phenomena—that is, natural phenomena in the sky such as thunder or lightning. From a practical perspective, these phenomena have led people to "tumble into myth," that is, to impute gods who intervene to cause these phenomena out of nothing.[12] The symptoms of such an effect are angst and anguish, which detract from a happy life. For those phenomena that can affect our wellbeing but for which we do not have conclusive explanations, Epicurus urges us to impute multiple explanations that conform to our empirical observations, so long as divine interventions are not entertained. Of course, there is only one causal explanation for meteorological phenomena, but if we cannot

---

12. Diogenes Laertius, "Epicurus," in *Lives of Eminent Philosophers*, trans. R.D. Hicks (Cambridge, MA: Harvard University Press, 1931), X. 89.

find their cause, then we should not forget that our wellbeing is served by instrumental knowledge. Epicurus does not merely urge us to distinguish the *causality* of meteorological phenomena from the *instrumental* explanations that have the practical effect of helping us reduce the anxiety that such phenomena may otherwise cause. He also regards the instrumental as primary insofar as a theory of action (an ethics and a politics) affects more than theoretical knowledge, which explains why he regards phronesis as the most significant kind of knowledge (§7).[13]

The epicurean emphasis on instrumentality was so strong that it was aptly attacked in antiquity. For instance, Cicero disparages it as a mercenary value (*macello peti*).[14] However, such critiques did not deter the epicureans who explicitly built their political program on the instrumental ends of actions, which ultimately meant foregrounding the practical judgments that calculate our utility. This is clear in what their politics is opposed to, namely, any figure of theological or political authority whose actions consist in the attempt to suspend the judgment of others so as to consolidate power. The most powerful example of this concerns another meteorological phenomenon, the lack of wind in Aulis where the Greek army was gathered to sail across the Aegean to lay siege to Troy. As Lucretius recounts the story at the beginning of his first book of *De rerum natura*, General Agamemnon, with the aid of the priests, sought to assuage his restless troops by persuading them that the gods were angry with them and that they needed to sacrifice Iphigeneia, Agamemnon's own daughter, in order for the winds to blow again. Lucretius pours scorn on the exploitation of a natural phenomenon for the purposes of consolidating the authority of the army general and the priesthood.[15] The epicurean political project includes a relentless critique of those who seek to expand their authority by exploiting and distorting the relation between causality and instrumentality.

In addition, the source of human interaction and the political is, according to the epicureans, the practical judgment calculating the instrumental ends of action. We find this most clearly articulated in Hermarchus's account of the formation of the laws. Hermarchus was a major epicurean figure, the immediate successor to Epicurus as head of the Garden, and a prolific and influential writer himself. Unfortunately, all his works have

---

13. Laertius, "Epicurus," X. 132–33.
14. Cicero, *De Finibus Bonorum et Malorum*, trans. H. Rackham (Cambridge, MA: Harvard University Press, 1931), 2. 50.
15. Lucretius, *On the Nature of Things*, trans. W.H.D. Rouse, rev. Martin F. Smith (Cambridge, MA: Harvard University Press, 1924), 1. 80–101.

been lost, except for his account of social formation that was preserved in *De absentia*, a book written about half a millennium later by Porphyry.[16] In his account, Hermarchus argues that the law prohibits the murder of human beings, not because of any inherent moral reason, but because it is expedient or utilius (*sympheron*) for the society as a whole. Indeed, all laws operate for the utility of the society, and Hermarchus even entertains the idea that, if all members of a society could correctly calculate the utility of the community, then there would not be a need (in principle) for any laws.

The contrast with the Judaic insistence on the proscription of the law could not be starker—which is perhaps why the word "epicurean" in Hebrew became a synonym for the word atheist. But it was also the Christians who found unpalatable the epicurean position about instrumentality. Not only is the epicurean ethics and politics premised on instrumentality that is, according to Augustine and the other Christian fathers, the source of sin, but the materialist metaphysics of the epicureans is also stringently opposed to transcendence and insists on an anthropology according to which the soul perishes with the body. The Christians attacked the epicureans more fiercely than any other ancient school of philosophy and they destroyed or simply stopped copying the epicurean manuscripts in monastic libraries, whereby for centuries scholars in Europe had no access to epicurean texts other than through the secondary sources that had attacked them.[17]

You can imagine the excitement of the humanists, then, when Emmanuel Chrysoloras, a Byzantine scholar, brought Diogenes Laertius's *Lives of Philosophers* with him to Florence in the early fifteenth century. In book 10 of *Lives*, the humanists gained access to three letters by Epicurus and a collection of maxims, the so-called *Principal Doctrines*, summarizing Epicurus's philosophy. The text was promptly translated into Latin and published in Florence. Through serendipity, Poggio Bracciolini discovered around the same time a manuscript of Lucretius's *De rerum natura* that was also published in Florence soon after. Suddenly, the humanists had access to two major epicurean texts. Lucretius became incredibly popular for his beautiful poetry, as the humanists loudly proclaimed, as they did not want to be perceived as epicureans and end up burned at the stake like

---

16. Porphyry, *De l'abstinence*, ed. and trans. Jean Bouffartigue (Paris: Belles Letters, 1977), 1. 7–12.

17. A collection of all the writings about epicureanism from ancient and Christian sources was published in 1887, but a reprint is available today: Hermann Usener, ed., *Epicurea* (Cambridge: Cambridge University Press, 2010).

Giordano Bruno. For a time in Europe, only the Bible had more printed editions than *De rerum natura*.

Alison Brown's *The Return of Lucretius to Renaissance Florence* recounts the initial impact of epicureanism on Renaissance humanism in Florence, where both Lucretius and Epicurus were published in the 1430s.[18] Brown's account is significant because it stresses that, insofar as ethical theory is concerned, the Renaissance humanists were not so much interested in the so-called epicurean hedonism—the idea that "the end of action is pleasure"—with which the Christians had vehemently disparaged epicureanism for centuries. Rather, they were fascinated by the instrumentality of epicurean ethics, or the epicurean account of phronesis. To avoid confusion with the Stoic and Christian conception of phronesis as *prudentia*, they translated it instead as utility or as effectivity. Thus, Machiavelli's conception of the centrality of the "effective truth of the matter" for politics in chapter 15 of *The Prince* is symptomatic of the epicurean influence on the Florentines (§7).

Through the resurfacing of instrumentality, or the unforgetting of instrumentality effected by the rediscovery of epicureanism, the distinction between instrumentality and causality resurfaces as well. This distinction is a feature of Machiavelli's thought. For instance, we can understand the dialectic of fate and virtue—described in chapter 25 of *The Prince*—as his iteration of the distinction. Fate is when the river swells from heavy rain and floods with destructive effects. Fate, then, is the unfolding of natural causality. Virtue is the anticipation that there will be a flood every time there is heavy rain, and the taking of measures, such as building dams and canals to tame the force of the water. Virtue, then, is the instrumental reasoning that finds the appropriate means to contend with natural causality (§7).

In *Spinoza, the Epicurean* I argue that the distinction is also central in Spinoza, especially in the *Theological Political Treatise*. For example, in chapter 4 of the *Treatise* Spinoza draws the distinction between divine and human law according to how each contributes different ends to living. The divine law is necessary and concerns the end of achieving beatitude, whereas the human law is contingent and concerns the utility of the community as a whole. Following that, Spinoza's discussion of the formation of the law and of communities echoes Hermarchus's. Spinoza argues that laws are established for the utility (*perutilius*) of the people and are operative even

---

18. Alison Brown, *The Return of Lucretius to Renaissance Florence* (Cambridge, MA: Harvard University Press, 2010).

before they are written as statutes, as without the utility provided by laws "each would find strength and time fail him if he alone had to plough, sow, reap, grind, cook, weave, stitch and perform all the other numerous tasks to support life."[19] The source of social formation is the calculation of utility, that is, the kind of practical judgment that calculates the ends of action, or what Aristotle and Epicurus call phronesis.

It is significant to trace another transformation of phronesis in the modern vernacular languages. In early modernity, phronesis and its cognates signifying the instrumental end were translated into Latin in terms of *utilitas* and its cognates. By the eighteenth and nineteenth centuries a further translation takes place: utility is translated to the discourse of interest. Thus, Adam Smith avers in *Wealth of the Nations* that "it is not from the benevolence of the butcher, the brewer, or the baker, that we expect our dinner, but from their regard to their own interest."[20] The similarity of this passage to the passage from chapter 5 of Spinoza's *Theological Political Treatise* suggests that Smith is employing the same idea as Spinoza, namely, the distinction between causal and instrumental ends. The final ends of production—that is, the products of the labor of the butcher, the brewer, and the baker—are distinct from the instrumental ends of their actions or their interests.

Through the discourse of interest, the distinction between final and instrumental ends becomes an assumption in political economy, even though its sources in antiquity are not foregrounded and the distinction itself is never articulated in a succinct manner. But as soon as we are aware of the distinction, we will not fail to see how indispensable it is for materialists such as Marx. This is true for his theory of class struggle, as articulated for instance in the *Communist Manifesto*. The bourgeoisie and the proletariat participate in the same processes of production, and yet their interests clash. Marx insists that the distinction between the classes is not a static one that is established by their status. Rather, it is a dynamic one, articulated through their competing interests. In the vocabulary that I have been using here, the two classes are distinct at the level of their competing instrumental ends—not at the level of the ends of production. The same distinction between the ends of production and the ends of interest is also

---

19. Spinoza, *Theological-Political Treatise*, trans. Samuel Shirley (Indianapolis, IN: Hackett, 2001), 63.

20. Adam Smith, *An Inquiry into the Nature and Causes of the Wealth of Nations*, ed. W.P. Todd, in *The Glasgow Edition of the Works and Correspondence of Adam Smith*, vol. 2, ed. R.H Campbell and A.S. Skinner (Oxford: Oxford University Press, 1976), 26–27.

indispensable for the theory of value in Marx's *Capital*. Production value corresponds to the former, surplus value to the latter, and exchange value mediates their relation.

At this point, one may be tempted to say that the distinction between causal and instrumental ends makes its triumphant return via the conception of interest in political economy. Assuredly. But just as importantly, one should not overlook the fact that this success also led to its second forgetting in the philosophy of the twentieth century. The language of interest progressively becomes associated with economic interest assumed to be separated from and juxtaposed to the political.[21] The most brilliant articulation of this move is Albert Hirschman's *The Passions and the Interests* from the 1970s. Insofar as the term "interest" refers to instrumental ends, Hirschman's point about its parallel operation with the emotions is nothing but a restatement of the position about phronesis as discovered in book 6 of the *Nicomachean Ethics*. Insofar as the parallel operation of interests and passions is supposed to have a pacifying effect that relies on economic activity as opposed to the political, as Hirschman claims, then the conclusion is the opposite of the one reached by Aristotle and the entire tradition that I have been sketching in the present section.

Whereas the function of the instrumental end is to indicate an acting with that is constitutive of the political, its reformulation as economic interest is mobilized by neoliberalism to argue that instrumentality is separate from the political and confined instead to economic activity. This reversal of the import of the distinction between causal and instrumental ends, so as to repress the political, constitutes the most impactful achievement of neoliberalism. The neoliberal notion of economic interest as separate from the political is a second coming of instrumentality but in fact it is now like a zombie concept, bereft of the political that was its lifeblood in antiquity and in the underground current of a materialism of instrumentality.

* * *

After such a mapping of the terrain of the distinction between causality and instrumentality, it is possible to see what is at stake in Heidegger's mistake that effects the concealment of the instrumental end. This is not merely a mistake that forgets the history of the distinction between causality

---

21. For the importance of Austrian neoliberal thought on the severing of economic from political interest, see Quinn Slobodian, *Globalists: The End of Empire and the Birth of Neoliberalism* (Cambridge, MA: Harvard University Press, 2018).

and instrumentality as I have sketched it here. Further, it is not merely a mistake that traps Heidegger into the theory of action that characterizes onto-theo-logy, or the metaphysics of morals, as I call it. It traps also all those philosophers working within the phenomenological tradition broadly conceived and who follow Heidegger in repressing instrumentality. In addition, Heidegger's position effectively separates instrumentality from the political and thereby offers a prospective apologetic of the neoliberal separation of interest from the political. The political stakes in Heidegger's seemingly minor mistranslations of Aristotle in the 1920s could not be higher, given that Heidegger agrees with neoliberalism on the apolitical nature of instrumentality. In this sense, Heidegger is a major participant in what I called above the second forgetting of instrumentality—that is, the forgetting that takes place in modernity and which infects the philosophy working on the phenomenological tradition since the middle of the twentieth century.

From our current vantage point, we see the enormous significance of Heidegger's mistake that conflates causality and instrumentality. The significance consists in whether a monist, materialist philosophy wants to retain a social and political relevance or not. This can be translated into a straightforward choice: Will philosophy continue hiding behind a putative, mysterious being so as to persist with the repression of instrumentality, thereby offering an apologetic to the neoliberal rupture between instrumentality and the political? Or will philosophy work through the metaphysics of the repression of instrumentality, a task that requires *both* a reevaluation of the underground current of a materialism of instrumentality *and* the resistance to be triggered by concepts, such as the ineffectual, that trap thought in the ruse of techne? This choice that I have already noted (§2, §14, §17, and §29) is not merely about philosophical proclivities, but about whether philosophy after the "death of god" or after transcendence wants to have a theory of action that is relevant to the current ethical and political predicament.

4

The Concealment of Instrumentality
The Conception of Action in Being and Time

33. The reason for focusing on the examples of action in *Being and Time*

The reading of *Being and Time* that I will offer in this chapter departs from an observation about what is missing in the examples of action that Heidegger presents throughout his book.[1] Heidegger presents action only in terms of causality, never in terms of instrumentality. Symptomatic of this absence of instrumentality is that the examples tend to focus on the technical or productive function of action. More emphatically, when Heidegger refers to the ends of action, he conceals the instrumental ends within the causal ends. The concealment of instrumentality is the variation of the ruse of techne characteristic of *Being and Time*.

One may object that, even if that is true, still soon enough Heidegger will turn his attention to the pernicious effects of instrumentality in modernity. In the 1930s, such a concern with instrumentality becomes central to his writings that focus on the social and political effects of the "nihilism of modernity" that is marked by the dominating power of technoscience. Instead, the project of *Being and Time* consists in the dismantling of the epistemology of mere presence or the "destruction of metaphysics."

---

1. Martin Heidegger, *Being and Time*, trans. Joan Stambaugh (Albany: SUNY Press, 2010) = *GA* 2. All refences to *Being and Time* in this chapter are given parenthetically in the text, English followed by German edition pagination.

To such an objection I would respond that Heidegger's focus on instrumentality in the 1930s marks a different variation of the ruse of techne that I will examine in chapter 5. For now, I see the concealment of instrumentality within causality as the culmination of Heidegger's distinction between techne and phronesis that he adumbrated in *Plato's Sophist*. As we saw in chapter 3, Heidegger conflates causality and instrumentality in his reading of book 6 of *Nicomachean Ethics*. Heidegger's mistake— as I put it—in this conflation was the absorption by techne of all the ends of action. That is what allowed Heidegger to determine, first, theoretical knowledge as the virtue of techne, thereby overcoming the metaphysical separation of theory and praxis; and second, a separate action, phronesis, as free of all ends. However, this conflation of causality and instrumentality was still imbued in metaphysics. For example, by employing the craft analogy that fails to distinguish between the causality of action and natural causality (§27). To hide the metaphysical provenance of the conflation of causality and instrumentality, Heidegger employed the ruse that repressed instrumentality so as to be able to determine an action without effects and without ends (§29).

Through the concealment of instrumentality, *Being and Time* radicalizes the earlier position that sophia is the virtue of techne (§27). In Division 1 of *Being and Time*, Heidegger shows how the metaphysical separation of theory and praxis is untenable because the technical use of equipment precedes theoretical knowledge. To put this in the vocabulary of *Plato's Sophist*, Heidegger is arguing now that techne is the virtue of sophia (§42). The action without ends that in the lecture course from 1924 Heidegger described as phronesis is thematized in *Being and Time* as the being-toward-death that, according to Heidegger, is an impossible possibility in the sense that no one experiences one's own physical death (§41). Thus, the temporality of being-toward-death is distinct from the temporality of the use of equipment since, strictly speaking, it has no end. The "end" of authenticity marked by the temporality of being-toward-death is only ever supposed to be internal, that is, about the being of Dasein, and hence without effects and without external ends.

This radicalization of the earlier position in *Being and Time* is only possible because of the trick, indicative of the use of the ruse of techne, to conceal instrumentality within causality. I will present here the three elements of the ruse, corresponding to the three areas denoted by techne, namely, monism (§§34–35), technology (§§36–40), and the action without ends (§§41–42). I will do so by focusing on the examples that Heidegger uses, such as the motto from Plato's *Sophist* about the forgetting of the single, unified being; or the famous example of the hammer; and the equally famous example of the myth of Care. In all these examples, the action is described as the final end of causality, characteristic of techne as craft or productive activity. But by concealing the instrumental ends of action within causality can Heidegger's determination of action retain any social and political significance? Is it possible to reconcile the concealing of instrumental ends with a consideration of the intersubjective impact of Dasein's action? Or to phrase the problem I am highlighting in the account of action in *Being and Time* in terms of the problematic of monism that I described in chapter 2, is Heidegger able to provide an account of action that is not merely an inconsequential modification of the single, unified being?

34. The epigraph and the problem of action in the *Sophist*

It is commonly held that Heidegger aimed in *Being and Time* to overcome metaphysics by dismantling its dualist epistemology exemplified in the Cartesian separation of subject and object. That is how Heidegger himself appears to present his project in §6 and §§19–21 of *Being and Time*. A key component of such a project is the overcoming of the traditional notion of the subject as opposed to the object, whose foundation is the designation of the subject as Dasein, the being for which its own being is a concern, which echoes the description of phronesis in *Plato's Sophist*.[2]

As Étienne Balibar has observed, the problem with such a conception of the project of *Being and Time* is not only that the notion of the subject as independent of the object is absent from Descartes; moreover the notion of the subject is also entrenched in the social and political determination of human action.[3] What remains inchoate in Balibar's criticism is the problematic of action in Heidegger's monism (§§11–13). Monism finds it difficult to account for difference in action, since all actions may appear to be modifications of the single, unified being. Dismissing Cartesian dualism is, at the same time, an affirmation of the monism of the single, unified being and as always monism has to contend with how to make actions matter.

This problematic of action in monism is inscribed at the very beginning of *Being and Time*. The book starts with an epigraph from Plato's *Sophist*

---

2. See Franco Volpi, "*Being and Time:* A 'Translation' of the *Nicomachean Ethics*?" in *Reading Heidegger from the Start: Essays in his Earliest Thought*, ed. Theodore Kiel and John van Buren, trans. John Protevi (Albany: SUNY Press, 1994), 195–211.

3. Étienne Balibar, *Citizen Subject: Foundation for Philosophical Anthropology*, trans. Steven Miller (New York: Fordham University Press, 2017), 19–39.

244a, that is, the text that Heidegger turned to in early 1925, immediately after lecturing on Aristotle's phronesis for close to three months as part of the *Plato's Sophist* course. The epigraph is part of an exordium that sets up the question of the book, namely, that we no longer have an answer to the question of being, just as noted in the *Sophist*. The task of *Being and Time* then is to raise anew the question of being.

Even though Heidegger does not note in his exordium the context within which the epigraph occurs in the *Sophist*, it is instructive to recall it as it leads straight to the problematic of action within monism. The dialogue starts with two of Socrates's students, Theodorus and Theaetetus, bringing to him a stranger from Elea. Soon they choose the topic of their conversation: the distinction between the sophist, the philosopher, and the statesman. Socrates probes the Eleatic stranger by asking him whether his school regards these as one, or two, or three distinct kinds of activity (217a).

The question that Socrates asks may seem nonsensical unless we recall the stranger's background. Elea is the place where Parmenides taught. The stranger is a Parmenidean. And, as we know, Parmenides defended the most extreme form of monism in antiquity by insisting that only being exists, or that nothing does not exist, or that being is one. Within this context, the question that Socrates asks refers to the problematic that I described earlier (§12): As soon as one posits a single, unified being, then it becomes difficult to demarcate an essential difference between actions. If there is only one being, which also suggests an identity of thought and action (§50), then should a Parmenidean have to assert that the actions of the sophist, the philosopher, and the statesman are mere modifications of that one being? Socrates's question frames the *Sophist* on the problematic of action that has challenged monism since antiquity.

The passage that Heidegger cites as the epigraph for *Being and Time*, occurs in response to this problem of how to differentiate between actions in monism. The Eleatic stranger guides Theaetetus through a succession of Rebelaiseque distinctions in an attempt to define the sophist.[4] These distinctions take up about half the dialogue in one of the most mischievous passages in Plato's work.[5] Instead of defining anything like the one being

---

4. For a more extensive discussion of Plato's *Sophist* and Heidegger's treatment of it, see Dimitris Vardoulakis, "Why Ancient Monism Matters Today: Heidegger and Plato's Sophist," *Review of Metaphysics* 77, no. 2 (2023): 299–326.

5. The proliferation of distinctions is also evident in the *Statesman*, which is set the day after the *Sophist* and whose main character is again the Eleatic stranger. But the *Statesman* is still not as exaggerated as the *Sophist*. It is notable that Plato has a propensity

of Parmenides, the distinctions proliferate a bewildering multiplicity of traits that would surely have made poor Theaetetus crave the less painful Socratic maieutic method.

Eventually, they reach a serious point when the Eleatic stranger and Theaetetus agree that the sophist is one who deals with fantasies that are lies referring to nonexistent things. But if nothing does not exist in Eleatic monism, then the monist lapses into self-contradiction when he claims that the sophist deals with nonexistent fantasies or lies. If we say that he is simply propagating nonexistent lies (ψευδῆ τολμήσαντας εἰπεῖν, 241a), the sophist will respond that we attribute to him nonbeing (τῷ γὰρ μὴ ὄντι τὸ ὄν προσάπτειν, 241a–b), which contradicts the monist position that nothing does not exist, or that being does not admit of negation (§11). In considering the implications of this difficulty, the Eleatic stranger delivers the passage used for the epigraph of *Being and Time*, according to which the question of being is not properly raised.

The key to the Eleatic stranger's solution to this problem is that actions are not distinguished according to a predetermined essence but rather depending on how they are oriented toward being. This is consonant with Heidegger's approach in *Being and Time*. No sooner does he determine the priority of existence over essence in chapter 1 than he underscores how this entails that the human or Dasein is a being for which being itself is an issue. In such a framework, Dasein is never objectively present but rather disclosed through what it can possibly do *("Dasein wesenhaft je seine Möglichkeit ist,"* 42/57). And Dasein has two essential possibilities, or there are two "Seinsmodi"—authenticity and inauthenticity (42/57). Authenticity and inauthenticity describe different actions depending on how they are oriented toward being, the criterion being whether the actions have external ends (§36).

In a sense, this adds nothing new to what we saw in *Plato's Sophist*. Still, instead of relying on exegesis, Heidegger investigates the single, unified being through a phenomenological analysis of experience. The principle that regulates this analysis is, following the epigraph, the forgetting of being. The task, then, is to undo this forgetting, which also means destroying the metaphysical tradition so as to construct a new sense of temporality "as a possible horizon for any understanding of being whatsoever" (1/1).

---

to treat Eleatic monism with mischief. See Mehmet Tabak, *Plato's* Parmenides *Reconsidered* (New York: Palgrave Macmillan, 2015).

35. Destruction and monism

The figure of destruction was a common topos in the first quarter of the twentieth century. Every modernist avant-garde movement of the time proclaimed a certain destruction. From Dadaism to Futurism, radical modernists sought to outdo themselves in their proclamations for destruction, advocating diverse aims such as the dismantling of representation, or the demolition of museums and the substitution of paintings with machines. "Out with the old, in with the new" was the mantra of this avant-garde obsession with destruction. Heidegger's call for a destruction of the tradition has been interpreted as such a call to leave the past behind, especially early on, such as in the important *Heidegger und die Tradition* by Werner Marx, first published in 1961.[6]

An attentive reading of the Introduction of *Being and Time* makes it clear that the modernist conception of a wholesale destruction of the past is far from Heidegger's mind. Destruction is intertwined with temporality: "destruction sees itself assigned the task of interpreting the foundation of ancient ontology in light of the problematic of temporality [*Temporalität*]" (24/32). That is why "destruction, taken as a task, is the prior and necessary step before the foundation: the latter is the analytic of Dasein in the horizon of temporality."[7] Destruction, then, is the way in which the question of being as single and unified (that is, the question of monism) is retrieved so as to be placed in the new framework of an analysis in terms of time. Monism as temporality—that is the thrust of the call to destruction. Far from an abandonment of the past, this is a call for a revival of the essential in the tradition, namely, the question of the single, unified being that has been obscured or "forgotten" (2/3) through its refraction into inessential questions.

Significantly, early in §1 of *Being and Time*, Aristotle is singled out as having understood "the unity" (2/4) of being as distinct from its manifold manifestation in beings. This indicates that Heidegger is calling for a destruction, not of tradition as such, but rather of the forgetting of the single, unified being in onto-theo-logy. Thus, as Sean Kirkland argues, destruction is a method in which the figure of Aristotle looms large.[8] This makes

---

6. For the English translation, see Werner Marx, *Heidegger and the Tradition*, trans. Theodore Kisiel and Murray Greene (Evanston, IL: Northwestern University Press, 1971).

7. Dominique Janicaud and Jean-François Mattéi, *Heidegger: From Metaphysics to Thought*, trans. Michael Gendre (Albany: SUNY Press, 1995), 3.

8. Sean Kirkland, *The Destruction of Aristotle: Reading the Tradition with the Early Heidegger* (Evanston, IL: Northwestern University Press, 2021).

sense as soon as we note the continuity of the question of action in monism between *Plato's Sophist* and *Being and Time*.

Even though the figure of destruction predates Heidegger's discovery of the importance of phronesis in resolving the problematic of action in monism, still destruction resonates from the very beginning of *Being and Time* with one key characteristic of phronesis, namely, the possibility of an action whose criteria of evaluation are provided through its own enactment (§§21–22). Andrew Barash traces Heidegger's first significant use of destruction to his review of Karl Jaspers's *Psychology of Worldviews*.[9] In this review, Heidegger conducts a critique of both neo-Kantianism and Husserl because they seek a theoretical foundation separate from life and as the ground of experience. Heidegger opposes such "life philosophy" because experience ought "not to be judged according to nonexperiential concepts." Barash clarifies further: "Heidegger emphasized that, rather than to reach outside the evidence of factical experience to grasp absolute standards of judgment, one had to remain faithful to the factical character of experience recalcitrant to such standards."[10] An important consequence follows from the kind of experience whose understanding does not rely on any external criteria or theoretical knowledge: "To grasp this primordial sense of experience, critical analysis had to begin from presuppositions or 'preconceptions' flowing from that experience."[11] Experience does not have external criteria or a theoretical foundation, but it also does not unfold in a vacuum.

This suggests a double temporal register of destruction. On the one hand, time is the time of Dasein's experience. On the other hand, time is also the tradition. The two times are intertwined: "Dasein not only has the inclination to be entangled in the world in which it is and to interpret itself in terms of that world by its reflected light; at the same time Dasein is also entangled in a tradition which it more or less explicitly grasps. This tradition deprives Dasein of its own leadership in questioning and choosing" (20/28–29). Destruction, then, effects a double response due to the dual temporal register of the experience in the world and the weight of the tradition. Destruction has to respond to the prejudices that prevent Dasein from the disclosure of its being in experience, and to the forgetting of being in the philosophical tradition.

---

9. Heidegger's review can be found in *Pathmarks*, ed. William McNeill (Cambridge: Cambridge University Press, 1998) = *GA* 9. The review was shared with Jaspers, but it was not published at the time.
10. Andrew Barash, *Martin Heidegger and the Problem of Historical Meaning* (New York: Fordham University Press, 2003), 103.
11. Barash, *Martin Heidegger and the Problem of Historical Meaning*, 103.

36. Inauthentic, indifferent, and authentic action

To destroy is a transitive verb, which means that destruction requires activity. Heidegger distinguishes between two fundamentally different kinds of activity, depending on whether they are driven by ends. Only action without ends can accomplish destruction and thus arrive at the single, unified being. This is the kind of action that Heidegger calls authenticity. By contrast, inauthenticity cannot accomplish the destruction because it is an end-oriented activity. But, Heidegger notes, "the inauthenticity of Dasein does not signify a 'lesser' being or a 'lower' degree of being [*nicht etwa ein 'weniger' Sein oder einen 'niedrigeren' Seinsgrad*]" (42/57). If being is one and there is no outside being, that is, so long as Heidegger espouses a monist position, he cannot distinguish between authenticity and inauthenticity as *qua* being as such. Rather, Heidegger draws a qualitative distinction between actions, depending on whether they have an end.

This is the solution to the problematic of monism in action that Heidegger faced with the adoption of a single, unified being (§§13–14) and which he worked out in the exegesis of Aristotle as part of *Plato's Sophist* (§§24–26). In *Being and Time*, the qualitative distinction between end-oriented actions and actions without end provides the organizing principle of the text, the former corresponding to the analysis of inauthenticity in Division 1 and the latter to authenticity in Division 2. I will concentrate for the moment on Division 1 where inauthenticity is the transformation of the concept of techne that Heidegger develops in *Plato's Sophist*, before turning to authenticity (§§41–42) to see how phronesis is also transformed in *Being and Time*.

The fundamental feature of techne in *Plato's Sophist* was its designation as a modality of theoretical knowledge. Designating sophia as a virtue of techne Heidegger hoped to have found a way to bridge the central binary organizing metaphysics, namely, the gap between theory and praxis (§27). To put the same point in terms of the destruction of the forgetting of being in metaphysics, Heidegger needed to show how inauthenticity is the kind of activity that can account for theoretical knowledge in conjunction with activity. Heidegger accomplishes this with the invention of one of the most powerful concepts in *Being and Time*, the concept of the world. The term "world" signifies where action takes place. It is the *totality* of the setting of action. This enables a series of important determinations.

First, the world is intertwined with being. This means that the world retains something of the mystery of being that can never be grasped in its totality (§14). Or, as is stated at the very beginning of *Being and Time*, "an enigma lies a priori in every relation and being toward beings as beings" (3/6). Thus, monism is inscribed in the notion of the world. Consequently, the destruction of the forgetting of being is a positive task as it forms new worlds. It is, as Gerhard Richter puts it, world-opening.[12]

Second, this provides the methodological framework of *Being and Time*, Heidegger's specific conception of phenomenology:

> One speaks of "appearances of symptoms of illness." What is meant by this are occurrences in the body that show themselves and in this self-showing as such "indicate" something that does *not* [*Nicht*] show itself. When such occurrences emerge, their self-showing coincides with the presence [*Vorhandensein*] of disturbances that do not show themselves. Appearance, as the appearance "of something," thus precisely does *not* mean that something shows itself; rather, it means that something which does not show itself announces itself through something that does show itself [*sondern das Sichmelden von etwas, das sich nicht zeigt, durch etwas, was sich zeigt*]. Appearing is a *not showing itself* [*Erscheinen ist ein* Sich-nicht-zeigen]. But this "not" must by no means be confused with the privative not. (27–28/39)

The last sentence is the key. Appearance, like being, does not admit of negation (§11), whereby it is placed within a monist framework. This entails that an appearance is never exhausted in what appears. The phenomenon is never self-contained. It has no completeness, which means that there is no experience complete in itself, but also there is no mental state or theoretical insight grounding the experience so that it can be understood completely. Since the monist framework means that the "negativity" of experience is not—underscores Heidegger—a privative negativity, in fact, registers being in its unity and multiplicity, a point that Heidegger develops elsewhere such as in *Introduction to Metaphysics*.

Third, such a concept of the world admits that material reality can be approached either as mere presence (*Vorhandenheit*) that effectively separates theory and praxis, whereby it falsely attempts to occlude the understanding of the world; or, in terms of the network of use that the world offers (*Zuhandenheit*), which understands the world as a totality of useful relations that can never be completed. This is a fundamental distinction in Division 1 of *Being and Time* because it indicates that end-oriented activity can either be on the right path toward being even if it does not attain its disclosure, or it can be profoundly disoriented away from being. This allows for three fundamental modalities of experience: "Dasein exists always in

---

12. Gerhard Richter, *This Great Allegory: On World-Decay and World-Opening in the Work of Art* (Cambridge, MA: MIT Press, 2022).

one of these modes [of authenticity and inauthenticity], or else in the modal indifference [*Indifferenz*] to them" (53/71).

The relation between inauthenticity and indifference has caused much confusion.[13] But the point of this distinction is straightforward if viewed as an attempt to qualitatively distinguish between actions depending on whether action includes ends or not. Heidegger cannot distinguish between actions directly as this will amount to introducing negation within the single, unified being (§13). So, the distinction is drawn according to whether action is end oriented. But as part of being, all action needs to have the possibility of attaining to its unconcealment. That is why Heidegger needs a further distinction within end-oriented actions: those that are on the path to being even though they cannot attain it, and those that are completely misdirected (§14).

Inauthenticity, insofar as it deals with the world in terms of a network of use (*Zuhandenheit*), has the potential to become authentic and disclose being. There is indeed an element of truth in inauthenticity (§42). Heidegger marks this connection through the resonance between care (*Sorge*) as the key comportment of Dasein in relation to being, which is etymologically connected to, and phonetically resonates with, *Besorgen*, the taking care of things characteristic of inauthenticity (§§40–41). Indifference, by contrast, is the activity that requires a separation between theory and praxis because it assumes the possibility of theoretical knowledge of objects that are independent of an indifferent observer, that is, it starts with objective presence (*Vorhandenheit*). Thus, indifference is the distinctive feature of the scientific attitude that attempts to occlude knowledge and which the epistemology of *Being and Time* wants to overcome since it cannot attain to the truth of being (§42).

The contention that I am making here is that the truth of being, or aletheia, is inseparable from the way that action is related to the world. Even though I am not aware of another scholar who puts this point in terms of the problematic of action in monism, still my contention is not incompatible with works such as Daniel Dahlstrom's *Heidegger's Concept of Truth*.[14] This book is the most comprehensive study of Heidegger's conception of truth and its key thesis is that Heidegger opposes the "logical prejudice," the practice in logic that occludes thinking. Dahlstrom masterfully navigates between the idea that truth is a property of the statement,

---

13. Robert J. Dostal, "The Problem of '*Indifferenz*' in *Sein und Zeit*," *Philosophy and Phenomenological Research* 43, no. 1 (1982): 43–58.

14. Daniel O. Dahlstrom, *Heidegger's Concept of Truth* (Cambridge: Cambridge University Press, 2001).

which is commensurate with the practice of indifference; the hermeneutics of facticity that leads to inauthentic accounts of truth; and authenticity that leads to disclosure. We can discover, then, in Dahlstrom the three orientations of action to truth that I have been highlighting as well. The difference is that, because Dahlstrom does not acknowledge the connection with the problematic of action in monism, he also does not recognize the qualitative distinction between actions that are end-oriented and those that are not. Hence, he misses the concealment of instrumentality in *Being and Time* and remains blind to the ruse of techne.

Fourth, the concept of the world suggesting the three conceptions of action that I have highlighted—inauthentic, indifferent, and authentic—organizes Heidegger's discourse beyond *Being and Time*. This concerns both Heidegger and the reception of his thought. We can discern the importance of this distinction in *The Fundamental Concepts of Metaphysics*, the lecture course from the winter semester of 1929 that develops the theme of the world from *Being and Time*. Heidegger expands the concept of the world beyond Dasein's totality of reference by explaining that "the stone is worldless, the animal is poor in world, the human is world-forming."[15] Several philosophers have observed how difficult it is to police the boundary between the lack of a world, being poor in the world, and Dasein as world-forming.[16] Roland Végső pushes this critique to its limit by arguing that "worldlessness is the disavowed centre of contemporary thought."[17] Other philosophers defend Heidegger's notion of the world on the grounds that it does not reduce reality to the operation of causes and effects characteristic of the technoscientific approach of the world. Thus, Markus Gabriel, working within a Heideggerian framework, argues that world as an objective presence does not exist because it can never be completely thematized.[18]

In all these discourses, there is one obvious point that is missing—Heidegger's world concerns action. An inanimate object, like the stone, is worldless because it cannot act. That is why science can take it as mere presence and study the laws of nature that determine it, such as the collision

---

15. Martin Heidegger, *The Fundamental Concepts of Metaphysics: World, Finitude, Solitude*, trans. William McNeill and Nicholas Walker (Bloomington: Indiana University Press, 1995) = GA 29/30, 185/ 273; cf. 177/ 263.

16. See for example, Jacques Derrida, *The Beast and the Sovereign*, vol. 2, trans. Geoffrey Bennington (Chicago: University of Chicago Press, 2011).

17. Roland Végső, *Worldlessness After Heidegger: Phenomenology, Psychoanalysis, Deconstruction* (Edinburgh: Edinburgh University Press, 2020), 5.

18. Markus Gabriel, *Why the World Does Not Exist*, trans. Gregory S. Moss (Cambridge: Polity Press, 2015).

between material objects like stones explained by the laws of gravity. Animals are poor in the world because the environment in which they act has a certain regularity that provides them with ends outside their control, like the final ends of techne. Heidegger uses the example of bees. They have a certain capacity to sense, to communicate, and to move. This capacity is delimited by causality whereby it can be studied by science. But in this case it is not the mathematical certainty of physics, but rather the study of bees by the biological sciences that presuppose the bees' use of their environment. This is not the case where the world of Dasein is concerned because—as we saw earlier—its world remains an enigma. This offers the human the possibility to mold its world through its actions.

Indifference, inauthenticity, and authenticity cannot be reduced to epistemology because they are actions. As actions—and that is the strong point that I am making—Heidegger presents them within a monism framework that requires the qualitative distinction between those actions that are end-oriented, either because they present the world as matter that is passively submitted to the laws of nature whereby it can be studied by an indifferent observer, or because they present the world in terms of the uses made possible in its totality of reference; and those actions that are without effects because they have no ends external to them, or what Heidegger calls authenticity. Recognizing that Heidegger is referring to actions matters because we can then ask: Is there something in action that Heidegger fails to consider in the way that he draws the qualitative distinction between inauthenticity, indifference, and authenticity? As soon as we ask this question, the answer suddenly appears self-evident: what Heidegger conceals in the way that he constructs his typology of action is instrumentality. Just as techne absorbed all ends of action in *Plato's Sophist*, similarly in *Being and Time* and the courses that immediately follow there is a qualitatively distinct category of activities that includes all ends to action, and in addition, these ends are only ever described as causal ends. Heidegger systematically and methodically conceals the instrumental ends of action.

37. Hammering and the concealing of instrumentality (*Being and Time* §15)

Following *Plato's Sophist*, Heidegger offered the course *History of the Concept of Time* in the summer semester of 1925.[19] The bulk of the course reads

---

19. Martin Heidegger, *History of the Concept of Time: Prolegomena*, trans. Theodore Kisiel (Bloomington: Indiana University Press, 1985) = *GA* 20.

as a first draft of Division 1 of *Being and Time*. Heidegger decided immediately after *Plato's Sophist* that the part of the argument that needed the most development concerned the idea that sophia is the virtue of techne. Or, differently put, Heidegger realized that he needed to work out the details of end-oriented action.

Hubert Dreyfus expresses the epistemological impetus for the use characteristic of end-oriented action in *Being and Time*: "Heidegger's examples start with involved acting in the world, using things such as hammers and doorknobs. Heidegger seeks to demonstrate that what is thus revealed is exactly the opposite of what Descartes and Husserl claim. Rather than first perceiving perspectives, then synthesizing the perspectives into objects, and finally assigning these objects a function on the basis of their physical properties, we ordinarily manipulate tools that already have a meaning in a world that is organized in terms of purposes."[20] The end-oriented action that uses tools is intertwined with knowledge, but this knowledge is not thematized, it is not theoretical—scientific knowledge comes after use (§§42–43). It is knowledge given within the relations of one's environment, the totality of which constitutes Dasein's world. This already suggests that use as described in *Being and Time*—much like techne in *Plato's Sophist*—bridges the gap between theory and praxis and works toward the undoing of the forgetting of being in metaphysics.

Heidegger calls "circumspection" the kind of knowledge whose activity is characteristic of the use of tools and bridges the gap between theory and praxis, thereby unraveling metaphysical conceptions of knowledge. Circumspection corresponds to different modalities of action. The most developed modality of practice characteristic of inauthenticity is *Besorgen*, which we can translate as dealing with, attending to, or taking care of. It indicates "to have to do with something, to produce, order and take care of something, to use something, to give something up and let it get lost, to undertake, to accomplish, to find out, to ask about, to observe, to speak about, to determine" (57/76). These are end-oriented activities where the activity "subordinates itself to the in-order-to constitutive for the particular tool in our dealings" (69/93). Consequently, their end is independent of the activity itself. They belong, then, to techne as Heidegger extrapolated it in his reading of book 6 of *Nicomachean Ethics*.

Inauthenticity determines the ends of actions in terms of their final ends, such as the final ends of craft. This *conceals* all instrumental ends of action.

---

20. Hubert L. Dreyfus, *Being-in-the-World: A Commentary on Heidegger's* Being and Time, *Division 1* (Cambridge, MA: MIT Press, 1991), 46–47.

This move is useful for Heidegger because it demonstrates how knowledge presupposes praxis, whereby knowledge cannot be understood in terms of the cognitive capacity of an indifferent observer. But the price that Heidegger has to pay for this move is that without the instrumental ends of action the end-oriented actions that he describes are abstracted from their social and political context. Thus, the world becomes an empty shell and the action appears trivial or vacuous. Let us see how this plays out in the famous example of the hammer.

In *Being and Time*, Heidegger describes activities that engage with their environment in terms of use tools to achieve certain ends. In such activities, Dasein is *immersed* in its world. In such an immersion, objects are in a network of useful relations (*Zuhandenheit*) that employ tools toward certain ends. "There 'is' no such thing as *a* useful thing" (68/92), because the activity concerns "a totality of useful things [*eine Zeugganzheit*]" (68/93). That is what Heidegger calls *Besorgen* or taking care of things. In §15 of *Being and Time*, Heidegger offers hammering as an example of such an action:

> Actions geared to useful things, which show themselves genuinely only in such actions, for example, hammering with the hammer, neither *grasps* these beings thematically as occurring things, nor does such using even know the structure of useful things as such. Hammering does not just have a knowledge of the useful character of the hammer; rather, it has appropriated this utensil in the most adequate way possible. In such useful actions, taking care [*das Besorgen*] subordinates itself [*unterstellt sich*] to the in-order-to constitutive for the particular tool in our actions [*für das jeweilige Zeug konstitutiven Umzu*]; the less we just stare at the thing called hammer, the more we take hold of it and use it [*zugreifender es gebraucht wird*], the more original [*ursprünglicher*] our relation to it becomes and the more undisguisedly [*unverhüllter*] it is encountered as what it is, as a useful thing. The act of hammering itself discovers the specific "handiness" [*Handlichkeit*] of the hammer. (68–69/93)

The description of the network of useful relations or handiness appears initially compelling. It describes something that we all experience in our everyday lives. This is the fact that we are not actively aware of our actions when we use things or when we are involved in processes of production. As soon as one starts focusing too much on how to use the hammer, the hammering activity becomes harder.

Another example would be skills such as driving. A competent driver does not think about changing gears when a sharp turn is coming up, she does not make a mental list of pros and cons before pressing the brake pedal when a child jumps in front of the car, and, unlike the computer of a self-driving car, a competent driver does not calculate steering all the time but simply "does" it. Heidegger claims that we are immersed in a network of useful relations when we act in our world toward certain useful or productive ends—immersed to such an extent that we are not even aware of our acting. This provides a "prethematic" kind of experience that reveals a certain truth about the being in question—such as hammering or driving.

This description of hammering is pivotal in Heidegger's destruction of metaphysics. If metaphysics assumes that there is theory independent of praxis, then hammering demonstrates that praxis precedes, and cannot be separated from, theory. This is sufficient to unsettle the epistemology of metaphysics. Significantly, the end of this praxis, the *Um-zu* as Heidegger puts it, is only ever amenable to the final end of causality, not to the provisional end of instrumentality. By focusing on production, which requires ends external to it, that is, the final ends of causality, the hammer example shows that causality absorbs within it the instrumental ends of action. This is the distinctive form of the conflation of causality and instrumentality that we find in *Being and Time*. The description provided by Heidegger leaves no room for the parallel function of both causal and instrumental ends. It is such a parallel function that is distinctive of the monist materialist theory of action (§7, §14, §22, and §32).

More specifically, I contend that a materialist monist would describe hammering as having two distinct ends, both of which can be a matter of praxis as it unfolds in a network of useful relations. From such a perspective, *Zuhandenheit* would require another layer to account for action in a framework that refutes the superiority of theory. If it is a premental state to pick up the hammer to put a nail in the wall, it is also premental whether that hammering is done as part of a Sunday morning house maintenance activity. When I do small tasks at home, I know what needs to be done to maintain my world within my household. I do not need to make a detailed plan to know that hanging the new picture will promote a sense of domestic well-being because it brightens the empty wall. These instrumental ends do not need to be thought and calculated explicitly as they are part of the world of the hammering subject just as much as the technical end of hammering.[21] Such instrumental ends are necessary, because without them there is no explanation as to why I might bother to pick up the hammer on a Sunday morning instead of staying in bed or going to the beach, but

---

21. See Ian H. Angus, *Technique and Enlightenment: Limits of Instrumental Reason* (Lanham, MD: University Press of America, 1984).

they are not reducible to anything like a phenomenological conception of intentionality, as they are premental. Without the instrumental ends, the account of action excludes its social and political dimensions, and this impoverishes the account of action.

The instrumental ends of our action are socially constructed while simultaneously constructing further social relations (§30). Ignoring them amounts to hiding the social, ethical, and political context of action. The technical and the instrumental work in parallel. My first car had a faulty gearbox and I knew that it was hard to put into the second gear. I developed techniques to counter that. For instance, if there was a green light at a busy intersection, I might persist in first gear and then go straight to third. That was the techne of driving an old, secondhand car that I could afford. But I was happy with that car as it gave me the mobility that I previously lacked, helping me realize my instrumental ends. Both the technical and the instrumental ends were present in my driving and I was not fully aware of either—they were both premental while I was driving. But the technical ends were insufficient to describe the social and economic aspects of my driving. The instrumental ends of my actions were also needed.

Now, imagine that there was a guy next to me at the traffic light who obtained his license at the same time as me but whose father bought him a brand-new BMW. He might also have aimed to go from first to third gear, but this same technique had very different instrumental ends. For him, it was a matter of enjoyment, of jumping ahead of the traffic at the green light, of getting pleasure out of his sports car. We may have both gone from first to third gear without thinking about it, just as in the example of hammering. But we also did not think about how different social and economic conditions led to the same technique. Such social and economic conditions can only be phenomenologically described if we resist abstracting the instrumental ends from the experience of changing gears, that is, by resisting the concealment of instrumentality of Heidegger's conception of circumspection.

Take another example: a craftsman who is hammering and shaping marble. Let us suppose that the craftsman is a famous sculptor, like Pheidias—who was Aristotle's example (in *Nicomachean Ethics* 1141a) for the Athenians saying that sophia is a virtue of techne (§27). We can imagine all sorts of instrumental ends as part of Pheidias's hammering the piece of marble that was to be formed into the statue of Athena in the Parthenon. Achieving recognition and fame as a sophos or wise sculptor could be one of them. Becoming an example in a famous philosopher's treatise could be another. Such instrumental ends are not "owned" by Pheidias, but they can arise within the social context that recognizes his art as great. Thus, the Athenians may have offered him the commission because they may have thought that his art would increase the prestige of the Parthenon. We can imagine also mundane ends in his everyday conduct in his studio, such as extracting the best of his assistants through means such as being nice or threatening to them. Without the instrumental ends, the hammering activity of Pheidias is cut loose from the social, economic, and political relations that made it possible in the first instance for him to obtain the commission for Athena's statue or for its successful completion.

Heidegger is focused on the hammer in the hand. Hammering becomes a practical action that demonstrates that, when the Dasein is in a state of attending to ends by using tools, the equipment used disappears from view and becomes invisible in the course of hammering. But, as if by a conjuring trick, Heidegger conceals that the hammering is not concerned only with the ends that pertain to the product of the action and the technical use of the tool. They are also intertwined with another realm of ends that are instrumental, which are also invisible and prethematic or premental. The two ends—the ends of techne and the instrumental ends—work alongside each other. Concealing the instrumental ends of action amounts to removing the object of its social context—that is, destroying the social, economic, legal, ethical, and political aspects of Dasein's world. The ruse makes all ends of action final but remains trapped within an abstracted description of action that offers an impoverished framework to grasp acting, because Dasein is *indifferent* to the social and political structure of its world.

38. The breakdown of ends (*Being and Time* §16)

Is it perhaps possible, according to *Being and Time*, to discover the social, ethical and political dimension of end-oriented action when we become aware of it? This is not the case. In §16, Heidegger describes how we notice the ends of our actions when the use of tools is disrupted, preventing them from reaching their final ends. He describes three kinds of disruption. First, a tool can become unusable (the head of the hammer falls off); second, a tool may be missing (for example, the hammer is lost in the mess of the workshop); and third, something gets in the way (a sore shoulder prevents the hand from hammering). All the forms of disruption that Heidegger describes indicate a breakdown of final ends of action, still concealing the instrumental ends, whereby the social and political fields also remain obscured.

We do not think about it when we drive a car. A car is part of the network of useful relations (*Zuhandenheit*) that make driving an immersive experience. We become aware of the car when something breaks down (there is a flat tire); something is missing (oops, I forgot to fill the gas tank); or something intervenes (traffic delays). Heidegger explains that such breakdowns bring to the fore the objective presence of the tools in the midst of their use in a network of useful relations (73/99): "the surrounding world announces itself [*meldet sich die Umwelt*]" in the action of the Dasein (74/101). Key to this description of the dominance of objective presence in the disruption of the final end of action is that, as soon as the cause of the breakdown is rectified, we revert back to the immersive experience as described with the example of hammering (74/100).

What is common to all these examples is that the disruption of use is registered through the breakdown of the final end of action. We know the final end, even if we are not actively thinking about it while acting. Then the world intervenes to disrupt that end, which is independent of our actions. If the tire is flat, or if we run out of gas, or if there is a traffic jam, we will not be able to reach our end destination. In all these cases, the end is the final end of techne that is independent of the action. The concealment of instrumentality persists in the description of how we become aware of tools when they break down. This has two important effects. The breakdown of the ends as the constitutive feature of a tool that is wrenched away from the network of useful relations and transported to mere presence resembles more the function of a robot than a human. Further, such a description forecloses any social and political implications to action. Let me provide an illustration of each of these points.

An intriguing theme resurfaces in Gary Kasparov's *Deep Thinking* that concerns the breakdown of a computer.[22] The book is Kasparov's account of his matches against Deep Blue, the computer that beat him when he was the world chess champion. This was a historic moment for AI because of the symbolic significance of a machine beating the best human chess player, which had been taken as standard proof of machine intelligence. In *Deep Thinking* Kasparov describes the regular breakdowns of Deep Blue that occurred for a variety of reasons, from electrical outages to software crashes. Kasparov points out how reboots from these breakdowns were only possible through the intervention of the programmers and operators. The reboots occurred in a complex matrix of relations that included instrumental ends such as the desire of the IBM engineers to "prove" machine intelligence by beating the world chess champion. None of this context was included in the published games or the reporting of the match.

---

22. Gary Kasparov with Mig Greengard, *Deep Thinking: Where Machine Intelligence Ends and Human Creativity Begins* (London: John Murray, 2017).

The rebooting of Deep Blue resembles the description of breakdowns in §16 of *Being and Time*. The context of handiness (*Zuhandenheit*) is disrupted, the tool can no longer be used, so the hardware becomes mere objective presence (*Vorhandenheit*). Heidegger assumes that "mere objective presence . . . withdraws again into handiness. . . . [when] it is put back into repair" (72/98). This "repair" concerns only the final ends of action—the causal structure of experience. It conceals any of the instrumental ends required for the action to revert back to being useful. For example, it cannot answer *why* we should fix a broken tool in the first place. By concealing the instrumental ends in the causal ends, the description of the breakdown of the network of useful relations resembles the reporting of the Deep Blue match that concealed the instrumental matrix of the programmers and engineers supported by a tech giant, which enabled the rebooting of the machine. The lapse from the handiness of the useful tool to its objective presence when it breaks down, and the reversal back to operation, conceals that the achieving of the final ends of action is only possible within a world that includes instrumental relations. The phenomenological description of the breakdown of *Besorgen*, or dealing with tools, is akin to the description of the breakdown of Deep Blue excluding any consideration of the programmers and engineers who actually performed the rebooting, obscuring the social structure of the breakdown.

We can use a related image to explain Heidegger's approach. There was once a chess-playing automaton dressed as a Turk that toured playing demonstration games. Hidden inside the automaton, was a chess player who actually chose the moves. The description of the breakdown of the taking care of things resembles a description of the Turk, but without mentioning the player hidden within it. This is the concealed instrumentality that, in fact, plays the game—that is, it is responsible for action—despite its silencing by Heidegger. Due to the concealed instrumentality, Heidegger's description of the breakdown is mechanistic and lacks its social and political context.

There are also significant political implications in concealing instrumentality in the description of dealing with tools. Lisa Guenther's work on the employment of solitary confinement in the prison system is particularly useful in this regard, not only because it exposes the political limits of the notion of breakdown that we find in §16 of *Being and Time*, but also because it demonstrates that phenomenology can attain a critical edge only when taking instrumentality and its socio-political context into consideration. Guenther describes solitary confinement as a "breakdown of meaningful experience" that makes those subjected to it targets of violence.[23] In other words, Guenther does not describe the disruption and collapse merely of one tool such as a hammer that prevents the accomplishment of one end associated with that tool. Rather, Guenther describes a kind of experience that exercises violence by being designed to deprive the person subjected to it of all tools and ends. Solitary confinement is not merely a disruption in the world of the prisoner, but the "unhinging" of the prisoner's being-in-the-world, which leads to dehumanization.[24]

Guenther's critical phenomenology is not confined to a description of the "unhinged experience" of solitary confinement. In addition, and just as importantly, it examines three historical movements that justified solitary confinement in the United States—religious reformers in the mid-nineteenth century; the 1960s and 1970s justification inspired by behaviorism; and the final wave lead by prison administrators. The three movements employed essentially the same technique that had a similar impact on the prisoners subjected to solitary confinement. But the *instrumental* justifications were significantly different, whereby the *critique* of these movements was, in each case, different. The lesson from Guenther's analysis is clear: For a critical phenomenology that is engaged with the political, the breakdown of the prisoners' experience cannot be conflated with the instrumental ends that affect the actions of the participants.

The political significance of disruption extends also to conceptualizations of political praxis. This was particularly pertinent in the industrial era of the nineteenth and early twentieth centuries, when so much of life was regulated by the introduction of machines in economic relations. In this context, political action was often conceived as the willful disruption of tools.[25] By the beginning of the twentieth century, such practices were so widespread that George Sorel theorizes them in terms of violence and the general strike.[26] The political import of disruption, then, as presented recently by Guenther but also as was presented in the political and social

---

23. Lisa Guenther, *Solitary Confinement: Social Death and its Afterlives* (Minneapolis: University of Minnesota Press, 2013), xiv.

24. The concept of the "unhinged" experience of solitary confinement runs throughout the entirety of Guenther's book.

25. For the example of how textile workers in England intentionally broke down machines of production, see Gavin Mueller, *Breaking Things at Work: The Luddites Are Right About Why You Hate Your Job* (London: Verso, 2021).

26. George Sorel, *Reflections on Violence*, ed. Jeremy Jennings (Cambridge: Cambridge University Press, 1999). Originally published in 1908.

discourse of the nineteenth and early twentieth centuries, presents a reverse thesis than the one defended by Heidegger. §16 of *Being and Time* presents the breakdown of the operation of tools as the way in which tools become noticed within the kind of action that Heidegger describes as the dealing with things in one's world. The political discourse and praxis of disruption, by contrast, suggests that political action disrupts tools because they are all too well noticed when they operate smoothly.

The description offered in *Being and Time* of how breakdowns make us aware of tools fails to account for the social and political context because it conceals the instrumental ends of action. Heidegger's description of the breakdown of ends describes a mechanical process that is more akin to the breakdown of AI than to human experience. As a result, the description of circumspective understanding of the kind of activity that Heidegger calls "dealing with things," (*Besorgen*) magically wishes away the ethical and political aspects of action, conjuring a world wrenched apart from the facticity of social reality. As a consequence, the account of action as *Besorgen* appears trivial as it occupies a vacuum created by the abstraction of instrumentality and its concealment in causality.

39. Sign and reference, understanding and interpretation (*Being and Time* §17)

The analysis of the breakdown of tools is followed by an examination of signs and reference in §17. This is an important turn in laying out the ontology of *Being and Time*, as it introduces themes that will ultimately be cashed out in the conceptions of understanding and interpretation in chapter 5 of *Being and Time*. Thus, the discussion of signs and reference in §17 forms the basis of the hermeneutics of facticity. It is a critical juncture, not only for the argument in *Being and Time*, but for Heidegger's project of an ontology of Dasein as a whole (and beyond), as the hermeneutics of facticity in turn becomes the basis for the Heideggerian conception of language and linguistic expression, such as in poetry.

Here again the concealment of instrumental ends persists unabated. Just as in the description of tools and their breakdown, the description of signs relies on a conception of action as directed exclusively toward final ends. The difference from earlier sections is that signs and reference introduce human interaction, which was not evident in the description of actions such as hammering where the relation was primarily between an agent of action and objects around her. The introduction of human interaction presents an additional facet of the problematic concealment of instrumentality: namely, it *presupposes* the structural operation of power while being unable to address it when it examines only the ends of use and production that characterize causality.

A guiding motivation for the development of a theory of reference and signs, just as for interpretation and understanding in chapter 5 of *Being and Time*, is Heidegger's need to bridge the gap between theory and praxis. His target remains the epistemology of metaphysics. Reference and the sign do "not come about with theoretical intent and by way of theoretical speculation" (80/109). It is not as if the subject can stand still in front of a sign to contemplate it indifferently as something external that needs to be deciphered. Rather, the sign, just like the hammer, is something that is intertwined with action. Heidegger's example is the car's indicators. At issue is not an isolated sign but how there is a "corresponding conduct [*Verhalten*]" (78/106) when we see a car indicating. And just as in the case of the hammer, the action in response to the sign is not an intentional act that presupposes a rational process of assessment—such as calculating the pros and cons as to whether we should yield to the turning car with the indicator on—but rather leads to an action without "thinking about it" or "automatically." Or, as Heidegger puts it, "Dasein is always somehow directed and underway" (78/106).

Reference and sign are intertwined and yet play distinct roles in such a description of action. Reference indicates the "in-order-to" or the end of the action. The world of utility that is characteristic of *Besorgen* is organized through reference to such ends. This corresponds to the "as-structure" of interpretation when the scope of action is broadened from the kind of modality that Heidegger calls *Besorgen*. Reference and interpretation on their own cannot forge a link between Dasein's world and language. Signs are also needed. Signs have two components relevant to the pursuit of ends made possible by reference: signs point to the totality of use within the matrix of reference; and they indicate the circumspection with which the Dasein surveys the world in a prethematic or pretheoretical manner. Heidegger will later describe these elements as constitutive of the "fore-structure" of understanding.

For example, the indicator sign of the car involves both the end of reference and the circumspective comprehension of the sign. When the indicator is switched on, the car references the end that it is going to turn. But this end is only possible within a totality of reference that includes a preunderstanding of traffic signs. To interpret the indicator, one needs foreknowledge of road rules and driving conventions. Such an understanding is not mentally present as something we are actively aware of—we do not recall the specific rule every time we see an indicator. Rather, the awareness is there, available to guide action without a self-aware mental process. The reference of the end of action and the sign's circumspective comprehension that points to the totality of references within a given context are inseparable and yet distinct. This interaction between reference and sign establishes the ground of the connection between existence and language, or the hermeneutics of facticity.

There is one problem that haunts the hermeneutics of facticity. What comes first, reference or the sign? Or, more broadly, what is more primary, interpretation or understanding? A hermeneutics of facticity means that the circle of understanding mirrors a question at the heart of ontology: What comes first in the world, the ontic (beings in the particularity and multiplicity), or the ontological (being in its singularity and unity)? This is a circularity about existence that Heidegger identifies early on in the Introduction to *Being and Time* (§2), and he resolves it with recourse to the hermeneutic circle in §32, when he famously argues that the crucial thing is not to try to avoid the circle but rather to find the right way to step into it.

We see at this juncture what is at stake in the discussion of the relation of reference and sign. We have here a first iteration of the connection between ontology and hermeneutics. Or, more accurately, the discussion of §17 forms the basis upon which the circularity that haunts being is to be resolved through hermeneutics. If we discover a problem with the analysis of reference and sign, then, it will shake the entire scaffolding of being and understanding in *Being and Time*.

Such a problem comes immediately into view as soon as we recognize that the concealment of instrumentality that undermines the analysis of tools (§15) and their breakdown (§16) also raises significant problems in the determination of reference and sign. The difficulty with the concealment of instrumentality is that it represses the political and the social. Let me illustrate, using Heidegger's kind of example, traffic signs.

Heidegger does not consider in §17 the institutional framework without which traffic signs are unable to function as signs. An authority that establishes the signs precedes the end of action characteristic of reference as well as the totality of references and the circumspection characteristic of the sign. One can unintentionally interpret a traffic sign only when one is imbued in a social-legal framework that regulates the meaning of the signs and ensures that they operate as intended. The last point is critical: policing is also constitutive of the sign. If one does not stop at a "stop" sign, one *may* be issued a ticket. If one lights a cigarette next to a "no smoking sign," one *may* be issued a fine. If a male enters a toilet whose sign indicates that it is for female use, one *may* cause alarm and a call to the police.

I have italicized "may" in these examples to indicate that policing is not merely an automatic response to not obeying the sign. Policing is not automatic—imagine if we were issued a ticket automatically, every time we went slightly over the speed limit. Rather, policing intersects between the referential end indicated by the sign and its application. If the ends of reference are final ends of action, the application of the ends of the sign are instrumental and include policing structures of power. The space between a rule, its signification and its application is vast and the range of actions occurring in this space is enormous and complex—with factors such as context or cultural specificity being paramount. The point that I am making is that Heidegger's analysis of signs abstracts from experience in such a way as to conceal that space of power and the instrumentality that evidences it. Such a concealing undermines the entire analysis of §17.

For example, Heidegger insists that circumspection "does not comprehend what is at hand" (78/106). Circumspection is not a self-reflexive mental activity. One does not "think about it" when pressing on the brake pedal when approaching a stop sign. And yet, the rule in Australia is that the car has to be completely stationary for three seconds at a stop sign. It is rare, but not unheard of, for police to strictly observe this time limit. A friend of mine, living in a small costal village, once told me of how the new policeman in their town made a habit of hiding at deserted intersections and issuing fines to drivers who did not stop for the full three seconds. Heidegger is correct that one does not comprehend what is at hand in a sign, but what one does not comprehend is not only the reference of the sign or the end of action suggested by the sign—such as the instruction to stop. In addition, what one does not comprehend is the power structure that establishes and polices that end—just like the "hey, you!" of the policeman in Althusser's famous example of ideology. At the same time, the power structure becomes very much visible and comprehensible when power intervenes in the implementation of the rule and its signification. My friend described the outrage of the entire village at the assertion of the new policeman's power. But this structure of power is obscured when the analysis of action conceals instrumental ends—such as the policeman's end of asserting his power at his new post so as to establish his authority.

Heidegger describes reference and signs as if signification is a relation between an object—the physical sign—and an observer. This is too narrow, as the signification of the sign includes both the institutions that establish the sign and the representatives of the institutions that enforce the sign's implementation. In other words, the sign is not a sign outside a structure of power. And power operates by establishing and implementing instrumental ends to action.

One may object at this point that I take Heidegger to mean, narrowly, what C.S. Peirce calls symbolic signs—that is, signs generated through a process of agreement that may include institutional processes. What if Heidegger merely refers to indexical signs, that is, signs that arise by custom? Such signs regulate all aspects of our behavior even though they are not formally established or policed, like traffic signs. Thus, for example, when we attend a talk by an invited speaker at our department, there are all sorts of customs that unfold via the use of signs. The sign about the start of the talk (the chair starts introducing the speaker), the sign from someone in the audience to ask a question (raising a hand), the chair's sign that one can ask that question, and so on. These are signs that arise over time and some of the specifics may vary from department to department. There may also be no specific end to the actions associated with such signs—one may want to ask a question as part of the process of educating oneself in general as opposed to a specific end to be derived from the answer. As such, the signs of the conduct of the participants at a talk are neither established nor policed in the same way as symbolic signs such as traffic signs.

And yet, instrumentality is strongly present in indexical signs as well. This is not indicated only by the fact that the ends of action of an indexical sign can be part of the action process as opposed to the ends of action of causality that are independent of the action—for instance, asking a question at a talk can have the instrumental end of furthering one's comprehension by clarifying an obscure point. More importantly still, indexicals are just as involved in power structures as symbolic signs. There are power structures—who can deny it?—that operate in departmental talks. An expert on the talk's topic might be allowed to ask the first question. Or the senior scholars might wait until the students ask their questions. In all these cases, power operates without comprehending what is at hand, as Heidegger puts it referring to signs.

But the clearest operation of power in indexical signs is when there is a clear comprehension of the signs because of the disruption of their operation. Imagine, for example, that there is a colleague who has been complaining to the chair about the seminars. The complaints could be about feelings of not been treated fairly because of her ethnicity, race, or gender. The complaints could even have been made in writing, and hence formalized. In such a situation, the participants in the discussion during the question period may be fearful of participating in the discussion in case they inadvertently become subjected to the colleague's habitual complaints. They may hesitate to raise their hand to ask a question before they look sideways in case the person who complains wants to speak. A new series of indexical signs that governs conduct and power relations is quickly established in such a situation. In such practice, indexical signs consolidate and perpetuate the power of the person who complains while they become the referents of the powerlessness of the rest.

If signs, as forms of language, presuppose the operation of power, and if the analysis of power requires the examination of the instrumental ends of action, then Heidegger's concealment of instrumentality in the analysis of reference and sign entails an impoverished conception of signs that abstracts from experience so as to exclude power. This undermines the assumption that the ontological circle between ontic and ontological can be resolved through the hermeneutical circle between interpretation and understanding. This brings us back to the unpalatable dilemma about the Heideggerian conception of action that should be familiar by now: The repression of instrumentality characteristic of the ruse of techne leads to a conception of action that is either vacuous or self-contradictory (§16).

This double bind also appears from a different angle here. Irrespective of whether it is a vacuous or performative contradiction, the concealment of instrumentality in Heidegger is ultimately also—or, maybe, *essentially*—the concealment of the power structures that operate within experience. Consequently, such a hermeneutics of facticity *is—pace* Heidegger—a political theory, one whose aim (its instrumental end) is to obscure and hence support and perpetuate established structures of power. The ruse of techne that the concealment of instrumentality effects is, in Althusserian terms, an ideological apparatus.

40. Dictatorship

The ideological import of the politics implied by Heidegger's ruse of techne that conceals instrumental within causal ends comes to the fore in chapter 4 of *Being and Time*, where Heidegger examines a second modality of inauthenticity, *Fürsorge*. We can translate this as concern. Expressions that come to mind are "mütterliche Fürsorge" (motherly care or concern) or even "göttliche Fürsorge" (divine care or providence). Just as in the case of *Besorgen*, the substantive care (*Sorge*) has a suffix. The idea is similar to the dealing indicated by *Besorgen*, except that the "being-with" of Dasein that Heidegger calls *Fürsorge* is not a useful thing, but another Dasein (118/162). In other words, *Fürsorge* is an engagement between humans that, as opposed to *Besorgen*, diverts from the path that leads to being.

It is in chapter 4 that we find the notions of Mitsein and Mitdasein that have provided the platform for various scholars to attempt the construction of a Heideggerian ethics and politics.[27] I remain skeptical about such attempts, at least to the extent that they claim to represent Heidegger's position. After all, Heidegger not only insists that "encountering *others* is, after all, oriented toward one's *own* Dasein" (115/158). Moreover, this means that "in being absorbed . . . in being-with toward others [*im Mitsein zu den Anderen*], Dasein is not itself" (122/167). Just like the dealing with objects that Heidegger calls *Besorgen,* the interaction with other humans (*Fürsorge*) prevents Dasein from unconcealing the being of its being.

The culmination of this argument occurs in the second part of chapter 5, where Heidegger describes the "fallness" (*Verfallen*) of Dasein through its interaction with others—the "they" or *das Man*—in terms of chatter, curiosity, and ambiguity. It is hard to find any redemptive quality in Dasein's interaction with others. By contrast, anxiety, what Heidegger calls the fundamental attunement of Dasein, is designated as an existential solipsism because it "individualizes and thus discloses Dasein" (182/250). Anxiety is about Dasein's own being—not about Mitsein or Mitdasein.

It is instructive to notice why modes such as chatter are inauthentic. If discourse (*Rede*) can lead to understanding, that is because it can keep "being-in-the-world open"; by contrast, chatter (*Gerede*) is "closing it off" (163/224–25). Closure is precisely the problem that Heidegger finds in end-oriented action. If the end is conceived as the end of techne or the final end of causality, then its attainment is simultaneously the end of the action. Activity is then closed off or exhausted. The existential solipsism of anxiety, by contrast, has no such impediment. It is solipsistic because it is directed toward the Dasein itself, instead of an independent end outside it. What is concealed in this contrast between closure and solipsism is the notion of the instrumental end, which I described as the end of phronesis (§21). Such an end is constitutive of action and as such it is not an independent end that can be reached when the product of the action is finalized, but rather a provisional end that morphs and adapts to the changing circumstances as the action unfolds.

The concealment of instrumentality in the way that we relate to others has a clear political implication that Heidegger admirably summarizes by designating the influence of the other (*das Man*) on Dasein as a dictatorship (*Diktatur*) (123/169). We see in this assertion the ancient trope of the multitude or *hoi polloi,* the masses that threaten to destroy the community

---

27. See Jean-Luc Nancy, *Being Singular Plural,* trans. Robert D. Richardson and Anne E. O'Byrne (Stanford, CA: Stanford University Press, 2000); and Frederick A. Olafson, *Heidegger and the Ground of Ethics: A Study of Mitdasein* (Cambridge: Cambridge University Press, 1998), see §5.

because they do not adhere to higher values of society and culture—such as authenticity.[28] This is a trope that we find constantly in philosophy at least since Plato, and it is partly to explain the long-lasting philosophical disdain for democracy.[29] Within this context, it comes as no surprise that these passages about the pernicious influence of the multitude as an impersonal *das Man* were at the center of the initial reception of *Being and Time* in 1927, just as Germany was tiring of the liberal democratic experiment of the Weimar Republic and anti-democratic forces were gathering strength.

I do not harbor the illusion that the people are all "good" and that they do not have a propensity to make bad choices—something that every populist movement is keen to exploit. The multitude, for the most part, "see the better and do the worse," as Ovid puts it. There is a certain truth to a suspicion, even a complaint, against the people. And yet, without the multitude, there is no possibility of social change and even the fabric of the political is threatened. The possibility that the multitude will overcome its shortcomings and function as a constituent power has not been lost to radical thinkers in modernity, as Antonio Negri recounts in *Insurgencies*.[30]

We can put it another way. There is certainly a possibility that the multitude will effect a dictatorship with disastrous consequences, something which eventuated six years after the publication of *Being and Time*. But also there is no possibility of overcoming dictatorship or any form of tyranny more generally without the participation of the multitude. Political change is not sui generis but effected through the multitude. That is what holds power in check, which is what effects change. This is only possible, underscores Negri, so long as we avoid the Bartelby trap. To any request for action, the hero of Melville's novella only ever responds that he would prefer not to. Negri warns against the chimera of a politics of the "useless," a politics that seeks to do away with instrumentality, which is exemplified by the figure of Bartelby.[31]

The fact that Heidegger cannot accommodate the danger of the Bartelby "uselessness" is due to the concealment of instrumentality. This ideological

---

28. Cf. the interpretation of the myth of the cave in Martin Heidegger, *The Essence of Truth: On Plato's Cave Allegory and Theaetetus*, trans, Ted Sadler (London: Continuum, 2002) = *GA* 34.

29. See Jacques Derrida, *Rogues: Two Essays on Reason*, trans. Pascale-Anne Brault and Michael Nass (Stanford, CA: Stanford University Press, 2005).

30. Antonio Negri, *Insurgencies: Constituent Power and the Modern State*, trans. Maurizia Boscagli (Minneapolis: University of Minnesota Press, 1999).

31. Michael Hardt and Antonio Negri, *Empire* (Cambridge, MA: Harvard University Press, 2000), 203–24.

baggage of his ruse of techne becomes constitutive of the politics implied in those pages of *Being and Time* that castigate the multitude so as to pave the way to the existential analytic of Division 2. It is there that we discover the third meaning of techne as action without effects or without ends. And with the third meaning, the ruse of techne is in full swing.

41. The temporality of death and the myth of Care

The key idea that forges the transition to the existential analytic of Division 2 of *Being and Time* is the transformation of all causal ends—and by implication of all instrumental ends too as they are concealed within causality—to death. "The 'end' [*'Ende'*] of being-in-the-world is death" (224/310). But "end" here does not mean the actual physical death of the individual; rather, death indicates a temporal structure that organizes Dasein's existence. Heidegger writes "Ende" within "scare quotes" to warn the reader that death as end has nothing to do with passing away, it is not something external or independent of Dasein's actions. Rather, it has to do with how "the potentiality-for-being-whole" of Dasein, or the authentic possibilities of Dasein's acting, are organized by a temporality that we can discovered through an examination of death (224/310). In *Plato's Sophist*, Heidegger had already realized that phronesis needs a particular temporal structure (§29). This suggestion in *Plato's Sophist* is now fully developed in Division 2 of *Being and Time* through the temporality introduced by the being-toward-death.

The concealment of instrumentality is paramount for the conception of authenticity. In chapter 7, the first chapter of Division 2, we can glean at least five essential characteristics of the repression of instrumentality through the temporality of death. All of them are well-known, so I will enumerate them here quickly before I turn to Heidegger's example meant to illustrate the temporality that he believes destructs metaphysics.

First, the distinction between vulgar time and projective time. The key difference between the two is that the "everyday vulgar [*alltäglich-vulgäre*] understanding of time" relies on a "calculation of time [*Zeitrechnung*]" (225/312). Such a calculation is possible by conceiving time on the model of causality as a linear sequence of moments upon which the sequence of causes and effects can be overlaid. Heidegger contrasts such an inauthentic conception of time that relies on calculation with the authentic conception of time that relies on the "projection [*Entwurf*] of a meaning of being in general" (225/312). Projective temporality does not concern itself with effects because it is "ek-static," as Heidegger calls it, meaning that it stands out of sequential causality and from all the final ends of action. Dasein's attunement characteristic of this temporality is anxiety, which arises from the fact that "the certainty of death cannot be calculated [*kann nicht errechnet werden*]" (253/351). An authentic Dasein uncovers its authentic emotional disposition within the world, only through a temporality that is beyond calculation, the being-toward-death.

Second, so long as death is not understood as physical demise but as the projective temporality of being-toward-death, death escapes representation: "in 'ending,' and in the being a whole of Dasein which is thus constituted, there is, according to its essence, no representation [*Vertretung*]" (231/320). Representation here does not mean only a mental representation made possible through calculation. It also, and primarily, means that there is no representative (*Vertrer*) for such authentic temporality. Here is the source of Heidegger's vehement opposition to representation in politics, expressed in his fierce rejection of liberal democracy as well as any form of representative politics. There is either the "existential solipsism" of authentic temporality (182/250), or representation. There is no in-between (§29).

Third, the truth of being as pursued by Dasein is only possible because of the projective temporality of death: "As the end of Dasein, *death is* in the being [*Sein*] of this being [*Seienden*] *toward* its end" (248/343). Dasein is suited to disclose its being because death as end, that is, the temporality of death, substitutes all other notions of end, both causal and instrumental. But the end of death is only the anticipation (*Vorlaufen*) of the possibilities that are near Dasein. In other words, the conception of the action of Dasein relies on such anticipation. But this is on condition that anticipation "knows no measure at all [*überhaupt kein Maß*] . . . but means the possibility of the measureless impossibility [*die Möglichkeit der maßlosen Unmöglichkeit*] of existence" (251/348). The possibility of action is "impossible" because it lacks effects whereby it cannot be measured. The temporality of death shows an action without calculation, a useless kind of acting—an action without effects.

Heidegger calls care (*Sorge*) the "formal existential totality of the ontological structural whole of Dasein" (186/256) that organizes the immeasurable, unrepresentable, anticipatory temporality of Dasein. For the key to care in terms of temporality, Heidegger cites an ancient myth about Care from Hyginus:

> Once when "Care" was crossing a river, she saw some clay; she thoughtfully took a piece and began to shape it. While she was thinking about what she had made, Jupiter came by. "Care" asked him to give it spirit, and this he gladly granted. But when she wanted her name to be bestowed upon it, Jupiter forbade this and demanded that it be given his name instead. While "Care" and Jupiter were

arguing, Earth (Tellus) arose, and desired that her name be conferred upon the creature, since she had offered it part of her body. They asked Saturn to be the judge. And Saturn gave them the following decision, which seemed to be just: "Since you, Jupiter, have given its spirit, you should receive that spirit at death; and since you, Earth, have given its body, you shall receive its body. But since 'Care' first shaped this creature, she shall possess it as long as it lives. And because there is a dispute among you as to its name, let it be called 'homo,' for it is made out of humus (earth)." (191/262–63)

According to Heidegger's interpretation, the human is made of mind and body, these being the contributions of Jupiter and Earth respectively. However, its origin is in Care, and it is "held fast and dominated by it, as long as this being 'is in the world'" (191/263). Thus, Care preempts and overcomes the metaphysical separation of mind and body, and of theory and praxis. Significantly, the origin of being is determined by Saturn's decision, the king of the gods who, Heidegger underscores, is time. From this, Heidegger concludes that "the whole of the constitution of Dasein itself is not simple in its unity [*in seiner Einheit nicht einfach*] but shows a structural articulation [*eine strukturale Gliederung*] which is expressed in the existential concept of care" (192/265). In other words, the primordial totality of the being of Dasein is composed by various elements whose unity relies on the temporality—immeasurable, unrepresentable, anticipatory—disclosed by Care. This temporality is reformulated in the next chapter of *Being and Time* as the end of death and the authentic temporality of Dasein. The fable, then, is an illustration of the authentic temporality of Dasein in terms of Care.

The pivot of Heidegger's interpretation of the myth of Care in terms of authentic temporality is the function of Saturn who, according to mythology, is time, *der "Zeit,"* as Heidegger puts it (191/263). The Greek name of Saturn is Cronus, which points to "chronus" or time. Heidegger's interpretation suggests that Saturn, as authentic time, overcomes the temporal structure of creation that relies on causality: Care is the formal cause as she gives shape to the human; Jupiter provides the efficient cause for the human, as the mind is responsible for the planning of the actions to be undertaken; the material cause of the human is Earth who gives it the body. Saturn as "the time" provides the name and, hence, the essence of this creation. In this interpretation, just as earlier in *Being and Time*, the end is associated exclusively with causality, leaving the instrumental ends of action concealed. Saturn—as the king of the gods that also stands for time—is contrasted to this temporality of causality.

But another interpretation of the same myth seems more obvious, or at least more consonant with the mythological tradition. Contrary to Heidegger's interpretation, in Hesiod's *Theogony*, the foundational text of how Greco-Roman mythology presents the genealogy of the gods and the creation of the human, Saturn (or Cronus) marks a double temporality that explicitly includes instrumentality.

The first notion of time that pertains to Cronus is determined by the operation of instrumentality. The key characteristic of Cronus is that he is *agkylometis*. This is a difficult epithet to translate. It is a compound. Metis refers to the kind of instrumental thinking that is characteristic of the Greek conception of action (§23 and §51). *Agkyle* means bend. So, an *agkylometis* is someone whose instrumental calculations are not obvious, or someone who is scheming. Hesiod uses this epithet in relation to the two most critical moments in Cronus's story. The first pertains to how he overthrew his father, *Ouranos*, to become the king of the gods, and the second to how he devoured his own children to prevent them from overpowering him in turn, and ending his reign as king of the gods.[32] The second kind of scheming failed, his time as king of the gods ended, and his son, Zeus, succeeded him. Tellingly, Hesiod describes Zeus as *metioenta*, that is, the most instrumental or the most skillful in calculating the instrumental ends of action.[33] According to Greco-Roman mythology, Cronus indicates the time of the genesis of the gods where time is determined steadfastly as the time of instrumentality.

The second temporality associated with Cronus relates to the human. Cronus's reign was during the time of the Greek heroes, the fourth stage of human development according to *Works and Days*.[34] But this all changed when Zeus succeeded him. That is when the humans had to negotiate a new contract with the gods. This is not a contract or testament in the Hebrew sense where it is bestowed upon humans by god. Rather, Hesiod uses the word *ekrinonto* to describe the negotiations between the gods and humans regarding the terms of their relationship.[35] The gods do not simply hand down the law but have to arrive at the law in negotiation with the humans. At this point Prometheus intervenes to help the humans when he

---

32. Hesiod, "Theogony," in *Theogony; Works and Days; Testimonia*, trans. Glenn W. Most (Cambridge, MA: Harvard University Press, 2006), 168, 471, 495

33. Hesiod, "Theogony," 467.

34. Hesiod, *Works and Days*, 156–73. The so-called "golden age" of the rule of Cronus is an oft-repeated motif. For example, Plato uses it in the *Statesman* in the story about the reversal of time.

35. Hesiod, "Theogony," 535.

tricks Zeus into agreeing to sacrifices to the gods only consisting of the fat and bones of animals and to the gods giving fire to the humans. The key characteristic of Prometheus's actions is that they are done *epi techne*, that is, they are crafty or carried out through a certain technique (§47).[36] The time after Cronus, or the time of the new Pantheon, is the time that introduces the technical alongside the instrumental in the lives of the humans.

The myth of Care, insofar as it is part of Greco-Roman mythology, evidences a kind of temporality that is, as Heidegger correctly observes, intertwined with Cronus as the deity representing time. But the time registered through the figure of Cronus has nothing to do with the overcoming of a temporality that reduces being to the linear time of causality by concealing instrumentality. To the contrary, the myth of Cronus demonstrates that Cronus evidences the parallel operation of instrumentality and causality in the unfolding of time. The human exists in a finite time that includes the *metis* that calculates instrumental ends and the *techne* that calculates final ends. In other words, the time of Cronus evidences the monist materialist distinction between causality and instrumentality. From the mythological perspective, human finitude, the end of time as death as Heidegger puts it, now emerges as being possible only when the action uncovers or discloses its instrumental ends alongside the technical ones.

Just as in the case of the mistranslations in *Plato's Sophist*, one could argue that Heidegger's misinterpretation of the temporality associated with Saturn is insignificant for his philosophical position. The misinterpretation, one could claim, does not affect the argument about a kind of temporality separate from calculation. And yet, just as in the lecture course, the supposedly insignificant mistranslation is in fact symptomatic of a mistake that Heidegger attempts to hide through the ruse of techne. Similarly, here too Heidegger can only designate the temporal structure of authenticity because his examples systematically conceal instrumentality as if in a conjuring trick. The calculation that authentic temporality overcomes is the sequential calculation of causality—but it leaves unaffected the concealed instrumental ends determined by and determining in turn power relations.

42. Techne as the virtue of theory

In *Plato's Sophist*, Heidegger argues that sophia or theoretical knowledge is the virtue of techne. This insight is further developed in Division 1 of *Being and Time*, where it is shown that circumspection, as the kind of knowing

---

36. Hesiod, "Theogony," 540, 547, 555.

characteristic of acting within a network of useful relations or handiness (*Zuhandenheit*), lifts tools from the mere objective presence (*Vorhandenheit*) characteristic of metaphysics. This bridges the gap between subject and object as well as between theory and praxis. In Division 2, the end-free temporality of being-toward-death is presented as contrasted to inauthentic temporality. These arguments address a determination of inauthenticity and its relation to authenticity, but they do not address the notion of theoretical knowledge and the kind of action that Heidegger describes as indifference (§36). Heidegger also needs to explain the relation between authenticity and theoretical knowledge. This task is taken up in §69 of *Being and Time*.

The direction of the argument in §69 is clear enough. Heidegger wants to argue that the objective presence of theoretical knowledge presupposes handiness. If he can demonstrate that, he will not need a detailed account of the direct relation between theoretical knowledge and authenticity, as he has already determined the relation between handiness and authenticity when he argued that handiness (*Zuhandenheit*) and its modality that takes care of things (*Besorgen*) in fact contain within themselves the possibility of the ecstatic temporality of care (*Sorge*). Differently put, if he can show that indifference presupposes handiness that in turn presupposes authentic action, Heidegger will have a neat account of the relation between theoretical knowledge and authenticity. This strategy essentially consists in accentuating the insight about the relation between techne and sophia from *Plato's Sophist* by reversing their priority (§27): techne now emerges as the virtue of sophia. Or as Don Ihde puts it, technology precedes science.[37]

Commentators have noticed all sorts of difficulties with this solution. In the German reception of Heidegger, the defense of this position took two seemingly incompatible routes. Some held that practice becomes primary.[38] Others that the very distinction between theory and praxis is completely overcome, whereby neither has priority.[39] Matters got worse when, in response to this dispute, scholars paid more attention to §69, and noticed that, far from an easy solution to the relation between science

---

37. Don Ihde, *Heidegger's Technologies: Postphenomenological Perspectives* (New York: Fordham University Press, 2010), chapter 2.
38. Ernst Tugendhat, *Der Wahrheitsbegriff bei Husserl und Heidegger* (Berlin: De Gruyter, 1970).
39. Walter Bröcker, "Heidegger und die Logik," *Philosophische Rundschau* 1 (1953): 48–56.

and authenticity, Heidegger's argument ends up assuming the priority of theory over praxis, thereby lapsing back into metaphysics.[40]

What remains unthought in these debates that concentrate on Heidegger's theory of knowledge is Heidegger's conception of action, which is indispensable if praxis precedes theoretical knowledge. What is the relation between scientific knowledge and the ecstatic temporality of Dasein in terms of the separation between an action that is end-oriented and an authentic action that is end-free? For a conception of theoretical knowledge, we have to contend yet again with the concealment of instrumentality that regulates Heidegger's account of action in *Being and Time*.

The attempt to resolve the relation between indifference and authenticity via an examination of the relation between taking care of things and theoretical knowledge is indicated in the examples that Heidegger chooses. He reminds his readers how the hammer is not really noticed when it is used but becomes noticed when it breaks down (§38). Such breakdown means that "praxis has its own specific sight ('theory')" (341/473). But insists Heidegger, the relation is reciprocal: "theoretical research is also not without its own praxis" (341/473). An empirical scientist reads the measurements of instruments, an archaeologist has to undergo the toil of the excavation before she can assert her theory, and any scientist needs the use of mundane tools such as pen and paper. Such a practical side to science is "by no means ontologically indifferent" because it shows that "it is by no means obvious where the ontological boundary between 'theoretical' and 'atheoretical' conduct [*Verhalten*] really lies!" (341/473–74). The boundary between the theoretical and "atheoretical" may be unclear, but as the word "conduct" indicates, the priority is given to action. There is such a thing as theory because of the correct measuring, the successful excavating, or the copious notetaking.

At this point, the question about action in monism arises again. This is the objection that Socrates raises against the Eleatic stranger when he asks him whether sophistry, philosophizing, and statesmanship are in fact one, two, or three kinds of action (§34). If there is really only one being whose unified structure is uncovered by ontology, then what justifies the distinction between different actions? This is a problem that is at the forefront of Heidegger's mind in §69. He explains that things within a network of useful relations do not have their being changed when they are viewed from a scientific perspective. Any modification (*Modifikation*) does not affect the

---

40. Gerold Prauss, *Knowing and Doing in Heidegger's* Being and Time, trans. Gary Steiner and Jeffrey S. Turner (Amherst, MA: Humanity Books, 1977).

being of the objects (344/478). The difficulty with this argument is that actions can collapse into insignificant differentiations of the single, unified being. Then, the reversal from sophia being the virtue of techne to circumspection becoming the virtue of science is ultimately inconsequential. If actions are mere differentiations or modifications of the single, unified being, the distinction between theory and praxis is not, strictly speaking, overcome. Rather, it collapses because the terms lose their determination.

Resoluteness is critical in how Heidegger seeks to avoid this problem. In chapter 2 of Division 2 of *Being and Time*, Heidegger describes resoluteness as the authentic form of care—as opposed to the inauthentic forms that he described in Division 1. In chapter 3 he describes the temporal structure of resoluteness, which is anticipatory—a conception that was prefigured in *Plato's Sophist* (§29). Anticipatory resoluteness becomes Dasein's structure for the disclosure of being (§41). Significantly, such an existential structure is a form of action, since "Dasein is already acting by virtue of being resolute [*als entschlossenes handelt das Dasein schon*]" (287/398). Every action contains within it the possibility of resoluteness, even those whose modality is indifference, reducing objects to mere presence and dealing with their environment by measuring and calculating, are still only possible because they contain the potential of resoluteness. This allows Heidegger to argue in chapter 4 that a full existential analysis will examine all the actions described as inauthentic in Division 1 and redescribe them from the perspective of anticipatory resoluteness. Thus, Heidegger holds *both* that there is a single, unified being that is common to both inauthentic and authentic acting, *and* that there are different kinds of acting depending on how they are related to the disclosure of being. We see, then, in chapter 4, *both* Heidegger's monism according to which actions as such are not different *and* his solution, differentiating between qualitatively distinct actions according to how they are positioned vis-à-vis being (§6, §§13–14, §26).

For instance, in section (a) of §68, he distinguishes between two ways of enacting understanding, *either* the inauthentic making present (*Gegenwärtigen*), *or* the authentic understanding in the moment (*Augenblick*). The distinction does not determine a quality intrinsic to being, but instead how the different actions realize the potential to be resolute and hence orient themselves toward the disclosure of being. Similarly, in (b) of §68, he distinguishes between two actions, depending on distinct attunements of Dasein, *either* inauthentic fear *or* authentic anxiety: "One who is resolute knows no fear, but understands the possibility of anxiety as *the* mood that does not hinder and confuse him. Anxiety frees one *from* 'nullifying' possibilities and lets one become free *for* authentic possibilities" (329/456).

Either one is caught in fear presenting the unconcealment of being, or one discovers the liberating action that arises from the authentic mood of anxiety. These are two qualitatively different ways of being in the world depending on how they are oriented toward being.

In section (b) of §69, Heidegger describes two inauthentic experiences, circumspective understanding and scientific knowledge, by elaborating on the qualitative distinction between the two actions (§§13–14, §§26–27, §36). The criterion for the distinction remains the same: it pertains to the action's orientation toward the being of Dasein, which depends on how action deals with ends. In this framework, theoretical knowledge is inferior because it is "only in the service of pure observation [*nur im Dienst der reinen Betrachtung*]" (341/474). This is the tendency of theoretical knowledge to separate praxis from theory, whereby it lapses into indifference and moves away from the disclosure of being. Differently put, science forgets the final ends of actions characteristic of circumspection, whereby—crucially—instrumentality remains concealed. Whereas authenticity is without ends, and inauthenticity is useful because of its final ends, indifference is reliant on use but pretends that it operates independently of ends. It is this mistake that, according to Heidegger, makes theoretical knowledge assume the metaphysical conception of the object as mere presence.

To illustrate the distinction between circumspection and science, Heidegger returns once more to the example of the hammer to explain the distinction between useful and indifferent action (§36). What does the weight of the hammer indicate? For circumspection, the weight is related to how it is used. For science, the weight is something measurable. Even though it may be the same thing, a hammer, "the understanding being [*Seinsverständnis*] guiding the heedful dealings with innerworldly beings has been transformed [*umgeschlagen*]" (344/477–78). Thus, it is one kind of action if Pheidias picks up a hammer, "feels" its weight, and decides to pick a lighter one instead to chisel Athena's helmet. It is an entirely different kind of action if a scientist measures two hammers and determines that one weighs 527 grams and the other 725 grams. The actions may appear similar—weighing a hammer—but actually, the circumspective handling of the hammer by the sculptor, and the scientist's handling of the hammer for "pure observation" are in fact qualitatively different. The weighing action is "transformed" depending on whether the final end is recognized or disavowed.

The qualitative distinction of actions according to their ends holds so long as we describe the action in terms of their final end—the shaping of the marble or the measuring of the weight of the hammer. So long as the end is external to the action and independent of it, then it is possible to distinguish between the creative action of the sculptor that uses the tool, and the action of the scientist that is "used" by measuring the hammer to arrive at the intended pure observation. This is a level that is equally shared by technical action and action that measures cause and effect. But this qualitative separation requires the concealment of instrumentality and thereby deprives action of any socio-political import. We saw earlier (§§37–39) this effect of the concealment of instrumentality in the dealing with things (*Besorgen*). We can see the same point with science. There is no such a thing as a pure observation. It is not scientific to simply "measure" a hammer, unless there is a question that this measurement intends to answer. And such a question is never purely theoretical but is rather imbued within social and power structures, whereby science, too, requires instrumental ends.

Take for example the COVID-19 vaccine developed by the University of Queensland. From the perspective of pure observation, this was a perfectly good vaccine. In the testing phase, it was effective and did not record any negative side effects. Further, it would have been an expedient vaccine for Australia to build sovereign capacity, as it could be produced locally. And yet, the government decided to abandon the vaccine when trials revealed a small chance of a false positive for HIV. The reason was that a protein found in HIV was used as a "molecular clamp" to bind parts of the vaccine. The HIV was inactive and there was no suggestion of any negative health effects. The abandonment of the vaccine was simply a matter of public perception and the "stigma" of potentially obtaining an HIV-positive test.[41] The causal question that the vaccine sought to answer was whether it would protect subjects from infection. The parallel set of instrumental questions concerned the socio-political issue as to whether there would be a negative perception of the vaccine, preventing usage in the community. The observations and measurements are never pure because they

---

41. See the ABC reporting of this issue: Nick Sas and Michael Slezak, "Coronavirus Vaccine from UQ and CSL Abandoned After HIV Response Which Scientists Say Was 'Unexpected,'" ABC News, December 11, 2020, www.abc.net.au/news/2020-12-11/covid19-vaccine-csl-uq-hiv-element-what-went-wrong/12973952; Barbara Miller and Stephanie Dalzell, "Coronavirus Vaccine Trials Run by UQ and CSL Abandoned Due to False Positive HIV Results," ABC News, December 11, 2020, www.abc.net.au/news/2020-12-11/uq-csl-coronavirus-vaccine-trial-to-be-abandoned/12973656; Michael Slezak, "How the UQ Coronavirus Vaccine Induced False-Positive HIV Test Results and Why Scientists Were Prepared," ABC News, December 11, 2020, www.abc.net.au/news/2020-12-11/how-the-uq-covid-19-vaccine-induces-false-positive-hiv-results/12975048; Jess Rendall and Lily Nothling, "Cancellation of University of Queensland's COVID-19 Vaccine Trial 'Reassuring,'" ABC News, December 12, 2020, www.abc.net.au/news/2020-12-12/coronavirus-queensland-vaccine-uq-trial-cancellation-setback/12973724.

are always intertwined with instrumental ends and, hence, with power structures that refract the "indifferent" scientific knowledge. Knowledge is power, as Foucault would say.

What does it matter if science is imbued with instrumental ends? Then the entire Heideggerian argument about science reducing objects to mere presence so as to make them measurable, which in turn is the reason why circumspection or techne becomes the virtue of theory, and which in turn presupposes the concealment of instrumentality—the entire architectonic in *Being and Time* of the distinction between actions depending on their ends—collapses as soon as instrumentality is admitted in the argument. There is no longer such a distinct technical action such as Pheidias's weighing of the hammer in his hand, nor a distinct scientific measurement such as the weighing of the hammer on precision scales, where their qualitative distinction relies on their different ends that at the same time conceal instrumentality. Both actions have instrumental ends that embed them in ethical, social, and political concerns. Further, if the transition to authenticity relies on an activity that is free of ends where the ends are defined only as final, then authenticity collapses as soon as instrumental ends are introduced.

In a moment of parapraxis, Heidegger discloses the instrumentality operating within scientific knowledge. It occurs in a single sentence that is the only reference to the economy in *Being and Time*: "The everyday context of useful things at hand [*zuhandene Zeugzusammenhang*], their historical origination and utilization, their factical role in Dasein—all these are the objects of the science of economics [*der Wissenschaft von der Wirtschaft*]" (344/478). This is a sentence uniformly ignored in the secondary literature. At first it may appear as an extempore remark with seemingly little significance. This remark is nonetheless revealing because it introduces instrumentality in the relation between handiness and objective presence. It introduces instrumentality because economics is a science that deals with instrumental ends. As Adam Smith memorably puts it, the baker, the brewer, and the butcher do not produce their goods out of the goodness of their hearts but because of their self-interest.[42] There are two parallel ends to their actions, the end of production (the bread, the beer, and the meat) and the instrumental end (whatever each individual producer wants to achieve by producing their goods). Economics is the science that

---

42. Adam Smith, *An Inquiry into the Nature and Causes of the Wealth of Nations*, ed. W.P. Todd, in *The Glasgow Edition of the Works and Correspondence of Adam Smith*, vol. 2, ed. R.H Campbell and A.S. Skinner (Oxford: Oxford University Press, 1976), 26–27. See §32 in the Excursus for a discussion of this passage.

explicitly studies both ends. It is this parallel operation of ends that is characteristic of epicurean monism's response to the problematic of action (§7, §22, and §32), but which is incompatible with Heidegger's ruse of techne (§14, §31, §36). Inadvertently, Heidegger demonstrates the operation of instrumentality in the science of economics. The reference to the science of economics betrays his trick to conceal instrumentality within the final ends of causality.

The concealment of instrumentality is the ruse that allows Heidegger to incorporate all ends to the final ends of action that are independent of the action itself and which can be identified as objects separate from the observer, whereby they can turn to mere presence. If it is impossible to reduce all ends of action to final ends, maybe the notion of objective presence as conceived by Heidegger requires reformulation to include the social and political construction of the instrumental ends, suggesting that maybe there never was such a thing as a "mere object" that was measured by science. Maybe, then, Heidegger has been shadowboxing all along and what he calls "metaphysics" never existed.

Let me express the same point, starting from Heidegger's remark about the economy. If there is such a thing as an economic science that is inextricable from the instrumental ends of action, then the objects of science can never be merely pure observations or subjects to measurement and calculation. This means that instrumentality is constitutive of circumspection and the dealing with things—instrumental ends can no longer be dissolved into causal ends. Therefore, the separation between qualitatively different actions required for Heidegger's solution to the problem of action in monism simply collapses. As soon as instrumentality is inscribed into the operation on indifference, inauthenticity, and authenticity—which is to say, as soon as these actions are situated within an ethical, social, and political context—the qualitative distinction between them as drawn according to the presence of final ends that presupposes the concealment of instrumental is simply no longer tenable.

The concealing of instrumental ends within causal ends is done surreptitiously. It is carried out like a conjuring trick that hides instrumentality from view by presenting the ends of action only in terms of final ends. A conjuring trick relies on diverting the spectator's eye from the action that performs the hiding. But a conjuring trick also always contains the possibility that this quick movement that effects the concealing can be observed when the spectator does not submit to how the conjurer wants to direct her vision. The reference to economics as a science that relies on a network of useful relations (*Zuhandenheit*) while it is the science that relies on interest and hence instrumentality is the swift movement that betrays Heidegger's conjuring trick. The moment that we see the concealed instrumental ends in Heidegger's movement of thought, the magic of his ruse dissipates, and his conception of action achieves an ethical and political significance.

43. Subjectum absconditum

One of the usual critiques of *Being and Time* is that the notion of authenticity is problematic. The description of the ecstatic temporality of the subject has puzzled some commentators. Much of the criticism leveled against *Being and Time* takes aim at Division 2. Even a sympathetic reader such as Hubert Dreyfus contends that Division 1 is better worked out and achieves its aim of presenting an ontology of Dasein in the world that has overcome the metaphysical separation of theory and praxis, whereas Division 2 slides back to a conception of the subject that is perilously close to metaphysics. This worry has often been proffered as the reason for Heidegger's "turn," as we will see later.

By contrast, I have shown that the problem with *Being and Time* starts with Division 1. It is here that the argument is developed for a kind of activity characteristic of the human, that supposedly incorporates within it all the ends of action. This inauthentic activity, however, only ever deals with the final ends of action. The instrumental ends of action are concealed within the final ends of circumspection and the taking care of things.

This leads to tensions in Heidegger's argument. The tensions are so great that they may even undermine the successful overcoming of the epistemology of metaphysics. If *Besorgen*, the premental action that effects the bridging of theory and praxis, in fact offers a deficient description because it contains instrumental ends that have been concealed, then the entire anti-metaphysical foundation of fundamental ontology is shaken.

Besides the epistemological implications, the concealment of instrumentality also has important repercussions in how action is conceived. Effectively, the concealment of instrumentality leads Heidegger to a position where his conception of action deprives it of impact. The descriptions of action are emptied of both ethical and political purchase. I described earlier the double bind encountered by Heidegger's solution to the problematic of action in monism: the qualitative distinction between actions according to whether they are end-oriented represses instrumentality, whereby action appears *either* as trivial *or* as self-contradictory and complicit in the operation of existing power (§16). The account of action in *Being and Time* takes the first alternative. By concealing instrumentality, Heidegger arrives at a vacuous account of action that is stripped of all its social and political significance. (We will see in the next chapter that in attempting to rectify this, his work in the 1930s falls into the other side of the double bind.)

After the reading of *Being and Time* that I have offered here, one thing comes to view: the concealment of instrumentality is never argued for. Nowhere can we find an argument as to why actions can only be described in terms of the final ends of techne and not the provisional ends of phronesis. In this absence, we can discern the ruse of techne. Redeploying the tactic worked out in *Plato's Sophist*, the instrumental ends are simply hidden behind the description of Dasein's useful action, never interrogated, and systematically repressed. References such as the one on the economy that—by accident or parapraxis—introduces the instrumental are merely confirmations of the ruse to hide that which has ethical and political import.

The ruse of techne aims at the forgetting of instrumentality. But its actual effect is different: The construction of the reformulated subject as "Dasein" fails to get a grip on finitude. Because of the concealed instrumentality supported by the ruse of techne, the subject of fundamental ontology appears vacuous. It is not a subject in the world of social and political relations. Rather, it is the subject whose sociality has vanished in a conjurer's trick, a *subjectum absconditum*.

5

The Ontology of Conflict
Conjuring Authority

44. The "turn" and action

A different approach emerges in Heidegger's work from the 1930s, often referred to as the "turn" or *die Kehre*. It is first described by Heidegger himself in the "Letter on Humanism" as "the turning from 'Being and Time' to 'Time and Being.'"[1] It is also memorably articulated by William Richardson, who distinguishes between Heidegger I, exemplified by the fundamental ontology whose starting point is Dasein in *Being and Time*, and Heidegger II, defined by the "reversal" that takes being itself as its starting point.[2] Despite the change of direction, Heidegger and Richardson insist that the focus throughout remains the same, namely, the question of the single, unified being.[3]

---

1. Martin Heidegger, "Letter on Humanism," in *Basic Writings*, trans. David Farrell Krell (London: Routledge, 2000) = GA 9, 231–32/328. More on the "Letter on Humanism" in chapter 6.
2. William J. Richardson, *Heidegger: Through Phenomenology to Thought*, revised edition (New York: Fordham University Press, 2003).
3. Richardson's interpretation had Heidegger's own imprimatur. Heidegger provided a preface for its first edition in 1963. There, he explicitly asserts: "Contrary [to what is generally supposed], the question of *Being and Time* is decisively fulfilled in the thinking of the reversal." Richardson, *Heidegger*, xviii.

There is a wide—even bewildering—array of interpretations that detail this turn.[4] But these interpretations, by and large, follow the framework set by Heidegger and Richardson, raising the suspicion that the turn has become an après-coup explanation that silences the reasons why Heidegger was forced to revise his ontology (cf. §55). What is the impasse that fundamental ontology encounters which motivates Heidegger to change course in the 1930s and which, after World War II, he describes as the turn in "Letter on Humanism"? To answer this question, I want to provide here an account of the turn that departs from the problematic of action in monism.

As we saw in chapter 4, Heidegger encountered an impassable problem when he tried to account for action through the concealment of instrumentality. As I explained in chapter 2, a monist ontology always faces the question of how to account for action. If there is one being outside of which nothing exists, then is action anything but the mere modification of being? Traditionally, monist materialists respond by giving an account of the distinct ends of action (§14, §§21–23, §32). Since the "Natorp report," Heidegger opted instead for a qualitative distinction between actions—whether action is end-oriented or whether it has abandoned external ends—whereby it has the potential to disclose the truth of being (§6, §§13–14, §26, §36).

But *Being and Time* was unable to sustain the separation between qualitatively different actions because the instrumental ends of action proved impossible to contain within circumspection, unraveling Heidegger's attempt to overcome the epistemology of metaphysics (§42). The implications for Heidegger's conception of praxis were even starker: by concealing instrumentality, action was bereft of any effects in the world (§§37–39), whereby it lapsed into triviality (§§40–41), echoing the indifference of the metaphysical conception of theoretical knowledge that Heidegger wanted to overcome (§43). That was the impasse at the end of *Being and Time*.

From this perspective, the key concern in the 1930s becomes the adumbration of a theory of action that is not trivial. The starting point now becomes the attempt to combine thought and action, so that the account

---

4. On the voluminous secondary literature on the turn, see James Risser, "Introduction," in *Heidegger Toward the Turn: Essays on the Work of the 1930s* (Albany: SUNY Press, 1999), 1–16; Thomas Sheehan, "*Kehre* and *Ereignis*: A Prolegomenon to *Introduction to Metaphysics*," in *A Companion to Heidegger's Introduction to Metaphysics*, ed. Richard Polt and Gregory Fried (New Haven, CT: Yale University Press, 2001), 3–16; Richard Fried, *Heidegger's Polemos: From Being to Politics* (New Haven, CT: Yale University Press, 2000), 66–79; and Richard Polt, *Time and Trauma: Thinking Through Heidegger in the Thirties* (London: Rowman & Littlefield, 2019).

of praxis is no longer based on the human's pursuit of truth, but rather on being itself, the aim being to provide a less subjective and a more materialist account of action. The conjunction of thought and action has a direct reference to monism, even if, in typical Heideggerian fashion, it is not named as such. Heidegger consistently turns to Parmenides, the thinker of the one being, to support the identity of thought and action. As *Introduction to Metaphysics* puts it: "Parmenides' saying [about thought and being] is a determination of the human essence on the basis of [*aus*] the essence of being itself" (153/152).[5] In statements such as this—and there are many similar ones (§50) culminating in the discussion of action at the opening of the "Letter on Humanism" (§60)—we can recognize the problematic of action in monism.

Significantly, being's truth that combines thought and action is now described as the conflictual relation between concealment and unconcealment. In this new ontology, the question of truth pivots around a conflict within being itself, as opposed to truth being located within the human pursuit of authenticity. This inflects the qualitative distinction between actions: actions are now separated according to how they deal with the conflict between concealment and unconcealment, which comes to determine both the repression of instrumentality and the conception of action without effects. I call this *conflictual ontology* the attempt to address action from the perspective of the strife between concealment and unconcealment within being as a way of overcoming the triviality of action.

The turn is not simply, not even primarily, about two different epistemologies, one that starts with Dasein and one that starts with being. Rather, the "turn"—or the multiple turns, as I will explore in chapter 6—consists in different responses to the problem of action in monism. The first account of action in Heidegger departs from the conjunction of technology with theoretical knowledge, that is, a conjunction of the forms of action contained in the second sense of techne (§25, §36). This is possible because of the techne or craft analogy (§26), which Heidegger employs to argue for the destruction of the metaphysical separation of theory and praxis—despite the fact that the craft analogy is imbued in metaphysics (§31). The first articulation of action most comprehensively expressed in *Being and Time* resulted in a trivial account of action.

---

5. Martin Heidegger, *Introduction to Metaphysics*, trans. Gregory Fried and Richard Polt (New Haven, CT: Yale University Press, 2000) = *GA* 40. Cited parenthetically in §§44–52, English translation followed by the German edition.

Conflictual ontology seeks to overcome this triviality. The move of the turn as described by Heidegger and Richardson—from Dasein back to being itself—is of secondary importance. The critical shift is that Heidegger no longer bases his argument on the craft analogy. The qualitative distinction between actions, and hence the "essence" of distinct actions (§15), does not start from the consideration, internal to the second sense of techne, of whether theoretical knowledge is the virtue of technology (§27) or vice versa (§42). The second sense of techne is split into science and technology (§46), but there is no longer any attempt to reconcile these two aspects, as was the case through the employment of the craft analogy in the concealment of instrumentality. The sense that refers to science is castigated as nihilism, whereas techne or craft is defined through its proximity to the third meaning of techne that is explicated as poetry, tragedy or the work of art. Nonetheless, by continuing to repress instrumentality—in new ways revolving around authority that I describe in the present chapter—Heidegger arrives at a conception of action that lapses into self-contradictions and betrays a complicity with preexisting structures of power (§16, §53).

45. Authority as the means to repress instrumentality

A significant effect of the abandonment of the craft analogy is that Heidegger can no longer conceal instrumentality within the second sense of techne—science and technology—which was the move first described in *Plato's Sophist* (§27) and then comprehensively employed in *Being and Time* (§36). It is symptomatic of the abandonment of the craft analogy that the optimism about technology in *Being and Time* on the grounds that theoretical knowledge is meant to presuppose handiness—or techne becoming the virtue of theory (§42)—gives way to a pervasive pessimism. For example, in his inaugural lecture at Freiburg University titled "What is Metaphysics?" Heidegger disparages technoscience as the "nihilism of modernity."

The transition to the ontology of conflict occurs gradually so it is next to impossible to determine a specific *terminus a quo*. Elements of the conjunction of techne and theoretical knowledge persist in the early 1930s, even as they are transformed through the engagement with the pre-Socratics and tragedy (§47). But by 1935, when Heidegger delivers the lecture course *Introduction to Metaphysics* as well as the public lectures later published as the essay "The Origin of the Work of Art," it is plain to see that the craft analogy has all but been replaced by the conflict between concealment and unconcealment. The ontological analysis now revolves around terms that denote conflict—such as *Auseinandersetzung*, *Streit*, and *Kampf*. Heraclitus's

Fr. 53—"war (*polemos*) is the father and king of all"—becomes perennial in Heidegger's lectures and writings of this period, emblematic of the new ontology of conflict. It is just as tricky to specify a *terminus ad quem*, but it is also plain to see that the use of terms denoting conflict decreases by the outbreak of WWII, signaling a move beyond the ontology of conflict (§55). We can take Heidegger's two major interpretations of the stasimon in Antigone as exemplifying conflictual ontology and its abandonment. The first in *Introduction to Metaphysics* revolves entirely around conceptions of struggle, conflict, and violence. By contrast, in the interpretation of the same stasimon in *Hölderlin's Hymn "The Ister"* from 1942 violence is no longer central, even though Heidegger appears to arrive at similar conclusions.[6]

If we are to understand the ontology of conflict from the perspective of the question of action within monism, then the most significant change in Heidegger's position consists in the different determination of the repression of instrumentality.

The rise of conflictual ontology coincides with Heidegger's only explicit and intense engagement with the political.[7] I do not mean by this only his foray into politics as a result of becoming rector of Freiburg University. Nor merely the highly unusual number of references to contemporary politics that we find in a text such as *Introduction to Metaphysics*. In addition, the emphasis on the political is an inevitable effect of the emphasis on conflict. There is no conflict in "existential solipsism." Conflict requires interaction, that is, it requires the political. The focus on the political, coupled with the intensification of the repression of instrumentality, is expressed by Heidegger's conception of the political in terms of poetic activity. Poetry or art are now the kind of action purified of ends that emerge as the political action *par excellence*, which explains the emphasis on tragedy, poetry, and the work of art in the period of conflictual ontology.

The ontology of conflict has to refashion the ruse of techne, that is, the technique used to repress instrumentality, since Heidegger can no longer draw on the craft analogy that he used for the repression of the instrumental in *Plato's Sophist* and *Being and Time*. I compared Heidegger's earlier engagement with Aristotle and then the discourse of authenticity in *Being*

---

6. Martin Heidegger, *Hölderlin's Hymn "The Ister,"* trans. William McNeill and Julia Davis (Bloomington: Indiana University Press, 1996) = *GA* 53. This interpretation of *Antigone* takes up more than one third of the entire course (§§10–20). For a review of the literature comparing the two versions of Heidegger's interpretation of the ode to the human in *Antigone*, see Clare Pearson Geiman, "Heidegger's Antigones," in Polt and Fried, *A Companion to Heidegger's Introduction to Metaphysics*, 161–82.

7. Cf. Fried, *Heidegger's Polemos*.

and Time to a conjurer's trick that makes something disappear—in Heidegger's case, instrumentality. The ontology of conflict develops the other stock-standard conjuring trick, that is, making something appear out of thin air. That something is authority, as I will argue here.

By authority I do not mean its modern conception whereby it becomes indistinguishable from sovereignty, but rather *auctoritas* that, from antiquity to the French Revolution, signified the cessation of practical judgment.[8] To the extent that practical judgment requires the calculation of means and ends, the emergence of authority is *eo ipso* a repression of instrumentality. Thus, authority is the obverse side of the repression of instrumentality, since both evade the instrumentality of practical judgments that the Greeks called phronesis. I identify, here, three constitutive characteristics of authority that will help us identify how it is conjured in Heidegger's ontology of conflict.

First, authority is *sui generis*, a spontaneous creation out of nothing.[9] This theme permeates the ontology of conflict. Paul Ricoeur notes that authority has a double source, theological and political.[10] The theological source makes authority *sui generis*. We can see it reflected in the conception of a nothing that makes the thinking of being possible in "What is Metaphysics?" and then again in more detail in *Introduction to Metaphysics*. This spontaneous creation is intertwined with the conception of an action without effects, exemplified by the work of art—poetry and tragedy, in particular. We will also see how this *sui generis* creation becomes responsible, according to Heidegger, for a conception of history and for the founding of the political.

Second, authority necessarily leads to conflict. From a Judeo-Christian perspective, this conflict refers to the double source of authority extrapolated by Ricoeur. As he demonstrates, the political source of authority is the law. The combination of the theological and the political sources of authority produces conflict. Moses exemplifies this double source of authority and its essential violence in early modernity. Emblematic of his theologico-political authority is the ascent to Mount Sinai where he

---

8. See Dimitris Vardoulakis, "The Antinomy of Frictionless Sovereignty: Inverse Relations of Authority and Authoritarianism," *boundary 2 online*, August 20, 2020, www.boundary2.org/2020/08/dimitris-vardoulakis-the-antinomy-of-frictionless-sovereignty-inverse-relations-of-authority-and-authoritarianism/.

9. Alexandre Kojève, *The Notion of Authority (A Brief Presentation)*, ed. François Terré, trans. Hager Weslati (London: Verso, 2014), 31–38.

10. Paul Ricoeur, "The Paradox of Authority," in *Reflections on the Just*, trans. David Pellauer (Chicago: University of Chicago Press, 2007), 91–105.

communed with god and received the Tablets of the Law. When he returned to the camp the Hebrews were venerating the golden calf. Enraged, Moses smashed the Tablets and, as *Exodus* 32: 26–28 says, he "put thousands to the sword."[11] Authority is inherently conflictual outside a Judeo-Christian metaphysics as well. As soon as we define the figure of authority as someone who cannot be argued with, the stage is set for conflict with those who want to argue and resist the figures of authority. Cicero's oldest definition of authority as residing with the Roman senate as opposed to the people's power (*potestas*) suggests such a conflict.[12] Machiavelli celebrates this conflict between the senate and the people as the cause of Rome's greatness.[13] We can discern the same notion of conflict in the distinction between everyday politics—the politics of the state— and the thinking of being as political, which is critical for Heidegger's metaphysico-political conflict (§48) and the notion of the founding of the state (§53).

Third, authority requires to be impervious to conflict itself. Or, more accurately, its source and its destination are immune to conflict. Hannah Arendt has best captured this feature of authority, which she expresses by pointing out its distinction from power (*potestas*) that is essentially instrumental and violent.[14] The conflict inherent in authority's relation to power needs to presuppose a space that is immune from conflict, and which is the reason why authority itself "does not permit of argumentation."[15] Or, as Alexandre Kojève puts it, authority resides with someone whose "action does not provoke a reaction."[16] In Arendt's formulation, "where arguments are used, authority is left in abeyance."[17] Differently put, authority is the structure of power that precludes the operation of phronesis because it

---

11. For an extensive discussion of the theologico-political source of authority in relation to Moses, see Dimitris Vardoulakis, *Spinoza, the Epicurean: Authority and Utility in Materialism* (Edinburgh: Edinburgh University Press, 2020), chapter 2.

12. Cicero, *De Legibus*, trans. Clinton W. Keyes (Cambridge, MA: Harvard University Press, 1928), 492.

13. Niccolò Machiavelli, "Discourses on the First Decade of Titus Livius," in *Machiavelli: The Chief Works and Others*, volume 1, trans. Allan Gilbert (Durham, NC: Duke University Press, 1989), 200–201.

14. Hannah Arendt, "Authority," in *Between Past and Future: Six Exercises in Political Thought* (New York: Viking, 1961), 91–141, and *On Violence* (New York: Harcourt, 1970).

15. Spinoza, *Theological-Political Treatise*, trans. Samuel Shirley (Indianapolis, IN: Hackett, 2001), 139.

16. Kojève, *The Notion of Authority*, 13.

17. Arendt, "Authority," 93.

presupposes a space that is purified of instrumentality.[18] A figure retains authority only in the absence of any residual resistance that arises from the fact that others might have conflicting instrumental ends from the one who has authority.[19] In other words, authority represses practical judgment—authority is the means for the repression of instrumentality.

So, authority is created spontaneously, it is violent, and it points to a space protected from conflict because it is free of instrumentality. We will see how Heidegger's ontology of conflict employs and combines these three constitutive characteristics thereby conjuring authority—even though he never names it as such—as the means to repress instrumentality and to perform the ruse of techne.

46. Conflict and the three senses of techne

As we have seen, the ruse of techne relies on three areas of signification related to techne, or the three senses of techne (§3). They denote a constellation of three conceptual fields that determine the structure of Heidegger's thought (§4, §6, §15, and §27). It is necessary to revisit the three senses of techne here—how are the three senses of techne configured in the ontology of conflict?

The first sense of techne points to the discovery of the single, unified being in Greek thought. This was described in *Being and Time* in terms of the destruction of metaphysics. Destruction is replaced in conflictual ontology by the rhetoric of the origin. The shift in language indicates, also, a conceptual shift. If destruction suggests that we need to dismantle the metaphysical conception of being, the new rhetoric emphasizes the metaphorics of the word "origin" in German, *Ur-spung*: the origin is not something confined to the distant past but rather a "primordial leap" from the past that determines our present and future. Or, in Heidegger's own words: "The beginning *exists* still [*ist* noch]. It does not lie *behind* us [*nicht* hinter uns] as something long past, but it stands *before* us [vor *uns*]. . . . The beginning has invaded our future."[20] The delineation of monism in terms of the origin coincides with a decreased focus on Plato and Aristotle and a

---

18. Vardoulakis, *Spinoza, the Epicurean*.

19. I use the example of "order, peace and stability" to describe how a sovereign logic also requires such a space beyond conflict. See Vardoulakis, *Sovereignty and its Other: Toward the Dejustification of Violence* (New York: Fordham University Press, 2013).

20. Martin Heidegger, "The Self-Assertion of the German University," in *The Heidegger Controversy: A Critical Reader*, ed. Richard Wolin, trans. William S. Lewis (Cambridge, MA: MIT Press, 1998) = *GA* 16, 32/110.

corresponding increased engagement with the pre-Socratics—especially Heraclitus and Parmenides—as well as tragedy, that Heidegger regards as the supreme expression of Greek poetry (§49). This change of focus facilitates the determination of a space immune from conflict, which is one of the constitutive characteristics of authority.

The most readily recognizable change from the concealment of instrumentality in *Being and Time* occurs within the second sense of techne—that is, the one that includes the useful dealing with things and theoretical knowledge. The structure of the argument in *Being and Time* required that the gap between useful dealings (*Zuhandenheit*) and theory was bridgeable, whence the reliance on the craft analogy. As we saw (§42), Heidegger argues that science, in fact, relies on practices such as measuring or notations with pen and paper, which means that praxis is inscribed in theoretical knowledge, whereby techne emerges as the virtue of theory. In the ontology of conflict, there is scant effort to bridge the gap. To the contrary, a widening gap offers the first determination of conflict. The activities of techne as craft are now systematically opposed to scientific activities, whence the impression that the craft analogy is all but abandoned. Heidegger designates this gap as constitutive of the essential decision that makes genuine history possible. It is no longer science *as* technology; it is now *either* technoscience *or* the essence of techne as conflict and violence (§49).

This opening up of the gap between the two kinds of activity in the second meaning of techne pushes techne as craft close to the third meaning of techne. In the transfiguration of craft, great techne becomes near identical with the thinking of being. That is why Heidegger underscores that Prometheus, who gave craft to the humans, was regarded by the Greeks as the first philosopher (§47). But the clearest indication of this move is Heidegger's elevation of the poet or the artist to the same level as the thinker or philosopher who can disclose being: "Only poetry [*Dichtung*] is of the same order as philosophical thinking" (28/28). It is not by accident that, even before the dust had settled from the ill-fated foray into the rectorship at Freiburg University, Heidegger turned to Hölderlin for the first time. The lecture course from the winter semester of 1934–1935—the first new course Heidegger offered after his rectorship—describes poetry as providing a nonmetaphysical conception of being or *Seyn* (an archaic spelling of Sein or being that he discovers in Hölderlin).[21]

---

21. Martin Heidegger, *Hölderlin's Hymns "Germania" and "The Rhine,"* trans. William McNeill and Julia Ireland (Bloomington: Indiana University Press, 2014) = *GA* 39.

By contrast, the scientific activity that belongs to the second meaning of techne is now presented in increasingly negative ways. "The Age of the World Picture" (1938) perhaps best captures this opposition to scientific knowledge as detrimental to the fate of the human in modernity. Theoretical knowledge grasps the world as a "picture" because it is representational. This means, according to Heidegger, both that the objects to be cognized are understood as mere presence, and simultaneously that the human is conceived as a subject that is positioned as an external observer to gain theoretical knowledge of the object. There is, in other words, the metaphysical separation of theory and praxis. What Heidegger finds most objectionable about this "world picture" is that it creates a "realm of human capacity [*Bereich der menschlichen Vermögen*] as the domain of measuring and execution for the purpose of the mastery of beings as a whole [*für die Bewältigung des Seienden im Ganzen*]."[22] Heidegger disparages the submission of human action to the measuring of nature, which he regards as the scourge of modern technology that dooms humans to subjection. Thus, Heidegger's political project becomes committed to the rejection of the mastery of technoscience. Consequently, the first site of conflict is the opposition to technoscientific mastery. The first site of conflict, then, is within the second meaning of techne: between the violence of craft and the domination of technoscience and, as I will show, it is related to the conflict constitutive of authority (§48).

The third sense of techne can be understood as the action that presents the conflict between concealment and unconcealment, which uncovers the truth of being. This second kind of conflict unfolds within being and it can take various forms. A recurring one is that between thinking (νοεῖν) and being (εἶναι). According to Parmenides—the most stringent monist of Greek thought—the two are the same (§50). Heidegger extrapolates this monism by insisting that its source is the unresolvable conflict between concealment and unconcealment at the heart of truth. Key to this conflict between concealment and unconcealment is that it is not constructed. Rather, it appears spontaneously, it is *sui generis*, which is a constitutive feature of authority.

The three senses of techne in conflictual ontology come together through the operation of authority. The origin that refers to Greek monism that, according to Heidegger, points to a space immune from conflict, is redeployed

---

22. Martin Heidegger, "The Age of the World Picture," in *Off the Beaten Track*, trans. Julian Young and Kenneth Haynes (Cambridge: Cambridge University Press, 2002) = *GA* 5, 69/92.

spontaneously—without any calculation of instrumental ends—through the political conflict between craft and the unity of being so as to impact our present predicament. This conjunction of the three senses of techne and the three constitutive characteristics of authority culminates in the figure of the preservers, conceived as the "people" who grasp their "destiny" in a spontaneous act that founds the polis (§53). Thus, the three senses of techne work in tandem with the three constitutive characteristics of authority to conjure the figure of authority in the ontology of conflict. Such an authority becomes the means for the repression of instrumentality and, as such, enacts the ruse of techne in this period of Heidegger's work.

47. The subjectivism of authority (*Prometheus*)

The positions that sophia is the virtue of techne in *Plato's Sophist* and that technology is the virtue of sophia in *Being and Time* both repress instrumentality by employing the craft analogy according to which the end of techne and the final end of causality are essentially related (§27). The opening up of a gap between techne and theory to instigate the conflict characteristic of the second meaning of techne seeks to abandon the craft analogy. This is first clearly established in a passage that records the earliest conjuring of authority and that is also the earliest substantive reference to tragedy in Heidegger's work. I am referring to the discussion of Aeschylus's *Prometheus* in the rectoral address.

It should come as no surprise that the conflictual ontology exhibits an increasing fascination with tragedy. After all, the core of Greek tragedies is the agon or dialogic conflict between the protagonists. Heidegger credits Jacob Burckhardt with the discovery of the "agonal principle" in ancient Greece, which he links to tragedy, going so far as to assert that "there is only *Greek* tragedy and no other besides it."[23] Following Burckhardt, the agonal or conflictual and the tragic are intertwined in Heidegger's mind (§51). The reference to *Prometheus* inaugurates a variegated and fascinating engagement with tragedy that marks Heidegger's conflictual ontology. This first engagement with tragedy shows how the ontology of conflict substitutes the craft analogy with authority as the new means to repress instrumentality. But this results in the opposite of what the purported turn is supposed to accomplish. Instead of eliminating any impression of the metaphysics of the subject in Dasein, authority in fact conjures a more

---

23. Martin Heidegger, *Parmenides*, trans. Andre Schuwer and Richard Rojcewicz (Bloomington: Indiana University Press, 1992) = *GA* 54, 18/26, 90/134.

robust subjectivism. Let us see how this works by examining the interpretation of techne in *Prometheus* according to the rectoral address.

The concept that organizes the rectoral address, "The Self-Assertion of the German University," is *Wissenschaft*, meaning both science in the narrow sense and knowledge more broadly.[24] Heidegger insists that we can discover the essence of science/knowledge only if "we submit to the power of the *beginning* of our spiritual historical existence," which he identifies with Greek philosophy because it distinguishes between the multiplicity of being from "the being that is," whereby for the Greeks "all science/knowledge is philosophy [*alle Wissenschaft ist Philosophie*]."[25] This establishes monism—the first sense of techne—as origin and provides the segue into *Prometheus*.

To demonstrate the Greek conception of knowledge, Heidegger quotes line 514 from Aeschylus's *Prometheus Bound*. The Greek is:

τέχνη δ' ἀνάγκης ἀσθενεστέρα μακρῷ

A standard translation would be:

Techne is weaker than necessity

Heidegger's translation emphasizes the power (*Kraft*) of the techne mentioned in this passage. This power is radically different from the power of scientific knowledge that aims to master nature:

"But knowledge [*Wissen*] is far less powerful [*weit unkräftiger*] than necessity." That means: all knowledge of things remains beforehand at the mercy of overpowering fate and fails before it [*der Übermacht des Schicksals und versagt vor ihr*].[26]

Heidegger's interpretation of this passage consists in identifying two notions of conflict that arise from the second sense of techne. The first is the impotence in the face of the external world's determinative causality. Such a "knowledge is presented to us as the 'theoretical' attitude."[27] This technoscientific knowledge functions by separating the subject from the object, constructing the metaphysics of mere presence. This has nothing to do with the second notion of conflict that relies on the necessity or compulsion

---

24. Recall, for instance, the great debate between Natur- und Geisteswissenschaften, or natural sciences and the science of the "spirit" (or the humanities) that was so important in Germany since the mid-nineteenth century.
25. Heidegger, "The Self-Assertion of the German University," 31/108–09.
26. Heidegger, "The Self-Assertion of the German University," 31/109.
27. Heidegger, "The Self-Assertion of the German University," 31/109.

(ἀνάγκη) as understood by the Greeks, insists Heidegger. For the Greeks, "science [*Wissenschaft*] is the questioning standing firm in the midst of the totality of beings as it continually conceals itself. This active perseverance," explains Heidegger, "knows of its impotence in the face of Fate [*seine Unkraft vor dem Schicksal*]."[28] The knowledge of techne recognizes that beings are concealed—they can never yield the truth of being. That is the impotence of techne that is concerned with particular beings: it is of necessity bound—just like Prometheus—to its fate, that is, to the single, unified being that remains a mystery.

We see here two differences from the earlier ontology of the concealment of instrumentality. First, the analysis of *Being and Time* sought to reconcile technology and theoretical knowledge, the two sides of the second sense of techne. Such a reconciliation was an essential feature of the destruction of the metaphysical separation of theory and praxis. By contrast, theory and praxis are here in an irreconcilable conflict. Second, this has significant implications for Heidegger's conception of praxis. We found the analysis of action in *Being and Time* blind to power. By contrast, the conflict between techne and scientific knowledge in *Prometheus* leads straight to references to power.

In these differences from the concealment of instrumentality, it is still unclear what the demand means that "we obey the distant decree of the beginning."[29] We can see this as a demand to remain attuned to the single, unified being or monism. Such a demand collapses an analysis of action into the "obedience" to being. Through such a collapse, the kind of power that emerges is authority. Let me demonstrate how this occurs by examining the conjuring of authority in Heidegger's reading of *Prometheus*.

We can start by contextualizing the line from *Prometheus* quoted in the rectoral address. Line 514 is part of an exchange between the Chorus and Prometheus. The Chorus accuses Prometheus that he was out of his mind to have stolen the fire from the gods and given it to the humans (cf. §41). Such an action aroused the ire of Zeus who punished Prometheus to be chained to a rock in the Caucasus where an eagle would eat his liver each day and the liver would grow anew each night—a perpetual torture since Prometheus was immortal. The severe punishment is justified because fire was the condition of the possibility of techne. Prometheus responds with a detailed description of how craft benefits humans. This concludes with the forceful assertion that all the arts of the mortals come from Prometheus. At this point, the Chorus

---

28. Heidegger, "The Self-Assertion of the German University," 32/110.
29. Heidegger, "The Self-Assertion of the German University," 32/110.

challenges Prometheus as a master technites—that is, as the master of techne. What good is your techne, says the Chorus, when in fact it is "less powerful [μεῖον ἰσχύσειν]" than Zeus, the king of the gods, who is punishing you for giving the humans too generous a gift?[30] Prometheus responds in line 514 that techne is less powerful (ἀσθενεστέρα) than necessity.

Necessity (ἀνάγκη) refers to something distinct from techne—clearly, Heidegger is correct on this. He is also correct to note that necessity has a double register. The first is the notion of causality, that is, the necessity that, as Prometheus knows, will ultimately lead Zeus to accept the gift of fire to the humans. The second notion of necessity, however, is contrasted with the power (ἰσχύς) of Zeus himself. Prometheus says to the Chorus that, even if he is weaker than Zeus, and his technical skills could not prevent his current punishment, still he can *calculate* that this will change in the future. He undertook the action to disobey the king of the gods and suffer the consequences because he judged that the power struggle with Zeus would ultimately resolve itself favorably.

The notion of necessity then creates a rupture between techne and causality. Their ends may be understood on the same model—they can both be configured as final ends independent of the action performed, as we have seen since chapter 1, but this does not entail that they are the same, as the craft analogy would suggest. The gap that opens up between them creates conflict (such as the conflict between Zeus and Prometheus). Heidegger is correct to see the split between techne and causality, and to also see how the split is constitutive of power and the agon that it precipitates. He is also correct that this is only possible on the condition that we understand being as one and unified. Monism essentially tells us that even Zeus, the king of the gods, cannot escape the totality outside of which nothing exists. Even Zeus is subject to the necessity of being.

Although Heidegger gets so much right about line 514, he misses one critical, indispensable point: the function of instrumentality in *Prometheus* in overcoming the craft analogy. The rupture between techne and causality, the power dynamic that this generates, and the way that the conflict is determined by the necessity of being, are all effected by Prometheus's calculation that leads to his judgment to give fire to the humans. This is the kind of calculation that the Greeks call phronesis. It is not a calculation with a clear end—Prometheus does not know how the power struggle with Zeus

---

30. Aeschylus, *Prometheus Bound*, in *Suppliant Maidens, Persians, Prometheus, Seven Against Thebes*, trans. Herbert Weir Smyth (Cambridge, MA: Harvard University Press, 1922), 510.

will unfold, as the end of the calculation is determined by the actions undertaken, it is not independent of them. As such, the end is instrumental and distinct from the ends of techne and causality. At the same time, Prometheus suggests, the instrumental calculation arises as a response to *both* the opening up of a gap between the ends of techne and causality *and* the resultant power configurations. It was Prometheus's instrumental decision or judgment of phronesis to give fire to the humans that effected the exercise of power from the king of the gods. Thus, the notion of power evidenced in line 514 operates via the distinction between causality and instrumentality indicative of materialist monism (§7, §14, §§22–23). Power relations arise as a result of Prometheus's instrumental judgments, whose ends are distinct from final ends.

In Aeschylus's play, the exercise of practical judgment by Prometheus constitutes a challenge to the authority of Zeus that results in his ire and the punishment of the titan. The tragic element consists in the relation between Prometheus's instrumental calculation, Zeus's authority, and how they are mediated by the foreknowledge that, in time, the dispute will be resolved.[31] The tragedy arises from Prometheus's calculation about Zeus's immediate power and the eventual acceptance of the gift of fire to the humans. This calculation is the operation of phronesis—the kind of calculation whose ends arise through its enactment, whereby they can never be calculated with any certainty. Line 514 establishes a distinction between causality and instrumentality—or between the *hou heneka* and *heneka tinos* (§21). Prometheus's instrumental calculation arising from this distinction between causality and instrumentality is a political act that challenges Zeus's authority (§32).

The tensions that arise as a result of the operation of instrumentality are absent from Heidegger's reading. Instead of a distinction between causality and instrumentality, Heidegger emphasizes the relation between concealment and the single, unified being. This brings techne as technology close to the single, unified being, thereby creating the two senses of conflict—against science and within being—that constitute the knowledge of techne. But such knowledge remains ignorant of instrumentality.

Heidegger's analysis of power in "The Self-Assertion of the German University" conjures authority through the operation of the three constitutive

---

31. I note in passing how the tragic in Aeschylus is related to an excess of knowledge, whereas from Sophocles onward the tragic arises from a lack of knowledge. Prometheus knows, while Oedipus is ignorant. This fundamental difference has not been sufficiently noted by scholars. But that is a huge topic that I cannot take up here—it deserves its own book.

characteristics of authority. The demand to "obey being" establishes a power that appears spontaneously and that suspends judgment, thereby making authority impervious to resistance. By repressing the contestable calculation of the ends of instrumentality, authority is quarantined from contestation, the possibility of resistance to authority disappears. Prometheus can challenge Zeus's authority because instrumentality mediates between the ends of techne and the necessity evidenced by the ends of causality. But when Heidegger associates necessity with the spontaneously created obedience to being, the space of contestation is eliminated. Even though there is conflict through techne, the authority of being itself is immune from any challenge or contestation. Obeying being is the protective harbor that shelters from conflict those who act in accordance with the single, unified being.

Heidegger's interpretation of *Prometheus* in the rectoral address shows how authority establishes the repression of instrumentality. The split of the ends of techne and the final ends of causality institute a conflict whose *end* is the repression of instrumentality. The instrumental end of the ontology of conflict—suggesting that, *pace* Heidegger, the ends of phronesis cannot be eliminated through their repression—is nothing but the establishment of the authority of being that annuls conflict. It is an ontology that allows for conflict in how being articulates itself through concealment and unconcealment, only so that conflict is eliminated from the authority of being that this conflictual relation establishes. It is, in other words, a conflictual ontology whose end is the end of conflict.

This has a significant political implication. Even if Heidegger says that it is being that needs to be obeyed, the authority of being, in fact, implies human authority. About a year after Heidegger delivered his rectoral address and resigned from his position, he visited Karl Jaspers again. Before 1933, the two philosophers would regularly work together at Jaspers's house for a week or two at a time. This meeting in June 1934 would be the last time that the two met face-to-face, and it was tense and awkward. Jaspers challenged Heidegger's position about the renewal of knowledge expressed in the rectoral address. Not only did Heidegger defend his position by calling "for judgment day on philosophy. . . . [Heidegger also] said, with anger and fury in his voice, that it was 'nonsense that there should be so many professors of philosophy, only two or three need be kept in Germany.' When Jaspers asked which ones, Heidegger remained meaningfully silent."[32] Jaspers challenged Heidegger to determine who judges who is obeying being.

---

32. Rüdiger Safranksi, *Martin Heidegger: Between Good and Evil*, trans. Ewald Osers (Cambridge, MA: Harvard University Press, 1999), 231.

Who judges the borders of the site that is protected from conflict? This suggests that, even though authority is supposed to reside in being, still it requires "representatives," endowed with authority, to make judgments about the matrix of command and obedience. The power of being turns out to be nothing but the exercise of the power of its representatives.

Heidegger's response to Jaspers was consistent throughout this period: authority is only ever met with silence. Authority determines knowledge and conflict and as such its presence is powerfully felt. But authority is never named as such. This authority is never spoken of—it appears out of thin air, as if it is *sui generis* (§§52–53). Jaspers's question suggests however that authority also needs to be effected by a representative. Even more emphatically, Jaspers suggests that Heidegger has appointed himself as the representative of the authority of being.

The move away from fundamental ontology that starts with Dasein is supposed, on the accepted account, to eliminate any residual impression of anthropocentricism. But the conjuring of authority in conflictual ontology in fact establishes a subjectivism that revolves around the figure of authority who demands obedience on behalf of being and silence about that authority. At the end of conflictual ontology, there emerges the subjectivism of a figure who represents authority—a subjectivism much more radical than the determination of Dasein in *Being and Time*.

48. The problem of the metaphysico-political conflict

The question thus becomes whether the conjuring of authority can provide an account of action that is preferable to the trivial action of the concealment of instrumentality in *Being and Time*. More than any other text, *Introduction to Metaphysics* stands out by explicitly linking the ontological argument to Heidegger's contemporary political situation. This pivotal text for conflictual ontology was delivered in 1935 and then became the first lecture course to be published in 1953, revised for publication by Heidegger himself. In this text, we discover the great problem faced by the ontology of conflict: the subjectivism of authority in fact suggests that instrumentality is still operative, which makes Heidegger's discourse self-contradictory and complicit with the political powers identified as the representatives of being.

We can read *Introduction to Metaphysics* as tackling the problem of action in monism, as the entire course is framed by the question of the nothing. "The question 'Why are there beings [*Seiendes*] at all instead of nothing [*Nichts*]?' is first in rank for us as the broadest, as the deepest, and finally as the most originary question" (2/2). It soon becomes clear that Heidegger sides with Parmenides's monist position according to which nothing does not exist (§11). But the nothing does not exist as the absence of being, or as the negation of a totality outside of which nothing exists. Thus, the question of the nothing leads to the conception of the single, unified being. It entails, as Heidegger puts it at the conclusion of "The Age of the World Picture," that being itself is nothing. *Introduction to Metaphysics* is structured around these two conceptions of the nothing, the metaphysical and the monist.

The metaphysical conception of the nothing sets up the conflict within a monist framework. The "nothing remains in principle inaccessible to all science" (27/28) because it understands nothing as mere absence that is opposed to mere presence. This metaphysical failure to comprehend the nothing in monist terms institutes the "pure nihilism" of modernity (26/26). This is the gateway to transfer the ontological conflict between concealment and unconcealment to the political realm as the conflict between those powers that adhere to monism and those that promote the nihilism of technoscience.

The ontological conflict becomes political by being translated into a specific geopolitics. The German *Volk* are "the metaphysical people" because they have access to the origin, the conception of the single, unified being. But they are surrounded by America and the Soviet Union—"we lie in the pincers [*wir liegen in der Zange*]" (41/41).[33] And again, "Europe . . . lies today in the great pincers [*in der großen Zange*] between Russia on the one side and America on the other" (40/40). The "metaphysical" identity of America and Russia is based on their common employment of technoscience in such a way as to be controlled by it and to lose all connection to the origin. "Russia and America, seen metaphysically [*metaphysisch gesehen*], are both the same: the same hopeless frenzy of unchained technology [*dieselbe trostlose Raserei der entfesselten Technik*]" (40/40–41). No wonder they are mired in liberal democracy and communism respectively, the two political regimes that actualize the nihilism of modernity, according to Heidegger (§15).

Ontological thinking has here been transformed into a geopolitical confrontation between those for and those against monism—not in an abstract way, but as specific political actors in the stage of world politics. This metaphysico-political conflict cannot be reduced to a message to obey the National Socialists whom Heidegger also criticizes as complicit in the

---

33. For the most informative discussion of the historical background to Heidegger's mobilization of such a political discourse in the mid-1930s, see Charles Bambach, *Heidegger's Roots: Nietzsche, National Socialism, and the Greeks* (Ithaca, NY: Cornell University Press, 2003).

nihilism of modernity because of the instrumentalism of their politics.[34] The translation of the ontological into the geopolitical stage appears to transform the account of action from *Plato's Sophist* and *Being and Time*. There is nothing trivial in the translation of the ontological conflict into a geopolitical conflict: the metaphysico-political call to liberation from the "pincers" intends to break the hold of vacuousness in the account of action that we discovered in the concealment of instrumentality.

A closer look, however, reveals that the conflation of the metaphysico-political conflict brings us back to the dilemma about action in Heidegger's thought (§16). The repression of instrumentality makes action either apolitical and hence trivial, or self-contradictory and hence potentially complicit in the exercise of the prevailing power. This dilemma is accentuated by the inchoate subjectivism of the conjuring of authority. The moment that the ontological is transformed into political terms by calling for a fight against the representatives of instrumentality, the question becomes, *who* issues the call? *Who* is authorized to bring the ontological and the political together? *Who* has the *authority* to translate an ontological "polemos" into a geopolitical confrontation?

With these questions, the operative presence of authority in Heidegger's discourse becomes visible—an authority that is never acknowledged and which appears out of nowhere, *ex nihilo*. Such a conjuring of authority lapses into a radical subjectivism caught in the familiar double bind (§16). As soon as there is a political call against instrumentality so as to effect a metaphysico-political liberation from the nihilism of modernity, *either* the call does not really pertain to action, in which case it is trivial, *or* it does and thus has effects in which case it is an instrumental call against those who represent the technoscientific instrumentalism in modernity, which is self-contradictory.

49. The historical decision and phusis (*Oedipus Rex*)

Introduction to Metaphysics presents the metaphysico-political conflict as history. The starting point of such a conception of history is monism. If there is one being outside of which nothing exists, then clearly there can be no complete knowledge of that one. Thus, being has always been thought

---

34. The implicit criticism of National Socialism in *Introduction to Metaphysics* was first pointed out by Heidegger himself who justifies the mildness of the criticism due to the presence of informers. This has often been discussed in the secondary literature. See the essays in Part 3 in Polt and Fried, *A Companion to Heidegger's Introduction to Metaphysics*.

of in relation to its opposites. History is the register of these oppositions to being. This conception of history, however, relies on phusis as the unity of the single, unified being. Phusis in itself is purified of conflict, thereby bringing to the fore one of the constitutive features of authority: namely, that the source of its conflictual nature is itself immune to conflict.

Chapter 4 of *Introduction to Metaphysics*—which, in fact, takes up more than half the course—is organized around four such fundamental oppositions to being that delineate Heidegger's framework for the entire history of thought as they are essentially the history of being in its unity. The fourth is the opposition between being and ought to that, Heidegger asserts, is exclusively modern and as such suffers from the forgetting of being. So, Heidegger concentrates on the other three oppositions. I will turn to the third opposition through an analysis of Heidegger's reading of *Antigone* (§§50–52), but this requires that we understand the first two oppositions that establish the notion of phusis.

The first and second oppositions concern the Greek way in which being and its opposite have been thought. They are the oppositions of being and becoming and being and seeming. As belonging to the origin of being in Greek thought, they attest an "inner connection" (107/109), which is the single, unified being. Thus, they are ultimately a single opposition seen from two perspectives characteristic of Greek thought (121–22/122–23). That explains why Heraclitus, who is usually associated with an argument about the priority of becoming, is for Heidegger, actually in agreement with Parmenidean monism, usually understood to hold the oneness of being as opposed to seeming. They both adhere to the single, unified being that Heidegger discovers in Greek thought (103/105) (§50).

Heidegger holds that Greek thought itself, specifically the sophists and Plato, establishes a separation between being and seeming that paves the way for onto-theo-logy (111/113). The "chasm" (*Kluft*) between being and seeming is consummated by Judeo-Christian metaphysics, which loses the unity and singularity of being. By contrast, Heidegger insists that the Greeks managed to "wrest being forth from beings" only by "embodying the struggle [*einzig im Bestehen des Kampfes*] between being and seeming" (111/113). In other words, the unity and singularity of being is sustained in the struggle or conflict that belongs to the opposition of being and seeming.

It is at this juncture that tragedy becomes important. The "unity and clash [*Einheit und Widerstreit*] of being and seeming" was "portrayed at its highest and purest in Greek tragic poetry [*Tragödiendichtung*]" (111–12/113–14). His example is Sophocles's *Oedipus Rex*. Oedipus initially seems to be the savior of Thebes, but then "he is unconcealed in his Being as the murderer of his father and the defiler of his mother." Heidegger infers that Oedipus's story presents "a unique struggle [*ein einziger Kampf*] between seeming (concealment and distortion) and unconcealment (being)" (112/114). From this, Heidegger concludes that "in Oedipus we must grasp that form of Greek Dasein . . . [namely] the passion for the unveiling of being, that is, the struggle over being itself [*d.h. des Kampfes um das Sein selbst*]" (112/114). The suggestion is clear. The conflict, struggle, or clash between being and seeming, characteristic of Heidegger's conception of Greek monism, is nothing but the unfolding of the truth of being as the strife between concealment and unconcealment.

This leads to Heidegger's conception of the historical. The Greek origin is not confined to a distant, irretrievable past. Heidegger emphasizes that truth, as the conflict between concealment and unconcealment, is determinative today because the genuine notion of history starts with the way in which our actions relate to that originary conflict. This entails the "decision" about whether one is "for or against" such a conflict. "With decision [*Ent-scheidung*], history as such begins." In a parenthetical remark added in 1953, Heidegger explains that "de-cision here does not mean the judgment and choice of human beings, but rather a division [*Scheidung*] in the aforementioned togetherness of Being" (116/118) insofar as it is articulated in the conflict of truth. Thus, the conflict between concealment and unconcealment within the Greek opposition of being and seeming determines our history. We experience "the nearness of future decision" because this origin remains active.[35] And this means that we have to decide—whether we want it or not, whether we are aware of it or not—the side we are on: the side of the Greek origin that adheres to monism or the side of the nihilism of modernity that forgets the original conflict of concealment and unconcealment (§52). This "decision for or against" is the monist origin of history (116/118).

Such a conception of history as fundamentally conflictual recalls Nietzsche's assertion that the struggle between the noble and the slave mentalities is the determinative event of history. Just like the *Introduction to Metaphysics*, the *Genealogy of Morality* also presents history as a conflict that arises from a distant origin that determines us today. But there is a determinative difference. The origin of morality or action in Nietzsche is *Schuld*, meaning both debt and guilt. Both meanings imply an instrumental calculation. The important aspect of such a calculation for Nietzsche is not whether it

---

35. Martin Heidegger, "On the Essence and Concept of *Phusis* in Aristotle's *Physics* B, 1," in *Pathmarks*, ed. William McNeill, trans. Thomas Sheehan (Cambridge: Cambridge University Press, 1998) = *GA* 9, 185.

is correct, but rather how it produces structures of power. The conflict between the noble and the slave mentalities is ultimately the conflict between two conflicting *strategies* about overpowering. The instrumental is inscribed in such a notion of calculating in Nietzsche.[36]

The instrumental is repressed in Heidegger's analysis of the originary conflict. The force of concealment in the Greek experience of the conflict of truth comes from what Heidegger understands as *phusis*. For Greek thought, insists Heidegger, "being and truth create [*schöpfen*] their essence out of *phusis*" (119/120). *Phusis*, according to Heidegger, provides the unity of being but in a concealed way. Heidegger reinforces this point with reference to Heraclitus's Fr. 123, which he renders as being "intrinsically inclined toward self-concealment [*Sichverbergen*]" (121/122). Heidegger's point will be misunderstood if we translate *phusis* as nature. As he points out at the beginning of the course, the term *phusis* was translated into the Latin *natura*, which in turn provided the word "nature" in European languages. The concept of nature indicates birth or growth. The problem with his conception of nature is that it starts with particular beings, assuming that it can arrive at being by examining them, measuring them, or placing them in a chain of causes and effects—what has come to be called a "natural process."[37] But, insists Heidegger, "the Greeks first experienced what *phusis* is . . . the other way around [*umgekehrt*]: on the basis of a fundamental experience of Being in poetry and thought, what they had to call *phusis* disclosed itself to them" (15–16/17). Just as *Oedipus Rex* shows in Heidegger's interpretation, the unity of the Theban city occurs simultaneously with the unity of Oedipus's nature.

Such a repression of instrumentality in the analysis of history as de-cision within the purview of the unity of phusis points to one of the constitutive features of authority—it designates a space immune from conflict. History may start with a de-cision that indicates the conflict against those who decide against monism, but still with the lodgment of history within phusis Heidegger arrives at a unity of being which is itself, as well as its historical representation, protected from conflict. As soon as Oedipus's phusis is disclosed and thereby we also discover the phusis of Thebes, the conflict of history ends in Heidegger's account. Phusis presents an essential unity that is the boundary of conflict. Phusis, as such a boundary, conjures one of the constitutive characteristics of authority, its being immune from conflict.

That such a boundary does not exist for the Greeks is evidenced by the story of Oedipus itself. When it was discovered that he had killed his father

---

36. See Vardoulakis, *The Agonistic Condition* (Edinburgh: Edinburgh University Press, 2025), §26.
37. Cf. Heidegger, "On the Essence and Concept of *Phusis* in Aristotle's *Physics* B, 1."

and defiled his mother, he could no longer be the king of Thebes. But his abdication eventually led to his two sons, Eteocles and Polynices, fighting for the throne. When they kill each other in battle and Antigone, their sister, breaks the order of Creon, the new king, to leave Polynices unburied, conflict continues to permeate the polis. The unity of the single being in Heidegger's construal requires a safe harbor from the conflict of history, whereas for the Greeks there is no such safe harbor as there is no outside to conflict.

50. Apolis and the spontaneous creation of authority (*Antigone* 1)

The grounding of history on the history of being, registered as the various oppositions to being, leads to the originary conflict determinative of the political as soon as phusis encounters what Heidegger refers to as "techne." *Introduction to Metaphysics* presents the political ontology of such a conflict through a reading of the stasimon or choral ode in *Antigone* that describes the human as *deinon*. Based on the assumption of a space immune from conflict in history, Heidegger's interpretation of the stasimon further conjures authority by invoking another one of its constitutive characteristics, its spontaneous creation. Central to this is the reading that he offers of the phoneme "*hyphipolis; apolis*" in line 370 of *Antigone*:

> The *polis* is the site of history, the Here, *in* which, *out of* which and *for* which history happens. To this site of history belong the gods, the temples, the priests, the celebrations, the games, the poets, the thinkers, the ruler, the council of elders, the assembly of the people, the armed forces, and the ships. All this does not first belong to the *polis,* is not first political, because it enters into a relation with a statesman and a general and with the affairs of state. Instead, what we have named is political—that is, at the site of history—insofar as, for example, the poets are *only* poets, but then are actually poets, the thinkers are *only* thinkers, but then are actually thinkers, the priests are *only* priests, but then are actually priests, the rulers are *only* rulers, but then are actually rulers. Are—but this says: use violence as violence-doers [*als Gewalt-tätige Gewalt brauchen*] and become those who rise high in historical being as creators, as doers [*als Schaffende, als Täter*]. Rising high in the site of history, they also become *apolis*, without city and site, lonesome, un-canny, with no way out amidst beings as a whole, and at the same time without ordinance and limit, without structure and fittingness, because they *as* creators [*Schaffende*] must first ground all this in each case. (163/161–62)

The entire analysis of metaphysics and its relation to politics grounded in the history of being through the conflict between phusis and techne is condensed in these few sentences that analyze the phoneme "*hypsipolis; apolis*." The interpretation of the stasimon collapses the distinction between *hypsipolis* and *apolis*, whereby the one who is held in high esteem by the city can simultaneously find themself "without city and site, lonesome." This may appear as an extravagant claim: how is it possible that those who are most profoundly imbued in actions of the polis—the priest, the thinkers, the ruler, and so on—are also excluded from the polis? What unites them is the logic of an action without effects, that is, the repression of instrumentality (§51) that presents a *sui generis* creation of political subjectivity. This, again, conjures authority as spontaneous creation is one of its constitutive features.

To discern the spontaneous creation of authority in the phoneme *hypropolis; apolis*, we need to start by contextualizing the passage within the development of the argument of *Introduction to Metaphysics*. After the analysis of the two specifically Greek oppositions to being—being as opposed to becoming and seeming (§49)—Heidegger turns to the third opposition, being and thinking. Heidegger makes it clear that he regards this as *the* critical opposition for metaphysics. He introduces the opposition as the one that has dominance (*Herrschaft*) in, and hegemony (*Vorherrschaft*) over, Western thought, that is, in philosophy (122–23/123–24). Its predominance means that "it does not set itself between and among [*zwischen und unter*] the other . . . divisions but represents all of them to itself" (123/124). As such, it functions as the ground of the ontology of conflict: "thinking [i.e., as the opposite of being] . . . becomes the basis and the pivot [*zum Boden und Fußpunkt wird*] on which one decides about what stands against it [*das Entgegenstehende entschieden wird*], so much so that being in general gets interpreted on the basis of thinking" (123/124). Consequently, in the opposition of being and thinking "we have to recognize that fundamental orientation of the spirit of the West that is the real target of our attack [*der unser eigentlicher Angriff gilt*]" (123–24/125). Metaphysics has completely misunderstood and missed the conflict of concealment and unconcealment within the single, unified being, and transformed it instead into the opposition between being and thinking. Any monism is compelled to set up this deceiving opposition as its primary target. This means that any monism has to resist the reduction of being into thought—which amounts to saying that monism ought to contend with problematic of action (§12).

There is an important historical dimension to this opposition between being and thinking. It is not only determinative for the present and future direction—for the "destiny"—of the West, whereby it ought to be our "real target." In addition, this target is only possible if we recognize that the opposition is in fact derivative. And this, in turn, is only possible on condition, according to Heidegger, that we see the origin of the thinking of being in Greek thought that holds together being and thinking. A large part of the chapter is taken up by an analysis of Heraclitus and Parmenides, "the founders [*Stifter*] of all thinking" (145/145), to demonstrate that, in their thought, being and thinking are connected. This is the fundamental point about action that all materialist monists agree upon, regardless of disagreements about the nature of action and thought. Heidegger pays particularly close attention to Fr. 5 from Parmenides, according to which thinking (*noein*) and being (*einai*) are one and the same, arguing that this becomes "the guiding principle of Western philosophy" (154/154). The analysis of Fr. 5 leads to the inference that "the type and direction of the opposition between being and thinking are unique because here the human being comes face to face with being [*der Mensch dem Sein ins Angesicht tritt*]. This happening is the knowing appearance of humanity as historical" (150–51/150). How we determine the relation between being and thinking subsequently determines our relation to being (§49). We can face being only with the correct determination of the relation between being and thinking that we find in Greek monism. Given that the relation between thought and being is determinative of history, it also forms the basis for Heidegger's conception of action.

Consequently, historical action is not to be discovered in the *res gestae* or the historical events. Heidegger insists that it was in "poetry in which Greek being and Dasein . . . were authentically founded" (154/153), a poetry that includes Parmenides, Heraclitus and, significantly, tragedy. To delineate this founding, he turns to *Antigone* to interrogate the originary conception of the human through the relation between being and thinking, prior to their separation in onto-theo-logy. Unlike the deficient separation between being and thinking, Heidegger demonstrates that the human as *deinon* exhibits an originary struggle or conflict: "The human [*der Mensch*] is *deinon,* first, inasmuch as it remains exposed to this overwhelming sway, because it essentially belongs to Being. However, the human is also *deinon* because it is violence-doing [*der Gewalt-tätige . . . ist*]" (160/159). The human is deinon because it incorporates the conflict between the unity of *phusis* and the violent act or "violence-doing" that Heidegger associates with techne.[38]

---

38. For the most perspicacious analysis of the relation between phusis and techne, see Walter Brogan, "The Intractable Interrelationship of *Physis* and *Techne*," in *Heidegger and the Greeks: Interpretative Essays*, ed. Drew A. Hyland and John Panteleimon Manoussakis (Bloomington: Indiana University Press, 2006), 43–56. We will return to

Heidegger introduces the conflict between phusis and techne at the beginning of the course: "*phusis* gets narrowed down by contrast with *techne*—which means neither art nor technology but a kind of *knowledge*, the knowing disposal over the free planning and arranging and controlling of arrangements. . . . *Techne* is generating, building, as a knowing pro-ducing [*Erzeugen, Erbauen, als wissendes Hervor-bringen*]" (18/19). We have already seen the conjunction of knowing and techne (§47), which is here further extrapolated through its conflictual relation between phusis and techne. This is represented, according to Heidegger, in the conflict between the unity of phusis and the human's violent technical activities such as seafaring, taming of animals, and cultivating of the land described in the stasimon, activities that seek to change the natural environment in which the human finds itself.

The conflictual relation between phusis and techne is carried out in the choice of words: Heidegger uses the verb *walten* and its cognates to describe *phusis* as a concealing that also unites. This double characteristic of *phusis* has led scholars to compare it to the concept of the "world" in *Being and Time*.[39] But there is something in the word *walten* that the comparison with the notion of the world in *Being and Time* does not fully capture, namely, an allusion to power.[40] The English translators opt for the expression "to hold sway."[41] This is a "correct" translation even though it suffers from the same shortcoming that Derrida identifies in the French translation: it "neutralizes and muffles" the sense of power in the word.[42] By contrast, Derrida insists that the *walten* of *phusis* is an activity that denotes a "dominant, governing power, as self-formed sovereignty, as autonomous, autarchic force, commanding and forming itself, of the totality of beings,

---

the relation between phusis and techne when examining "The Origin of the Work of Art" (§53).

39. For example, Charles Guignon, "Being as Appearing: Retrieving the Greek Experience of *Phusis*," in Polt and Fried, *A Companion to Heidegger's Introduction to Metaphysics*, 42.

40. Cf. Charles E. Scott, "The Appearance of Metaphysics," in Polt and Fried, *A Companion to Heidegger's Introduction to Metaphysics*, 27

41. See "Translators' Introduction," in Heidegger, *Introduction to Metaphysics*, xiii.

42. Jacques Derrida, *The Beast and the Sovereign*, vol. 2, trans. Geoffrey Bennington (Chicago: University of Chicago Press, 2011), 32. Derrida is not discussing here *Introduction to Metaphysics* but rather the course *The Fundamental Concepts of Metaphysics* from six years earlier. Heidegger developed his position about phusis over a number of years by interpreting a number of texts. *Introduction to Metaphysics* gathers and summarizes the earlier discussion, and then presents it in explicitly conflictual terms.

beings in their entirety, everything that is."[43] Derrida suggests that *phusis* affirms the unity of structures of power. This is confirmed by Heidegger's position that *dike* (justice) belongs to *phusis* (e.g., 177/175), and that *nomos* (law) is a "counterphenomenon" of phusis (17/18). The entire unity of the polis through the legal sphere is incorporated with the *walten* of phusis. Within this context, the determination of the activity of techne as *Gewalt* (violence) is telling: The term *Gewalt* as the key characteristic of techne is derived from *walten* as the key characteristic of phusis. The conflictual relation of phusis and techne is registered within this etymological convergence of the words *walten* and *Gewalt* that in fact signify incongruence and conflict. The originary conflict erupts—spontaneously—in the echo of the *walten* of phusis in the *Gewalt* of techne.

The critical point where this spontaneous originary conflict between phusis and techne is translated into political terms thereby conjuring authority is Heidegger's interpretation of the contrast between *hypsipolis* and *apolis* in line 370 of the stasimon. The *polis*, understood not as a legally defined state, but as a site that gathers together all those activities—of the gods, the priests, the poets, and so on—that constitute its history. The unity of the polis, its phusis, determines its gods, its priests, its poets, and its thinkers. The activities of those historical actors, and the effects of those actions, is *not* what determines them as priests, poets, and so on, it is the other way around. By being placed within the phusis of the polis, they engage in the conflicts of being through their techne and as a result they can direct themselves toward certain ends. That is why a poet is first a poet and then an actual poet who produces poetry, as Heidegger explains. They are "only" poets, thinkers, rulers, and so on, insofar as their activity takes place within the structure of the whole of the polis, that is, within the phusis of the polis. At the same time, this is only possible if they perform an act of violence that establishes specific ends which change the structure of the polis. This violence belongs to techne. The conflict of phusis and techne is the spontaneous force that allows the political actors to define themselves as *sui generis*.

The poets, priests, leaders, and so on are "only" so before they are who they are *sui generis* before they need to act toward certain instrumental ends. They act because they incorporate the struggle of phusis and techne within the polis, just like authority is a *sui generis* creation. This spontaneous creation is encapsulated in the phoneme *hypsipolis; apolis*. Following the standard editions of *Antigone*, I insert a colon between *hypsipolis*, that

---

43. Derrida, *The Beast and the Sovereign*, vol. 2, 39.

literally means someone who is held high in the city, and *apolis*, someone without a polis. Heidegger deletes this semicolon in this rendering of the stasimon (157/157) so as to collapse the distinction between *hypsipolis* and *apolis* in order to conjure authority.[44] From this perspective it is indeed irrelevant whether one is *hypsipolis*, one highly regarded within the city, or *apolis*, one outside the city. Both *hypsipolis* and *apolis* are *sui generis* creations of the being outside conflict, and hence their authority does not need grounding in any "real" polis. One can be *apolis*, expelled from the polis—or alienated from the Party, as Heidegger was in 1935—and yet retain all their political authority.

51. The human as *deinon* and the repression of instrumentality (*Antigone* 2)

The spontaneous creation of the political actors becomes the means for the repression of instrumentality. This is accomplished through the key focus of Heidegger's reading of the stasimon, the interpretation of the human as *deinon*. Exploring the source of Heidegger's repression of instrumentality in his interpretation of *Antigone* will help us evaluate the conjuring of authority. This will show us again the importance of instrumentality for Greek thought (§23, §32).

The description of the conflict between *phusis* and *techne* that determines the human as *deinon* excludes consideration of the instrumental ends for action. This is evident in Heidegger's description of the activities listed in the stasimon, all of which are described as forms of techne without any acknowledgment of the parallel operation of instrumental ends. Activities such as sailing and taming animals are technical and the word "technas"—techne in the plural—is mentioned on line 366. But there is ample linguistic evidence in the stasimon that instrumentality is operative alongside techne. For example, the term "pantoporos" that Heidegger discusses at length just prior to turning to "*apolis*" is in fact, as Gourgouris observes, "like the Homeric *polymechanos* or *polytropos*, an Odyssean figure, all-resourceful, making one's passage everywhere ... indeed, much like *deinos*."[45] Ulysses is not a man of techne, he is the archetypical man of instrumental means. So, what is it that justifies Heidegger to read tragedy in

---

44. There is no doubting the willfulness of Heidegger's translation of the stasimon, examined with forensic accuracy by Stathis Gourgouris, *Does Literature Think? Literature as Theory for an Antimythical Era* (Stanford, CA: Stanford University Press, 2003), 134–46.

45. Gourgouris, *Does Literature Think?*, 138.

a fashion that comprehensively represses the instrumentality operative within the description of the human in the stasimon?

The answer is not to be found in *Introduction to Metaphysics*, nor in the Hölderlin seminar from the summer of 1942 which contains the other extensive discussion of *Antigone*. Rather, the answer emerges in the lecture course on Parmenides from the winter semester of 1942–43. The connection between tragedy and Eleatic monism is established since *Introduction to Metaphysics*, where Heidegger turns to *Antigone* to support his argument that the conflict of concealment and unconcealment is constitutive of how Parmenides constructed the relation between being and thought. It is to explicate the same relation that precipitates the turn to *Antigone* in *Parmenides*. Heidegger wants to show how "*aletheia* possesses a conflictual essence" as it unfolds within the polis that "gathers originally the unity of everything."[46] The short reference to *Antigone* adds *almost* nothing significant to the analysis familiar from *Introduction to Metaphysics*.

Almost. Because there is one brief, but revealing, comment. Referring to the conflict of concealment and unconcealment, Heidegger observes: "Here lies concealed the primordial ground of that feature Jacob Burckhardt presented for the first time in its full bearing and manifoldness: the frightfulness, the horribleness, the atrociousness of the Greek polis."[47] Heidegger needs no footnote because his comment on Burckhardt's "lectures at Basel from 1872" that "Nietzsche had in his possession [in the form of] an auditor's transcript" leaves no doubt that he is referring to the lectures published posthumously as *Griechische Kulturgeschichte*, translated as *The Greeks and Greek Civilization*. The most famous chapter of this book, titled "The Agonal Age," describes the Greek city precisely in terms of a conflict free of instrumentality.[48] More specifically, Burckhardt argues that "nobility

---

46. Heidegger, *Parmenides*, 90/133–34.

47. Heidegger, *Parmenides*, 90/133.

48. There is considerable debate in Nietzsche studies about Burckhardt's influence on the development of Nietzsche's notion of agonism. Some downplay this connection. See Christa Davis Acampora, *Contesting Nietzsche* (Chicago: University of Chicago Press, 2013), 211. Others place a lot of emphasis on it. See Yunus Tuncel, *Agon in Nietzsche* (Milwaukee, WI: Marquette University Press, 2013), 8. Heidegger seems to suggest that Nietzsche follows Burckhardt's anti-instrumental interpretation of the agonal. As I argue elsewhere, in fact, Nietzsche reverses Burckhardt's position by making the agonal instrumental. See Vardoulakis, *The Agonistic Condition*, §6. This reversal, I argue, is particularly evident in Friedrich Nietzsche, "Homer's Contest," in *On the Genealogy of Morality and Other Writings*, ed. Keith Ansell-Pearson, trans. Carol Diethe (Cambridge: Cambridge University Press, 2006).

reigned everywhere" in the agonal age.[49] The key feature of aristocratic rule was the prevalence of competition, for instance, in athletic and tragic festivals, whence the "agonal" or competitive nature of the age. Crucially, Burckhardt describes the period as "a non-utilitarian world" whereby "the agon occupied the whole of existence."[50] Following this noninstrumental agon, *Parmenides* indicates that Burckhardt's "agonal age" is the source of the idea of a Greek conflictual ontology purified from instrumentality that Heidegger translates into the political as the unity of the polis.

The problem is that Burckhardt is wrong: Greek culture was anything but anti-instrumental. The most significant work on this is Marcel Detienne and Jean-Pierre Vernant's *Cunning Intelligence in Greek Culture and Society*. The notion of "cunning intelligence" that they argue is central to Greek culture is an expression rendering a number of words that denote acting guided by instrumental ends. The main word that they examine, *metis*, has multifarious significations and applies to a vast array of fields, ranging from everyday life to the gods. *Metis* involves a calculation "applied to situations . . . which do not lend themselves to precise measurement, exact calculation or rigorous logic."[51] It concerns—to put it in the vocabulary from chapter 1—the *tinos heneka* of action. Detienne and Vernant describe cunning intelligence as a fundamental comportment of the ancient Greek psyche that consists in an instrumentality without illusion to a complete calculation.

The translation cunning intelligence is somewhat misleading as the word "cunning" has negative connotations in English. The difficulty of translating *metis* into English, as well as other European languages, is the metaphysical inflection on instrumentality, which associates the calculation of means and ends with sin (§31). No such negative connotation is implied in Greek. Even if Ulysses is perhaps the archetypical master of cunning intelligence, he is not alone—the gods, as we find in myths, historical actors, as we see in Thucydides, and tragic characters, as we saw in the analysis of *Prometheus*, all engage in cunning intelligence. *Metis* is not simply *not* negative, it is, rather, that it does not even occur to the Greek mind to consider whether it is negative or positive. Cunning intelligence as such is beyond "good and evil." It is only its *effects* that can be judged as good or evil—and we will see in a moment how this leads to conceptions of deficient judgment.

---

49. Jacob Burckhardt, *The Greeks and Greek Civilization*, trans. Sheila Stern (New York: St. Martin's Griffin, 1998), 160.
50. Burckhardt, *The Greeks and Greek Civilization*, 185.
51. Marcel Detienne and Jean-Pierre Vernant, *Cunning Intelligence in Greek Culture and Society*, trans. Janet Lloyd (Chicago: University of Chicago Press, 1991), 3–4.

Just as any conception that organizes action in a culture, cunning intelligence is denoted by many words. Besides *metis*, there is a wide array of synonyms. One is *deinotes*, the substantive, and *deinos*, the epithet. Detienne and Vernant explicitly engage with Aristotle's discussion of the *deinon* in book 6 of *Nicomachean Ethics*, where cunning intelligence is philosophically articulated under the concept of phronesis.[52] This is to be expected, since phronesis is the philosophical term that captures the idea of an instrumental calculation that is situated and provisional since its ends form part of the action whereby it is impossible to calculate their outcome with any certainty.

Not only does Heidegger fail to note the deep connection between *to deinon* and phronesis in his analysis of *Antigone* in *Introduction to Metaphysics* or any of its iterations, such as the course on Hölderlin in 1942 and the course on *Parmenides* in 1942–43. He also does not mention *to deinon* in the detailed reading of book 6 of *Nicomachean Ethics* in *Plato's Sophist*, even though it occupies a critical position in the argument about the relation between phronesis and theoretical knowledge. It is not hard to see why. Heidegger *could not* analyze the function of *to deinon* in *Nicomachean Ethics* without also acknowledging that phronesis concerns the calculation of instrumental ends, exposing his mistake to repress instrumentality, which would have been nothing short of giving away his ruse. It would be instructive to examine the role *to deinon* plays in *Nicomachean Ethics*, as this will lead to a renewed appreciation of what Heidegger says—or, rather, does *not* say—in his interpretation of human as *to deinon*, as "uncanny," in the stasimon from *Antigone*.

As already noted, the key difference between techne and phronesis is that the final ends of techne can be verified with some certainty (§22). If the end of action is to make a cup that holds tea, all we have to do to measure the successful completion of techne is to pour some liquid to test the final product. This is not the case with phronesis. There are no predetermined means to achieve the end as its accomplishment is part of the action that includes the judgment of phronesis. The fallibility of phronesis poses various problems. It is in the context of the analysis of these problems that Aristotle employs the epithet *deinos*.

Specifically, a problem concerns the correct means used toward the wrong end. We can agree that drawing a correct judgment about the means of carrying out the action and the accomplishment of its end is a characteristic of the political good (ἀγαθοῦ, 1142b22). But is it still a political good

---

52. Detienne and Vernant, *Cunning Intelligence*, 316–17.

when a bad person (φαῦλος) uses a correct calculation to arrive at something evil (κακὸν δὲ μέγα, 1142b18–21)? The second but related problem concerns the situation when the correct ends are achieved through the employment of incorrect means. Is it still a political good if it is achieved by accident without correct calculation (1142b23–24)?

These problems are not a minor aside to the discussion of phronesis in *Nicomachean Ethics* but central to the comparative evaluation of phronesis and sophia. Everybody knows that Aristotle regards sophia as superior to phronesis, but few seem to pay attention to the sentence announcing this relation: "phronesis is inferior [χείρων] to wisdom but it is nonetheless more impactful [κυριωτέρα]" (1143b34). The comparative *kyrioteros* that I translate as "more impactful" is derived from *kyrios*, the noun indicating the one who is in control or who holds power. It is the Greek word that comes closest to the modern "sovereign." Why does Aristotle say that phronesis is both inferior and more powerful?

The inferiority and greater impact of phronesis are related in a way that points straight to *deinotes*. Sophia is superior because it does not need anything external to achieve its good, consisting in the knowledge of the universal. Wisdom is therefore self-sufficient. Or, as Aristotle puts it, wisdom possesses its whole virtue (τῆς ὅλης ἀρετῆς, 1144a6). With wisdom, the good ends are only ever achieved through good means. By contrast, phronesis is not self-sufficient because of its fallibility. The instrumentality of phronesis also requires natural virtue (ἀρετὴ φυσικὴ, 1144b16) to be able to distinguish a good from a bad action. According to Aristotle, without natural virtues such as bravery or justice we cannot evaluate whether the means and ends operations of phronesis achieve the good. Thus, the calculative virtue of the judgment of phronesis is not self-sufficient since it requires the mediation of natural virtues.

In this context, Aristotle calls *deinotes* the fallibility of phronesis (1144a24). Deinotes denotes the fact that there is no certain or complete calculation of means and ends. Thus, a *deinos* could be someone who employs means at this disposal for both good and bad ends. Or as Sophocles puts it in the stasimon, "wise [σοφόν] beyond hope is the instrumentality [τὸ μηχανέον] of the human's skills [τέχνας], whereby the human advances sometimes to evil, at other times to good."[53] *To deinon* consists in the employment of means that are never good nor bad as such. No matter what

---

53. Sophocles, *Antigone*, in *Antigone. Women of Trachis. Philosctetes. Oedipus at Colonus*, trans. Hugh Lloyd-Jones (Cambridge, MA: Harvard University Press, Loeb, 1994), 365–67.

technical skills are employed, it is the context of their employment that determines their virtue. But, at the same time, such instrumental actions have significant *effects* in the world. The calculation, regardless of whether their means and their ends are good or bad, impact the city. Consequently, the *deinotes* of phronesis is more powerful (*kyriotera*) than sophia.

This paradoxical power of phronesis—its deficiency because it errs and its impact on the polis—is registered in the stasimon through the contrast *hypsipolis; apolis*. The Chorus points out that those who make the correct judgments are *hypsipolis* or highly regarded in the polis. By contrast, those who err in their calculations become *apolis*. Their wrong judgments make them unwanted in the polis and at our abode (παρέστιος): we do not want to exercise our practical judgments with them (μήτ' ἴσον φρονῶν).[54] Thus, the contrast *hypsipolis; apolis* captures what Aristotle indicates as the *deinotes* of phronesis in book 6 of *Nicomachean Ethics*, namely, its fallibility, but also its powerfulness because the judgments of phronesis exercise a great impact on the polis. The danger of *deinotes* is the combination of its fallibility and its impactfulness which is intertwined with instrumentality. From this perspective, the entire stasimon is about that which Heidegger silences so as to repress—instrumentality.

That the entire stasimon is about the instrumentality of the *deinotes* of phronesis is also indicated by what happens immediately after the stasimon.[55] Antigone appears on stage just as the Chorus says that they do not want someone in the city who calculates incorrectly. Seeing Antigone, the Chorus addresses her by saying that her actions are carried out "in folly" (ἐν ἀφροσύνῃ).[56] The privative alpha indicates a lack of phronesis. The Chorus is kind to Antigone. Her judgments are not bad, whereby she will be an *apolis*, someone to be thrown out of the city, but her actions lack calculation, they are sheer folly, whereby they do not have an impact and she is not required to be expelled from the polis.[57]

By contrast, the Chorus is not so kind to Creon. At the conclusion of the play, a despondent Creon contemplates (with horror) the multiple deaths that have occurred as a result of his faulty judgments—not only Antigone

---

54. Sophocles, *Antigone*, 373–74.

55. As Andrew Benjamin puts it, "the necessity for judgment resides in what the Ode formulates in terms of the reality of the *apolis*," with the clarification that this judgment "involves *phronesis*." Benjamin, *Place, Commonality and Judgment* (London: Continuum, 2010), 109, 113.

56. Sophocles, *Antigone*, 383.

57. There are further significant references to phronesis in *Antigone* that I cannot discuss here, e.g., see Sophocles, *Antigone*, 707, 755.

is dead, but also his son and his wife. Left alone on stage with the Chorus, he laments that he is "no more than nothing [οὐκ ὄντα μᾶλλον ἢ μηδένα]" and describes himself as a useless (μάταιον) man.[58] Creon puts himself in the position of the *apolis*, of the one who experiences isolation as a result of his deficient instrumental calculations. We can also say that he was *deinos*: he did try to calculate, and his ends included the protection of the polis, but he failed in his calculations. After he departs and there is no actor left on the stage, the Chorus delivers *le fin mot de l'histoire*: "Phronesis is by far the chief part of happiness [πολλῷ τὸ φρονεῖν εὐδαιμονίας πρῶτον ὑπάρχει]."[59] These are harsh words, accusing Creon that his practical judgments of phronesis were deficient and his instrumental calculations failed, which is the reason that he finds himself an *apolis*, even though he is the ruler of Thebes—he rules over an empty place, as his son Haemon puts it.[60]

From such a perspective, not only the stasimon but the entire play is about the instrumentality of phronesis. Heidegger is perfectly correct to identify the stasimon as a pivotal moment in *Antigone* because it determines the human as *deinon*. But he merely repeats the mistake from *Plato's Sophist* when he defines the *deinon* simply as the conflict between phusis and techne, thereby repressing the function of instrumentality in the *deinotes* of how technical skill is applied. No, the human is *deinon* because the conflict between phusis and techne is mediated by the calculation of instrumental ends, characteristic of phronesis and inseparable from the political.

52. A politics without reaction or an agonistic politics

A conception of political action that focuses on the instrumental ends of action is different in two crucial respects from Heidegger's. First, Heidegger insists that one is first a ruler, a poet, or a priest and then acts like one, which means that such roles are *sui generis*. This is the constitutive characteristic of their authority. In *Antigone*, the opposite is the case. Creon is a ruler, but when his judgments fail, whereby his actions effect ruin, he becomes *apolis*. If one's political status is determined by the *effects* of their instrumental calculations, then one is political by virtue of the fact that one participates in a space of judgment and contestation that is never *sui generis* and, hence, it is incommensurable with authority. That is the Greek conception of the polis: not as a unity within which the originary conflict

---

58. Sophocles, *Antigone*, 1325, 1339.
59. Sophocles, *Antigone*, 1347.
60. Sophocles, *Antigone*, 739.

spontaneously creates authority, but as the conflict between means and ends of action whose effects delineate the political field and constitute history.

Second, according to Heidegger the *hypsipolis* and the *apolis* are both derived from *phusis* and, hence, created spontaneously from the unity of being whereby they are both endowed with the same political authority. Such a framing of the conflict brackets out instrumentality. By contrast, the operative presence of instrumentality and phronesis in *Antigone* indicates a lack of guarantee for how conflict will resolve itself. Following the Greek conception of phronesis as the pursuit of instrumental ends that can err at any turn, both *hypsipolis* and *apolis* are inherently vulnerable figures. Their actions are constantly subject to the scrutiny of the polis. This means, *contra* Heidegger, that both the *hypsipolis* and the *apolis* are stripped of authority. Their position in the polis is precarious, subject to dispute, and open to contestation.

These two differences summarize a fundamental incompatibility in the conception of the ontology of conflict in Heidegger and the agon that is so important in monist materialism.[61] According to Heidegger, the poet, the priest, and the ruler are who they are prior to their actions having any effect. This means that the originary conflict is confined to their actions but they themselves are immune from conflict. Heidegger's authority requires a space immune from conflict. Thus, we can define the metaphysico-political authority of Heidegger's discourse as those figures whose enactment of the originary conflict protects them from conflict. In other words, it is an authority that builds itself on a conflictual site by being itself separated—or immune—from conflict. This has a concrete effect. The fact that authority is separate from conflict means that it is impervious to challenge. One will look in vain at Heidegger's text for any indication of how someone who obeys being can potentially be challenged. There is no indication of how someone who obeys being can be wrong. Truth, as the unfolding to concealment and unconcealment, is impervious to falsity—and so are its representatives, like the poet, the priest, and the ruler.

By contrast, the agon of monist materialism pertains to the contestation of the ends of instrumentality. Its source is the impossibility to calculate means and ends with any certainty (§§21–22). The fact that someone can become *apolis* in such an agon, even if that someone is the sovereign like Creon, suggests that the agon of the monist materialist tradition is squarely

---

61. I use the term agon, here, in the sense that I have developed it in *Stasis Before the State: Nine Theses on Agonistic Democracy* (New York: Fordham University Press, 2019), and *The Agonistic Condition*.

directed against any vestige of authority—no one is beyond reaction. Here, the political space is not immunized from conflict but both producing and being produced by the agon. As a result, the agon is not confined to any one individual—be that a poet, a priest, or a ruler. Rather, the agon of the monist materialist tradition unfolds within a transindividual space, since the determination of the means and ends of action includes others (§30).

We are offered here, then, here two contrasting political visions of the conflictual nature of two monist ontologies. The Heideggerian ontology of conflict holds that it is possible to account for political action by confining all the ends of action to the violence of techne that establishes a conflict with phusis. In this set up, certain figures appear—the poet, the priest, the ruler—whose identity is determined by the *sui generis* doubling of justice (*dike*) that belongs to phusis and the violence that belongs to techne. This establishes them as figures of authority, removing them from conflict and also from any potential challenge. Their actions are impervious to argumentation because they are beyond effects as they are who they are before the operation of any instrumental ends.

The politics of monist materialism, by contrast, locates the agon in contestations about the instrumental ends of action. The agon concerns the effects of action, whereby the conflict can never be described as *sui generis*. The agon is not about individual figures and it is directed against any authority that, by definition, aims to suspend the judgments of phronesis about the instrumental ends of action. Further, because the means and ends of action cannot be owned by anyone, they demarcate a commonality and a transindividuality that is conducive to democratic politics.

Heidegger's ontology of conflict conjures an authority that systematically represses instrumentality. It achieves this by the ruse of hiding the instrumental ends of action behind the *sui generis* authority. The repression of instrumentality through the conflict between phusis and techne creates the figures of authority that regulate Heidegger's discourse of conflictual ontology: the poet, the priest, and the ruler. Such a politics of authority relies on the conjuring trick of making authority appear out of nowhere to repress instrumentality.

The politics of monist materialism is more plain, more modest. There are no figures here that are impervious to contestation. There are no guarantees that the ends of our actions will be reached. The human is *deinon*—both cunning and miserable at the same time since the cunning is inherently errant and yet impossible to evade. It establishes a space where one assumes the responsibility and the danger to calculate means and ends, knowing all along that the calculation is both fallible and impacting the community. Despite the difficulties and aporias of such a determination of the political, despite the precarity that permeates it, it has one distinct advantage over the Heideggerian politics of the metaphysico-political authority. It is a politics attuned to instrumentality, which allows it to see the ruse of techne as what it really is: an ideological trap that seeks to suffocate being with others so as to allow, not the single, unified being, but the single, unified authority of the self-proclaimed unconcealer of being.

53. The preservers and the magical founding of the city

"The Origin of the Work of Art" offers the most powerful conjuring of authority.[62] In this sense, the essay can be seen as the apex of conflictual ontology. Philippe Lacoue-Labarthe points to the convergence between the discussion of *apolis* in *Introduction to Metaphysics* and the argument about the founding of the political community in "The Origin of the Work of Art."[63] This is not surprising if we recall that "The Origin of the Work of Art" was initially a series of talks delivered in 1935, shortly after *Introduction to Metaphysics*.[64] But "The Origin of the Work of Art" goes further. There, authority finds its ideological fulfillment in the notion of the people as preservers, who thus emerge as the apex of conjuring of authority in Heidegger's ontology of conflict. The artwork in Heidegger's sense has—to echo what Heidegger says about technology—nothing to do with works of art. In the ontology of conflict, the artwork's primary function is to conjure the preservers as founding the polis and as figures of authority.

To recognize the authority of the preservers, we need to pay attention to the conflictual ontology of "The Origin of the Work of Art." This is one of Heidegger's most famous essays, and there is an enormous amount of secondary literature on it. And yet, there is scant appreciation of how much conflict permeates every turn of the argument. For example, in the first section of the essay, Heidegger discusses three deficient determinations of the thing in the history of philosophy, all of which are described in vocabulary that invokes conflict. The realist description of a thing as a

---

62. Martin Heidegger, "The Origin of the Work of Art," in *Basic Writings*, trans. David Farrell Krell (London: Routledge, 2000), 143–212 = *GA* 5. All parenthetical references in §53 are to this work.

63. Philippe Lacoue-Labarthe, *Heidegger, Art and Politics: The Fiction of the Political*, trans. Chris Turner (Oxford: Blackwell, 1990), 17–18.

64. The publication history is more complex than I can go into here. For a perceptive account, see Peter Fenves "'As on the First Day': Nine Notes on Heidegger's 'First Elaboration' of his *Ursprung des Kunstwerkes*," *Modern Language Notes* 136 (2021): 561–80; see also Françoise Dastur, "Heidegger's Freiburg Version of the Origin of the Work of Art," in Risser, *Heidegger Toward the Turn*, 119–42.

carrier of traits is a kind of "assault" (*überfallen*, 151/10); the idealist conception of the thing as the unity of the manifold makes the thing "press excessively upon us" (*rückt... es uns zu sehr auf den Leib*, 152/11); as for understanding the thing as the combination of matter and form, this is nothing but a "deprivation" (Entblößung) of the thing's useful context of relations—what *Being and Time* calls *Zuhandenheit*—which is ultimately also an assault (*Überfall*) upon the thing (156/15). Regardless of who the assailant is, the subject or the object, in all three onto-theo-logical determinations of the thing, conflict is paramount.

In the second section of the artwork essay, Heidegger focuses on the conflict characteristic of the relation between world and earth, or between what *Introduction to Metaphysics* calls phusis and techne. Here is one description:

> The world grounds itself on the earth, and earth juts through world. Yet the relation between world and earth does not wither away into the empty unity [*in der leeren Einheit*] of opposites unconcerned with one another. The world, in resting upon the earth, strives to surmount it. As self-opening it cannot endure anything closed. The earth, however, as sheltering and concealing, tends always to draw the world into itself and keep it there. The opposition of world and earth is strife [*Streit*]. (174/35)

The terms are already familiar from the 1935 lecture course: the world points to the unity of beings, whereas earth indicates the violent "thrust" into beings characteristic of techne's final ends. This conflict is the "original strife [*des ursprünglichen Streites*]" because the "essence of truth is, in itself, the primal strife [*Urstreit*]" (180/42). Thus, the truth of the work of art turns out to be the ontological conflict of world and earth, or phusis and techne.

I will not repeat here how this thrust or violence of techne represses instrumentality. Is not the interplay of matter and form, which Heidegger describes as the most determinative of the three "assaults" of the conception of the thing, premised on the distinction between the four causes, two of which are the material and the formal cause? We have already seen, many times over, how Heidegger uses the analysis of final ends within the purview of causality to repress the instrumental ends of action. I will not repeat either how the obscuring of the instrumental ends elides any consideration of power structures. Heidegger takes an ancient temple as an example of the strife between phusis and techne so as to argue that the temple gives people the truth of being. There is nothing in Heidegger's description about the fact that the temple is also imbued in structures of power that require an ontology to be grounded in history. Recall, for instance, how the Parthenon was built from the taxes that the Athenians collected from their allies—or, perhaps, satellite states—which was a major contributing factor to the eruption of the Peloponnesian War and the destruction of classical Athens. No, I will not repeat all that about the repression of instrumentality and the obscuring of power, since there is nothing particularly new about all this in "The Origin of the Work of Art."

What is new here is the way in which the artwork conjures authority in relation to a conception of the people that Heidegger calls the preservers of the work. Heidegger acknowledges the importance of this point, signaling just before mentioning the preservers that he is about to "take the step toward which everything thus far said tends [*den Schritt . . . auf den alles bisher Gesagte zustrebt*]" (191/54). The whole point of the discussion of the work of art is about the preservers:

> The more solitarily the work, fixed in the figure, stands on its own and the more cleanly it seems to cut all ties to human beings, the more simply does the thrust come into the open that such a work *is,* and the more essentially is the extraordinary thrust to the surface and what is long-familiar thrust down. But this multiple thrusting is nothing violent, for the more purely the work is itself transported into the openness of beings—an openness opened by itself—the more simply does it transport us into this openness and thus at the same time transport us out of the realm of the ordinary. To submit to this displacement means to transform our accustomed ties to world and earth and henceforth to restrain all usual doing and prizing, knowing and looking, in order to stay within the truth that is happening in the work. Only the restraint of this staying lets what is created be the work that it is. This letting the work be a work we call preserving [*die Bewahrung*] the work. Just as a work cannot be without being created, but is essentially in need of creators, so what is created cannot itself come into being without those who preserve it [*die Bewahrenden*]. (191/54)

This is a complex passage, and I will not be able to do justice to every claim it contains. I will raise four points to show how the preservers are the culmination of the conflictual ontology, conjuring authority in such a way as to disavow any possibility of resistance to the power signified by their historical destiny.

First, it is important to acknowledge a point that is often made in the analysis of the preservers, namely, that this idea is prefigured in *Being and Time,* specifically in chapter 5 of Division 2 that concerns historicity in a dimension that transcends the individual and pertains to the world as a whole. Drawing this parallel, Lacoue-Labarthe highlights the mythological element in Heidegger's conception of the historical significance of poetry.[65] As soon as Lacoue-Labarthe discerns the parallels between fundamental ontology and the mythological construction of the people in the 1930s, he is inevitably led to the conclusion that Heidegger's ontology has Nazi commitments, despite the fact that Heidegger distanced himself from the Nazi Party in 1934.

Although there is truth in Lacoue-Labarthe's analysis, we should not forget a significant difference between the ontology of the concealment of instrumentality and the ontology of conflict. The discourse on historicity in *Being and Time* is framed as a fundamental ontology: authenticity is arrived at by starting with an understanding of the everyday, by what we experience "initially and for the most part," only to then discard the vulgar conceptions of experience, temporality, and historicity.[66] In the conflictual ontology of "The Origin of the Work of Art," by contrast, there is no such progression from a fundamental ground. Here, creation, creator, and preserver *spontaneously* come together. There is a historically grounded "chemical reaction" that affects the spontaneous generation of work, creator, and preserver. Perhaps it is more apt to say "magic" instead of chemical reaction—or maybe we can compromise with "alchemy." All these metaphors express the *sui generis* creation of the preservers through the conflict of phusis and techne, or world and earth, thereby conjuring authority.

Second, the notion of preserving is intertwined with a semantics of founding. This makes the historically grounded preserving political. Or, more precisely, the political is defined through such a founding. Following this thought, Heidegger does not hesitate to note that the primal strife of world and earth responsible for the creation of the work of art is also an "act that founds a state [*die staatgründende Tat*]" (186/49). So much so that "founding . . . is actual only in preserving [*Stiftung ist . . . nur in der Bewahrung wirklich*]" (199/63). So, the notion of the preservers appears also as the figure endowed with political authority.

Such a founding that is related to people and poetry is not an entirely new idea. We find it in the first set of lectures on Hölderlin from 1934: "poet is the one who grounds being [*der Dichter ist der Begründer des Seyns*]. What we call the real in our everyday life is, in the end, what is unreal. In the beckoning of the gods being, as it were, built into the foundational walls [*Grundmauern*] of the language of a people by [*durch*] the poet . . . beyng is founded

---

65. Philippe Lacoue-Labarthe, *Heidegger and the Politics of Poetry*, trans. Jeff Fort (Urbana: University of Illinois Press, 2007).

66. Cf. *Being and Time*, §§72–73.

in the historical Dasein of the people [*im geschichtlichen Dasein des Volkes*].... Poetizing... [is] the founding of being [*Dichtung... Stiftung des Seyns*]."[67] As well as in *Introduction to Metaphysics*: "poetizing-thinking, [is] grounding and founding of the historical Dasein of a people [*dichtend-denkende Gründen und Stiften des geschichtlichen Daseins eines Volkes*]."[68] But, despite the similarity in the nomenclature, there is a significant difference. In the earlier works, poetry and the poet found the people.[69] In the artwork essay, the preservers are equally participating in the founding.

We can understand this difference as the consummation of the notion of authority characteristic of Heidegger's ontology of conflict. In "The Origin" essay, authority includes not only individuals, but also the entire community. The historical grounding of the ontology of conflict into a spontaneously formed and founding people creates the most powerful figure of authority in Heidegger's work, the preservers. Here artwork, especially the "projective saying [*Sagen*] of poetry" that is "the saying of the arena of strife" between concealment and unconcealment, between world and earth, between phusis and techne—this saying *spontaneously* creates the poet. At the same time, "actual language at any given moment is the happening of this saying, in which a people world historically arises." The poetic saying, however, is nothing without the people, which is why "founding... is actual only in preserving" (198–99/61–63). We see in this movement from the saying of poetry, to the poet, to the people, and back to the saying itself through the preservers an *immediate* movement without resistance.[70]

Third, if the conjuring of authority is the major political lesson of the ontology of conflict, then "The Origin of the Work of Art" is the most

---

67. Heidegger, *Hölderlin's Hymns "Germania" and "The Rhine,"* 31–32/33.

68. Heidegger, *Introduction to Metaphysics*, 176/174.

69. This point is made quite clearly in the discussion of Hölderlin. Here is another citation: "the historical Dasein of the peoples—its rise, its pinnacle, and its decline—springs from poetry [*aus der Dichtung entspringt*], and from this [*aus dieser*] a proper knowing in the sense of philosophy, and from both [*aus beiden*] the effecting of the Dasein of a people as a people through the state: politics [*die Erwirkung des Daseins eines Volkes als eines Volkes durch den Staat—die Politik*]. This originary, historical time of the peoples is therefore the time of the poets, thinkers, and creators of the state—that is, of those who properly ground and found the historical Dasein of a people. They are those who properly create." Heidegger, *Hölderlin's Hymns "Germania" and "The Rhine,"* 49–50/51. Here, the poet is founder. In the "Origin" essay, the preservers are constitutive of the founding.

70. Without resistance, or immediately, as I put it in "A Matter of Immediacy: The Artwork and the Political in Walter Benjamin and Martin Heidegger," in *Sparks will Fly: Benjamin and Heidegger*, ed. Andrew Benjamin and Dimitris Vardoulakis (Albany: SUNY Press, 2015), 237–57.

comprehensive articulation of conflictual ontology because it is the most comprehensive articulation of authority. There are, of course, a legion of questions coming to mind here. Are the preservers possible only if they are connected somehow—and *how*?—to the Greek origin? Are "people" destined to not achieve the status of the preservers if they have not come into contact with Heraclitus, Parmenides, Sophocles and, of course, Hölderlin? Is this notion of the preserver a political ideal? If so, can it be actualized? How will political change happen after such preservers found a state? What happens in a state of such authoritative preservers if a portion of the population cannot understand the origin? Does everyone have to "obey" the saying that precipitates the founding? What happens if one does not obey? Who is to determine whether disobedience has taken place? And who will determine the punishment? What is the law that the authority conjured by preserving requires?

All these questions suggest that the construction of the authority of the preservers in fact presupposes a radical subjectivism (§47). Even though the preservers are constitutive of the authority that emanates from being, still there need to be figures who safeguard the obedience to being. Arendt suggests in "Authority" that the Greeks lacked the concept of authority and they did not even have a word for it. The reason may be that they did not regard anyone as impervious to argumentation. But it is also important to remember that subjectivism was foreign to the Greek mind. As the questions above suggest, Heidegger suffers from a profound blindness to the political implications of a spontaneously created community of preservers who are also authorized for historical destiny by the *dike* (justice) that belongs to phusis. Heidegger does not see—or, at least, does not mention—that the *effects* of such an authority of the preservers are always mediated by historical actors who assert their subjectivity as judges and defenders of being. Law and power structures are not *sui generis*, but historically constructed.

Fourth, the Heideggerian response would likely be that all these questions, and their implied subjectivism, demote an ontological thought to the drudgery of the "ontic." The inadequacy of such a response is obvious as soon as we recall that the ontological is constructed through a magic trick, and as such, a trick is itself grounded on the ontic. The trick has been the repression of instrumentality, whose characteristic articulation in the ontology of conflict has been the conjuring of authority. The entire analysis of the ontology of "primal strife" represents the instrumental ends of action, which finally allows for the transformation of power into authority as that which needs no scrutiny—of the kind provided by the questions above—since it is impervious to argumentation and its "poetic sayings" invite no reaction. As soon as the trick is recognized, the self-contradictory basis of Heidegger's position is exposed. Primal strife can never be purely ontological, it is always also ontic, and as such it is never *sui generis* and never devoid of resistance. In other words, *pace* Heidegger, the notion of the preservers cannot be separated from the calculations of instrumentality.

The moment that we recognize the self-contradiction at the heart of Heidegger's conjuring of the authority of the preservers, we can also discern its uglier and more dangerous underside: its complicity with constructed and established structures of power. So long as authority is created "spontaneously" and that process includes the people as a whole so that they become the preservers of the state, then any instituted—or ontic—law or power remains beyond reproach, impervious to argumentation, shielded from scrutiny. The political, here, emerges as the unfolding of this complicity between the "spontaneously" created preservers and the constructed powers that they support. There is no prospect in this construal of any democratic politics, no possibility of resistance. Is this the utopia of a harmonious obedience inscribed in the conflict of concealment and unconcealment disclosing the truth of being in the destiny of a people? Or is it a dystopia that deprives action of any vestige of freedom, a form of what La Boétie calls "voluntary servitude"? We cannot determine this dilemma because—thankfully—such an authority of the preservers has never existed in history.

Despite all that, I ought to acknowledge my admiration for Heidegger's extraordinary skill to pull off the conjuring of the authority of the preservers in "The Origin" essay. It surely requires significant technical competence to repress the instrumental ends of action within the political. It is also not a small feat to conjure individual figures of authority out of the poets, the thinkers, or the ruler. But to create a multiple authority, a whole *polis* of authority, is surely a magic trick of extraordinary proportions—not the pulling of a rabbit, but rather a whole rabbit warren, out of a hat!

But, if we are not looking for magical tricks to reenchant the political, and if we are also concerned with pursuing a politics that retains the agonistic space where no authority can establish itself unchallenged, then Heidegger's work of art will be of little use to us. In that case, we will be better off to stop lingering admiringly at the artifice of Heidegger's preservers and move on to an analysis of the *effects* of the calculation of the means and ends of action which—despite its fallibility—is intent on challenging any historically determined political authority. We will then gain a notion of the agon that is attuned to the dangers and difficulties inherent in phronesis, without being enchanted with a supposedly spontaneously created political community that is meant to be impervious to challenge and remains magically immune from resistance.

6

The Ontology of the Ineffectual
The Purloined Letter of Instrumentality

54. The reversal of the critique of monism

There is a shift in the vocabulary that characterizes the third articulation of Heidegger's ontology. In the second phase, the emphasis is on conflict, which takes two fundamental guises: first, the conflict between technoscience and the pursuit of the truth of being; and second, within being itself as the strife between concealment and unconcealment. By contrast, in the third articulation of his ontology, the place of conflict is taken by various terms that indicate the placing or "clearing" where being emerges or "propriates." For example, we read in "Letter on Humanism" that "language is the clearing-concealing advent [*Ankunft*] of Being itself" (230/326).[1] In the mid-1930s, the relation between concealment and unconcealment would have been described as a struggle, not in topological terms.

Such an advent of being has a profound implication. The typical move of the third phase of Heidegger's thought is an emphasis on the kind of action that becomes indistinguishable from thinking and whose main feature is that it lacks effects or consequences. Thus, we read in the "Letter on Humanism" that the thinking of being "has no result [*kein Ergebnis*]. It has no effect [*keine Wirkung*]" (259/358). And in another example, in

---

1. Martin Heidegger, "Letter on Humanism," *Basic Writings*, trans. David Farrell Krell (London: Routledge, 2000) = *GA* 9. All references to the "Letter" parenthetically in the text, in all sections of chapter 6 *except* §§57–59.

the late text "The End of Philosophy and the Task of Thinking" from the 1960s, Heidegger insists that "there is a thinking outside [*außerhalb*] of the distinction of rational and irrational, more sober-minded still than scientific technology, more sober-minded and hence removed, without effect [*ohne Effekt*], yet having its own necessity."[2] Such a convergence of thought and action produces the *ineffectual*. It is this thinking that appears in the clearing of being, a place unconcerned with beings, which becomes the substitute for conflict in the ontology of the ineffectual.

A related rhetorical change is the avoidance of any political engagement in Heidegger's public discourse. One may dismiss this change as precipitated by the disaster of his membership in the National Socialist Party with regard to the rectorship of Freiburg University. The fateful decision in 1933 haunted Heidegger for many years. It was particularly damaging after World War II, when the process of denazification in Germany meant that Heidegger was banned from teaching at the university. This led to a significant personal crisis but also provided a context where the fervent political rhetoric of the 1930s was out of place. In this third phase, then, there is scant reference to any destiny of the people and no compulsive return to any political "founding" made possible by the poem and its preservers. Thus, the key markers that conjure the authority characteristic of the ontology of conflict have been all but displaced from Heidegger's later discourse.

These personal circumstances, however, are an inadequate explanation for the transformation of the political in the ontology of the ineffectual. There is a more significant change within the structure of the argumentation itself related to the new articulation of the concealment of instrumentality. Suddenly, instrumentality appears as a term within Heidegger's discourse. Initially, this takes place in texts that Heidegger did not publish in his lifetime—although he cared for their preservation and posthumous publication, especially the *Contributions to Philosophy* (first published in 1989) and the *Black Notebooks* (whose publication started in 2014).

In such texts, the references to instrumentality and calculation are numerous and distinctive. In *Contributions to Philosophy*, they take the guise of a critique of machination (*Machenschaft*) or technologization. Alongside the scientific pursuit of knowledge through causality, instrumental rationality or calculation is responsible for the nihilism of modernity and the forgetting of being. Such hectoring will develop further in subsequent works, such as the lectures on Nietzsche. The references to calculation in

---

2. Martin Heidegger, "The End of Philosophy and the Task of Thinking," in *Basic Writings* = GA 14, 449/89.

the *Black Notebooks* are more sinister, as calculation is regularly attributed to the "Jews." Blaming the Jews for machination is key to what Donatella Di Cesare calls the "coded"—as opposed to racial—anti-Semitism of the *Black Notebooks*.³ Maybe that is true, but we should remember that it is also symptomatic of an ingrained anti-Hellenism, albeit one never explicitly stated, but rather operating in the interstices of Heidegger's writing as the compulsive repetition to repress instrumentality (§6, §26, §45, §51). In any case, it seems that the references to calculation now also become a coded political commentary while the kind of direct political observations characteristic of texts such as *Introduction to Metaphysics* recede into the background.

Even though there are numerous references to calculation as the distinctive feature of machination, still instrumentality never receives anything like the close attention paid to causality, which is most starkly presented in the "Question Concerning Technology" (§57). There are various texts in which Heidegger scrutinizes the theory of causality, such as Aristotle's theory of the four causes. The most important, perhaps, is "On the Essence of Ground" from 1928, which associates causality with transcendence as understood by onto-theo-logy while at the same time proposing a new meaning of transcendence as the world-forming activity of Dasein—what he elsewhere calls "ek-stasis."⁴

Not only is there no systematic analysis of instrumentality and a lack of its grounding in the history of philosophy, moreover the typical Heideggerian move is to reduce instrumentality to causality. An example can be found in §61 of *Contributions to Philosophy*, in an oft-quoted section on machination. It is here that Heidegger notes how machination is etymologically related to making and hence conceptually linked to techne. This leads to a discussion of production familiar from other texts, and then to the inference that "the cause-effect connection [*Ursache-Wirkungs-Zusammenhang*] comes to dominate everything (god as *causa sui*). That is an essential deviation from phusis and is at the same time the transition to the emergence of *machination* as the essence of beingness in modern thought."⁵ Instrumentality here collapses into causality. The conflation of causality and theoretical

---

3. Donatella Di Cesare, *Heidegger and the Jews: The Black Notebooks*, trans. Murtha Baca (Cambridge: Polity Press, 2018).

4. Martin Heidegger, "On the Essence of Ground" in *Pathmarks*, ed. William McNeill (Cambridge: Cambridge University Press, 1998) = *GA* 9.

5. Martin Heidegger, *Contributions to Philosophy (Of the Event)*, trans. Richard Rojcewicz and Daniela Vallega-Neu (Bloomington: Indiana University Press, 2021) = *GA* 65, 100/127.

knowledge characteristic of the craft analogy employed in *Plato's Sophist* and *Being and Time* (§27, §42) returns here, but with one difference: in the earlier writings, the analogy is facilitated by hiding instrumentality from view; here, it is clearly presented so as to be incorporated within causality.

This move is *the* way in which instrumentality is repressed in Heidegger's third ontology. Although as Heidegger now starts naming it in the texts through various words such as calculation and machination, instrumentality remains repressed as it is still conflated with causality that receives all the attention. For this reason, the distinctive repression of instrumentality in the third phase of Heidegger's thought resembles the concealing technique that Edgar Allan Poe describes in "The Purloined Letter." In the short story, the stolen letter is hidden by keeping it on the desk in plain sight, whereby the most thorough police search fails to locate it. Similarly, in ineffectual ontology, instrumentality is hidden in plain sight, attached to causality to produce together the lethal concoction of machination characteristic of the metaphysics of modernity as Heidegger understands it.

I regard this hiding in plain sight as an essential feature of the ontology of the ineffectual, and that is why I locate the earliest articulations of the third phase of Heidegger's ontology in *Contributions to Philosophy*. This means that the ontology of conflict and the ontology of the ineffectual co-exist for about a decade, from around 1936 to the end of WWII. For example, we readily find the theme of the conflict of world and earth in *Contributions to Philosophy* where Heidegger starts referring to calculation. I regard the "Letter on Humanism" as the text where conflictual ontology has all but been replaced by the ontology of the ineffectual. This is understandable also, given that the "Letter" is Heidegger's calling card to a new audience in France, to whom he needs to talk directly, just as he is denied access to students and limited in his academic pursuits in Germany. The search for a new audience consolidates the new approach.

As soon as we regard the ontology of the ineffectual from the perspective of the problem of action in monism (§§12–13), then we can see the most significant effect of the third phase of Heidegger's ontology. Whereas the ontology of the concealment of instrumentality was caught in the determination of action as trivial, and whereas the ontology of conflict lurched toward a self-contradictory account of action that emerged as complicitous to structures of power, the ineffectual ontology fully recommits to the trivial, even vacuous account of action.

In chapter 2 I described the initial reaction to Spinoza, the great monist of early modernity. This consisted of a frontal assault on Spinoza's theory of action. Bayle, synthesizing this assault, argued that a monism entails that actions are mere modifications of the single, unified god or nature, whereby they are completely inconsequential. In his famous quip, he noted that Spinozists should not be saying that the German army killed ten thousand Turks, but rather that god, modified into Germans, killed himself, modified into Turks. The implication is clear: monism lacks an ethics and a politics since its account of action is trivial and vacuous.

Even though the ontology of the ineffectual resurrects the craft analogy employed in the concealment of instrumentality, still there is one fundamental difference insofar as action is concerned. In the earlier work, the triviality of action is concealed in what Heidegger does not say (§§37–39). By contrast, Heidegger's ontology of the ineffectual fully embraces the critique of monism so as to make a virtue out of it. Instead of acknowledging the problem of establishing an ontology for which action has no effect, Heidegger insists that the distinctive feature of metaphysics—understood as machination or technology in modernity—is an ontology that conceives of action as having an effect. This is the problem of rationality, of what Heidegger also calls the "essence of ground," which aspires to universal truth only to be consumed in production. In a stunning *reversal* of the critique of the possibility of an account of action in monism, Heidegger's position becomes that the more ineffectual action is, the more it frees itself from the dominance of rationality, thereby seeking to entirely void the modern critique of monism.

This emphasis on the ineffectual is distinct from the pursuit of authenticity as the completeness of Dasein's transition to the truth of being through the everyday and through that which is experienced initially and for the most part. It is also distinct from the founding action that characterizes the figures of authority in the ontology of conflict. The advent of the ineffectual is then a new phase in Heidegger's thought, one that marks a more insistent monism to the point of turning upside down the traditional objection to monism's conception of action so as to celebrate it and going so far as to make it the linchpin of the third articulation of his ontology.

There is no doubt that this notion of ineffectual action has had a profound influence on French thought, and from there to structuralism, poststructuralism, and all post-WWII continental philosophy in general. No doubt there is also something heroic, even divine-like, in an action without effect. For Bataille, in works such as *The Accursed Share*, this is the model of action distinctive of god that was also the only model fit for the sovereign—a model of such excess that it was impossible to accommodate within the quotidian concerns about means and ends. Maybe that is why Heidegger also avers that "only yet another god can save us." But let us not forget that the source of this boastfulness in monism is nothing if not a proud admission that Bayle was correct—which Heidegger's reversal transfigures into the strength and virtue of a thinking that is simultaneously an acting "without effect."

The price that Heidegger has to pay for this reversal of the critique of monism is to be led to the renunciation of the possibility of any ethics and any politics. The conception of action as trivial and vacuous and the impossibility of ethics and politics are two sides of the same coin. It is around this nexus that the entire ontology of the ineffectual revolves.

55. The turn, the return, and the other turn (the critique of Sartre as self-critique)

That Heidegger, in the third phase of his ontology, argues for the impossibility of ethics and politics does not mean in the least that he is unconcerned with a theory of action. Nothing could be further from the truth. The "Letter on Humanism," the text that consolidates the transition to the ontology of the ineffectual, can be understood as a meditation on action.

It is not just any kind of action that the "Letter" is concerned with. Here, it is important to recall the context. Heidegger's text was a response to a letter by Jean Beaufret, who sent him a series of questions, the first of which concerned the meaning of "humanism" (219/315). This was not an arbitrary question; rather, it was occasioned by "Existentialism is a Humanism," a lecture recently delivered by Jean-Paul Sartre. The lecture was important for Heidegger, since Sartre was relying on his thought to expound his own existential philosophy in *Being and Nothingness* and then simplify it for a more general audience in "Existentialism is a Humanism." Thus, shortly after the end of WWII, just as Heidegger is looking for a new audience, he is given the opportunity to engage with one of the—if not *the*—most important conduits of his thought in France at that point.[6]

Heidegger's response to Beaufret's letter, which is also a response to existentialism, is in addition an extraordinary attempt from Heidegger to self-interpret his own philosophy and to present it in a new key that could resonate with the concerns of French philosophers. As such, it was also a unique opportunity for Heidegger to take stock and to map a clear path forward for his own thought as well. No doubt this set of circumstances was a contributing factor in finally abandoning the ontology of conflict after a decade of prevaricating.

---

6. For the most thorough and erudite account of Heidegger's reception in France, see Dominique Janicaud, *Heidegger in France*, trans. François Raffoul and David Pettigrew (Bloomington: Indiana University Press, 2015).

This double context—the circumstances of Beaufret's letter in the context of the French reception of Heidegger's work, as well as Heidegger's concerns to clarify and promote his own work—still does not provide an adequate explanation for the reconfiguration of the notion of action that we find in the "Letter." From the philosophical perspective, the most important factor is the difficulties that hampered the development of the ontology of conflict. As we saw in chapter 5, the various kinds of conflict—such as the struggle against technoscience and the strife between concealment and unconcealment—were resolved into the figures of the poet, the thinker, and the preservers. As spontaneously created and as founding figures, the poet and the preservers are endowed with authority. This leads to the inevitable question about who becomes a representative of that authority—a question that carries within it the danger of extreme subjectivism. Whoever becomes the representative of authority will be called upon to decide on issues such as how to defend and perpetuate that authority. That is the endpoint of the ontology of conflict (§52).

We should read Sartre's "Existentialism is a Humanism" with this endpoint and the specter of subjectivism in mind. Sartre's famous paper is usually summarized as holding three mutually supporting positions: first, existence precedes essence; second, as a result of the first point, all that exists is the actions we undertake; and third, following from the previous two, that human existence is an affirmation of a radical freedom of the subject. The combination of these points leads Sartre to present existentialism as an engaged philosophy against any form of "quietism." The price that existentialism has to pay for turning Heidegger's ontology into an engaged philosophy is that it lapses into subjectivism—or what Heidegger also defines as humanism in his "Letter."

Such a customary summary of Sartre's lecture elides a crucial point, namely, that the subjectivism of Sartre's position is a product of the repression of instrumentality in action so as to create a free human *spontaneously*. The engaged political subject of existentialism is a *sui generis* human being that arises out of the repression of instrumentality. For instance, we read, "A man who joins a communist or revolutionary group wills certain concrete aims that imply an abstract will to freedom, yet that freedom must always be exercised in a concrete manner. We will freedom for freedom's sake."[7] The act of freedom as conceived in existentialism is defined in opposition to any concrete end-oriented action, exactly in the way that the

---

7. Jean-Paul Sartre, *Existentialism is a Humanism*, trans. Carol MaComber (New Haven, CT: Yale University Press, 2007), 48.

political founding of the state by the poets, the thinkers, and the priests in collaboration with the preservers is possible through the repression of instrumentality. From this perspective, the subjectivism of the human conceived in existentialist terms as "willing freedom for freedom's sake" and the authority ensconced in conflictual ontology appear as akin notions. We can see why Sartre was happy to invoke Heidegger as an ally in his project.

The fact that Sartre clearly and succinctly drew out the subjectivist implications of the ontology of conflict made the humanism of existentialism a frenemy to Heidegger.[8] The affinity of existentialism and the ontology of conflict only highlights the impasse of subjectivism into which Heidegger found himself in the 1930s. Sartre takes Heidegger at his word to the point of extending his "engaged" political thought characteristic of the ontology of conflict—but such a subjectivism implied by authority in the ontology of conflict undermines Heidegger's entire project of retrieving a forgotten and impersonal being that is one and unified.

If we see the dynamic between Heidegger and Sartre from the perspective of the impasse reached by the ontology of conflict that is taken over and reaffirmed by Sartre, then we can also see the strategy that presents itself to Heidegger in how to respond to Beaufret's question about humanism. The only viable strategy is to deny everything. Or, rather, to reinterpret his work in such a way as to avoid the trap of subjectivism set up by the ontology of conflict. Hence the repeated *return*—I underscore this word that I will explain shortly—to *Being and Time* in the "Letter" culminating in the self-proclaimed "turn" that Heidegger proffers as the key to this thought (§44).

However, the turn that Heidegger announces in "Letter on Humanism," if there is one, is not away from the earlier fundamental ontology into a position that starts with being—since, as Heidegger and then later Richardson correctly point out, the concern was with being all along. Rather, the actual turn is back to the original dilemma about action. If in the first phase of Heidegger's ontology action hides its triviality by repressing instrumentality, and if the second phase of conflictual ontology advances an authority that ends up being a self-complicitous contradiction, then the third turn is back to the earlier ontology, but in such a way as to choose again, and this time by foregrounding and celebrating action as trivial.

---

8. I am thinking here of Derrida's discussion of the intertwinement of host and hostis in *Of Hospitality: Anne Dufourmantelle Invites Jacques Derrida to Respond*, trans. Rachel Bowldy (Stanford, CA: Stanford University Press, 2000).

Let me express this in a different way. The first articulation of Heidegger's ontology sought to give an account of action within a single, unified being by separating different kinds of action. In particular, we discovered three kinds of actions: authentic actions that disclose being, inauthentic actions that prepare the way for disclosure, and indifferent actions that prevent disclosure (§36, §42). The problem with this position is that it was sitting on the fence insofar as the main problem of action in monism is concerned, namely, whether action is a mere modification of being and hence inconsequential, or whether it has consequences and thereby implies certain instrumental ends, which makes it self-contradictory. The impossibility of navigating this dilemma became Heidegger's limit of the first articulation of his ontology.

The second exposition of his ontology repressed instrumentality within a series of conflicts—especially the opposition to the nihilism of modernity and the conflict between world and earth—through the conjuring of authority that was meant to be engaged and political because it facilitated the "founding of the state" (§53). The second ontological articulation constitutes a *first turn* to one side of the dilemma, namely, the side of self-contradiction. Heidegger sought to eliminate any vestige of instrumentality by emphasizing the completely uninstrumental activity of poetry that is registered in the actions of the poet and the preservers of the poem. The problem is that the authority implied in this position not only reintroduces instrumentality but also raises the specter of subjectivism.

The third ontology is a *turn away* from the ontology of conflict that is simultaneously a *return* to the original dilemma between triviality and self-contradiction, but now as an attempt to *turn the other way* by putting his wager with triviality. This new turn is perhaps best summarized in the directive "to think being without beings," as Heidegger expresses it in his late essay "Time and Being."[9] Remember that Heidegger describes the turn in "Letter on Humanism" as the turn from "being and time" to "time and being" (§44). Thus, this late essay from 1962 can be read as an *apres coup* justification of the turn. Except that it is a return to the earlier dilemma so as to choose the other turn this time, the turn to the trivial.

Within the context of all these turns we can see that when Heidegger turns his back to Sartre he in fact turns his back to himself as well—to that self who put Heraclitus's polemos at the center of his philosophy and who signed up for membership to the National Socialist Party. At the same

---

9. Martin Heidegger, "Time and Being," in *On Time and Being*, trans. Joan Stambaugh (New York: Harper & Row, 1972) = *GA* 14, 2/5.

time, turning his back to Sartre is the only possible move for Heidegger to turn to France and to face it in the aftermath of WWII—facing it with the return to the dilemma from before 1933, but this time opting for the other turn, not the political, engaged one advocated by conflictual ontology and existentialism, but the one of triviality. Thus, a turn of fate (Beaufret's letter) precipitated a philosophical turn (the decisive abandonment of conflictual ontology in favor of the ontology of the ineffectual) that was simultaneously an expedient and necessary political turn (the turn to France), all of which was possible because of a return to the old problem of action in monism so as to give it a different turn akin to the initial response from the time of reading Aristotle's phronesis and from *Being and Time*.

If one gets dizzy with so many turns, and one complains that these twists and turns are of more biographical than philosophical value, they would not be entirely incorrect. Except that the twists and turns that end with the account of action as ineffectual, supported by the repression of instrumentality by hiding it in plain sight has had a profound influence in philosophy from the late 1940s onward. The reception of Heidegger's ontology of the ineffectual—that is, the Heidegger after he has performed all these twists and turns—has deeply marked the direction of French thought and consequently what has come to be called "continental philosophy" (§2). I will trace some of this influence back to the "Letter on Humanism" after I first present the repression of instrumentality by hiding it in plain sight through the use of the three senses of techne. This will show us how the ruse of techne operates in the ontology of the ineffectual.

56. Transformations of the ruse of techne

All these various turnings are possible only if Heidegger sustains the repression of instrumentality. That is where the ruse of techne is needed. The ontology of the ineffectual refashions the three senses of techne. Let me outline the changes relying on what we learn in the "Letter on Humanism."

If in the ontology of conflict the first sense of techne was the monism of the origin that the founding of the poem and its preservers was meant to resurrect in the present, then monism in the ineffectual ontology is derived straight from being itself whereby its historical grounding is no longer primary. The second sense of techne again concerns the contrast between technoscience and the articulation of being in language, "the house of being." But whereas in conflictual ontology the second side was the site of a struggle, here the description insists on the derivative nature of the modern conception of technology from the originary conception of techne in the Greeks. The poetic saying remains the center of the third sense of techne, however, its historical and political significance all but evaporate in the ontology of the ineffectual, replaced by a conception of being that can only ever be approached discretely as the mystery that can never be revealed, no longer as the site that stages a strife translatable into politics. The endpoint of the third sense of techne in ineffectual ontology is the discourse of the late Heidegger, where even being is replaced by the event (*Ereignis*) that is separate from the ontic and hence set adrift from any effectivity.

The ruse of techne is accomplished by hiding instrumentality in plain sight. The third articulation of the ruse is a mind game. Whereas in the ontology of the concealment of instrumentality the ruse of techne consisted in making instrumentality disappear altogether; and in conflictual ontology in making authority appear out of thin air; the ruse in ineffectual ontology consists in making instrumentality disappear by making it appear as nothing but a derivative of causality. The third iteration of the ruse is the most extraordinarily paradoxical one from the perspective of power, since it is asking its audience to willingly refuse to see something that is there. This is the power of hegemony as understood by Gramsci and then rearticulated by Laclau and Mouffe: the power to insist on the transience of materiality—on the impossibility of presenting the mystery of being in any specific act—while at the same time presenting it as the repression of instrumentality with all the institutional controlling apparatuses that this entails—such as publications, conferences, entire careers that rely on denying the presence of that which has appeared.

The most intricate and at the same time the most explicit articulation of the ruse of techne in the ontology of the ineffectual can be found in "The Question Concerning Technology." This essay was written initially as a series of three lectures Heidegger presented at Bremen four years after the "Letter on Humanism." The final draft of the essay presents each lecture reworked into a section of the essay. Each section presents one sense of techne. The most direct approach to dispelling the enchanted mystique of the hiding of instrumentality in plain sight is to examine each sense of techne as it is presented in its distilled purity in the technology essay.

57. Instrumentality incorporated into causality (the first sense of techne)

The most significant change to the ruse of techne that we can observe in "The Question Concerning Technology" is not only that instrumentality is hidden in plain sight but also that it is registered in the first sense of techne.[10] In the first and second iterations of Heidegger's ontology, the repression of instrumentality was accomplished in the second sense of techne. In the ontology of the concealment of instrumentality, it consisted in the employment of the craft analogy to make sophia into the virtue of techne (§27) or vice vera (§42). In conflictual ontology, it was the struggle against technoscience. In the ontology of the ineffectual, the first sense of techne shows that the instrumental is incorporated into causality, while causality is reinterpreted in a more "essential" way as the *aition* that establishes the single, unified being.

The greatest misconception about the technology essay is that the most daring idea, and the one that organizes the entire essay, is that "the essence of technology is by no means anything technological [*das Wesen der Technik ganz und gar nichts Technisches*]" (311/7). This is not a novel idea. The same idea is articulated, for instance, about art in the "Origin of the Work of Art" essay (§53), and in any case it is typical of all discourse on "essence." The idea—ubiquitous in Heidegger's writings—is that the forgetting of being effects a distortion of action. The work of art and the work of techne are distorted unless their essence is discovered by examining how truth is disclosed in these practices. If we keep in mind the centrality of essence in Heidegger's ontology, this sentence about technology is no more than a familiar repetition of the need to point to something inessential so that the essential can come into being. We have seen this in the drawing of the qualitative separation between actions in Heidegger—some actions include all ends, others are purified of ends—that is connected with the discourse of essence (§15): there is an (inessential) action that is driven by the pursuit of ends, and an (essential) action that is free of ends and without effects.

What is new in the essay, and at the same time functions as the pivot of the entire argument, is the assertion that "instrumentality . . . is based on causality [*das Instrumentale . . . im Kausalen beruht*]" (316/11). In the secondary literature, this assertion is simply taken for granted, whereby it has actually remained thoroughly unexamined. It seems that everyone takes it as self-evident that the chain of causes and effects and the enactment of means and ends are one and the same. This conflation of causality and instrumentality remains blind to those materialisms in the history of thought that insist on the separation of causal and instrumental ends (§7, §14, §22, §32, §41, §51). It is also blind to the other move in the history

---

10. Martin Heidegger, "The Question Concerning Technology," in *Basic Writings* = *GA* 7. All references to the technology essay in-text parenthetically in §§57–59.

of thought that naturalizes the conflation of causality and instrumentality in what has come to be called the craft analogy (§15, §27, §42). The distinctive feature of the conflation of causality and instrumentality in the technology essay is that it is now repositioned from the second to the first sense of techne that indicates monism, or the singularity and unity of being. Let us see how Heidegger makes this move.

Heidegger's argument has two parts. The first consists in identifying the technological—as opposed to the essence of technology—with instrumentality, whereby the technological becomes an expression of the subjectivism of onto-theo-logy. The second consists in showing that the notion of causality taken as self-evident in modernity is in fact different from Aristotle's notion of the cause (*aition*) that actually points to the singularity and unity of being. This notion of the *aition* that Heidegger reconstructs can give us the essence of techne. The fulcrum between the two arguments is the assertion that instrumentality is based on causality. With this move, the instrumental is reduced to the metaphysical conception of causality that privileges the efficient cause, while also examining the Greek notion of causality which points to the monist essence of technology.

It is easiest to elaborate on Heidegger's position by starting with the second part of the argument. The argument that Aristotle's presentation of causality has nothing to do with the metaphysical conception of causality is nothing new. We can find the same argument, not only in "On the Essence of Ground" written shortly after *Being and Time*, but also in numerous other essays such as "Plato's Doctrine of Truth" from 1931 and "On the Essence and Concept of Phusis in Aristotle's *Physics* B, 1" from 1939.[11] We can also find the same argument in lecture courses such as *Aristotle's Metaphysics Theta 1–3* from the summer semester of 1931.[12] Heidegger's argument is that, with the translation of the Greek *aition* into the Latin *causa*, a fundamental misunderstanding sets in. The Latin translation separates the four causes that Aristotle identifies in *Physics* and *Metaphysics*—the material, formal, efficient, and final causes. This separation is fateful for the development of Western metaphysics, since it leads to a privileging of the efficient cause, the agent of the action, with the resultant humanism and subjectivism. It is as if one acts as an individual endowed with freedom from within themselves, independently of the unity of the other causes.

---

11. Both of these essays are contained in *Pathmarks*.
12. Martin Heidegger, *Aristotle's* Metaphysics *Theta 1–3: On the Essence and Actuality of Force*, trans. Walter Brogan and Peter Warnek (Bloomington: Indiana University Press, 1995) = *GA 33*.

This unity of the four causes through a proper reading of causality in Aristotle, contends Heidegger, points to the singularity and unity of being. The Greek *aition* does not indicate a series of effects produced by their causes. Rather, "the four causes are the ways, all belonging at once to each other, of being responsible for something else [*die unter sich zusammengehörigen Weisen des Verschuldens*]" (314/10). That is why the Aristotelian doctrine of causality, in fact, does not know the efficient cause (315/11). That is also why the unified structure of the four causes is a "bringing-forth" that consists in disclosure—it "brings out of concealment into unconcealment" (317/13). In other words, whereas causality as understood in modernity lapses into subjectivism, the *aition* in Aristotle and the Greeks leads to the single, unified being.

When this part of the argument about the *aition* in Greek monism is presented in the works from the 1930s, Heidegger does not link causality and instrumentality. When he does link them in works before the technology essay, such as in *Contributions to Philosophy*, he does so fleetingly, without combining the metaphysical conception of causality with an analysis of the *aition* in Greek thought.[13] In other words, prior to "The Question Concerning Technology," Heidegger does not explicitly incorporate instrumentality within monism. Or, differently put, he does not inscribe instrumentality within the first sense of techne.

This inscription demonstrates in Heidegger's schema that the essence of techne belongs to the *aition* while the technological merely corresponds to the distorted notion of causality that predominates in metaphysics. That is why the two definitions of the technological—as a means to an act and as a human activity—in fact "belong together" (312/7). The instrumental and the anthropological definitions of the technological, as Heidegger calls them (312/8), are united because they are both based on the metaphysical conception of causality: "A means is that whereby something is effected and thus attained [*bewirkt und so erreicht wird*]. Whatever has an effect as its consequence [*Wirkung zur Folge*] is called a cause [*Ursache*]. But not only that by means of which something else is effected is a cause. The end [*Zweck*] that determines the kind of means to be used is also considered a cause [*gilt als Ursache*]. Wherever ends are pursued, and means are employed [*Zwecke verfolgt, Mittel verwendet werden*], wherever instrumentality reigns, there causality holds sway [*wo das Instrumentale herrscht, da*

---

13. The most explicit linking of the metaphysical conception of causality and instrumentality (but without reference to Greek causality) is in §61 and §76 of *Contributions to Philosophy*.

waltet Ursächlichkeit, Kausalität]" (313/9). The means-and-ends relation is reduced to the metaphysical conception of the cause-and-effect relation. The predominance of metaphysics where the technological reigns (*herrscht*), also entails the dominance of causality—which Heidegger emphasizes by using both terms available for it in German, *Ursächlichkeit* and *Kausalität*.

One may wonder here whether Heidegger's account of the metaphysical conception of causality, is anything more than his version of the critique of technoscience in modernity according to which technoscience is never neutral but always self-interested and hence political (§2). It is instructive to pause and consider the difference of Heidegger's argument from the Frankfurt School argument against instrumentality (§6). Adorno has a much more modest argument against instrumentality. His argument is directed against the reason of the Enlightenment. Such a reason sought to attain universality by pretending to rise above the tumult of causality. This intensifies with the project of idealism, but the trick is that the universal reason can only ever register in particularity. It can only appear through the means and ends that it regulates, which enable its supposed universality. This tense relation between reason and history culminates in the philosophy of Hegel, who seeks to marry the two in the absolute. Adorno's critique is directed against the possibility of such a conciliation between reason and history. The supposed absolute always has effects that are in fact contingent. From this perspective, not only is there no indication in Adorno's argument of what I call "the repression of instrumentality"; moreover, we could paraphrase his argument by saying that his negative dialectics seeks to show how instrumentality is concealed within the supposed universality of reason. His argument is against the Enlightenment's employment of instrumentality, not against instrumentality as such. The argument that I am presenting in this book about monist materialism and the Adornian argument can be compatible.

The Heideggerian argument against the nexus of instrumentality and causality is different. As we saw in chapter 5, not only is Heidegger still striving to discover a historical "destiny" of being—not merely a critique of Enlightenment reason—but further, he is attempting to do that by indicating that causality, just like the Greek conception of phusis, holds sway (*waltet*) even where the technological reigns (*herrscht*). In other words, instrumentality is incorporated into causality because causality points to the single, unified being. Consequently, unlike Adorno's critique of instrumentality which consists in pointing out its effects, Heidegger's critique is the opposite: it asserts that instrumentality, in reality, has no effects because it is merely a modification of the *aition* and the only reason this is not understood is because of its Latin mistranslation and distortion into *causa*.

Or, differently put, whereas Adorno critiques a specific historical employment of reason that illegitimately appeals to instrumentality, Heidegger merges instrumentality with causality to argue against any "giving of grounds" or reasons that would explain reality as a whole, as that would be incompatible with the mystery of the single, unified being. Consequently, whereas Adorno focuses on the effects of the conflation of causality and instrumentality within a specific historical frame, Heidegger has to understand the *aition* as a mere modification of being without any determinative effect beyond any historical specific but rather through the "essence" of techne.

The comparison with Adorno highlights how Heidegger has transformed the critique of technoscience in modernity into a grand historical and philosophical narrative for the critique of metaphysics and for the discovery of the essence of technology. The conjunction of instrumentality and causality, characteristic of reason and technoscience, is not simply something that occurs in modernity, according to Heidegger, but it is rather nothing but "the will to mastery [*Meistern-wollen*]" (313/8) by effecting things. This is the inessential form of acting, and this also suggests that the essential is a freedom that consists in letting being be—abandoning all ends of action and escaping all effects. The transfer of instrumentality into the first sense of techne and its incorporation into the monist conception of the *aition* is then essentially the assertion of the ineffectual.

58. The ambivalence of the calculable and enframing (the second sense of techne)

If we pause for a moment to consider Heidegger's two arguments—one about the nature of instrumentality and one about the nature of causality and the *aition*—it is striking that their connection is never argued for. It is only ever asserted that the instrumental is based on causality as if it is self-evident. But even if the instrumental relies on an anthropological principle—the description of the human as a doer—it is still not obvious why this anthropological principle is reduced into the idea of the efficient cause. Perusing other texts by Heidegger, I have been unable to find any thematization of the connection between instrumentality and causality, and in fact the discussion in the first section of "The Question Concerning Technology" is the most detailed assertion of the collapse of instrumentality within modern causality that I am aware of, despite its highly elliptical nature.

The problem with the lack of an explicit argument about the collapse of instrumentality into causality is not only that it brushes it aside, without examining the long tradition that holds onto this distinction, thereby undermining the credibility of the historical part of Heidegger's argument (§15, §23, §32, §41, §51). And it is not also merely that it goes against "common sense," since the final cause by definition denotes the carrying out of an action, whereas the determination of an instrumental end does not guarantee that any acting will be undertaken—after all, we hatch plans that we never act upon all the time (§§21–22). Also, and most importantly, the conflation of instrumentality with causality leads to the unpalatable conclusion that the causal ends of the agent of action and the instrumental ends of acting are one and the same—which is incorrect because the instrumental ends are never owned by anyone in particular, whereby instrumentality is not reducible to individual agency or any efficient cause (§30). Consequently, the conflation of instrumentality with causality is nothing more than an evasion of the ethical, social, and political.

Of course, Heidegger cannot acknowledge, let alone address, all these difficulties, as this would betray the hiding place of instrumentality behind causality. And the whole point of making causality the basis of instrumentality was to hide instrumentality in plain sight!

The inability to tackle these difficulties so as to sustain the ruse of techne leads Heidegger to what seems like a simplistic mistake about the calculable, which embarrassingly enough has been taken over by continental philosophy. This consists in failing to recognize an ambivalence in the notion of the calculable. The calculable means, first, something that can be calculated with some certainty, for example, the weight of an object such as a hammer is calculable in the sense that it can be calculated with accuracy using scales. But it can also mean something that has to be calculated, even though we know that such a calculation can never be certain or secure as it lacks a determinate measurement, given that the calculation is part of its enactment.

The distinction between the two senses of the calculable corresponds to the two categories of verbal adjectives in ancient Greek: those with the suffix *teo* indicate that which has to be done; those with the suffix *to* indicate the possibility that something could be done. So, for example, we can say *logisteon* (something that must be calculated), and *logiston* (an action that is liable to calculation). The Latin derived suffix *able* translates both kinds of ancient Greek verbal adjectives, even though their meaning is quite distinct. Something is *logisteon* when we assume that it can be calculated. By contrast, something is *logiston* when it could be calculated without any certainty that such a calculation can ever be carried out. Given that the English language does not have a grammatical form to designate this distinction for verbal adjectives, I will use here "calculated" to indicate that which can be calculated, and "calculating" for the prospect of calculating without knowing with any certainty that it is possible.

We have of course encountered this distinction already. It is the final ends that can be calculated and the instrumental ends that are calculating (§§21–22). The conflation of the two senses of the calculable suggests, then, that Heidegger *still* persists with the same mistake of confusing causality and instrumentality that he first registered in the Natorp report, hastily written in October 1922 and then consolidated in the more detailed reading of book 6 of *Nicomachean Ethics* as part of *Plato's Sophist* in the autumn of 1924. If the mistake back then was due to mistranslations, now the mistake is due to the construction of a concept of the calculable as exclusively related to the calculated. In the "Technology" essay, that concept is the *Ge-stell*, or enframing in English.

Heidegger states two key positions about enframing. First, it indicates "the essence of modern technology" or of the technological (325/21). In other words, enframing is the inessential sense of technology as such. And second, modern physics is "the herald" of enframing (327/23). The reason for both of these points is that technology is not merely a mathematically exact calculation (326/22), but a process that makes something "calculable in advance" (326/22) and that seeks to peg calculation to causality:

> Physics . . . will never be able to renounce this one thing: that nature report itself in some way or other that is identifiable through calculation [*rechnerisch*] and that it remain orderable as a system of information [*als ein System von Informationen*]. This system is then determined by a causality that has changed once again [*noch einmal gewandelten Kausalität*]. Causality now displays neither the character of the occasioning that brings forth nor the nature of the *causa efficiens*, let alone that of the *causa formalis*. It seems as though causality is shrinking [*schrumpft*] into a reporting—a reporting challenged forth—of standing-reserves that must be guaranteed either simultaneously or in sequence. (328/23–24)

Enframing then according to Heidegger consists in the further devaluation of causality. If the translation of *aition* to the Latin *causa* "shrunk" causality by losing the unity between the four causes, the modern submission to the calculated that becomes a mere piece of information is a further shrinking of causality. The essence of the technological in the onto-theo-logy of modernity is the collapse of everything to a measure for exact calculation. This is the essence of the dominance of technology in modernity.

Such a conception of technology that is only calculated, or that is reducible to an exact measurement pertaining to causality, cannot provide a sufficient account of action, whereby action becomes merely trivial. The problem with enframing is not the fact that it demands calculation, but rather that the calculated controls the human and nature, who are treated as "standing reserves," that is, as measurable depositories ready to be used. For example, says Heidegger, "agriculture is now the mechanized food industry" (320/16). When action is analyzed merely with reference to the calculated, without regard to the calculating, as if it possible to neatly incorporate instrumentality within causality, then the resultant account of action appears trivial and vacuous. Let me provide one example.

When "The Question Concerning Technology" was delivered for the first time as a series of three lectures in Bremen, a leaflet with extracts from the talks was printed. One such leaflet survived, and it was reproduced by Philippe Lacoue-Labarthe. The corresponding passage from the citation above reads:

> Agriculture is now a mechanized food industry, the same thing in its essence as the production of corpses in the gas chambers and the extermination camps, the same thing as blockades and the reduction of countries to famine, the same thing as the manufacture of hydrogen bombs.[14]

Since the publication of this extract, it has attracted significant criticism, starting with Lacoue-Labarthe himself who calls it "strictly—and eternally—intolerable."[15] The reason proffered is that it is inappropriate to reduce the critique of metaphysics and modern technology as enframing to the actuality of the Holocaust. Without wanting to defend Heidegger, I would only point out that this comparison, no matter how abhorrent or monstrous, is in fact entirely in keeping with his ontology of the ineffectual—to which Lacoue-Labarthe otherwise subscribes. If the calculable can only be understood as the calculated, then it is indeed possible to argue that the process is the same, a process of counting, in one case kilos of vegetables or meat, in another corpses—in the macabre sense implied here, they can both be accurately weighed. If we accept the repression of instrumentality by failing to distinguish between the calculated and the calculating, Heidegger's point about the dominance of modern technology is consistent with his critique of the concept of causality in modernity.

---

14. Cited in Philippe Lacoue-Labarthe, *Heidegger, Art and Politics: The Fiction of the Political*, trans. Chris Turner (Oxford: Blackwell, 1990), 34.

15. Lacoue-Labarthe, *Heidegger, Art and Politics*, 35.

What is truly abhorrent is that the ethical and political are elided through a conflation of the two senses of the calculable. What is profoundly monstrous is the construal of a monist ontology that lacks a distinction between the calculated and the calculating—or between causality and instrumentality—whereby it washes its hands of any effects. What is hugely disturbing is that the illusion that action as ineffectual is celebrated as a political position. What is unbearable is that one can either arrive at or critique the assertion that the mechanized food industry is on the same plane as the Holocaust without questioning the repression of instrumentality that has validated this thought. What is, finally, truly extraordinary is that the same logic is still repeated, many years later, by other philosophers such as Agamben, who argues that, from the perspective of power, the Führer and *Musselmänner*, the most abject inmates of the concentration camps, refer to the same calculation of life and death.[16] When will we manage—or least try!—to break the spell of Heidegger's ruse of techne that hides instrumentality in front of our eyes?

59. The killing power of the saving power (the third sense of techne)

Well, one thing is for sure, the magic spell will persist for as long as the poem is supposed to grant us a "saving power." The third sense of techne in the ineffectual ontology of "The Question Concerning Technology" is consistent with the earlier articulations of Heidegger's ontology in that it is one purified of instrumentality. That is what Heidegger calls its saving power and that is why he associates it with the poem.

This saving power justifies the assertion at the beginning of the essay that the essence of technology is nothing technological. Let me quote a long passage that summarizes all the key elements of the ruse of techne in the ontology of the ineffectual:

> The essential unfolding of technology harbors in itself what we least suspect, the possible rise of the saving power [*birgt . . . das Wesende der Technik den möglichen Aufgang des Rettenden in sich*].
>
> Everything, then, depends upon this: that we ponder this rising and that, recollecting, we watch over it. How can this happen? Above all through our catching sight of the essential unfolding in technology [*das Wesende in der Technik*], instead of merely gaping at the technological [*nur . . . das Technische*]. So long as we represent technology

---

16. Giorgio Agamben, *Homo Sacer: Sovereign Power and Bare Life*, trans. Daniel Heller-Roazen (Stanford, CA: Stanford University Press, 1998), 187.

as instrumental [*als Instrument*], we remain transfixed in the will to master it [*im Willen . . . zu meistern*]. We press on past the essence of technology.

When, however, we ask how the instrumental [*das Instrumentale*] unfolds essentially as a kind of causality [*als eine Art des Kausalen*], then we experience this essential unfolding as the destining [*Geschick*] of a revealing.

When we consider, finally, that the essential unfolding of the essence of technology propriates in the granting that needs and uses man so that he may share in revealing, then the following becomes clear:

The essence of technology is in a lofty sense ambiguous [*zweideutig*]. Such ambiguity points to the mystery [*Geheimnis*] of all revealing, i.e., of truth.

On the one hand, enframing [*das Ge-stell*] challenges forth into the frenziedness of ordering [*das Rasende des Bestellens*] that blocks [*verstellt*] every view into the propriative event of revealing and so radically endangers [*von Grund auf gefährdet*] the relation to the essence of truth.

On the other hand, enframing [*das Ge-stell*] propriates for its part in the granting that lets man endure—as yet inexperienced, but perhaps more experienced in the future—that he may be the one who is needed and used for the safekeeping of the essence of truth. Thus the rising of the saving power [*der Aufgang des Rettenden*] appears. (337–38/53–54)

What is the starting point of the saving power? The recognition that the instrumental unfolds as causality. But not all causality—not the Latin conception that splinters the unity of the four causes, nor the modern that shrinks causality. Rather, this is causality as the *aition* that, according to Heidegger, points to the singularity and unity of being. This is the first sense of techne. As soon as the monism contained in causality is grasped, then, holds Heidegger, we can recognize a fork in the road. Technology is either reduced to the calculated and to enframing (the second sense of techne); or technology preserves the mystery of the truth of being whereby it lets the saving power arise (the third sense of techne). This saving power, contained within the technological, is the reason that the essence of technology is nothing technological.

But what is this mysterious third sense of techne? What does the saving power consist in? Heidegger's answer is clear and stated without any ambiguity: "Because the essence of technology is nothing technological, essential reflection upon technology and decisive confrontation with it must happen in a realm [*in einem Bereich*] that is, on the one hand, akin to the essence of technology and, on the other, fundamentally different from it." In other words, the ruse of techne establishes a realm, region, domain, or zone (*Bereich*) where action is purified of instrumentality and where the ineffectual can thrive. Heidegger continues: "Such a realm is art [*Ein solcher Bereich ist die Kunst*]" (340/36). The ineffectual that has the capacity to reveal being is art. Only art can "save" us.

Pondering on the word "Bereich," denoting certain borders and hence a certain sovereignty, one may wonder whether the conclusion here is not just as political as the conclusion in the "Origin of the Work of Art." Is this Bereich similar, or even the same, as the founding of the state that art is supposed to perform through the preservers according to the artwork essay? Despite the similarities, the structure of the argument—which is to say, the construction of the ruse of techne—is markedly different here. In the artwork essay, the essential feature of being was the conflict between concealment and unconcealment. As a result, the third sense of techne was a rearticulation of this conflict, now in a way that affected the political and the historical. In the technology essay, the essential feature of monism is the unifying force of being that stifles anything instrumental. Thus, the third sense of techne is art in the sense that art is anti-instrumental and ineffectual.

If we are to return to the question of action within monism at this point, then we can draw the inference that what Heidegger calls "art" here is thoroughly ineffectual. It is the separation of being from beings, to put it in the vocabulary from "Time and Being." The price that Heidegger has to pay for adopting this position, or for moving to this realm or domain of the ineffectual, is that action in the third articulation of his ontology appears thoroughly trivial. This means that the ontology of the ineffectual is not political—unlike conflictual ontology.

Or is it really apolitical? Is it perhaps possible to construct a politics out of a trivial account of action? Not only is it possible, but it has been done! The most prominent exponent of a politics of the ineffectual nowadays is Giorgio Agamben. His politics of the ineffectual leads of necessity to a radical anti-statism, as it frowns upon dual citizenship to two "realms," the ontological realm of the ineffectual and the political realm where a *Bereich* has borders and laws that define citizenship. That is why, for example, the ontological realm of the ineffectual in Agamben is a "zone of indistinction," a realm without definite or definable borders; or differently put, a realm whose borders are supposedly outside calculation. Such an anti-statism tapped into a certain distaste for the complicity of state power and high capitalism in the late 1990s that only intensified with the rush to "political theology" in the aftermath of 9/11, making the anti-statist politics of the ineffectual both a respectable and a popular position that catapulted Agamben to the center stage of continental philosophy and theory.

The problem with such a "trivial" politics is that the political may lead to anti-statism when it is assumed that it can be calculated with certainty *but*—to return to the distinction from §58—the anti-statism of the ontology of the ineffectual appears in a totally different light when the state is viewed from the perspective of a calculating that cannot be carried out with any exactitude. Just like Heidegger, who was consistent with his premises to compare the mechanized food industry to the Holocaust on the grounds that they both relied on the calculable (§58), Agamben was perfectly consistent philosophically to refuse the distinction between the calculated and the calculating, as the ontology of the ineffectual relies on the repression of instrumentality that effaces the distinction between causal and instrumental ends. But in the face of the enactment and the effects of this distinction with the outbreak of the COVID-19 pandemic and the imposed lockdowns, the anti-statism of the ineffectual in Agamben's castigation of the lockdowns as an expression of a carceral state logic appeared nonsensical and attracted severe criticism.[17]

The case of Agamben's editorializing during the pandemic teaches us something important about the trivial conception of action that celebrates art *because* it is ineffectual. It teaches us that the real danger may not be in instrumentality as such, but rather in its hiding in plain sight behind causality.[18] It also teaches us that the anti-statism implied in the politics of the ontology of the ineffectual may have a saving power whose *effects* could be lethal as it remains opposed to any effective measures to save lives from

---

17. Agamben's numerous short articles on the government responses to the pandemic were gathered into one volume, see Agamben, *Where Are We Now? The Epidemic as Politics*, trans. Valeria Dani (London: Rowman & Littlefield, 2021). These articles attracted wide condemnation and often virulent attacks. I concur with Carol Salzani that Agamben's description of the lockdown as a generalization of the "state of exception" is consistent with his general philosophical position—although for this, highlights the untenability of the anti-statism implied in such a politics of the ineffectual. See Salzani, "COVID-19 and State of Exception: Medicine, Politics, and the Epidemic State," *dePICTions*, March 12, 2021, https://parisinstitute.org/depictions-article-covid-19-and-state-of-exception-medicine-politics-and-the-epidemic-state/.

18. See Dimitris Vardoulakis, "The C** Word: Covid-19 and Calculation," *The Philosophical Salon*, May 14, 2020, https://thephilosophicalsalon.com/the-c-word-covid-19-and-calculation/.

threats such as COVID-19. The saving power of a trivial account of action harbors a killing power.

60. Metaphysical or materialist monism?

To further nuance the account of action as ineffectual and to trace the influence of this idea in continental philosophy and theory, we have to return to the "Letter on Humanism." It is here that we find the most explicit account of action in Heidegger's work. This account of action, just like "The Question Concerning Technology," insists that ineffectual action is the only way to attain being. But because the "Letter" is forced to confront the question of "materialism," it also offers a unique insight into the relation of the ineffectual to monism.

The engagement with materialism is not accidental. The "Letter on Humanism" is directed to a French audience, and French philosophy at the time was influenced by, or at least in conversation with, Marxism. To speak to the French, Heidegger needed to develop a position about Marxism. To discern Heidegger's conception of action in the "Letter," we need to view it within the context of his response to Marxism. The most stunning feature of this response is that Heidegger poses a dilemma: materialism or monism? In other words, he suggests that the truth of the single, unified being can be attained only on condition that we overcome materialism. This is the complete opposite of the position that, as I have suggested, is the viable solution for a materialist philosophy, which consists in its combination with monism: a materialist monism (§7, §14, §29, §32, §41, §52).

Heidegger's strategy is to define Marxism as the culmination of metaphysics and thereby designate Marx as the logical outcome of subjectivism and the machination of technoscience. Thus, Marxism becomes a critical component of the technique of hiding instrumentality in plain sight characteristic of the ontology of the ineffectual. More precisely, Heidegger argues that Marx has entirely missed the third sense of techne, that is, action as purified of instrumentality. This is certainly true: Marx does not entertain the idea that action can occur without ends and without effects. And yet, stating the obvious does not make Heidegger's diagnosis correct. Heidegger fails to discern the basis of Marx's materialist conception of action on a distinction between causality and instrumentality, thereby forcefully fitting Marxism into the framework of his own conception of metaphysics characterized by the repression of instrumentality. Let us examine his argument.

In the "Letter on Humanism," Heidegger praises Marx as the culmination of onto-theo-logy, or what he calls "absolute metaphysics." This means that Marx, like Nietzsche, performs an "inversion [*Umkehrung*]" whereby immanence replaces transcendence (239/336). The same point is repeated years later in the "The End of Philosophy and the Task of Thinking." Here, referring to Marx only, Heidegger notes that "with the inversion [*Umkehrung*] of metaphysics that was already accomplished [*vollzogen wird*] by Karl Marx, the uttermost possibility of philosophy is attained. It has entered into its end."[19] Philosophy in this context stands for metaphysics—as opposed to thought that is supposed to be able to lead to the truth of being.

The end or completeness of metaphysics in Marx consists, first, in the affirmation of subjectivism or the humanism that Heidegger is disparaging in his "Letter": "Because Marx by experiencing alienation [*Entfremdung*] attains an essential dimension of history [*eine wesentliche Dimension der Geschichte*], the Marxist view of history is superior to that of other historical accounts" (243/340). Heidegger praises Marx on the grounds that he has a "more essential" conception of history than Husserl or Sartre. However, such a conception of history is premised on alienation, which is nothing but the outcome of the tortured subjectivity at the highest point of metaphysics. Marx is "superior" to Husserl and Sartre, not because he has come any closer to being, but because he has gone as far away as is conceivably possible from being, thereby bringing to "completion" the project of metaphysics.

Immediately after this praise that is in fact a renunciation, Heidegger also dismisses materialism: "The essence of materialism [*das Wesen des Materialismus*] does not consist in the assertion that everything is simply matter [*alles sei nur Stoff*] but rather in a metaphysical determination according to which every being appears as the material of labor [*alles Seiende als das Material der Arbeit erscheint*]" (243/340). This is a false appearance, of course, and nothing but the obverse side of subjectivism, namely, technoscience or machination. Hence, "the essence of materialism conceals itself [*verbirgt sich*] in the essence of technology" (243–44/340). Materialism, then, becomes indistinguishable from Marxism and it is now merely another name for the end of metaphysics and the end of philosophy.

In a television interview from 1969, Richard Wisser pressed Heidegger on this interpretation of Marx by pointing out that the famous Thesis 11—"philosophers have only interpreted the world thus far whereas the point is to change it"—seems to suggest that Marx is leaving metaphysics and philosophy behind. Undeterred, Heidegger responds that Marx suggests that the world still needs to be interpreted in order to be changed,

---

19. Heidegger, "The End of Philosophy and the Task of Thinking," 433/71.

whereby Marx is making a demand on behalf of philosophy.[20] Perhaps Wisser's point cannot be so easily brushed aside. As soon as Heidegger notes the Marxist inversion that leads to absolute metaphysics, he also notes its opposite, namely, that "all refutation in the field of essential thinking is silly [*alles Widerlegen im Felde des wesentlichen Denkens ist töricht*]" (239/336). The single, unified being cannot be negated in "essential" thought—an idea that metaphysics is oblivious to because of the forgetting of being, according to Heidegger. Two important points follow from this contrast between Marx and the impossibility—the "silliness"—of negating being.

First, the conjunction of an absolute metaphysics with materialism is only possible by defining both in narrow terms. As we saw, Heidegger holds that materialism is the determination of all particular beings through the operation of labor, which aligns with Marx's subjectivism—the "alienation" of the human by technoscience. However, there is a different notion of materialism that is anything but subjectivist. This consists in the kind of monism that rejects the distinction between transcendence and immanence by affirming that there is a single totality outside of which nothing exists. This is not only the monism of Parmenides that Heidegger compulsively references, but also materialism as defined by Friedrich Lange.[21] Even though I have not found direct references to Lange in Heidegger, still it is highly likely that Heidegger was aware of his book on materialism. Lange was a significant figure in Neo-Kantianism, the school in which Heidegger himself was educated and from which he eventually meticulously distanced himself. Moreover, as was well-known in Germany, Lange's book on materialism was a major influence on Nietzsche. An alternative conception of materialism as monism makes it hard to dismiss Wisser's point about Thesis 11 and the end of metaphysics in Marx while undermining the reduction of Marxism to the subjectivism of alienation. Moreover, such a conception of monist materialism could explain the notion of historical necessity in Marx since then labor is not merely reducible to "particular beings" but rather forges the link between particular beings and—to use

---

20. The transcript of the interview is available here: Richard Wisser, "Martin Heidegger in Conversation with Richard Wisser," in *Martin Heidegger and National Socialism: Questions and Answers*, ed. Günter Neske and Emil Kettering, trans. Lisa Harries (New York: Paragon, 1990), 82. For a fascinating discussion of Heidegger's response to Thesis 11, see Gerhard Richter, *This Great Allegory: On World-Decay and World-Opening in the Work of Art* (Cambridge, MA: MIT Press, 2022), chapter 9.

21. Friedrich Lange, *Geschichte des Materialismus und Kritik seiner Bedeutung in der Gegenwart* (Iserlohn: Baedeker, 1887).

Heidegger's nomenclature—that which is essential and as such silly to refute since there is nothing outside it.

Second, I am not suggesting that Heidegger willfully distorts or misrepresents Marx. Rather, given his repression of instrumentality, Heidegger is unable to acknowledge the function of the economy in the relation between being and beings (§42) and to admit to any mediation between the "defective" necessity of causality and the true necessity of the call of being (§47). All this amounts to saying that Heidegger's reference to Marxism and political economy confronts him with the instrumentality that his own discourse must at all costs repress if it is to qualitatively distinguish between actions depending on how they are related to being (§§13–15). In other words, Heidegger is dragged kicking and screaming to a position where he has to acknowledge the operation of instrumentality in materialism, even though his own discourse cannot admit to it.

The famous, short opening section of "Letter on Humanism" on the "essence of action [*das Wesen des Handelns*]" (217/313) provides Heidegger's solution to this conundrum. The solution consists in the ruse of hiding instrumentality in plain sight—the trick of "The Purloined Letter" (§54). Heidegger here uses a series of terms that denote an end-oriented action, such as *das Bewirken, Wirkung, wirken*, and so on. To this he contrasts thinking as neither making nor effecting anything because thinking knows that "only what already is can really be accomplished." Heidegger immediately clarifies that what really is, is being (*Vollbringbar ist deshalb eigentlich nur das, was schon ist. Was jedoch vor allem "ist," ist das Sein*, 217/313). There is a Kierkegaardian "either/or" operating here: *Either* action is oriented toward ends whereby it is effective as it makes or produces, paying the price that it misses being. This includes indiscriminately all ends, both final and instrumental. *Or* the Parmenidean convergence of thinking and acting (§46, §50) that "lets being be" and where "thinking is *l'engagement* through and for [*durch und für*] the truth of being" (218/314) by virtue of being outside all calculation of ends. What is lost between the two extremes—one where ends are external to the thinking whereby it is separated from action, and another where thinking and action converge by eliminating all ends and becoming ineffectual—is the *effects* of the kind of thinking whose ends are part of the action itself, whereby they cannot be determined with any certainty. In other words, what is lost in the "abyss" between measurable effects and the ineffectual is the immeasurable effectivity of instrumentality of phronesis. Using the vocabulary from §58, what is lost between the calculated and the incalculable is the calculating—that which must be calculated even though there is no clear measure for its calculation and, hence, is impossible to calculate with certainty.

As a result, we can infer that Heidegger sets up a wrong either/or. The dilemma that he poses in the "Letter on Humanism" is materialism (as the culmination of the subjectivism of metaphysics) *or* the ineffectual (as the ek-stasis that leads to the truth or event of the single, unified being). This is the dilemma characteristic of Heidegger's metaphysical materialism and responsible for a trivial account of action. As soon as we undo the repression of instrumentality, we arrive at a fundamentally different "either/or": *Either* the ineffectual (that is unable to provide an ontology of action) *or* materialist monism (that accounts for actions depending on the effects of their different ends, final and provisional). This is the side where Marx is positioned in materialist monism that, *pace* Heidegger, cannot be reduced to the main characteristic of metaphysics, such as subjectivism, the separation of theory and praxis or to mere presence (§§30–32).

I am dubious that any attempt to bridge the gap between Heidegger's disjunction and the one between metaphysical monism and materialist monism has any hope of succeeding.[22] The reason is that the first "either/or" is premised on the repression of instrumentality, whereas the second one sees this repression as a purely ideological construct and as a significant remnant of the metaphysics of morals (§4). Between a metaphysical materialism and a materialist monism, there is not much room for compromise. One celebrates an action that stands over materiality and beyond any effects, whereas the other determines action through its effects while it regards as either trivial or as laden with ideology any attempt to ignore the effects of action. For anyone who holds a materialist monist position, the dilemma, as presented by Heidegger, is merely smoke and mirrors. The real dilemma is a monism without effects or a monism of the effect. If we define materialism as the overcoming of the onto-theo-logical notion of transcendence, and if we recall—as I argued in the Excursus—that the repression of instrumentality is a characteristic of the metaphysics of morals, then the dilemma can be presented as either metaphysical monism or materialist monism.

61. The French appropriation of the repression of instrumentality

There is little doubt that, if the dilemma about the conception of action is presented as metaphysical or materialist monism, then the Heideggerian solution has triumphed in the century following the publication of *Being*

---

22. Gianni Vattimo and Santiago Zabala, *Hermeneutic Communism: From Heidegger to Marx* (New York: Columbia University Press, 2011).

and Time. The repression of instrumentality has become such a dogma in continental philosophy that the distinction between causal and instrumental ends remains entirely unexamined in the analyses of praxis, which has meant that the option of a materialist monism cannot even be entertained for consideration.

There is also little doubt of the strategic importance of the "Letter on Humanism" in promulgating the repression of instrumentality. Through the "Letter," the ruse of techne makes instrumentality disappear from view by hiding it behind causality. The third iteration of the ruse in the ontology of the ineffectual relies on the previous two. Hiding instrumentality in plain sight presupposes the interpretation of phronesis in such a way as to allow Heidegger to describe an activity that is purified of instrumental ends that are transferred to, and incorporated with, the final ends of causality. The first articulation of the ruse establishes the conception of action premised on the repression of instrumentality, but the third iteration is the most determinative in the development of continental philosophy after WWII. The reason is the publication history, in which the "Letter on Humanism" becomes the first text by Heidegger to be widely read in France, long before the whole of *Being and Time* was translated, with the result that the "Letter" set much of the agenda in the late 1940s and 1950s, which were the formative years of a whole generation of French intellectuals who indelibly marked the development of continental philosophy and theory in the twentieth century.[23]

I do not mean that the French embraced Heidegger uncritically. The reception was always intense and engaged, often tersely critical. One need only recall Levinas's reformulation of the question of being to the question of ethical responsibility to the Other to see how critically Heidegger's ideas were processed. The French reception takes up Heidegger's thought and transforms it in many significant ways, thereby establishing the terms of what came to be called continental philosophy after WWII.

Because the reception following WWII starts with the "Letter," the tendency is to focus on the late Heidegger, or as Rainer Schürmann memorably puts it, to read Heidegger backwards.[24] This is significant since the

---

23. Janicaud, *Heidegger in France*, 6. See also Tom Rockmore, *Heidegger and French Philosophy: Humanism, Antihumanism and Being* (London: Routledge, 1995), 69–75.

24. Reiner Schürmann, *Heidegger on Being and Acting: From Principles to Anarchy*, trans. Christine-Marie Gros (Bloomington: Indiana University Press, 1987). For a German perspective on this common French approach, see Hans-Georg Gadamer, Review of *Heidegger on Being and Acting: From Principles to Anarchy*, by Reiner Schürmann, *Graduate Faculty Philosophy Journal* 13, no. 1 (1988): 155–58.

"Letter on Humanism" introduces a number of themes that became stock-in-trade of continental philosophy. The most prominent are the critique of value and the critique of subjectivity usually referred to as anti-humanism. For instance, François Raffoul's work on subjectivity indicates the anti-humanism that the French reception takes from the ontology of the ineffectual, whereby it seeks to construct a Heideggerian conception of the subject without falling into the humanist traps of the separation of interior and exterior, the proliferation of binaries, and subjective freedom.[25] Another theme of fundamental significance is the notion of the event that signifies an action supposed to be immeasurable and unpredictable by virtue of the fact that it is not oriented toward any ends. Thus, a host of concepts develops that organize different and often competing discourses in France, setting the parameters of the discussion in continental philosophy as well as theory, whose provenance is the ineffectual ontology of Heidegger's third iteration of the repression of instrumentality.

Let me provide one illustration of how the post-WWII French reception of Heidegger's ineffectual ontology has spread the repression of instrumentality and the ineffectual in numerous discourses. In his last interview, Michel Foucault unexpectedly reveals his debt to Heidegger:

> Heidegger has always been for me the essential philosopher. I started by reading Hegel, then Marx, and I began to read Heidegger in 1951 or 1952. . . . I still have the notes I took while reading Heidegger—I have tons of them!—and they are far more important than the ones I took on Hegel or Marx. My whole philosophical development was determined by my reading of Heidegger. . . . I don't know Heidegger well enough: I practically don't know *Being and Time* nor the things recently published. . . . I probably wouldn't have read Nietzsche if I hadn't read Heidegger. I tried to read Nietzsche in the fifties, but Nietzsche by himself said nothing to me. Whereas Nietzsche and Heidegger—that was the philosophical shock! . . . I think it's important to have a small number of authors with whom one thinks, with whom one works, but on whom one doesn't write. Perhaps someday I'll write about them, but at that point they will no longer be instruments of thought for me.[26]

---

25. François Raffoul, *Heidegger and the Subject*, trans. David Pettigrew and Gregory Recco (Atlantic Highlands, NJ: Humanities Press, 1998).

26. Michel Foucault, "The Return of Morality," in *Politics, Philosophy, Culture: Interviews and Other Writings 1977–1984*, ed. Lawrence D. Kritzman, trans. Thomas Levin and Isabelle Lorenz (New York: Routledge, 1988), 250.

There are two ways to view this statement. One can look at it from the perspective of an understanding of Foucault's work.[27] He suggests that the notion of power he derives from Nietzsche makes no sense unless it resonates with the critique of subjectivity in the late Heidegger—Foucault admits that he does not know *Being and Time*. The so-called "structuralist" analysis we find in Foucault, such as the work on discipline or on biopolitics, derives its "anti-humanism" from Heidegger. Foucault's work was part of the intellectual milieu in France after WWII whose agenda was set through a series of themes established by the "Letter on Humanism."

From another perspective, recognizing the Heideggerian influence—or, more accurately, the influence of the ontology of the ineffectual—in Foucault's work also opens up a radically different perspective on the spread of the influence of the repression of instrumentality. This does not apply only to Foucault's interaction with "poststructuralism," such as, for example, the notion of the "outside" as—to repeat Heidegger's words from "The End of Philosophy"—"a thinking outside of the distinction of rational and irrational . . . and hence removed, without effect."[28] The idea of an outside to calculation marks continental philosophy, theory, and any discourse that arises from structuralism and poststructuralism. This discursive hegemony of the repressed instrumentality thus extends on a broad array of discourses that use as a springboard Foucault and the intellectual milieu developing from the study of Heidegger in the early 1950s. For instance, "posthumanism" has had a powerful impact in theory, and one might legitimately say, after studying the numerous posthumanist books, that their lack of reference to Heidegger signifies his minimal impact on posthumanism. And yet, the notion of the ineffectual is determinative for the move away from humanism and the way in which posthumanism understands the bridging of the gap between mind and body as well as of materiality, which shows that Heidegger's repression of instrumentality permeates—even *defines*—the direction of the posthumanist discourse.

It seems, then, that Heidegger has worked his magic. Unnoticed and yet in plain sight, his repression of instrumentality has become an absolute presupposition of continental philosophy and of theory. Scholars who scorn Heidegger and who may not even have studied his texts are actually working using the main trick of his ineffectual ontology, the repression of instrumentality, by producing thought whose terms are set by French thought

---

27. See Stuart Elden, *The Early Foucault* (Cambridge: Polity Press, 2021).
28. Cf. Michel Foucault, "Maurice Blanchot: The Thought from Outside," in *Foucault/Blanchot*, trans. Brian Massumi (New York: Zone Books, 1987).

with roots in the 1950s reception of the "Letter on Humanism." Thus, scholars are building upon various forms of anti-humanism or the critique of value without realizing that they are performing the ruse of techne (§64).

62. The new Kantianism

Insofar as continental philosophy more narrowly defined is concerned—that is, leaving aside "theory" in general—perhaps the most determinative effect of the "Letter on Humanism" is the emergence of a new Kantianism. This has been dimly glimpsed by Quentin Meillassoux. In *After Finitude*, he critiques the epistemological reliance on Kantianism, according to which subjectivity provides the unifying structure of experience and he advocates instead an epistemology grounded in concepts prior to Kant's "Copernican turn." The problem with this critique of continental philosophy is that epistemology has hardly been its mainstay. Instead, it is power and conceptions of action that are center stage in continental philosophy. The question, then, ought to be whether there is a residual—or even resurgent—Kantianism in the repression of instrumentality that arises from Heidegger's answer to the problem of action in monism. This is a question that Meillassoux cannot even ask, as he does not recognize the repression of instrumentality.

The best way to present the new Kantianism that emerges through the ontology of the ineffectual, and which disperses into continental philosophy as the privileging of ineffectual action, is through the argument for the rejection of the possibility of ethics in the "Letter on Humanism." Heidegger acknowledges that a "longing [*Verlangen*] necessarily awakens for a peremptory directive and for rules" in the time of the dominance of technology (255/353). But he rejects the possibility that such a search for an "ought to" can be fruitful. He insists instead that, rather than moral precepts, we need to look for the "ethos [that] immediately comes to light" in the work of those poets and thinkers who have grasped the singularity and unity of being (256/354). Such an ethos, according to Heidegger's interpretation of Heraclitus's Fr. 119, is available everywhere "insofar as he is man, in the nearness of god" (256/354–55). Heidegger recounts the anecdote of visiting admirers who are surprised to find Heraclitus warming up near an oven in the kitchen. Heraclitus responds to them that even here the gods are present.[29] This is meant to show "the original ethics [*die ursprüngliche Ethik*]" (258/356). That is, not ethics in the traditional sense, but rather the same as "the thinking that inquires into the truth of being" (259/357).

---

29. The anecdote is preserved in Aristotle's *Parts of Animals*.

The new Kantianism that arises as a result of the repression of instrumentality can be understood in two steps. First, the ethos sketched here is concerned with preserving singularity. Heidegger makes this clear as he immediately dismisses the possibility that there are any guidelines about how to think of being. Insofar as there is an ethos, or an intermeshing of thinking and action, there are no rules appropriate to it. This preserves the singularity of being: "Historically, only one saying belongs to the matter of thinking, the one that is in each case appropriate to its matter" (259/358). This idea is indebted to Kant. Without being the same as his categorical imperative, it shares the impossibility that it can be articulated in a rule because its expression is every time unique to the circumstances. And this Kantian singularity has spread from Heidegger to other French thinkers. Thus, despite being fiercely critical of Heidegger, the retention of singularity is an essential feature of Levinas's ethics. In fact, Levinas is fond of noting that the Other, the neighbor of the Jewish tradition, and the Kantian categorical imperative, have a family resemblance.[30] Levinas means by this that the ethics of the Other seeks to preserve the singularity of the ethical moment in the context of the impossibility of providing a regulatory framework for action. This is the first step with a Kantian provenance that we find in Heidegger's reformulation of ethics.

Heidegger expresses the second step by saying that the thinking that is intertwined with action characteristic of ethos, "has no result [*kein Ergebnis*]. It has no effect [*keine Wirkung*]" (259/358). Such an ethos is ineffectual. The provenance of this point is again Kantian, namely, the position that practical reason and its expression in the categorical imperative are separate from natural causality. The two steps are strictly connected. According to the new Kantianism, singularity is only possible because of the ineffectual. We can only escape the dominance of rules by positing something outside that evades all calculation and all ends. The impact of an ineffectual ethics in post-WWII French philosophy is keenly felt. Levinas's Other—around which his entire ethics pivots—is an expression of the ineffectual. We can see this also in the function that the unconditioned plays in Jacques Derrida's philosophy. This takes many guises (such as unconditioned hospitality) which are indebted to the transcendental conception of the "as if" in Kant's practical philosophy—a conception, moreover, that is

---

30. See for example, Emmanuel Levinas, *Alterity and Transcendence*, trans. Michael B. Smith (London: Athlone, 1999), 80, or *Otherwise Than Being: Or Beyond Essence*, trans. Alphonso Lingis (Dordrecht: Kluwer, 1991), 4.

important precisely in order, as Derrida explains, to counter the hold of calculation in the way that the operation of reason is conceived.[31]

John Llewelyn neatly captures this double step of the new Kantianism in the wake of the Heidegger by calling it "the middle voice." The middle voice indicates a verb that is both active and passive, both theory and praxis. Llewelyn uses this linguistic feature of the verb to describe a kind of ethical action that is indebted to its environment always in a singular manner, while retaining a kind of transcendental separation from the material. Not by coincidence, his analysis of the ethics of continental philosophers continuously returns to Kant and Heidegger.[32]

The most illuminating insight into the new Kantianism predominating continental philosophy, which follows the route charted in the "Letter on Humanism," actually concerns what its theory of action—both in terms of ethics and politics—actually does *not* address. Thus, whereas the analytic philosophical tradition is circumscribed by the dilemma "deontology or consequentialism," the continental tradition fails to even acknowledge the possibility of a "utilitarian" ethics. In a sense, that is regrettable, as continental philosophy and consequentialism have the *same* fundamental conception of the calculable: the calculable is invariably understood as that which can be calculated with some certainty, that which can be made to fit within a certain measure, thereby ignoring the sense of the calculable as that which has to be calculated even though it is certain that the calculation is impossible—what I called the calculating (§58). Despite the fact that continental philosophy rejects, and consequentialism embraces, the notion of the calculable only as that which can be calculated, the calculable is defined in the same one-sided manner that excludes the calculating. This has been possible because of the other of the calculable: either the deontology of analytic philosophy, or the new Kantianism of continental philosophy chiseled out in the "Letter on Humanism."

What is most regrettable in this lack of communication between continental philosophy and consequentialism is that a dialogue may have led them to reassess the commitment to only one of the meanings of calculable, namely, as something that can be calculated. Maybe a confrontation might have led them to realize that we are often (in fact, most of the time) confronted with the exigency to calculate in the face of the provisional ends

---

31. See for example, Jacques Derrida, *Rogues: Two Essays on Reason*, trans. Pascale-Anne Brault and Michael Nass (Stanford, CA: Stanford University Press, 2005), 132–35.

32. John Llewelyn, *The Middle Voice of Ecological Conscience: A Chiasmic Reading of Responsibility in the Neighborhood of Levinas, Heidegger and Others* (New York: St. Martin's Press, 1991).

of instrumentality, or to perform the judgment that the Greeks called phronesis. The calculating determines our actions much more than the calculated or any notion of the incalculable, not because we can measure how much we are acting according to either, but because the calculated and the incalculable presuppose the calculating (§13, §32).

That which has to be calculated, no matter how provisionally, is *not* the incalculable so often invoked by continental philosophers as another name for the transcendental aspect of the ineffectual. For a philosophy cognizant of the distinction between causality and instrumentality—that is, not in the grip of Heidegger's ruse—the place for such a transcendental incalculable is ceded to the agonism that arises from the fallibility of phronesis (§52). But such agonism is only discernible in how phronesis strives—but fails to—calculate with certainty. Consequently, an ontology of the ineffectual is hopelessly impaired in discerning the agonistic ontology that arises from the calculation characteristic of the instrumental ends of phronesis.[33] The new Kantianism reaffirms a transcendental. Materialist monism substitutes the transcendental with the conflicts inherent in the fallibility of phronesis, or what I call "the agonistic condition."[34] That is the dilemma—*either the ineffectual or agonism*—that continental philosophy will be forced to confront as soon as it breaks the spell cast by Heidegger's ruse.

63. Technophobia and the repression of instrumentality

As an extension of the conception of action in continental philosophy and theory, the repression of instrumentality has played a determinative role in the conception of the technological. The most significant figure in this discourse is Bernard Stiegler, whose monumental *Technics and Time* series has done more than any other book to adumbrate a philosophy of technology in the last few decades.[35]

Stiegler's trilogy can be understood as an engagement with Heidegger's position that is at the same time searching for a foothold beyond a strict

---

33. See Dimitris Vardoulakis, *Spinoza, the Epicurean: Authority and Utility in Materialism* (Edinburgh: Edinburgh University Press, 2020).

34. Dimitris Vardoulakis, *The Agonistic Condition* (Edinburgh: Edinburgh University Press, 2025).

35. The technics trilogy is Barnard Stiegler, *Technics and Time, 1: The Fault of Epimetheus* (Stanford, CA: Stanford University Press, 1998), *Technics and Time, 2: Disorientation* (Stanford, CA: Stanford University Press, 2009), and *Technics and Time, 3: Cinematic Time and the Question of Malaise* (Stanford, CA: Stanford University Press, 2010).

Heideggerian ontology. Moreover, this is enacted in the form of a critique of Heidegger's assertion from "The Question Concerning Technology," according to which the essence of technology is nothing technological. The reason, as we saw earlier, is that technology as the culmination of metaphysics offers an ontology that is inadequate to present being. Against this position, Stiegler holds that the determinative forgetting in the history of thought is not that of being, but rather of technics. We see in Stiegler the importance of the move in the ontology of the ineffectual to move instrumentality to the first sense of techne referring to monism (§57): technics becomes Stiegler's term to indicate the underlying singularity and unity of being. Even though Stiegler suggests that this leads to a reformulation of the existential analytic from *Being and Time*, it is in fact consonant with the ontology of the ineffectual that we find in the "Letter on Humanism."

The key elements of Stiegler's position are presented via an interpretation of the recounting of the myth of Epimetheus and Prometheus as it is told in Plato's *Protagoras*.[36] According to this version of the myth, Epimetheus was tasked with equipping living beings for their survival. But the titan miscalculated and when he came to the human at last he had no skills left to give them. Stiegler describes this lack as a fault in human finitude, arising from the existential *forgetting* of technics, characteristic of the human. To rectify his brother's miscalculation, Prometheus stole technics from the gods and gave them to humanity. This transgression is the second *fault* characteristic of the human. Thus, the forgetting of technics indicates, according to Stiegler, a double fault—both a human that requires the prosthesis of technics for its survival, and the illegitimate way in which technics are obtained.

It is clear to see what Stiegler's main target is: He wants to resist Heidegger's move, according to which the authentic, or the event of the truth of being, is purified from technics. From this perspective, Stiegler's reading of Heidegger's philosophy is the one closest to my position that I am aware of. In the reading offered throughout this book I, too, have consistently questioned how tenable Heidegger's argument is to separate qualitatively between end-oriented activities from actions that are purified of ends so as to attain to the truth of being.

At the same time, there is a fundamental divergence in the argument offered in this book from the one put forward by Stiegler. Specifically, Heidegger considers a forgetting of technics without any consideration of instrumentality. By contrast, I have presented a forgetting and repression

---

36. See Stiegler, *Technics and Time, 1*, Part 2.

of instrumentality by way of employing a specific technique, the ruse of techne. This points to a fundamental difference. Whereas Stiegler focuses on the final ends of action, I have been focusing on the interaction between the final and the instrumental ends. The distinction between causality and instrumentality as well as the materialist tradition that employs this distinction in its theory of action are both entirely absent from Stiegler's discourse. This difference is telling: the repression of instrumentality is still an absolute presupposition of Stiegler's discourse, even as he is attempting to battle its effects in Heidegger's discourse, namely, the purification of authenticity from all ends. Stiegler remains under the spell of the ruse of techne.

The persistent repression of instrumentality in Stiegler's discourse means that he accepts the Heideggerian solution to the problem of action in monism. Stiegler never questions the veracity of Heidegger's single, unified being. His ontology is monist. But without the distinction between final and instrumental ends, he is still forced to account for action by distinguishing between two kinds of actions—one that fails the truth of being and one that attains it. The distinction between inauthenticity and authenticity remains critical for his ontology of technics. The most paradoxical outcome of Stiegler's adherence to the Heideggerian solution to the account of action within monism is that ultimately Stiegler embraces the technophobia that is so characteristic of the Heideggerian discourse. The unforgetting of technics is cashed out in the castigation of the threats of modern technology in high capitalism.[37] Despite Stiegler's efforts, his notion of technics barely touches the second sense of techne that leads to the "nihilism of modernity."

In the end, the distinction between technics and technology is nothing but the scholastic reassertion of the distinction between two qualitatively distinct actions, one that is oriented toward the end truth of being and one that is not. By contrast, as I have been arguing, materialist monism does not distinguish between actions directly, but rather between the different ends of action, whereby it requires the distinction between causality/technicity and instrumentality. I hold, then, that the only viable option for a monist philosophy is to adhere to the distinction between causality and instrumentality.

37. See, for instance, the *Disbelief and Discredit Series*: Bernard Stiegler, *The Decadence of Industrial Democracies: Disbelief and Discredit 1*, trans. Daniel Ross and Suzanne Arnold (Cambridge: Polity Press, 2011), and *Uncontrollable Societies of Disaffected Individuals: Disbelief and Discredit 2*, trans. Daniel Ross and Suzanne Arnold (Cambridge: Polity Press, 2013).

64. The paradox of the final end

Another way of presenting the fault of Stiegler's thought, whereby his unforgetting of technics leads to nothing but technophobia, is by recalling that Epimetheus and Prometheus had another brother, Atlas, who is not discussed by Stiegler. I will use Atlas here as a figure that indicates Heidegger's influence in the thinking of the most cutting-edge technologies even—or *especially*—when Heidegger's name is not mentioned and his work is not examined. The reason is that the unconscious of a large part of the philosophical and theoretical considerations of technology today is formed by the repression of instrumentality. I will suggest at the same time that Stiegler's work has opened up avenues to interrogate the distinction between the technical and the instrumental.

We often see Atlas today in logos for maps because of his position in Greek mythology. Having chosen the wrong side in the *titanomachia* (the battle of the titans), Atlas was condemned to hold the world on his shoulders. Atlas, then, can function as a metonymy for the current reach of technology, especially AI technologies and big data that seem to have a complete hold over us given how they are omnipresent—from our mobile phones to sophisticated policing algorithms. That is why Kate Crawford in her recent books employs the figure of Atlas to refer to AI.[38] Even though there is no hint, Atlas as a metonymy in Crawford's book restates Heidegger's notion of the *Ge-stell*, denoting the essence of modern technology that makes everything calculable in such a way as to assert the domination of technology over the human.

There is, however, a different way of interpreting Atlas other than as simply a metonymy of the *Ge-stell*. Atlas is a figure that combines the most powerful and the most powerless, thereby referring to the efficient cause as understood in metaphysics (§31). Atlas is the most powerful as he literally holds the world on his shoulders. He is the most powerful, not only in the sense that he has the strength to prop up the world, but also in the sense that, if he stops doing so, the world will collapse. At the same time, his position of power evidences his utter powerlessness. He holds the world as a form of punishment. His power is an effect of his powerlessness to resist the deprivation of his freedom.

The shift from a view of Atlas as a metonymy of the *Ge-stell* to the recognition of Atlas as the combination of powerfulness and powerlessness

---

38. Kate Crawford, *The Atlas of AI: Power, Politics, and the Planetary Costs of Artificial Intelligence* (New Haven, CT: Yale University Press, 2021).

indicates that Atlas is also a figure of techne. As I explained in the Excursus, the combination of powerfulness and powerlessness is an effect of the understanding of action in terms of the final end (§31). Action, then, is powerful insofar as the end is achieved, but powerless to the extent that the end is conditioned by materiality. Atlas achieves the end of holding the world on his shoulders, but he is powerless because of the conditions that forced him to attain this power. This is the paradox of the final end: its completion is also its undoing, its success is by definition also its failure.

The most succinct and clear presentation of the paradox of the end can perhaps be found in chapter 21 of Hannah Arendt's *The Human Condition*. Arendt refers to it as "the perplexity of utilitarianism."[39] And she describes it by saying that "an end, once it is attained, ceases to be an end and loses its capacity to guide and justify the choice of means, to organize and produce them."[40] Thus, any activity that is governed by ends is caught in a never-ending spiral according to which the end is consumed and used up the moment it is attained, unable to guide action any longer. The end here can only be the final end—as the instrumental end is never, by definition, something that can be reached with any certainty, which is what protects it from the perplexity of utilitarianism. Because it can be reached, by contrast, the final end is power empowering (we can successfully achieve it) and utterly divesting us of power (as its function disappears the moment it has been reached).

The paradox of the final end is important in the context of modern theories of technology. A lot of the discourse on modern technologies is caught up in this paradox as a way to determine power. An excellent example of this is Crawford's *Atlas of AI*. The way that the paradox articulates in the discourse of modern technology is that there is an increasing pessimism about the possibility of finding a rupture or an outside to the totalizing power of AI. The more powerful human technology becomes by inventing new data mining technologies and algorithms, the less power is granted to the human to disrupt the totalizing power of AI that determines it. The paradox of the end leads to a vision about modern technology that is bleakly dystopian.

The paradox of the final end is intertwined with the paradox of power that is so prevalent in the anti-humanism which arose in the aftermath of the French reception of the "Letter on Humanism." This anti-humanism

---

39. Hannah Arendt, *The Human Condition* (Chicago: University of Chicago Press, 1998), 154.
40. Arendt, *The Human Condition*, 154–55.

embraces the various Heideggerian critiques we find in the "Letter," such as the critiques of subjectivism and value. But it also tends to be unsatisfied with Heidegger's elision of the social and the political. To address this deficiency, anti-humanism renounces the central Heideggerian question, namely, the recovery of the question of being. This does not mean however that it renounces the central Heideggerian preoccupation with monism. Instead of being, the one now becomes power. In the anti-humanist ontology, no one can escape the structures of power. Power, then, is conceived as something outside of which nothing exists. The monism of the single, unified being lives on in the anti-humanist determination of power.

The great difficulty of embracing monism while translating it into a discourse of power so as to address social and political questions is that it reanimates the paradox of the final end. A well-known illustration of this is Foucault's position in "Subject and Power" that power presupposes resistance.[41] Even if we grant this, and even if we grant that resistance can "disrupt" the calculative operation of a specific power dispositif, still the fact remains that there is no outside to power as such. If power presupposes resistance, resistance too (Foucault forgot to add) presupposes power. "To resist" is a transitive verb. Resistance is resistance *to* a preexisting power. To form any conception of the resistance to power, power needs to be presupposed. This entails a vicious circle or, in more technological nomenclature, a feedback loop that seems inescapable—the simultaneous powerfulness and powerlessness that is the end result of conceiving the ends of action as final ends.

A large part of the theory and philosophy of technology today is caught up in the paradox of the final end. As a result, the social function of such a philosophy is conceived as a critique of existing structures of power. Such critique is valuable and important. For instance, it has highlighted the "algorithmic injustice" that establishes itself on the basis of AI.[42] Or it discerns new forms of imperialism through the assertion of military power by technological means.[43] And, in one of its most sophisticated formulations

---

41. Michael Foucault, "The Subject and Power," in *Michel Foucault: Beyond Structuralism and Hermeneutics*, second edition, ed. Hubert L. Dreyfus and Paul Rabinow (Chicago: University of Chicago Press, 1983), 208–26.

42. See for example, Andrew Ferguson, *The Rise of Big Data Policing: Surveillance, Race, and the Future of Law Enforcement* (New York: NYU Press, 2017); and Safiya Noble, *Algorithms of Oppression: How Search Engines Reinforce Racism* (New York: NYU Press, 2018).

43. See for example, Grégoire Chamayou, *Manhunts: A Philosophical History*, trans. Steven Rendall (Princeton, NJ: Princeton University Press, 2012).

in Davide Panagia, it leads to a conception of *#datapolitik* that is a significant attempt to think of the political in the era of the algorithm.[44] But the problem is always the same: the entrapment of the dialectic of powerfulness and powerlessness in the paradox of the final end. Here, the dialectic articulates itself in the rejection of the possibility of any conception of change—which is to say, of any effectual action—within the purview of power. Funny how we have returned full circle back to the problematic of action in monism (§12) that questions how change is possible!

The effects of this incapacity instigated by the paradox of final end is that theories of technology readily cede their position to humanist discourses that reduce the examination of power in AI and big data to subjectivism. These are usually normative discourses that offer a juridical remedy to problems of power. Instead of the search for an outside of the calculations of technology—what Heidegger calls the ineffectual—the humanist discourses concentrate on the importance of regulation. According to this normative approach, the question is not about the totalizing import of power—the question is no longer one that presupposes any kind of monism. Rather, the question is about particular articulations of power that need to be restrained through law and regulation.[45] The dystopianism of the power critique of technology is now replaced by a utopia of liberal representative democracy. Maybe that is the dialectical opposite of the ruse of techne (§8).

So here, then, is the antinomy of the current debate in the theory and philosophy of technology: *either* an anti-humanism that is informed by French philosophy and which is attuned to the critique of subjectivity and value but which is unable to find an outside to the social phenomenon of a totalizing power; *or* a resurgent humanism that regards anti-humanism as irrelevant because of how ineffectual it is but that itself falls back into a humanism that presupposes the very structures of liberal democracy and high capitalism that any tinkering with legislation and regulation is thoroughly hopeless to address. The common denominator of both is the repression of instrumentality. Both sides of the antinomy are determined by different articulations of incapacity and powerlessness that account for

---

44. Davide Panagia, "On the Possibilities of a Political Theory of Algorithms," *Political Theory* 49, no. 1 (2021): 109–33.

45. This is implied in all discourses that lament the deficient regulation of modern technologies. See for example, Frank Pasquale, *The Black Box Society: The Secret Algorithms that Control Money and Information* (Cambridge, MA: Harvard University Press, 2015); and Shoshana Zuboff, *The Age of Surveillance Capitalism: The Fight for a Human Future at the New Frontier of Power* (New York: PublicAffairs, 2019).

action relying exclusively on final ends. Even though most of those participating in the debates about modern technology are far from experts on Heidegger—if they have read any of his work at all—still his ruse of techne as transmitted through continental philosophy and theory determines their discourse.

The appeal to an ineffectual that results from the paradox of the final end will retain its hold as long as we fail to distinguish final from instrumental ends—which is to say, as long as the repression of instrumentality persists and pervades our thought and as long as we remain blind to the materialist monist tradition. At this point, we can see the potential contained within Stiegler's work. By recognizing the forgetting of technics in Heidegger—that is, by recognizing the three senses of techne as I have described them—Stiegler's work has inadvertently started opening the door for a way to overcome the paradox of final ends through a reinscription of instrumentality in the philosophy of technology. An example of this is the work of Yuk Hui.

Working in the wake of Stiegler, Hui has made two significant contributions to the philosophy of technology. First, he has forcefully shown that the origin of technology is never only one. There is not only one "cosmotechnics" that arises from the myth of Prometheus, understood as the narrative that starts with the human obtaining the divine gift of technics only to be overrun by the *Ge-stell* of technology. Instead, Hui demonstrates that there are many different cosmotechnics that resonate within cultural and historical specificities.[46] Second, this entails that a new ontology is needed, one that no longer reduces the conception of the object to the natural object. Hui insists to the contrary that we have to take seriously the question that there are what he calls "digital objects."[47] On both of these counts, Hui demonstrates that the technological ought not to be reduced to the kind of exact calculation characteristic of the final ends and Heidegger's conception of the *Ge-stell*.

And yet Hui is not aware that the specificity of calculation where its end is not independent of its enactment, and the concept of his "digital" that is a calculation without any exact result but a fallible and negotiable one, are in fact characteristics of instrumentality. Hui does not know the materialist monist tradition. We encounter then in Hui's work the unraveling of the repression of instrumentality even though the instrumental

---

46. Yuk Hui, *The Question Concerning Technology in China: An Essay in Cosmotechnics* (Falmouth: Urbanomic, 2016).

47. Yuk Hui, *On the Existence of Digital Objects* (Minneapolis: University of Minnesota Press, 2016).

remains unnamed and unthematized. *Like* Heidegger's ineffectual ontology, the instrumental remains hidden in plain sight, but *unlike* the ontology of the ineffectual—and that is the critical point—Hui hides the name of instrumentality even though he describes its effects. As such, Hui forges a way forward to break the hold of the paradox of the final end on the philosophy of technology.

We will never be free of the hold of the paradox of the final end unless we are in a position to name what it presupposes—the repression of instrumentality. This requires a double task. Both a description of the effects of the instrumental ends of action in the social and political—which is to say technological, legal, economic, and so on—domains of action, and at the same time the construction of the history of the nexus of causal and instrumental ends within materialist monism. Such a reconstruction of the history of thought can only start by identifying and working through the repression that has allowed the hold of the ruse of techne. *The Ruse of Techne* is a contribution to this task insofar as Heidegger's ruse of techne emerges as the major technique for the repression of instrumentality in continental philosophy and theory over the past century. Maybe it is high time that we negate this Heideggerian technique, as opposed to merely critiquing parts of his thought and thereby reaffirming its repressed content—namely, instrumentality.

Peroratio

Is *The Ruse of Techne* a book about Heidegger? The subtitle would suggest so, as well as the fact that the argument within proceeds for the most part as a series of close readings of Heidegger's most important works, covering the development of his thought from the early 1920s to after World War II. The material is predominately on and about Heidegger. And yet, from another perspective, Heidegger is only the protagonist of another story that is not his own. This is the story about his invention of the ruse of techne as the technique to repress instrumentality. When Heidegger interpreted phronesis in such a way as to conceal instrumentality, first rather tentatively in October 1922, he established something that has remained unchallenged in philosophy and theory: the repression of instrumentality.

Heidegger is by no means the only character in this story. I have suggested that the renunciation of instrumentality is a key characteristic of the metaphysics of morals and it has become a constitutive feature of what has come to be called "continental philosophy" and "theory." The repression of instrumentality is not a new phenomenon.

Heidegger is the protagonist in the story of the repression of instrumentality since the publication of *Being and Time* because he constructs an account of the history of philosophy that claims to "destruct" the epistemology of the metaphysics of presence. This large historical trajectory, going all the way back to the dawn of philosophy, distinguishes his critique of the instrumental from other accounts that are confined to a critique of modern rationality, such as the Adornian critique. The Heideggerian account of the history of philosophy has prevailed in continental philosophy and theory as evidenced by the fact that the monist materialist account of action that departs from the distinction between causal and instrumental ends has all but disappeared from view.

The acceptance of Heidegger's account of a history of philosophy that discovers a single unified being—or monism—as the starting point of thought has consolidated Heidegger's position in the philosophical canon, but it is also its the major weakness. Such an account requires the determination of an action that is free of ends and effects, which means that it is still mired in the metaphysics of morals. Heidegger's philosophy is materialist and monist to the extent that it examines existence through the single, unified being. But it is a magical materialism because of the ruse to repress instrumentality, which is incompatible with materialist monisms such as epicureanism that rely on the distinction between causal and instrumental ends to provide an account of praxis.

How can we break the spell of the ruse of magical materialism?

The only way is to recognize the provenance of the trick—the monist difficulty to account for action as effective, that is, to account for action as capable of change and not as mere differentiation. If materialism signifies at its most basic the rejection of transcendence, and if monism adds to this that there is a totality outside of which nothing exists, then the problem of a satisfactory account of action is clear: How is it possible to give an account of action that is not merely a modification of this totality?

In order to break the spell of the repression of instrumentality, continental philosophy needs to recognize that it is operating on a monist framework. This requires sidestepping the confusion of monism with a metaphysical doctrine of the Middle Ages. Such a dismissal of monism only obscures its connection to materialism, as well as its importance for the history of thought, given that monism was critical at the dawn of philosophy in ancient Greece.

As soon as continental philosophy and theory realize that their ontology is monist, then they cannot help but confront the problematic of action. Heidegger's thought forces us to make a decision: *either* the Heideggerian acceptance of the triviality and vacuousness of any account of action, whereby ineffectual action is celebrated as supposedly the only way to avoid the humanism of metaphysics; *or* an account of action that relies on an analysis of the effects of action, which requires the distinction between two different kinds of ends—final and instrumental.

The great significance of Heidegger is that he established the possibility of this decision by introducing in modernity its first side, namely, the ineffectual. (In *The Logic of Living* I argue that it is actually Stoicism that invents the first iteration of the ineffectual within a monist ontology.) His consolidation in the history of continental philosophy as one of the most, if not *the* most, important philosopher in the twentieth century, is because he has managed to convince three generations of philosophers that there is only one solution to the problematic of action in monism that consists in the repression of instrumentality. It is only by recognizing the ruse of Heidegger's thought that the true power of his philosophy—namely, the decision it demands of us—will also be recognized.

I have traced the ways in which Heidegger sought to repress, hide, or forget the distinction between the causal and instrumental ends of action. This consisted in particular readings of the philosophical canon, such as his reading of Aristotle's conception of phronesis, where for the first time he argues for the incorporation of instrumentality within causality. After this was achieved, the next move was to carve out a field of action that is purified of all ends—causal and instrumental—of action. He thereby established two qualitatively distinct actions, one that is end-oriented and one that is end-free and thereby ineffectual. Thus, he responded to the problematic of action within a monist framework by separating two kinds of action, one that is, as he argued, dominated by ends and that is in turn dominating "us"; and another that has no ends and hence no effects whereby it discloses being, which is simultaneously the true sense of freedom.

The development of this argument in Heidegger's thought was anything but smooth or linear. I have identified three stages of its development: the ontology of the concealment of instrumentality, the ontology of conflict, and the ontology of the ineffectual. Despite their differences, they all faced the same conundrum: the end-free action appeared either trivial and vacuous, or in fact presupposed instrumentality whereby it was self-contradictory and complicit in the perpetuation of existing structures of power. The late Heidegger solves this conundrum with a sheer power of will. He insists that the greatness of the end-free action is the fact that it is ineffectual, and moreover he defines (great) art or poetry as the authentic expression of the ineffectual.

We can find three dominant ways in which Heidegger's magical materialism is operative in continental philosophy. First, the celebration of the event. This can take many forms, but they all insist on the incalculable in action. The difficulty with these solutions is that they fail to distinguish between the two senses of the calculable: the calculated as something that can be measured with certainty, and the calculating as something that requires calculation, even though such a calculation will always be provisional (§58). This is the solution that is favored by those philosophers and theorists working in the phenomenological and postphenomenological traditions broadly defined, such as Jacques Derrida. They fail to understand that the failure to distinguish between the two senses of the calculable has its provenance in Heidegger's mistaken interpretation of phronesis as an action that is end-free, which is the overlooked source of the "event."

Second, the plane of immanence. The most influential figure for this articulation of the repression of instrumentality is Gilles Deleuze. The plane of immanence and the rhizome do not admit of an outside—they are monist—but without distinguishing between causality and instrumentality. As such, they propose a sense of action that is merely modification. Whence the emphasis on modulations or quantities of power, whence the entire theory of expressionism. This side of the extension of the repression of instrumentality bases itself on an interpretation of Spinoza based on the Stoic ontological distinction between activity and passivity, but, as I have argued in *Spinoza, the Epicurean*, it fails to acknowledge the import of the definition of the good as that which is utilius in Part IV of the *Ethics*—which is Spinoza's way of introducing phronetic instrumentality in his conception of action. As such, the Deleuzean route, as well as its extension in various subdisciplines such as affect theory and posthumanism, merely perpetuate the repression of instrumentality.

Third, a philosophy of power. The radical anti-humanism of Foucault's analysis of the structures of power culminates in his conception of biopower as the kind of articulation of power in high capitalism that has achieved the most thorough, the most intricate, and hence the most effective technique of measuring power: calculating, not on the basis of the human, but on the basis of populations as a whole. There is a glimmer of hope in the late Foucault, when he insists that power always presupposes resistance. But such hope is quickly scattered when we realize that resistance by definition always presupposes a power to be resisted. Foucault's philosophy of resistance attempts to mediate between an event that is "outside" calculation and a modulation of power within a plane of immanence but is thoroughly unable to offer any resolution as long as it persists with the repression of instrumentality.

Once, I asked someone who had been close to Derrida why he had never written on Spinoza. The response—not without a certain playfulness—was that Spinoza was the province of Deleuze. It was wrong to think, as Deleuze suggested, that Spinoza was the prince of philosophy; rather, Deleuze was the prince of Spinozism, and Derrida could not transgress in that region. For many years I thought that this answer was correct, and it is indeed partially true insofar as it addresses the academic politics in the French scene. But it fails to note something more important: that in fact Spinoza proposes a theory of action that challenges one fundamental assumption of both Deleuze and Derrida, namely, the repression of instrumentality. Derrida could not transgress into Spinoza because Deleuze had used Spinoza to construct the repression of instrumentality in a way that was incompatible with his own. To write on Spinoza would have necessitated a tacit acknowledgment of their complicity in the repression of instrumentality.

Derrida, Deleuze, and Foucault—philosophies of the event, of immanence, and of power—stand united in the camp opposed to the monist materialism that determines praxis through the distinction between causality and instrumentality. They stand in Heidegger's corner.

Tracing the repression of instrumentality to October 1922, when Heidegger interpreted phronesis for the first time as an end-free action, provides us with the infrastructure to challenge the repression of instrumentality in continental philosophy. This will mean, inter alia, looking at monism with fresh eyes. For instance, as the title of Spinoza's magnum opus—*Ethics*—suggests, he regards a monist ontology as a theory of action. The two are intermeshed, as was the case in Epicurus as well. Maybe we should follow their lead and examine monism from the perspective of action.

The intermeshing of monism and a conception of action requires reexamining the distinction between final and instrumental ends. A theory of action is impossible, suggests Spinoza, if we rely solely on the final ends of action. Causality can lead to a conception of the totality outside of which nothing exists—what Spinoza variably calls god, nature, substance, or immanent cause. But to think of action on the basis of causality is merely, as he puts it at the end of Part I of the *Ethics*, the "sanctuary of ignorance." The reason is that we will then be trapped in a position where god, nature, or causality will determine action as a mere modification of being without any real effects.

The problem with such a solution is not only that it provides a trivial account of action, but it establishes a sense of authority of the one who becomes a representative, spokesperson, or guardian of the "one." And such an authority demands the voluntary submission of everyone else to their power.

The solution that Spinoza proposes is to remember that the good is intertwined with the calculation of utility. This is a calculation of the instrumental ends of actions—no matter how provisional and incomplete, no matter how inaccurate and fallible such a calculation is since we are determined by our external conditions and by the influence of others, so that "we regularly see the best but do the worse." And yet, the recognition of such a fallible calculation is still a huge achievement because it breaks the hold of the dilemma between a trivial and a complicit account of action. In other words, it raises the prospect of a conception of freedom that relies on a calculation of the effects of action.

Such a reappraisal of Spinoza also has far-reaching implications for a conception of the history of philosophy. In particular, as soon as we recognize that Greek philosophy is essentially monist, and that the monist theory of action in antiquity culminates in the epicurean conception of phronesis as the calculation of instrumental ends, then we are forced to reconsider the entire history of philosophy from the perspective of materialist monism. The history of philosophy appears very different when our view is not distorted by the ruse of techne.

The Ruse of Techne is about Heidegger's technique to repress instrumentality, which has been adopted by twentieth-century European philosophy under the spell of Heidegger's ruse. As such, it is a call to work through the technique of this repression by recognizing the importance of the distinction between final and instrumental ends. Such a call does not suggest the delusion that a completely illuminated philosophy free of repressions is possible. It does suggest though that philosophy has the responsibility to be vigilant to work through its repressed content, and that the major one that we have inherited from Heidegger is the repression of instrumentality. To break the spell of Heidegger's ruse will be a major commitment, but a rewarding task that will challenge ingrained philosophical prejudices.

Acknowledgments

The Ruse of Techne is part of a larger project that attempts to reintroduce the instrumental into a thinking of radical politics. This is simultaneously a critique of the idea that ethical and political action proper ought to be separated from ends or effects, whose provenance goes back to Heidegger. I refer to this idea as *the ineffectual* and I argue that philosophy has systematically repressed instrumentality as the means to define action without effects.

I am acutely aware that the critique of the ineffectual in the name of a revival of the idea of instrumentality would sound preposterous to anyone schooled in phenomenology, structuralism, or post-structuralism. We have been trained to notice the "evils" of instrumentality and to ignore—to forget or repress—its positive function in the construction of a philosophy that is opposed to Judeo-Christian metaphysics and is also concerned with praxis or with giving an account of action. Thus, I have often worried that such a project would make me a lot of enemies. And yet, I have been lucky enough to have met many friends along the way who have supported me on this project.

In particular, I am grateful for the contribution of the students in my graduate seminar on Heidegger in 2019. In particular, I would like to thank Yuval Bar Shalom, Daniel Carey, Bahar Mirteymouri, Reginald Nagaiya, Lewis Rosenberg, and Andrew Song. Thanks to Zheng Guo for preparing the index.

Thanks to Peg Birmingham, Walter Brogan, Timothy Campbell, Justin Clemens, Richard Colledge, Rebecca Comay, Alex Lefebvre, Makis Kakolyris, Pavlos Kontos, Jeff Malpas, Gerhard Richter, Angelika Seppi, and Shaun Terry whose engagement with the material has enriched the book. Ryan Bishop invited me to a workshop organized under the auspices of *Theory, Culture and Society*, where the first version of this book's argument was presented in June 2019. Sean Kirkland and Ian Moore have been perceptive and generous readers, for which I thank them. My colleague Charles Barbour has made himself available to read and discuss drafts in a way that is free of Heideggerian dogmatism. Finally, I am grateful to Ingrid Diran and Vassilis Lambropoulos whose invitation to Michigan University in October 2019 gave me a further chance to expand upon the ideas; and to Anne O'Byrne, who was not only a graceful host at SUNY Stonybrook (also in October 2019), but also a supportive colleague and a provocative correspondent about the book.

Besides those who have directly read, listened, and commented on *The Ruse of Teche*, there is a large number of colleagues and friends—too many to name—who have responded to parts of the larger project to redeem a sense of instrumentality for political philosophy. The project consists of a series of four books: the first book, *Spinoza, the Epicurean*, was published in 2020; the second book is the present one; the third book is *The Agonistic Condition*, which examines notions of agonistic democracy in the context of both political theory and the history of philosophy; and the final book, *The Logic of Living*, is on ancient Greek thought.

I had the rare privilege to be invited to contribute the lead article for a special issue of the *Australasian Philosophical Review* and I took the opportunity to present an early version of chapter 3 of *The Ruse of Teche*. I thank Andrew Benjamin, who edited the special issue, and the respondents to my paper: Charlotta Weigelt, Ian Moore, Adriel Trott, Richard Lee, Marilyn Stendera, Roland Végső, Lachlan Liesfield, Bernando Ainbinder, and Martin Black. Their responses enriched my thinking and helped me revise my own argument.

The love of Amanda, Alexis, and Lukas helped me get through especially trying circumstances, due to the pandemic and, primarily, professional difficulties. They give meaning to the world.

I am indebted to Gregg Lambert for pushing me to clarify the concept of agonistic monism contained in *Stasis Before the State*. This prompted me to develop how monism requires a theory of action. Already knowing that the most significant example of this is Heidegger, I did my graduate seminar from March to June 2019 on Heidegger's work. The seminar helped me crystalize what I call "the problematic of action in monism," namely, the sense of loss of meaning and the erasure of difference when one adopts an ontology without transcendence, or monism. This, in turn, led to the realization that there are two responses to the "problematic of action": either by inscribing difference to the ends of action, which places instrumentality and the conflict about ends at the center of practical philosophy; or by securing difference through the distinction between end-oriented actions and actions free of ends and effects. The former is the route of philosophers such as Spinoza, and the latter is Heidegger's. The notes from that seminar became the basis for *The Ruse of Techne*.

The notes were converted into a manuscript between June and December 2021. Most of it was written while enjoying the hospitality of Bob Paulsen and Jo Third, to whom I am grateful.

During that period, Andrew Benjamin was my constant interlocutor. He became my critical sounding board, especially in the context of the closure of the Australian borders due to COVID-19, which prevented me from traveling to "road test" the argument of the book. Andrew's enthusiasm, his eagerness to read and vigorously discuss drafts, and his unwavering support were indispensable for bringing it to completion. I could not have imagined a better reader. For this reason, *The Ruse of Techne* is dedicated to him.

Works by Martin Heidegger

Unless otherwise specified, all references to Heidegger's work in German are to the *Gesamtausgabe* published by Vittorio Klostermann, abbreviated as *GA* followed by the volume number. The in-text page references to *GA* follow the English editions, separated by a forward slash.

Aristotle's Metaphysics *Theta 1–3: On the Essence and Actuality of Force.* Translated by Walter Brogan and Peter Warnek. Bloomington: Indiana University Press, 1995. [= *GA* 33]

The Basic Problems of Phenomenology. Translated by Albert Hofstadter. Bloomington: Indiana University Press, 1982. [= *GA* 24]

Basic Writings. Translated by David Farrell Krell. London: Routledge, 2000.

The Beginning of Western Philosophy: Interpretation of Anaximander and Parmenides. Translated by Richard Rojcewicz. Bloomington: Indiana University Press, 2012. [= *GA* 35]

Being and Time. Translated by Joan Stambaugh. Albany: SUNY Press, 2010. [= *GA* 2]

"Being-There and Being-True According to Aristotle." In *Becoming Heidegger: On the Trail of His Early Occasional Writings, 1910–1927*, edited by Theodore Kisiel and Thomas Sheehan, 211–34. Seattle: Noesis Press, 2007. [= *GA* 80]

Contributions to Philosophy (Of the Event). Translated by Richard Rojcewicz and Daniela Vallega-Neu. Bloomington: Indiana University Press, 2021. [= *GA* 65]

Early Greek Thinking. Translated by David Farrell Krell and Frank A. Capuzzi. New York: Harper Collins, 1984.

The Essence of Truth: On Plato's Cave Allegory and Theaetetus. Translated by Ted Sadler. London: Continuum, 2002. [= *GA* 34]

The Fundamental Concepts of Metaphysics: World, Finitude, Solitude. Translated by William McNeill and Nicholas Walker. Bloomington: Indiana University Press, 1995. [= GA 29/30]

History of the Concept of Time: Prolegomena. Translated by Theodore Kisiel. Bloomington: Indiana University Press, 1985. [= *GA* 20]

Hölderlin's Hymn "The Ister." Translated by William McNeill and Julia Davis. Bloomington: Indiana University Press, 1996. [= *GA* 53]

Hölderlin's Hymns "Germania" and "The Rhine." Translated by William McNeill and Julia Ireland. Bloomington: Indiana University Press, 2014. [= *GA* 39]

Identity and Difference. Translated by Joan Stambach. New York: Harper & Row, 1969. [= *GA* 11]

Introduction to Metaphysics. Translated by Gregory Fried and Richard Polt. New Haven, CT: Yale University Press, 2000. [= *GA* 40]

Kant and the Problem of Metaphysics. Translated by Richard Taft. Bloomington: Indiana University Press, 1997. [= *GA* 3]

"Letter on Humanism." In *Basic Writings.* Translated by David Farrell Krell. London: Routledge, 2000. [= *GA* 9]

"Moira (Parmenides VIII, 34–41)." In *Early Greek Thinking.* Translated by David Farrell Krell and Frank A. Capuzzi. New York: Harper Collins, 1984. [= *GA* 7]

Nietzsche I: The Will to Power as Art. Translated by David F. Krell. New York: Harper & Row, 1979. [= *GA* 43]

Nietzsche II: The Eternal Recurrence of the Same. Translated by David F. Krell. New York: Harper & Row, 1984. [= *GA* 44]

Nietzsche III: The Will to Power as Knowledge and Metaphysics. Translated by Joan Stambaugh, Frank A. Capuzzi, and David F. Krell. New York: Harper & Row, 1987. [= *GA* 47]

Nietzsche IV: Nihilism. Translated by Frank A. Capuzzi. New York: Harper & Row, 1982. [= *GA* 6]

On Time and Being. Translated by Joan Stambauch. New York: Harper & Row, 1972).

Off the Beaten Track. Translated by Julian Young and Kenneth Haynes. Cambridge: Cambridge University Press, 2002. [= *GA* 5]

Parmenides. Translated by Andre Schuwer and Richard Rojcewicz. Bloomington: Indiana University Press, 1992. [= *GA* 54]

Pathmarks. Edited by William McNeill. Cambridge: Cambridge University Press, 1998. [= *GA* 9]

"Phenomenological Interpretations with Respect to Aristotle: Indication of the Hermeneutical Situation." Translated by Michael Baur. *Man and World*, 25 (1992): 355–93 = "Phänomenologische Interpretationen zu Aristoteles (Anzeige der hermeneutischen Situation)." *Dilthey-Jahrbuch*, 6 (1989): 235–74.

Plato's Sophist. Translated by Richard Rojcewicz and Andre Schuwer. Bloomington: Indiana University Press, 1997. [= *GA* 19]

"The Self-Assertion of the German University." In *The Heidegger Controversy: A Critical Reader*, edited by Richard Wolin, 29–39. Translated by William S. Lewis. Cambridge, MA: MIT Press, 1998. [= *GA* 16]

Supplements: From the Earliest Essays to Being and Time and Beyond. Edited by John van Buren. Albany: SUNY Press, 2002.

"Why Do I Stay in the Provinces?" In *Philosophical and Political Writings*, edited by Manfred Stassen, 16–19. Translated by Thomas Sheehan. New York: Continuum, 2003.

Bibliography

Acampora, Christa Davis. *Contesting Nietzsche*. Chicago: University of Chicago Press, 2013.
Adorno, Theodor W. *The Jargon of Authenticity*. Translated by Knut Tarnowski and Frederic Will. Evanston, IL: Northwestern University Press, 1973.
Aeschylus. *Suppliant Maidens, Persians, Prometheus, Seven Against Thebes*. Translated by Herbert Weir Smyth. Cambridge, MA: Harvard University Press, 1922.
Agamben, Giorgio. *Homo Sacer: Sovereign Power and Bare Life*. Translated by Daniel Heller-Roazen. Stanford, CA: Stanford University Press, 1998.
———. *Where Are We Now? The Epidemic as Politics*. Translated by Valeria Dani. London: Rowman & Littlefield, 2021.
Althusser, Louis. "The Underground Current of the Materialism of the Encounter." In *Philosophy of the Encounter: Later Writings, 1978–87*, edited by François Matheron and Oliver Corpet, 167–207. Translated by G.M. Goshgarian. London: Verso, 2006.
Angus, Ian H. *Technique and Enlightenment: Limits of Instrumental Reason*. Lanham, MD: University Press of America, 1984.
Annas, Julia. *The Morality of Happiness*. Oxford: Oxford University Press, 1993.
Aquinas, Thomas. *The Summa Theologica*. Translated by Daniel J. Sullivan. Chicago: Benton, 1952.
———. *Commentary on Aristotle's Nicomachean Ethics*. Translated by C. J. Litzinger. Notre Dame, IN: Dumb Ox Books, 1993.
Arendt, Hannah. *Between Past and Future*. New York: Viking, 1961.
———. *The Origins of Totalitarianism*. Cleveland, OH: Meridian, 1962.

———. *The Human Condition*. Chicago: University of Chicago Press, 1998.
———. *On Violence*. New York: Harcourt, 1970.
———. *The Life of the Mind*. New York: Harcourt, 1978.
———. "Martin Heidegger at Eighty." In *Heidegger and Modern Philosophy*, edited by Michael Murray, 293–303. Translated by Albert Hofstadter. New Haven, CT: Yale University Press, 1978.
Aristotle. *Metaphysics*. Translated by Hugh Tredennick. Cambridge, MA: Harvard University Press, 1933.
———. *Nicomachean Ethics*. Translated by H. Rackham. Cambridge, MA: Harvard University Press, 2003.
———. *Physics*. Translated by H. Wicksteed and F.M. Cornford. Cambridge, MA: Harvard University Press, 1957.
———. *Nikomachische Ethik VI*. Edited and translated by Hans-Georg Gadamer. Frankfurt am Main: Vittorio Klostermann, 1998.
Axelos, Kostas. *Alienation, Praxis and Techne in the Thought of Karl Marx*. Translated by Ronald Bruzina. Austin: University of Texas Press, 1976.
———. *Introduction to a Future Way of Thought: On Marx and Heidegger*. Translated by Kenneth Mills. Lüneburg: Meson Press, 2015.
Augustine. *The City of God Against the Pagans*. Edited and translated by R.W. Dyson. New York: Cambridge University Press, 1998.
Backman, Jussi. *Complicated Presence: Heidegger and the Postmetaphysical Unity of Being*. Albany: SUNY Press, 2015.
Badiou, Alain. *Manifesto for Philosophy*. Translated by Norman Madarasz. Albany: SUNY Press, 1992.
Badiou, Alain, and Barbara Cassin. *Heidegger: His Life and his Philosophy*. Translated by Susan Spitzer. New York: Columbia University Press, 2016.
Baker, Gideon. *Nihilism and Philosophy: Nothingness, Truth and World*. London: Bloomsbury, 2018.
Balibar, Étienne. *Citizen Subject: Foundation for Philosophical Anthropology*. Translated by Steven Miller. New York: Fordham University Press, 2017.
Bambach, Charles. *Heidegger's Roots: Nietzsche, National Socialism, and the Greeks*. Ithaca, NY: Cornell University Press, 2003.
Barash, Andrew. *Martin Heidegger and the Problem of Historical Meaning*. New York: Fordham University Press, 2003.
Bataille, Georges. *The Accursed Share: An Essay on General Economy*, volumes 2 and 3, *The History of Eroticism and Sovereignty*. Translated by Robert Hurley. New York: Zone Books, 1993.
Bayle, Pierre. *Historical and Critical Dictionary: Selections*. Translated by Richard H. Popkin. Indianapolis, IN: Bobbs-Merrill, 1965.
Bernasconi, Robert. "Heidegger's Destruction of Phronesis." *The Southern Journal of Philosophy* 28 (1989): 127–47.
Benjamin, Andrew. *The Plural Event: Descartes, Hegel, Heidegger*. London: Routledge, 1993.

———. *Place, Commonality and Judgment*. London: Continuum, 2010.
Bianchi, Emanuela. *The Feminine Symptom: Aleatory Matter in the Aristotelian Cosmos*. New York: Fordham University Press, 2014.
Blanchot, Maurice. *The Infinite Conversation*. Translated by Susan Hanson. Minneapolis: University of Minnesota Press, 1997.
Blattner, William. "Ontology, the A Priori, and the Primacy of Practice: An Aporia in Heidegger's Early Philosophy." In *Transcendental Heidegger*, edited by Steven Crowell and Jeff Malpas, 10–27. Stanford, CA: Stanford University Press, 2007.
Bourdieu, Pierre. *The Political Ontology of Martin Heidegger*. Translated by Peter Collier. Cambridge: Polity Press, 1991.
Bowler, Michael. *Heidegger and Aristotle: Philosophy as Praxis*. London: Continuum, 2008.
Broadie, Sarah. "Nature, Craft and Phronesis in Aristotle." *Philosophical Topics* 15, no. 2 (1987): 35–50.
Bröcker, Walter. "Heidegger und die Logik." *Philosophische Rundschau* 1 (1953): 48–56.
Brockelman, Thomas. *Žižek and Heidegger: The Question Concerning Techno-Capitalism*. London: Bloomsbury, 2008.
Brogan, Walter. *Heidegger and Aristotle: The Twofoldness of Being*. Albany: SUNY Press, 2005.
———. "The Intractable Interrelationship of *Physis* and *Techne*." In *Heidegger and the Greeks: Interpretative Essays,* edited by Drew A. Hyland and John Panteleimon Manoussakis, 43–56. Bloomington: Indiana University Press, 2006.
Brook, Peter. *The Empty Space*. New York, Atheneum, 1968.
Brown, Alison. *The Return of Lucretius to Renaissance Florence*. Cambridge, MA: Harvard University Press, 2010.
Brown, Wendy. *Undoing the Demos: Neoliberalism's Stealth Revolution*. New York: Zone Books, 2015.
Burckhardt, Jacob. *The Greeks and Greek Civilization*. Translated by Sheila Stern. New York: St. Martin's Griffin, 1998.
Caputo, John. *Heidegger and Aquinas: An Essay on Overcoming Metaphysics*. New York: Fordham University Press, 1982.
Chamayou, Grégoire. *Manhunts: A Philosophical History*. Translated by Steven Rendall. Princeton, NJ: Princeton University Press, 2012.
Cicero. *De Finibus Bonorum et Malorum*. Translated by H. Rackham. Cambridge, MA: Harvard University Press, 1931.
———. *De Legibus*. Translated by Clinton W. Keyes. Cambridge, MA: Harvard University Press, 1928.
———. *De Rerum Deorum* and *Academica*. Translated by H. Rackham. Cambridge, MA: Harvard University Press, 1933.
Coetzee, J. M. "Australia's Shame." *New York Review of Books*. September 26, 2019. www.nybooks.com/articles/2019/09/26/australias-shame/.

Colledge, Richard. "Heidegger on (In)finitude and the Greco-Latin Grammar of Being." *Review of Metaphysics* 74, no. 2 (2020): 289–319.
Connolly, William. *The Augustinian Imperative: A Reflection on the Politics of Morality*. Lanham, MD: Rowman & Littlefield, 2002.
Corngold, Stanley. "Error in Paul de Man." *Critical Inquiry* 8, no. 3. (1982): 489–507.
Crowell, Steven Galt. *Husserl, Heidegger, and the Space of Meaning: Paths Toward Transcendental Phenomenology*. Evanston, IL: Northwestern University Press, 2001.
Dahlstrom, Daniel O. *Heidegger's Concept of Truth*. Cambridge: Cambridge University Press, 2001.
Dastur, Françoise. "Heidegger's Freiburg Version of the Origin of the Work of Art." In *Heidegger Toward the Turn: Essays on the Work of the 1930s*, edited by James Risser, 119–42. Albany: SUNY Press, 1999.
Davies, Margery. *Woman's Place is at the Typewriter: Office Work and Office Workers, 1870–1930*. Philadelphia: Temple University Press, 1982.
de Man, Paul. "A Letter from Paul de Man." *Critical Inquiry* 8, no. 3 (1982): 509–13.
Detienne, Marcel, and Jean-Pierre Vernant. *Cunning Intelligence in Greek Culture and Society*. Translated by Janet Lloyd. Chicago: University of Chicago Press, 1991.
Della Rocca, Michael. *The Parmenidean Ascent*. Oxford: Oxford University Press, 2020.
Derrida, Jacques, *Margins of Philosophy*. Translated by Alan Bass. Chicago: University of Chicago Press, 1984.
———. *Of Spirit: Heidegger and the Question*. Translated by Geoffrey Bennington and Rachel Bowlby. Chicago: University of Chicago Press, 1989.
———. *Of Hospitality: Anne Dufourmantelle Invites Jacques Derrida to Respond*. Translated by Rachel Bowldy. Stanford, CA: Stanford University Press, 2000).
———. "Autoimmunity: Real and Symbolic Suicides." In *Philosophy in a Time of Terror: Dialogues with Jürgen Habermas and Jacques Derrida*, edited by Giovanna Borradori, 85–136. Chicago: University of Chicago Press, 2003.
———. *Rogues: Two Essays on Reason*. Translated by Pascale-Anne Brault and Michael Nass. Stanford, CA: Stanford University Press, 2005.
———. *The Beast and the Sovereign*, vol. 2. Translated by Geoffrey Bennington. Chicago: University of Chicago Press, 2011.
———. "A Conversation with Jacques Derrida about Heidegger." Translated by Katie Chenoweth and Rodrigo Therezo. *Oxford Literary Review* 43, no. 1 (2021): 1–61
Derrida, Jacques, Hans-Georg Gadamer, and Philippe Lacoue-Labarthe. *Heidegger, Philosophy, and Politics: The Heidelberg Conference*. Translated by Jeff Fort. New York: Fordham University Press, 2016.
Di Cesare, Donatella. *Heidegger and the Jews: The Black Notebooks*. Translated by Murtha Baca. Cambridge: Polity Press, 2018.

Dihle, Albrecht. *The Theory of Will in Classical Antiquity*. Berkeley: University of California Press, 1982.
Diogenes Laertius. *Lives of Eminent Philosophers*. Translated by R.D. Hicks. Cambridge, MA: Harvard University Press, 1931.
Dostal, Robert J. "The Problem of '*Indifferenz*' in *Sein und Zeit*." *Philosophy and Phenomenological Research* 43, no. 1 (1982): 43–58.
Drabinski, John E., and Eric S. Nelson, eds. *Between Levinas and Heidegger*. Albany: SUNY Press, 2014.
Dreyfus, Hubert L. "Between Techne and Technology: The Ambiguous Place of Equipment in Being and Time." *Tulane Studies in Philosophy* 32 (1984): 23–35.
———. *Being-in-the-World: A Commentary on Heidegger's Being and Time, Division 1*. Cambridge, MA: MIT Press, 1991.
———. "Heidegger's History of the Being of Equipment." In *Heidegger: A Critical Reader,* edited by Hubert Dreyfus and Harrison Hall, 173–85. Oxford: Blackwell, 1992.
———. "Interpreting Heidegger on Das Man." *Inquiry* 38, no. 4 (1995): 423–30.
Düttmann, Alexander García. *The Memory of a Thought: An Essay on Heidegger and Adorno*. Translated by Nicholas Walker. London: Continuum, 2002.
Elden, Stuart. *Speaking Against Number: Heidegger, Language and the Politics of Calculation*. Edinburgh: Edinburgh University Press, 2006.
———. *The Early Foucault*. Cambridge: Polity Press, 2021.
Fagenblat, Michael. "Levinas and Heidegger: The Elemental Confrontation." In *The Oxford Handbook of Levinas*, edited by Michael L. Morgan, 103–33. Oxford: Oxford University Press, 2019.
Farias, Victor. *Heidegger and Nazism*. Translated by Paul Burrell and Gabriel R. Ricci. Philadelphia: Temple University Press, 1989.
Faye, Emmanuel. *Heidegger: The Introduction of Nazism into Philosophy in Light of the Unpublished Seminars of 1933–1935*. Translated by Michael B. Smith. New Haven, CT: Yale University Press, 2009.
Feenberg, Andrew. *Alternative Modernity: The Technical Turn in Philosophy and Social Theory*. Berkeley: University of California Press, 1995.
———. *Heidegger and Marcuse: The Catastrophe and Redemption of History*. New York: Routledge, 2005.
———. *Between Reason and Experience: Essays in Technology and Modernity*. Cambridge, MA: MIT Press, 2010.
———. *Technology, Modernity, and Democracy*. London: Rowman & Littlefield, 2018.
Fenves, Peter. "'As on the First Day': Nine Notes on Heidegger's 'First Elaboration' of his *Ursprung des Kunstwerkes*." *Modern Language Notes* 136 (2021): 561–80.
Ferguson, Andrew Guthrie. *The Rise of Big Data Policing: Surveillance, Race, and the Future of Law Enforcement*. New York: NYU Press, 2017.

Fóti, Véronique M. *Heidegger and the Poets: Poiesis/Sophia/Techne*. Atlantic Highlands, NJ: Humanities Press, 1992.

Foucault, Michel. "Maurice Blanchot: The Thought from Outside." In *Foucault/Blanchot*. Translated by Brian Massumi. New York: Zone Books, 1987.

———. *Politics, Philosophy, Culture: Interviews and Other Writings 1977–1984*. Edited by Lawrence D. Kritzman. New York: Routledge, 1988.

———. "The Subject and Power." In *Michel Foucault: Beyond Structuralism and Hermeneutics*, second edition, edited by Hubert L. Dreyfus and Paul Rabinow, 208–26. Chicago: University of Chicago Press, 1983.

Fried, Richard. *Heidegger's Polemos: From Being to Politics*. New Haven, CT: Yale University Press, 2000.

Führich, Angelika. "Woman and Typewriter: Gender, Technology, and Work in Late Weimar Film." *Women in German Yearbook*, 16 (2000): 151–66.

Furley, David. *The Greek Cosmologists: The Formation of Atomic Theory and its Earliest Critics*. Cambridge: Cambridge University Press, 1987.

Gabriel, Markus. *Why the World Does Not Exist*. Translated by Gregory S. Moss. Cambridge: Polity Press, 2015.

Gadamer, Hans-Georg. *Philosophical Hermeneutics*. Edited and translated by David E. Linge. Berkeley: University of California Press, 1976.

———. Review of *Heidegger on Being and Acting: From Principles to Anarchy*, by Reiner Schürmann. *Graduate Faculty Philosophy Journal* 13, no. 1 (1988): 155–58.

———. *Truth and Method*. Translated by Joel Weinsheimer and Donald G. Marshall. New York: Continuum, 1989.

———. *Gesammelte Werke*, vols. 1–10. Mohr: Tübingen, 1985–2010.

Golob, Sascha. *Heidegger on Concepts, Freedom, and Normativity*. Cambridge: Cambridge University Press, 2014.

Gourgouris, Stathis. *Does Literature Think? Literature as Theory for an Antimythical Era*. Stanford, CA: Stanford University Press, 2003.

Guenther, Lisa. *Solitary Confinement: Social Death and Its Afterlives*. Minneapolis: University of Minnesota Press, 2013.

Grassi, Ernesto. *Heidegger and the Question of Renaissance Humanism*. Binghamton, NY: Center for Medieval and Early Renaissance Studies, 1983.

Grunenberg, Antonia. *Hannah Arendt and Martin Heidegger: History of Love*. Translated by Peg Birmingham, Kristina Lebedeva, and Elizabeth von Witzke Birmingham. Bloomington: Indiana University Press, 2017.

Guignon, Charles. "Being as Appearing: Retrieving the Greek Experience of *Phusis*." In *A Companion to Heidegger's Introduction to Metaphysics,* edited by Richard Polt and Gregory Fried, 34–56. New Haven, CT: Yale University Press, 2001.

Hadot, Pierre. *What is Ancient Philosophy?* Translated by Michael Chase. Cambridge, MA: Harvard University Press, 2004.

Hardt, Michael, and Antonio Negri. *Empire*. Cambridge, MA: Harvard University Press, 2000.

Harman, Graham. *Tool-Being: Heidegger and the Metaphysics of Objects*. Chicago: Open Court, 2002.
Hegel, Georg Wilhelm Friedrich. *Lectures on Logic: Berlin, 1831*. Translated by Clark Butler. Bloomington: Indiana University Press, 2008.
———. *Lectures on the History of Philosophy, 1825–6*. Edited by Robert F. Brown. Translated by R.F. Brown and J.M. Stewart with the assistance of H.S. Harris. Oxford: Clarendon, 2009.
Hesiod, *Theogony. Works and Days. Testimonia*. Translated by Glenn W. Most. Cambridge, MA: Harvard University Press, 2006.
Hirschman, Albert O. *The Passions and the Interests: Political Arguments for Capitalism Before Its Triumph*. Princeton, NJ: Princeton University Press, 1977.
Hodge, Joanna. *Heidegger and Ethics*. London: Routledge, 1995.
Hopkins, Burt. *Intentionality in Husserl and Heidegger: The Problem of the Original Method and Phenomenon of Phenomenology*. Dordrecht: Kluwer, 1993.
Hui, Yuk. *The Question Concerning Technology in China: An Essay in Cosmotechnics*. Falmouth: Urbanomic, 2016.
———. *On the Existence of Digital Objects*. Minneapolis: University of Minnesota Press, 2016.
Hume, David. *Dialogues Concerning Natural Religion and Other Writings*. Edited by Dorothy Coleman. Cambridge: Cambridge University Press, 2007.
Ihde, Don. *Technics and Praxis: A Philosophy of Technology*. Dordrecht: Reidel, 1979.
———. *Heidegger's Technologies: Postphenomenological Perspectives*. New York: Fordham University Press, 2010.
Janicaud, Dominique. *Heidegger in France*. Translated by François Raffoul and David Pettigrew. Bloomington: Indiana University Press, 2015.
Janicaud, Dominique, and Jean-François Mattei. *Heidegger: From Metaphysics to Thought*. Translated by Michael Gendre. Albany: SUNY Press, 1995.
Jonas, Hans. "Heidegger and Theology." *Review of Metaphysics* 18, no. 2 (1964): 207–33.
Kant, Immanuel. *Critique of Pure Reason*. Translated by Paul Guyer and Allen W. Wood. Cambridge: Cambridge University Press, 1998.
———. *Groundwork of the Metaphysics of Morals*. Translated by Mary Gregor. Cambridge: Cambridge University Press, 2002.
Kasparov, Gary, with Mig Greengard. *Deep Thinking: Where Machine Intelligence Ends and Human Creativity Begins*. London: John Murray, 2017.
Kirkland, Sean. *The Destruction of Aristotle: Reading the Tradition with the Early Heidegger*. Evanston, IL: Northwestern University Press, 2022.
Kisiel, Theodore. *The Genesis of Heidegger's Being and Time*. Berkeley: University of California Press, 1995.
Kisiel, Theodore, and Thomas Sheehan, eds. *Becoming Heidegger: On the Trail of His Early Occasional Writings, 1910–1927*. Seattle: Noesis Press, 2007.

Kittler, Friedrich. *Gramophone, Film, Typewriter*. Translated by Geoffrey Winthrop-Young and Michael Wurz. Stanford, CA: Stanford University Press, 1999.
Kiverstein, Julian, and Michael Wheeler, eds. *Heidegger and Cognitive Science*. New York: Palgrave Macmillan, 2012.
Kojève, Alexandre. *The Notion of Authority (A Brief Presentation)*. Edited by François Terré. Translated by Hager Weslati. London: Verso, 2014.
Kontos, Pavlos. "Aristotle in Phenomenology." In *Oxford Handbook of the History of Phenomenology*, edited by Dan Zahavi, 5–24. Oxford: Oxford University Press, 2018.
Krell, David Ferrell. "On the Manifold Meaning of Aletheia: Brentano, Aristotle, Heidegger." *Research in Phenomenology* 5 (1975): 77–94.
———. *Ecstasy, Catastrophe: Heidegger from Being and Time to the Black Notebooks*. Albany: SUNY Press, 2015.
Lacoue-Labarthe, Philippe. *Heidegger, Art and Politics: The Fiction of the Political*. Translated by Chris Turner. Oxford: Blackwell, 1990.
———. *Heidegger and the Politics of Poetry*. Translated by Jeff Fort. Urbana: University of Illinois Press, 2007.
Lange, Friedrich Albert. *Geschichte des Materialismus und Kritik seiner Bedeutung in der Gegenwart*. Iserlohn: Baedeker, 1887.
Lee, Richard. "Willing the Means: On Vardoulakis on Heidegger on Aristotle," *Australian Philosophical Review* 6, no. 3 (2022): 271–81.
Levinas, Emmanuel. *Totality and Infinity: An Essay on Exteriority*. Translated by Alphonso Lingis. Pittsburgh, PA: Duquesne University Press, 1969.
———. *Otherwise Than Being: Or Beyond Essence*. Translated by Alphonso Lingis. Dordrecht: Kluwer, 1991.
———. *Alterity and Transcendence*. Translated by Michael B. Smith. London: Athlone, 1999.
Llewelyn, John. *The Middle Voice of Ecological Conscience: A Chiasmic Reading of Responsibility in the Neighborhood of Levinas, Heidegger and Others*. New York: St. Martin's Press, 1991.
Loraux, Nicole. *The Divided City: On Memory and Forgetting in Ancient Athens*. Translated by Corinne Pache and Jeff Fort. New York: Zone Books, 2006.
Löwith, Karl. *Mein Leben in Deutschland vor und nach 1933: Ein Bericht*. Stuttgart: J. B. Metzlersehe, 1986.
Love, Jeff, and Michael Meng. "The Political Myths of Martin Heidegger." *New German Critique* 42, no. 1 (2015): 45–66.
Lucretius. *On the Nature of Things*. Translated by W.H.D. Rouse. Revised by Martin F. Smith. Cambridge, MA: Harvard University Press, 1924.
Lyotard, Jean-François. *Heidegger and "The Jews."* Translated by Andreas Michel and Mark S. Roberts. Minneapolis: University of Minnesota Press, 1990.
MacIntyre, Alasdair. *After Virtue: A Study in Moral Theory*. Notre Dame, IN: University of Notre Dame Press, 2007.

Machiavelli, Niccolò. *The Prince*. Edited by Quentin Skinner and Russell Price. Cambridge: Cambridge University Press, 1988.

———. "Discourses on the First Decade of Titus Livius." In *Machiavelli: The Chief Works and Others*, volume 1. Translated by Allan Gilbert. Durham, NC: Duke University Press, 1989.

Malabou, Catherine. *The Heidegger Change: On the Fantastic in Philosophy*. Translated by Peter Skafish. Albany: SUNY Press, 2011.

Malpas, Jeff. *Heidegger's Topology: Being, Place, World*. Cambridge, MA: MIT Press, 2006.

———. *Heidegger and the Thinking of Place: Explorations in the Topology of Being World*. Cambridge, MA: MIT Press, 2012.

Marcuse, Herbert. *Heideggerian Marxism*. Edited by Richard Wolin and John Abromeit. Lincoln: University of Nebraska Press, 2005.

Marion, Jean-Luc. *Mystics: Presence and Aporia*. Translated by Christian Sheppard and Michael Kessler. Chicago: University of Chicago Press, 2003.

Marx, Karl, and Friedrich Engels. "Manifesto of the Communist Party." In *Collected Works of Karl Marx and Friedrich Engels, 1845–48*, vol. 6, 474–519. New York: International Publishers, 1976.

Marx, Werner. *Heidegger and the Tradition*. Translated by Theodore Kisiel and Murray Greene. Evanston, IL: Northwestern University Press, 1971.

McNeill, William. *The Glance of the Eye: Heidegger, Aristotle, and the Ends of Theory*. Albany: SUNY Press, 1999.

———. *The Time of Life: Heidegger and Ethos*. Albany: SUNY Press, 2006.

Meillassoux, Quentin. *After Finitude: An Essay on the Necessity of Contingency*. Translated by Ray Brassier. London: Continuum, 2009.

Menning, Laurence Paul. *Heidegger and Marx: A Productive Dialogue Over the Language of Humanism*. Evanston, IL: Northwestern University Press, 2013.

Merleau-Ponty, Maurice. *Phenomenology of Perception*. Translated by Donald A. Landes. London: Routledge, 2012.

Miller, Barbara, and Stephanie Dalzell. "Coronavirus Vaccine Trials Run by UQ and CSL Abandoned Due to False Positive HIV Results." ABC News, December 11, 2020. www.abc.net.au/news/2020-12-11/uq-csl-coronavirus-vaccine-trial-to-be-abandoned/12973656.

Mitchell, Andrew. *Heidegger Among the Sculptors: Body, Space, and the Art of Dwelling*. Stanford, CA: Stanford University Press, 2010.

Moore, Ian Alexander. *Eckhart, Heidegger, and the Imperative of Releasement*. Albany: SUNY Press, 2019.

———. "The End of Instrumentality? Heidegger on *Phronēsis* and Calculative Thinking." *Australian Philosophical Review* 6, no. 3 (2022): 255–61.

Mueller, Gavin. *Breaking Things at Work: The Luddites Are Right About Why You Hate Your Job*. London: Verso, 2021.

Nancy, Jean-Luc. *Being Singular Plural*. Translated by Robert D. Richardson and Anne E. O'Byrne. Stanford, CA: Stanford University Press, 2000.

———. "Heidegger's 'Originary Ethics.'" In *Heidegger and Practical Philosophy*, edited by François Raffoul and David Pettigrew, 65–85. Albany: SUNY Press, 2002.

Negri, Antonio. *Insurgencies: Constituent Power and the Modern State*. Translated by Maurizia Boscagli, Minneapolis: University of Minnesota Press, 1999.

———. *The Political Descartes: Reason, Ideology, and the Bourgeois Project*. Translated by Matteo Mandarini and Alberto Toscano. London: Verso, 2006.

Nietzsche, Friedrich. *On the Genealogy of Morality and Other Writings*. Edited by Keith Ansell-Pearson. Translated by Carol Diethe. Cambridge: Cambridge University Press, 2006.

Noble, Safiya Umoja. *Algorithms of Oppression: How Search Engines Reinforce Racism*. New York: NYU Press, 2018.

Olafson, Frederick A. *Heidegger and the Ground of Ethics: A Study of Mitdasein*. Cambridge: Cambridge University Press, 1998.

Panagia, Davide. "On the Possibilities of a Political Theory of Algorithms." *Political Theory* 49, no. 1 (2021): 109–33.

Pasquale, Frank. *The Black Box Society: The Secret Algorithms that Control Money and Information*. Cambridge, MA: Harvard University Press, 2015.

Pearson Geiman, Clare. "Heidegger's Antigones." In *A Companion to Heidegger's Introduction to Metaphysics*, edited by Richard Polt and Gregory Fried, 161–82. New Haven, CT: Yale University Press, 2001.

Perkams, Matthias, "Aquinas on Choice, Will, and Voluntary Action." In *Aquinas and the Nicomachean Ethics*, edited by Tobias Hoffmann, Jörn Müller, and Matthias Perkams, 72–90. Cambridge: Cambridge University Press, 2013.

Phillips, James. *Heidegger's Volk: Between National Socialism and Poetry*. Stanford, CA: Stanford University Press, 2005.

Polt, Richard. *Time and Trauma: Thinking Through Heidegger in the Thirties*. London: Rowman & Littlefield, 2019.

Polt, Richard, and Gregory Fried, eds. *A Companion to Heidegger's Introduction to Metaphysics*. New Haven, CT: Yale University Press, 2001.

Porphyry. *De l'abstinence*. Edited and translated by Jean Bouffartigue. Paris: Belles Letters, 1977.

Prauss, Gerold. *Knowing and Doing in Heidegger's* Being and Time. Translated by Gary Steiner and Jeffrey S. Turner. Amherst, MA: Humanity Books, 1977.

Protevi, John. *Time and Exteriority: Aristotle, Heidegger, Derrida*. Lewisburg, PA: Bucknell University Press, 1994.

Raffoul, François. *Heidegger and the Subject*. Translated by David Pettigrew and Gregory Recco. Atlantic Highlands, NJ: Humanities Press, 1998.

———. *Thinking the Event*. Bloomington: Indiana University Press, 2020.

Raffoul, François, and David Pettigrew, eds. *Heidegger and Practical Philosophy*. Albany: SUNY Press, 2002.

Rendall, Jess, and Lily Nothling. "Cancellation of University of Queensland's COVID-19 Vaccine Trial 'Reassuring.'" ABC News, December 12, 2020. www.abc.net.au/news/2020-12-12/coronavirus-queensland-vaccine-uq-trial-cancellation-setback/12973724.

Richardson, William J. *Heidegger: Through Phenomenology to Thought*, revised edition. New York: Fordham University Press, 2003.

Richter, Gerhard. *This Great Allegory: On World-Decay and World-Opening in the Work of Art*. Cambridge, MA: MIT Press, 2022.

Ricoeur, Paul. "The Paradox of Authority." In *Reflections on the Just*. Translated by David Pellauer. Chicago: University of Chicago Press, 2007.

Risser, James, ed. *Heidegger Toward the Turn: Essays on the Work of the 1930s*. Albany: SUNY Press, 1999.

Rockmore, Tom. *Heidegger and French Philosophy: Humanism, Antihumanism and Being*. London: Routledge, 1995.

Rubenstein, Mary-Jane. *Pantheologies: Gods, Worlds, Monsters*. New York: Columbia University Press, 2018.

Safranksi, Rüdiger. *Martin Heidegger: Between Good and Evil*. Translated by Ewald Osers. Cambridge, MA: Harvard University Press, 1999.

Sallis, John. *Echoes: After Heidegger*. Bloomington: Indiana University Press, 1990.

———. *Being and Logos: Reading the Platonic Dialogues*. Bloomington: Indiana University Press, 1996.

Salzani, Carolo. "COVID-19 and State of Exception: Medicine, Politics, and the Epidemic State." *dePICTions*, March 12, 2021. https://parisinstitute.org/depictions-article-covid-19-and-state-of-exception-medicine-politics-and-the-epidemic-state/.

Sartre, Jean-Paul. *Existentialism is a Humanism*. Translated by Carol Macomber. New Haven, CT: Yale University Press, 2007.

Sas, Nick, and Michael Slezak. "Coronavirus Vaccine from UQ and CSL Abandoned After HIV Response Which Scientists Say Was 'Unexpected.'" ABC News, December 11, 2020. www.abc.net.au/news/2020-12-11/covid19-vaccine-csl-uq-hiv-element-what-went-wrong/12973952.

Schürmann, Reiner. *Heidegger on Being and Acting: From Principles to Anarchy*. Translated by Christine-Marie Gros. Bloomington: Indiana University Press, 1987.

Scott, Charles E. *The Question of Ethics: Nietzsche, Foucault, Heidegger*. Bloomington: Indiana University Press, 1990.

———. "The Appearance of Metaphysics." In *A Companion to Heidegger's Introduction to Metaphysics*, edited by Richard Polt and Gregory Fried, 17–33. New Haven, CT: Yale University Press, 2001.

Sheehan, Thomas. "*Kehre* and *Ereignis*: A Prolegomenon to *Introduction to Metaphysics*." In *A Companion to Heidegger's Introduction to Metaphysics*, edited by Richard Polt and Gregory Fried, 3–16. New Haven, CT: Yale University Press, 2001.

Slezak, Michael. "How the UQ Coronavirus Vaccine Induced False-Positive HIV Test Results and Why Scientists Were Prepared." ABC News, December 11, 2020. www.abc.net.au/news/2020-12-11/how-the-uq-covid-19-vaccine-induces-false-positive-hiv-results/12975048.

Slobodian, Quinn. *Globalists: The End of Empire and the Birth of Neoliberalism*. Cambridge, MA: Harvard University Press, 2018.

Sluga, Hans. *Heidegger's Crisis: Philosophy and Politics in Nazi Germany*. Cambridge, MA: Harvard University Press, 1993.

Sorel, George. *Reflections on Violence*. Edited by Jeremy Jennings. Cambridge: Cambridge University Press, 1999.

Smith, Adam. *An Inquiry into the Nature and Causes of the Wealth of Nations*. In *The Glasgow Edition of the Works and Correspondence of Adam Smith*, vol. 2. Edited by R.H Campbell and A.S. Skinner. Oxford: Oxford University Press, 1976.

Sophocles. *Antigone. Women of Trachis. Philoctetes. Oedipus at Colonus*. Translated by Hugh Lloyd-Jones. Cambridge, MA: Harvard University Press, 1994.

Spinoza, Baruch. *Ethics*. Translated by Edwin Curley. London: Penguin, 1996.

———. *Theological-Political Treatise*. Translated by Samuel Shirley. Indianapolis, IN: Hackett, 2001.

Stiegler, Bernard. *Technics and Time, 1: The Fault of Epimetheus*. Stanford, CA: Stanford University Press, 1998.

———. *Technics and Time, 2: Disorientation*. Stanford, CA: Stanford University Press, 2009.

———. *Technics and Time, 3: Cinematic Time and the Question of Malaise*. Stanford, CA: Stanford University Press, 2010.

———. *The Decadence of Industrial Democracies: Disbelief and Discredit 1*. Translated by Daniel Ross and Suzanne Arnold. Cambridge: Polity Press, 2011.

——— *Uncontrollable Societies of Disaffected Individuals: Disbelief and Discredit 2*. Translated by Daniel Ross and Suzanne Arnold. Cambridge: Polity Press, 2013.

Strauss, Leo. *Das Erkenntnisproblem in der philosophischen Lehre Fr. H. Jacobis*. In *Gesammelte Schriften*, Band 2: Philosophie und Gesetz, Frühe Schriften, edited by Heinrich Meier, 237–92. Stuttgart: J.B. Metzler, 2013 [1921].

———. *Die Religionskritik Spinozas als Grundlage seiner Bibelwissenschaft: Untersuchungen zu Spinozas Theologisch-politischem Traktat*. Berlin: Akademie-Verlag, 1930.

———. "An Introduction to Heideggerian Existentialism." In *The Rebirth of Classical Political Rationalism: An Introduction to the Thought of Leo Strauss*. Edited by Thomas L. Pangle. Chicago: University of Chicago Press, 1989.

Szendy, Peter. *Listen: A History of Our Ears*. Translated by Charlotte Mandell. New York: Fordham University Press, 2008.

Tabak, Mehmet. *Plato's* Parmenides *Reconsidered*. New York: Palgrave Macmillan, 2015.

Taminiaux, Jacques. "Phenomenology and the Problem of Action." *Philosophy and Social Research* 11 (1986): 207–19.

———. "Poiesis and Praxis in Fundamental Ontology." *Research in Phenomenology* 17 (1987): 137–69.

———. *Heidegger and the Project of Fundamental Ontology*. Translated by Michael Gendre. Albany: SUNY Press, 1991.

Thanassas, Panagiotis. "Phronesis vs. Sophia: On Heidegger Ambivalent Aristotelianism." *The Review of Metaphysics* 66 (2012): 31–59.

Thomson, Ian. *Heidegger on Ontotheology: Technology and the Politics of Education*. Cambridge: Cambridge University Press, 2005.

Trawny, Peter. *Freedom to Fail: Heidegger's Anarchy*. Translated by Ian Alexander Moore and Christopher Turner. Cambridge: Polity Press, 2015.

———. *Heidegger and the Myth of a Jewish World Conspiracy*. Translated by Andrew J. Mitchel. Chicago: University of Chicago Press, 2015.

Trott, Adriel M. *Aristotle on the Matter of Form: A Feminist Metaphysics of Generation*. Edinburgh: Edinburgh University Press, 2019.

Tuncel, Yunus. *Agon in Nietzsche*. Milwaukee, WI: Marquette University Press, 2013.

Tugendhat, Ernst. *Der Wahrheitsbegriff bei Husserl und Heidegger*. Berlin: De Gruyter, 1970.

Usener, Hermann, ed. *Epicurea*. Cambridge: Cambridge University Press, 2010.

Vardoulakis, Dimitris. "A Matter of Immediacy: The Artwork and the Political in Walter Benjamin and Martin Heidegger." In *Sparks will Fly: Benjamin and Heidegger*, edited by Andrew Benjamin and Dimitris Vardoulakis, 237–57. Albany: SUNY Press, 2015.

———. *The Agonistic Condition* (Edinburgh: Edinburgh University Press, 2025).

———. "The Antinomy of Frictionless Sovereignty: Inverse Relations of Authority and Authoritarianism." *boundary 2 online*, August 20, 2020. www.boundary2.org/2020/08/dimitris-vardoulakis-the-antinomy-of-frictionless-sovereignty-inverse-relations-of-authority-and-authoritarianism/.

———. "Autoimmunities: Derrida, Democracy and Political Theology." *Research in Phenomenology* 48 (2018): 29–56.

———. "Behrouz Boochani and the Biopolitics of the Camp: The New Primo Levi?" Public Seminar, February 16, 2019. https://philarchive.org/archive/VARBBA.

———. "The C** Word: Covid-19 and Calculation." *The Philosophical Salon*, May 14, 2020. https://thephilosophicalsalon.com/the-c-word-covid-19-and-calculation/.

———. "The Invention of Nihilism: Political Monism, Epicureanism, and Spinoza." *Crisis and Critique* 8, no. 2 (2021): 510–35.

———. *The Logic of Living: The Materialism of Greek Thought* (forthcoming).

———. "Phronesis and Instrumentality: The Import of Aristotle's Book 6 of *Nicomachean Ethics* Today." *Graduate Faculty Philosophy Journal* 44, nos. 1–2 (2023): 99–122.

———. "Why Ancient Monism Matters Today: Heidegger and Plato's *Sophist*." *Review of Metaphysics* 77, no. 2 (2023): 299–326.

———. *Sovereignty and Its Other: Toward the Dejustification of Violence*. New York: Fordham University Press, 2013.

———. *Spinoza, the Epicurean: Authority and Utility in Materialism*. Edinburgh: Edinburgh University Press, 2020.

———. *Stasis Before the State: Nine Theses on Agonistic Democracy*. New York: Fordham University Press, 2019.

Vattimo, Gianni, and Santiago Zabala. *Hermeneutic Communism: From Heidegger to Marx*. New York: Columbia University Press, 2011.

Vaysse, Jean-Marie. *Totalité et Finitude: Spinoza et Heidegger*. Paris: Vrin, 2004.

Végső, Roland. *Worldlessness After Heidegger: Phenomenology, Psychoanalysis, Deconstruction*. Edinburgh: Edinburgh University Press, 2020.

———. "Ends Without a Cause: A Response to Dimitris Vardoulakis." *Australian Philosophical Review* 6, no. 3 (2022): 288–94.

Villa, Dana R. *Arendt and Heidegger: The Fate of the Political*. Princeton, NJ: Princeton University Press, 1996.

Volpi, Franco. "Dasein as *Praxis:* The Heideggerian Assimilation and the Radicalization of the Practical Philosophy of Aristotle." In *Martin Heidegger: Critical Assessments, Volume II: History of Philosophy*, edited by Christopher Macann, 90–129. London: Routledge, 1992.

———. "*Being and Time:* A 'Translation' of the *Nicomachean Ethics*?" In *Reading Heidegger from the Start: Essays in His Earliest Thought*, edited by Theodore Kiel and John van Buren, 195–211. Translated by John Protevi. Albany: SUNY Press, 1994.

——— "In Whose Name? Heidegger and 'Practical Philosophy.'" *European Journal of Political Theory* 6, no. 1 (2007): 31–51.

Wendland, Aaron James. "Rethinking Intentionality in *Being and Time*." *International Journal of Philosophical Studies* 29, no. 1 (2021): 44–76.

Williams, Bernard. *Shame and Necessity*. Berkeley: University of California Press, 1993.

Wisser, Richard. "Martin Heidegger in Conversation with Richard Wisser." In *Martin Heidegger and National Socialism: Questions and Answers*, edited by Günter Neske and Emil Kettering, 81–87. Translated by Lisa Harries. New York: Paragon, 1990.

Wolin, Richard. *The Politics of Being: The Political Thought of Martin Heidegger*. New York: Columbia University Press, 1990.

———, ed. *The Heidegger Controversy: A Critical Reader*. Cambridge, MA: MIT Press, 1991.

Ziarek, Krzysztof. *The Force of Art*. Stanford, CA: Stanford University Press, 2004.

Žižek, Slavoj. *In Defense of Lost Causes*. London: Verso, 2008.

Zuboff, Shoshana. *The Age of Surveillance Capitalism: The Fight for a Human Future at the New Frontier of Power*. New York: PublicAffairs, 2019.

Index

Acampora, Christa Davis, 214
Adorno, Theodor W., 5, 20, 33, 111, 243–44
Aeschylus, 196–97, 199–200
Agamben, Giorgio, 39, 248, 250–51
Althusser, Louis, 35, 122, 126, 167, 169
Angus, Ian H., 158
Annas, Julia, 136
Aquinas, Thomas, 18, 109–111, 132–33
Arendt, Hannah, 6, 39, 66, 69, 76, 89, 121, 125, 192, 227, 267
Aristotle, 2, 5, 12, 14, 18–19, 28, 35, 42, 50–51, 63–64, 76–106, 108–115, 118, 123, 126–27, 129–30, 132, 134–35, 141–43, 147–151, 159, 190, 193, 216–18, 231, 238, 241–42, 260, 274
Axelos, Kostas, 21–22
Augustine, 65–66, 121, 129–32, 139

Backman, Jussi, 49
Badiou, Alain, 4, 29
Badiou, Alain, and Barbara Cassin, 21
Baker, Gideon, 54
Balibar, Étienne, 146
Bambach, Charles, 203
Barash, Andrew, 150

Bataille, Georges, 29, 233
Bayle, Pierre, 53–54, 232–34
Bernasconi, Robert, 100, 108
Benjamin, Andrew, 25, 218, 226
Bianchi, Emanuela, 110
Blanchot, Maurice, 4, 25, 39
Blattner, William, 17
Bourdieu, Pierre, 21, 32
Bowler, Michael, 97
Broadie, Sarah, 109
Bröcker, Walter, 177
Brockelman, Thomas, 22
Brogan, Walter, 18, 51, 77, 89, 97, 210
Brook, Peter, 135
Brown, Alison, 140
Brown, Wendy, 39–40
Burckhardt, Jacob, 94, 196, 214–15

Caputo, John, 18
Chamayou, Grégoire, 268
Cicero, 58–59, 134–35, 138, 192
Coetzee, J. M., 68
Colledge, Richard, 50
Connolly, William, 132
Corngold, Stanley, 100
Crowell, Steven Galt, 17

Dahlstrom, Daniel O., 106, 153–54
Dastur, Françoise, 222
Davies, Margery, 69
de Man, Paul, 100
Detienne, Marcel, and Jean-Pierre Vernant, 215–16
Della Rocca, Michael, 52–53, 56
Derrida, Jacques, 4, 20, 24–25, 38, 154, 171, 211–12, 236, 261–62, 274–76
Derrida, Jacques, Hans-Georg Gadamer, and Philippe Lacoue-Labarthe, 20
Di Cesare, Donatella, 21, 231
Dihle, Albrecht, 131
Diogenes Laertius, 36, 50, 137, 139
Dostal, Robert J., 153
Drabinski, John E., and Eric S. Nelson, eds., 25
Dreyfus, Hubert L., 27, 156, 184
Düttmann, Alexander García, 33

Elden, Stuart, 26, 259

Fagenblat, Michael, 25
Farias, Victor, 20
Faye, Emmanuel, 20
Feenberg, Andrew, 34, 87
Fenves, Peter, 222
Ferguson, Andrew Guthrie, 268
Foucault, Michel, 7, 182, 258–59, 268, 275–76
Fried, Richard, 187
Führich, Angelika, 69
Furley, David, 45, 50–51

Gabriel, Markus, 154
Gadamer, Hans-Georg, 19–20, 22, 87, 93, 96, 257
Golob, Sascha, 17
Gourgouris, Stathis, 213
Guenther, Lisa, 162–63
Grassi, Ernesto, 18–19
Grunenberg, Antonia, 69
Guignon, Charles, 211

Hadot, Pierre, 136
Hardt, Michael, and Antonio Negri, 171
Harman, Graham, 28–29

Hegel, Georg Wilhelm Friedrich, 5, 13, 25, 54–55, 133–34, 243, 258
Heidegger, Martin, *Aristotle's Metaphysics Theta 1–3: On the Essence and Actuality of Force*, 241; *The Basic Problems of Phenomenology*, 117; *Basic Writings*, 33, 45, 186, 222, 229–30, 240; *The Beginning of Western Philosophy: Interpretation of Anaximander and Parmenides*, 49–50; *Being and Time*, 1–3, 11, 14, 17, 21, 25, 27–28, 44, 47, 57, 60, 67, 77–79, 96, 98, 105, 107, 115–117, 121, 124–25, 144–158, 160 ,162, 164–66, 169, 171–72, 174, 176–79, 182, 184–190, 193–94, 196, 198, 202, 204, 211, 223–24, 232, 236–38, 241, 257–59, 264, 272; "Being-There and Being-True According to Aristotle." In *Becoming Heidegger: On the Trail of His Early Occasional Writings*, 112; *Contributions to Philosophy (Of the Event)*, 230–32; *Early Greek Thinking*, 50; *The Essence of Truth: On Plato's Cave Allegory and Theaetetus*, 161, 249; *The Fundamental Concepts of Metaphysics: World, Finitude, Solitude*, 154, 211; *History of the Concept of Time: Prolegomena*, 155; *Hölderlin's Hymn "The Ister,"* 190; *Hölderlin's Hymns "Germania" and "The Rhine,"* 194; *Identity and Difference*, 47; *Introduction to Metaphysics*, 21, 45, 152, 188–91, 202–6, 208–9, 211, 214, 216, 222–23, 226, 231; *Nietzsche I: The Will to Power as Art, Nietzsche II: The Eternal Recurrence of the Same, Nietzsche III: The Will to Power as Knowledge and Metaphysics, Nietzsche IV: Nihilism*, 51; *On Time and Being*, 237; *Off the Beaten Track*, 62, 159; *Parmenides*, 12, 48–51, 60–62, 66–67, 69–70, 147–48, 188, 194–96, 203, 210, 214–16, 227, 254; *Pathmarks*, 150, 206, 231, 241; "Phenomenological Interpretations with Respect to Aristotle: Indication of the Hermeneutical Situation," 77; *Plato's Sophist*, 28, 87, 96–97, 100–1,

103–5, 107–9, 112–113, 115, 117–118, 145–48, 150–51, 155–56, 172, 176–77, 179, 185, 189–90, 196, 204, 216, 219, 232, 246; "The Self-Assertion of the German University." In *The Heidegger Controversy: A Critical Reader*, 193, 197–98; "Why Do I Stay in the Provinces?" In *Philosophical and Political Writings*, 69
Hesiod, 175–76
Hirschman, Albert O., 40, 142
Hodge, Joanna, 24
Hopkins, Burt, 17
Hui, Yuk, 30, 170–71
Hume, David, 110–112

Ihde, Don, 27–28, 67, 177

Janicaud, Dominique, 234, 257
Janicaud, Dominique, and Jean-François Mattei, 47, 149
Jonas, Hans, 18

Kant, Immanuel, 128–29, 133, 260–62
Kasparov, Gary, with Mig Greengard, 161
Kirkland, Sean, 47, 149, 280
Kisiel, Theodore, 77
Kisiel, Theodore, and Thomas Sheehan, eds., 112
Kittler, Friedrich, 67
Kiverstein, Julian, and Michael Wheeler, eds., 17
Kojève, Alexandre, 191–92
Kontos, Pavlos, 115, 280
Krell, David Ferrell, 21, 106

Lacoue-Labarthe, Philippe, 20, 222, 225, 247
Lange, Friedrich Albert, 47, 254
Levinas, Emmanuel, 4, 25, 39, 55, 257, 261–62
Llewelyn, John, 262
Loraux, Nicole, 31
Löwith, Karl, 3–4
Love, Jeff, and Michael Meng, 31–32
Lucretius, 138–40
Lyotard, Jean-François, 20

MacIntyre, Alasdair, 136
Machiavelli, Niccolò, 36–37, 89, 124, 127, 140, 192
Malabou, Catherine, 26
Malpas, Jef, 17–18, 280
Marcuse, Herbert, 21, 39
Marion, Jean-Luc, 18
Marx, Karl, and Friedrich Engels, 37
Marx, Werner, 149
McNeill, William, 18, 77, 117
Meillassoux, Quentin, 260
Menning, Laurence Paul, 12
Merleau-Ponty, Maurice, 120
Miller, Barbara, and Stephanie Dalzell, 146, 181
Mitchell, Andrew, 30
Moore, Ian Alexander, 15, 18, 66, 83, 280
Mueller, Gavin, 163

Nancy, Jean-Luc, 23–24, 170
Negri, Antonio, 171
Nietzsche, Friedrich, 15, 47, 56, 64, 67, 206–7, 214, 230, 253, 254, 258–59
Noble, Safiya Umoja, 268

Olafson, Frederick A., 24, 170

Panagia, Davide, 269
Pasquale, Frank, 269
Pearson Geiman, Clare, 190
Perkams, Matthias, 132–33
Phillips, James, 21
Polt, Richard, 187
Polt, Richard, and Gregory Fried, eds., 187–88, 190, 204, 211
Porphyry, 139
Prauss, Gerold, 178
Protevi, John, 117

Raffoul, François, 24, 258
Raffoul, François, and David Pettigrew, eds., 23, 234
Rendall, Jess, and Lily Nothling, 181
Richardson, William J., 186–87, 189, 236
Richter, Gerhard, 152, 254
Ricoeur, Paul, 191
Risser, James, ed, 187, 222

Rockmore, Tom, 257
Rubenstein, Mary-Jane, 50

Safranksi, Rüdiger, 48, 201
Sallis, John, 18
Salzani, Carolo, 251
Sartre, Jean-Paul, 234–38, 253
Sas, Nick, and Michael Slezak, 181
Schürmann, Reiner, 22–23, 113–114, 257
Scott, Charles E., 15, 211
Sheehan, Thomas, 187
Slezak, Michael, 181
Slobodian, Quinn, 40, 142
Sluga, Hans, 21
Sorel, George, 163
Smith, Adam, 141, 182
Sophocles, 12, 200, 205, 217–19, 227
Spinoza, Baruch, 6, 37–38, 46, 53–60, 64, 72, 74, 124, 140–41, 192, 232, 275–76
Stiegler, Bernard, 30, 263–66, 270
Strauss, Leo, 55, 77
Szendy, Peter, 71

Tabak, Mehmet, 148
Taminiaux, Jacques, 89, 100
Thanassas, Panagiotis, 107

Thomson, Ian, 106
Trawny, Peter, 21
Trott, Adriel M., 110
Tuncel, Yunus, 214
Tugendhat, Ernst, 177

Usener, Hermann, ed, 139

Vardoulakis, Dimitris, 6–8, 24, 33, 35–37, 41, 52, 54–55, 59, 68, 74, 80, 86, 91, 133, 136, 147, 191–93, 207, 214, 226, 251, 263
Vattimo, Gianni, and Santiago Zabala, 256
Vaysse, Jean-Marie, 56
Végső, Roland, 41, 154
Villa, Dana R., 66
Volpi, Franco, 115, 146

Wendland, Aaron James, 17
Williams, Bernard, 74
Wisser, Richard, 253–54
Wolin, Richard, 20–22, 193

Ziarek, Krzysztof, 29–30
Žižek, Slavoj, 26
Zuboff, Shoshana, 269

Dimitris Vardoulakis is Professor of Philosophy at Western Sydney University. He is the author of *Spinoza, the Epicurean: Authority and Utility in Materialism* (2020); *Stasis Before the State: Nine Theses on Agonistic Democracy* (2018); *Freedom from the Free Will: On Kafka's Laughter* (2016); *Sovereignty and Its Other: Toward the Dejustification of Violence* (2013); and *The Doppelgänger: Literature's Philosophy* (2010).

Perspectives in Continental Philosophy
John D. Caputo, series editor

Recent titles:

George Pattison, *A Philosophy of Prayer: Nothingness Language, and Hope.*
Irving Goh, ed., *Jean-Luc Nancy among the Philosophers.*
Neal DeRoo, *The Political Logic of Experience: Expression in Phenomenology.*
John D. Caputo, *Radical Theology: Expositions, Explorations, Exhortations.*
Michael Naas, *Class Acts: Derrida on the Public Stage.*
Adam Kotsko, *What is Theology? Christian Thought and Contemporary Life.*
Galen A. Johnson, Mauro Carbone, and Emmanuel de Saint Aubert, *Merleau-Ponty's Poetics: Figurations of Literature and Philosophy*
Ole Jakob Løland, *Pauline Ugliness: Jacob Taubes and the Turn to Paul.*
Marc Crépon, *Murderous Consent: On the Accommodation of Violent Death.* Translated by Michael Loriaux and Jacob Levi, Foreword by James Martel
Emmanuel Falque, *The Guide to Gethsemane: Anxiety, Suffering, and Death.* Translated by George Hughes.
Emmanuel Alloa, *Resistance of the Sensible World: An Introduction to Merleau-Ponty.* Translated by Jane Marie Todd. Foreword by Renaud Barbaras.
Françoise Dastur, *Questions of Phenomenology: Language, Alterity, Temporality, Finitude.* Translated by Robert Vallier.
Jean-Luc Marion, *Believing in Order to See: On the Rationality of Revelation and the Irrationality of Some Believers.* Translated by Christina M. Gschwandtner.
Adam Y. Wells, ed., *Phenomenologies of Scripture.*
An Yountae, *The Decolonial Abyss: Mysticism and Cosmopolitics from the Ruins.*
Jean Wahl, *Transcendence and the Concrete: Selected Writings.* Edited and with an Introduction by Alan D. Schrift and Ian Alexander Moore.

Colby Dickinson, *Words Fail: Theology, Poetry, and the Challenge of Representation.*

Emmanuel Falque, *The Wedding Feast of the Lamb: Eros, the Body, and the Eucharist.* Translated by George Hughes.

Emmanuel Falque, *Crossing the Rubicon: The Borderlands of Philosophy and Theology.* Translated by Reuben Shank. Introduction by Matthew Farley.

Colby Dickinson and Stéphane Symons (eds.), *Walter Benjamin and Theology.*

Don Ihde, *Husserl's Missing Technologies.*

William S. Allen, *Aesthetics of Negativity: Blanchot, Adorno, and Autonomy.*

Jeremy Biles and Kent L. Brintnall, eds., *Georges Bataille and the Study of Religion.*

Tarek R. Dika and W. Chris Hackett, *Quiet Powers of the Possible: Interviews in Contemporary French Phenomenology.* Foreword by Richard Kearney.

Richard Kearney and Brian Treanor, eds., *Carnal Hermeneutics.*

A complete list of titles is available at http://fordhampress.com.

www.ingramcontent.com/pod-product-compliance
Lightning Source LLC
Chambersburg PA
CBHW020354080526
44584CB00014B/1011